A+ CERTIFICATION OPERATING SYSTEM TECHNOLOGIES LAB GUIDE

Editor in Chief: Stephen Helba
Assistant Vice President and Publisher: Charles E. Stewart, Jr.
Production Editor: Alexandrina Benedicto Wolf
Design Coordinator: Diane Ernsberger
Cover art: Michael R. Hall
Production Manager: Matt Ottenweller
Marketing Manager: Ben Leonard

This book was set in Futura MD BT, Times New Roman, and Arial by Cathy J. Boulay, Marcraft International, Inc. It was printed and bound by Courier/Kendallville. The cover was printed by Phoenix Color Corp.

Written and edited by Marcraft Production Staff: Charles Brooks, Caleb Sarka, Paul Havens, Wanda Dawson, Evan Samaritano, Cathy Boulay, and Anthony Tonda

Technical review: Caleb Sarka, Wanda Dawson, and Stuart Palmer

Copyright © 2004 by Marcraft International Corporation and published by Pearson Education, Inc., Upper Saddle River, New Jersey 07458.
Pearson Prentice Hall. All rights reserved. Printed in the United States of America. This publication is protected by Copyright and permission should be obtained from the publisher prior to any prohibited reproduction, storage in a retrieval system, or transmission in any form or by any means, electronic, mechanical, photocopying, recording, or likewise. For information regarding permission(s), write to: Rights and Permissions Department.

Pearson Prentice Hall™ is a trademark of Pearson Education, Inc.
Pearson® is a registered trademark of Pearson plc
Prentice Hall® is a registered trademark of Pearson Education, Inc.

Pearson Education Ltd.　　　　　　　　　　Pearson Education Australia Pty. Limited
Pearson Education Singapore Pte. Ltd.　　　　Pearson Education North Asia Ltd.
Pearson Education Canada, Ltd.　　　　　　 Pearson Educación de Mexico, S.A. de C.V.
Pearson Education—Japan　　　　　　　　　Pearson Education Malaysia Pte. Ltd.

10 9 8 7 6 5 4 3 2 1
ISBN 0-13-114339-5

Trademark Acknowledgments

All terms mentioned in this book that are known to be trademarks or service marks are listed below. Marcraft cannot attest to the accuracy of this information. Use of a term in this book should not be regarded as affecting the validity of any trademark or service mark.

IBM®, IBM-PC, PC/XT®, PC-AT, EGA, MicroChannel, OS/2, PS/2, and XGA are registered trademarks of IBM Corporation.

CGA and VGA are trademarks of International Business Machines Corporation.

Microsoft®, MS-DOS®, MS-Windows, Windows 95, Windows 98, and Windows Me are registered trademarks of Microsoft Corporation.

Windows NT and Windows 2000 are trademarks of Microsoft Corporation.

Centronics is a registered trademark of Centronics Data Computer Corporation.

Freon and Mylar are registered trademarks of E. I. du Pont de Nemours and Co., Incorporated.

CompuServe is a registered trademark of CompuServe, Incorporated.

America Online is a registered trademark of America Online, Incorporated.

Apple, AppleShare, AppleTalk, and Macintosh are registered trademarks of Apple Computer, Incorporated.

AMI is a registered trademark of American Megatrends, Incorporated.

Award BIOS is a trademark of Award Software Incorporated.

Panasonic is a registered trademark of Matsushita Communication Industrial Co., Ltd.

Hercules is a registered trademark of Hercules Corporation.

Motorola and PowerPC are registered trademarks of Motorola Corporation.

Intel, 386, 387, 386SX, 387SX, i486, 486, Pentium, Pentium II, Pentium III, Pentium Pro, and Pentium MMX are trademarks of Intel Corporation.

Cyrix is a registered trademark of the Cyrix Corporation.

NetWare, Novell, and UNIX are registered trademarks of Novell, Incorporated.

Microcom is a registered trademark of Microcom Systems, Incorporated.

Sound Blaster is a trademark of Creative Technology, Limited.

ArcNet is a registered trademark of Datapoint Corporation.

Hayes is a registered trademark of Hayes Microcomputer Products, Incorporated.

Hewlett-Packard and LaserJet are registered trademarks of Hewlett-Packard Company.

Netscape and Netscape Navigator and Communicator are registered trademarks of Netscape/AOL.

Shockwave is a registered trademark of Macromedia.

RealPlayer is a registered trademark of RealPlayer Networks.

Adobe Acrobat is a registered trademark of Adobe.

PREFACE

The authors, and Marcraft International, have been producing computer services training materials since 1988. In particular, Marcraft publishes comprehensive theory and hands-on lab texts that assist students in studying for and passing the Computing Technology Industry Association (CompTIA) certification exams.

CompTIA is an organization that has established introductory certification criteria for service professionals in the computer industry. Most notably, CompTIA has created and sponsors the A+, Network+, i-Net+, Server+, and Security+ Certification Examinations. The A+ exam is designed to certify entry-level technicians for the installation, maintenance, and repair of desktop computer hardware and software. The Network+ exam is designed to serve as an introductory certification for network administration, focusing on Client/Server operating systems used with Local Area Networks (LANs). The i-Net+ Certification is designed specifically for any individual interested in pursuing Internet-related careers. The Server+ exam is designed for individuals who will be supporting and repairing servers. The Security+ exam is for individuals who will be supporting networks and websites that have direct Internet access and need to be protected from intruders.

For more information on CompTIA and these exams, visit *http://www.comptia.org*.

Organization

The *A+ Certification Operating System Technologies Lab Guide* provides an excellent hands-on component to emphasize the theoretical materials provided in the *A+ Certification Operating System Technologies Training Guide*. Applying chapter concepts developed in the textbook to these lab exercises is crucial in preparing for a successful career as a computer technician. The Lab Guide contains forty-one lab procedures:

Lab Group 1 – *Operating Systems* – Provides extensive instruction on the operation of the Windows Millennium Edition, Windows 2000 Professional, and Windows XP Professional operating systems. Operational features include navigation, Plug-and-Play, tools and resources, computer management, and installing peripheral equipment for operation under the operating systems.

Lab Group 2 – *System Administration Tools* – Covers the administration of computer operating systems and covers all operational aspects of the computer and its operating system. Utilization of the included operating system tools is also covered in depth. This includes system information, disk management, accessories, domain names, the Registry, safe operating system mode, log files, and virus protection.

Lab Group 3 – *Network Management* – Provides instruction on setting up and maintaining a computer network, which includes connecting to the Internet. The student will acquire the knowledge and skill sets that will enable them to troubleshoot a computer network with an understanding of the different features of the Internet.

Lab Group 4 – *System Maintenance* – Consists of maintaining a computer system, which includes keeping the system current with the latest updates and upgrades. This group concludes with operating system faults, which will provide an understanding of problems that can occur with many operating systems.

These labs are written to be performed on single operating system computers. However, they have been tested on multi-boot machines. There will be variances in lab procedures when running them on the multiple operating system computers. The OS fault labs will cause major problems in the system and SHOULD NOT be performed on multi-boot machines. Contact Marcraft International if you have any questions concerning how these labs are to be performed.

Pedagogy

Each lab begins with a set of objectives to be achieved through the procedure and a list of items required to carry out the procedure. Icons are employed throughout each procedure to describe its nature.

Each procedure ends with a set of lab-specific questions designed to permit students to assess their understanding of the lab.

Upon completion, the student should have learned the required knowledge and skill sets as defined by the CompTIA A+ Certification objectives.

Table of Contents

LAB GROUP 1 – OPERATING SYSTEMS

Lab Procedure 1 – Windows Me Video Drivers 3
    Objectives 3
    Resources 3
    Discussion 3
    Procedure 4
    Tables 7
    Lab Questions 8

Lab Procedure 2 – Windows Me Navigating 9
    Objectives 9
    Resources 9
    Discussion 9
    Procedure 10
        My Computer 13
        Windows Explorer 13
        Moving Folders Around 15
        Formatting a Blank Floppy Disk 18
        The Control Panel 19
        Windows Setup 20
    Tables 21
    Lab Questions 23

Lab Procedure 3 – Windows Me Command Prompt Navigating 25
    Objectives 25
    Resources 25
    Discussion 25
    Procedure 26
    Tables 31
    Lab Questions 33

Lab Procedure 4 – Advanced Windows Me 35
    Objectives 35
    Resources 35
    Discussion 35
    Procedure 36
        Creating a Startup Disk 36
        Booting to the Windows Me Startup Disk 37
        Using RegEdit 37
        RegEdit Screen 38
        HKEY_CLASSES_ROOT 38

HKEY_LOCAL_MACHINE	39
HKEY_CURRENT_USER	39
Adjusting Color Values	40
Tables	41
Lab Questions	44

Lab Procedure 5 – Windows 2000 Navigation 45
- Objectives 45
- Resources 45
- Discussion 45
- Procedure 45
- Tables 50
- Lab Questions 52

Lab Procedure 6 – Windows 2000 Administrative Tools 53
- Objectives 53
- Resources 53
- Discussion 53
- Procedure 54
- Tables 60
- Lab Questions 62

Lab Procedure 7 – Windows 2000 Computer Management 63
- Objectives 63
- Resources 63
- Discussion 63
- Procedure 63
- Tables 67
- Lab Questions 69

Lab Procedure 8 – Windows XP Navigating 71
- Objectives 71
- Resources 71
- Discussion 71
- Procedure 72
- Tables 79
- Lab Questions 80

Lab Procedure 9 – Windows XP Control Panel 81
- Objectives 81
- Resources 81
- Discussion 81
- Procedure 81
- Tables 83
- Lab Questions 84

Lab Procedure 10 – Windows 2000 Plug-and-Play 85
- Objectives 85
- Resources 85
- Discussion 85
- Procedure 85

Tables	88
Lab Questions	88

Lab Procedure 11 – Windows XP Plug-and-Play 89
Objectives 89
Resources 89
Discussion 89
Procedure 89
Tables 90
Lab Questions 90

Lab Procedure 12 – Windows Me Printers 91
Objectives 91
Resources 91
Discussion 91
Procedure 91
Tables 94
Lab Questions 95

Lab Procedure 13 – Windows 2000 Printers 97
Objectives 97
Resources 97
Discussion 97
Procedure 97
Tables 100
Lab Questions 100

Lab Procedure 14 – Installing Printers in Windows XP 101
Objectives 101
Resources 101
Discussion 101
Procedure 101
Tables 104
Lab Questions 104

LAB GROUP 2 – SYSTEM ADMINISTRATION TOOLS

Lab Procedure 15 – Windows Me System Information 107
Objectives 107
Resources 107
Discussion 107
Procedure 107
    Viewing the Tools that are Available in the Tools Menu 108
Tables 110
Lab Questions 113

Lab Procedure 16 – Windows Me Disk Management 115
Objectives 115
Resources 115
Discussion 115

Procedure	116
Tables	119
Lab Questions	120

Lab Procedure 17 – Windows 2000 Accessories 121
- Objectives 121
- Resources 121
- Discussion 121
- Procedure 121
- Tables 124
- Lab Questions 125

Lab Procedure 18 – Windows 2000 Disk Management 127
- Objectives 127
- Resources 127
- Discussion 127
- Procedure 127
- Tables 131
- Lab Questions 132

Lab Procedure 19 – Windows 2000 Registry 133
- Objectives 133
- Resources 133
- Discussion 133
- Procedure 134
- Tables 136
- Lab Questions 137

Lab Procedure 20 – Windows Me Safe Mode 139
- Objectives 139
- Resources 139
- Discussion 139
- Procedure 140
- Tables 142
- Lab Questions 142

Lab Procedure 21 – Windows Me Setup Log Files 143
- Objectives 143
- Resources 143
- Discussion 143
- Procedure 144
    - BOOTLOG.TXT 144
    - DETLOG.TXT 146
    - NETLOG.TXT 147
    - SETUPLOG.TXT 148
- Tables 148
- Lab Questions 150

Lab Procedure 22 – Windows 2000/XP Startup Modes 151
- Objectives 151
- Resources 151

  Discussion 151
  Procedure 152
  Tables 155
  Lab Questions 156

Lab Procedure 23 – Windows XP System Restore 157
  Objectives 157
  Resources 157
  Discussion 157
  Procedure 157
  Lab Questions 162

Lab Procedure 24 – Windows 2000 Virus Protection 163
  Objectives 163
  Resources 163
  Discussion 163
  Procedure 163
  Tables 166
  Lab Questions 168

LAB GROUP 3 – NETWORK MANAGEMENT

Lab Procedure 25 – Windows Me Dial-Up Access 171
  Objectives 171
  Resources 171
  Discussion 171
  Procedure 173
    Configure the Dial-Up Networking Feature 173
  Tables 175
  Lab Questions 175

Lab Procedure 26 – Windows Me Network Operations 177
  Objectives 177
  Resources 177
  Discussion 177
  Procedure 178
  Tables 183
  Lab Questions 184

Lab Procedure 27 – Windows Me Accessories 185
  Objectives 185
  Resources 185
  Discussion 185
  Procedure 185
  Tables 189
  Lab Questions 190

Lab Procedure 28 – Windows 2000 TCP/IP 191
  Objectives 191
  Resources 191

  Discussion 191
  Procedure 192
    IPCONFIG 193
    ARP 193
    NETSTAT 194
    NBTSTAT 195
    NET VIEW 196
    TRACERT 197
    PING 198
  Tables 200
  Lab Questions 202

Lab Procedure 29 – Windows 2000 Networking 203
  Objectives 203
  Resources 203
  Discussion 203
  Procedure 203
  Tables 207
  Lab Questions 208

Lab Procedure 30 – Windows XP TCP/IP Setup 209
  Objectives 209
  Resources 209
  Discussion 209
  Procedure 210
  Tables 213
  Lab Questions 214

Lab Procedure 31 – Windows XP Network Operations 215
  Objectives 215
  Resources 215
  Discussion 215
  Procedure 215
  Tables 220
  Lab Questions 220

Lab Procedure 32 – Windows XP Remote Troubleshooting 221
  Objectives 221
  Resources 221
  Discussion 221
  Procedure 221
  Lab Questions 228

Lab Procedure 33 – Internet Client Setup for IE 6.0 229
  Objectives 229
  Resources 229
  Discussion 229
  Procedure 230
  Tables 234
  Lab Questions 235

Lab Procedure 34 – Windows Me FTP/Telnet ... 237
   Objectives ... 237
   Resources ... 237
   Discussion ... 237
   Procedure ... 238
      Transferring Files Using an FTP Client ... 239
   Tables ... 244
   Lab Questions ... 246

Lab Procedure 35 – Windows Me Internet Domain Names ... 247
   Objectives ... 247
   Resources ... 247
   Discussion ... 247
   Procedure ... 248
   Tables ... 251
   Lab Questions ... 252

LAB GROUP 4 – SYSTEM MAINTENANCE

Lab Procedure 36 – Windows Me Software Version Update Management ... 255
   Objectives ... 255
   Resources ... 255
   Discussion ... 255
   Procedure ... 256
      Updating Windows Me ... 256
      Using an Application's Upgrade Feature ... 258
      Manually Downloading and Installing a Driver Update ... 259
   Tables ... 263
   Lab Questions ... 264

Lab Procedure 37 – Windows 2000 Software Version Update Management ... 265
   Objectives ... 265
   Resources ... 265
   Discussion ... 265
   Procedure ... 265
   Tables ... 269
   Lab Questions ... 270

Lab Procedure 38 – Windows XP Software Version Update Management ... 271
   Objectives ... 271
   Resources ... 271
   Discussion ... 271
   Procedure ... 271
   Tables ... 275
   Lab Questions ... 275

Lab Procedure 39 – Windows Me OS Faults ... 277
   Objectives ... 277
   Resources ... 277
   Discussion ... 277

Procedure 277
　　Tables. 279
　　Lab Questions 280

Lab Procedure 40 – Windows 2000 OS Faults 281
　　Objectives 281
　　Resources. 281
　　Discussion 281
　　Procedure. 281
　　Tables. 286
　　Lab Questions 288

Lab Procedure 41 – Windows XP OS Faults 289
　　Objectives 289
　　Resources. 289
　　Discussion 289
　　Procedure. 290
　　Tables. 293
　　Lab Questions 294

LAB GROUP 1

OPERATING SYSTEMS

LAB PROCEDURE 1

Windows Me Video Drivers

OBJECTIVES

1. Install new video drivers.
2. Change display resolutions.
3. Change the desktop size.
4. Change desktop appearance.
5. Configure the power settings.

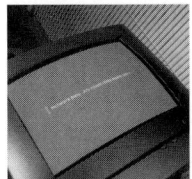

Operating
System
Technology

RESOURCES

1. PC-compatible desktop/tower computer system—Customer-supplied desktop/tower hardware system **OR** Marcraft MC-8000 Computer Hardware Trainer **OR** suitable PC hardware trainer running Windows Millennium
2. Manufacturer's driver installation disk for the display adapter

DISCUSSION

The first thing that anyone does after installing Windows 9x or Windows Me is to update the display driver. Windows Me usually installs its own generic version of the manufacturer's drivers. There are a few incompatibilities between Windows Me and third-party software, so you should read Display.txt located in the Windows directory to see if your configuration matches anything on the list.

Windows Me upgrades all Microsoft-provided drivers from Windows 9x and DirectX releases. Windows Me also upgrades certain third-party Windows 9x drivers that might experience problems running in Windows Me.

If the Windows Me CD does not contain a driver for your display, Windows Me converts the driver to standard VGA to allow the system to start. In this case, you need to obtain an updated driver, either by following the procedure in Windows Update or by contacting your display hardware manufacturer.

Windows Me Setup Wizard configures your adapter type based on the type of video controller it uses (e.g., S3, Cirrus Logic, or ATI). However, you may find a more exact match for your adapter's make and model by using the Update Device Driver Wizard. If your computer works with the display driver that Windows Me automatically installed, there's no need to make a change.

If Windows Me does not contain a driver for your monitor type, select one of the standard monitor types instead. This selection will not adversely affect the performance or quality of the Windows Me display output. Before you can change to a higher resolution on certain video cards, you will have to specify the exact monitor type. This is by the design of the newer drivers. Windows Me also supports multiple monitors. You can use one computer to control two to nine monitors through a common desktop. The multiple-monitors feature increases the size of your screen, so you can see multiple programs or windows simultaneously.

PROCEDURE - 1

After all drivers have been updated, Windows 9x and Windows Me provide you with many different graphics for decorating your desktop appearance. If you don't like any of these, you can use one of your own, customizing the appearance to whatever suits your fancy.

Operating System Technology

PROCEDURE

1. **Boot the computer to Windows Me**
   ___a. Turn on the computer and select **Windows Millennium** from the Operating System (OS) selection menu.

2. **Change the video display adapter driver**
   ___a. Right-click the desktop and choose **Properties**.
   ___b. Click on the **Settings** tab.
   ___c. Click on the **Advanced** button.
   ___d. Click on the **Adapter** tab.
   ___e. Click on the **Change** button.
   ___f. Insert the manufacturer's driver installation disk into the proper drive.
   ___g. Accept the default option of letting Windows search for the best drivers and click on **Next**.
   ___h. Click on **Finish** once Windows has found and installed the new drivers.
   ___i. Remove the manufacturer's disk.
   ___j. Click on **YES** to restart the computer.
   ___k. If you are prompted to install the monitor, follow the steps at startup.

3. **Change the display resolutions**
   ___a. From the Windows Me desktop, navigate the *Start/Settings/Control Panel* path.
   ___b. Double-click the **Display** icon.
   ___c. Click on the **Settings** tab and, in Table 1-1, list how many colors are used and the Screen area setting.
   ___d. Click on the arrow next to the color settings to display the color options, as shown in Figure 1-1.

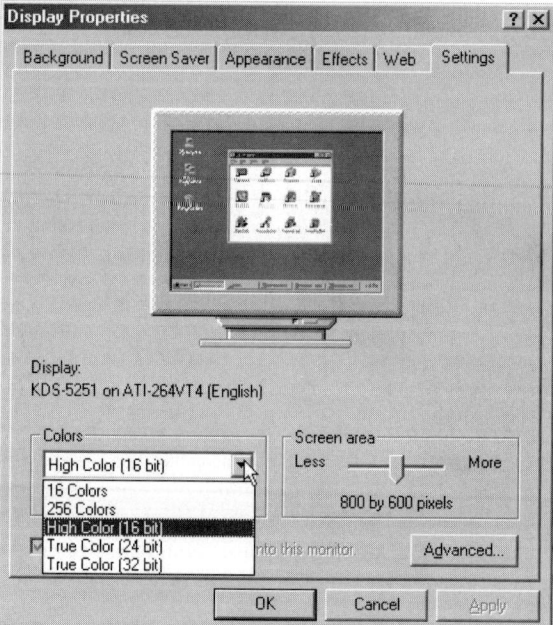

**Figure 1-1:
Changing the Color Settings**

4 - LAB GROUP 1

PROCEDURE - 1

    ___e.   In Table 1-2, list the optional color settings available.
    ___f.   Choose the highest color setting available for your video adapter and click on **Apply**.
    ___g.   Click on the radio button next to **Apply the new color.**
    ___h.   Click on **OK**.
    ___i.   Click on **OK** again to close the display.

4.   Verify the Interrupt and Input/Output system settings of the display adapter
    ___a.   From the Control Panel, double-click the **System** icon.

NOTE: If you do not see the option that you are looking for, click on "View all Control Panel options."

    ___b.   Click on the **Device Manager** tab.
    ___c.   Double-click on **Display Adapters**.
    ___d.   Double-click the name of your display adapter to bring up its properties.
    ___e.   Click on the **Resources** tab.
    ___f.   In Table 1-3, list the Memory ranges, Input/Output ranges, Interrupt requests, and DMI, if given.
    ___g.   Close your adapter's properties window and the system properties window.
    ___h.   Close the Control Panel.
    ___i.   Right-click the desktop and choose **Properties**.
    ___j.   Click on the **Settings** tab.
    ___k.   At the bottom right under Screen area, change the setting to 1027x768 pixels and click on **Apply**.
    ___l.   Click on **OK** twice to resize the desktop.
    ___m.   Notice the difference in the screen area and icon sizes. Click on **No** to save your current 800x600 pixel settings or **Yes** to accept the new settings.

5.   **Change the desktop appearance**
    ___a.   Click on the **Background** tab.
    ___b.   Scroll through the list of Wallpaper and click on **Windows Millennium**.
    ___c.   Under *Picture Display*, select **Stretch** as shown in Figure 1-2.

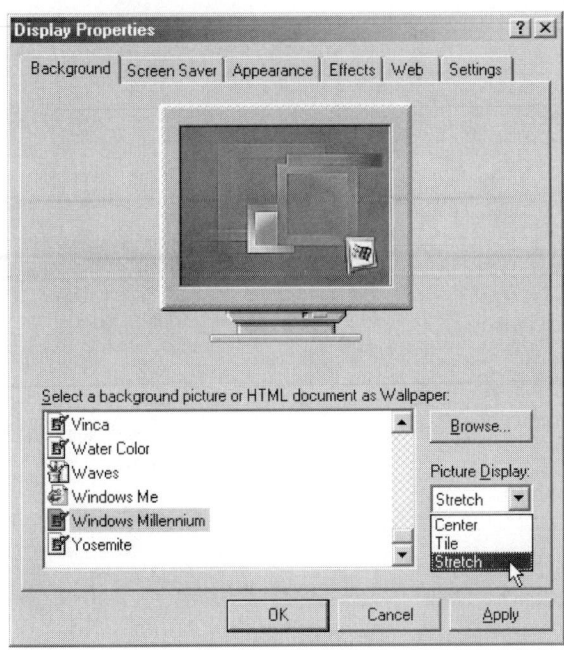

Figure 1-2: Setting the Windows Desktop Wallpaper

PROCEDURE - 1

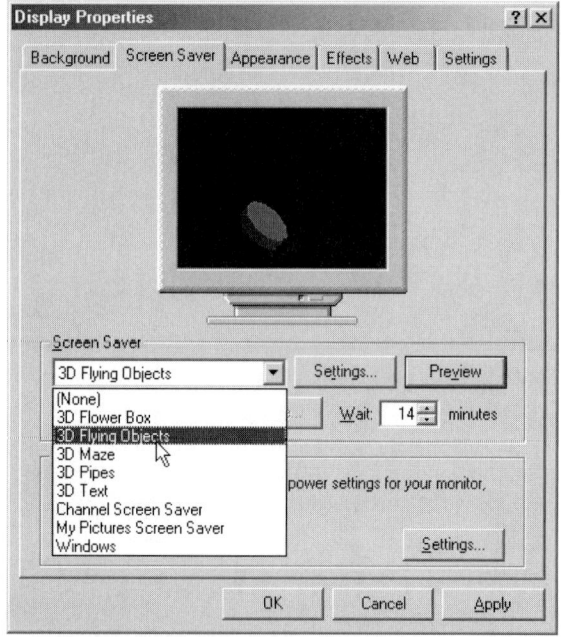

Figure 1-3: Selecting a Screen Saver

    ____d.   Click on **Apply**.

NOTE: You may be prompted to enable Active Desktop; click on yes to enable it.

    ____e.   Click on the **Screen Saver** tab.
    ____f.   Click on the down arrow next to the *Screen Saver* box to open the menu.
    ____g.   Select **3D Flying Objects** as shown in Figure 1-3.
    ____h.   Click on the **Settings** button.
    ____i.   In the *Style* menu, select **Splash**.
    ____j.   Check the box next to **Color-cycling** and click on **OK**.
    ____k.   Change the number of minutes to wait for the screen saver to activate to **1**, as shown in Figure 1-4.
    ____l.   Click on the **Apply** button.

6. **Configure the Power Scheme**
     ____a. Click on the **Settings** button in the *Energy saving features of monitor* box.
     ____b. In Table 1-4, list the *Power Scheme* options from the menu.
     ____c. Select the **Home/Office Desk power** scheme and select **1** minute to "*Turn off Monitor*".
     ____d. Next to *System Stand By*, select **After 2 Minutes**.
     ____e. Click on **Apply**.
     ____f. Click on **OK**.
     ____g. Click on **OK** to close the Display Properties.
     ____h. Sit back for a few minutes without touching the mouse or the keyboard.
     ____i. In Table 1-5, describe what happens.
     ____j. Move the mouse.
     ____k. In Table 1-6, describe what happens.
     ____l. Right-click the desktop and choose **Properties**.
     ____m. Click on the **Screen Saver** tab.
     ____n. Click on the **Settings** button in the *Energy saving features of monitor* box.
     ____o. Next to *System Stand By*, select **1** hour.
     ____p. Next to *Turn Off Monitor*, select **1** hour.
     ____q. Click on **Apply**, then **OK**.
     ____r. Next to *Wait*, click the mouse cursor next to the 1 and press the **DELETE** key.
     ____s. Type in **15** and click on **OK** to close Display Properties.

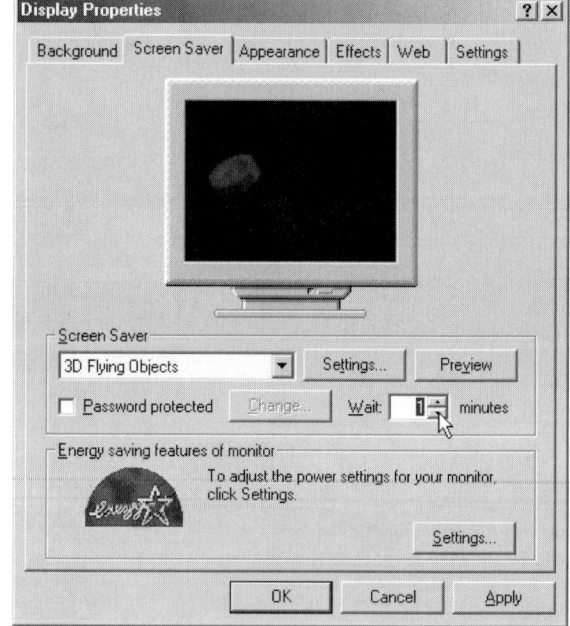

Figure 1-4: Setting the Screen Saver Activation Delay

PROCEDURE - 1

TABLES

Table 1-1

No. of Colors:	
Screen Area Setting:	

Table 1-2

Table 1-3

PROCEDURE - 1

Table 1-4

Table 1-5

Table 1-6

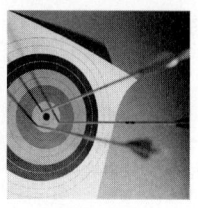

Feedback

LAB QUESTIONS

1. How can you open the display adapter properties window?

2. What are the typical screen areas (in pixels) found in most contemporary computers?

3. How do you configure the settings for a screen saver?

4. What two features can be controlled in the Power Options Properties window?

5. If Windows Me identifies your video adapter, either during the installation of the operating system or by using Plug-and-Play installation afterwards, what kind of driver does it install?

LAB PROCEDURE 2

Windows Me Navigating

OBJECTIVES

1. Explore the Start menu.
2. Start an application.
3. Multi-task between applications.
4. Moving folders and files around.
5. Use Control Panel settings.

Operating System Technology

RESOURCES

1. PC-compatible desktop/tower computer system — Customer-supplied desktop/tower hardware system **OR** Marcraft MC-8000 Computer Hardware Trainer **OR** suitable PC hardware trainer
2. Student work disk

DISCUSSION

A Windows Me desktop display, similar to that depicted in Figure 2-1, should be on the screen. The Desktop program manager is the application coordinator that associates related software applications and data into groups. The default groups installed by Windows Me may include: My Computer, Outlook Express, the Recycle Bin, and, if a network adapter is detected, the Network Neighborhood.

Double-clicking on the *My Computer* icon provides access to the system's drives and the Control Panel. Outlook Express is the default e-mail client installed with Windows. The Recycle Bin is a temporary storage place for deleted files. Double-clicking this icon allows the user to view and retrieve deleted files. The Network Neighborhood utility allows the user to view network resources, provided the computer is connected to a network. This utility is used to connect to other computers attached to the Local Area Network (LAN).

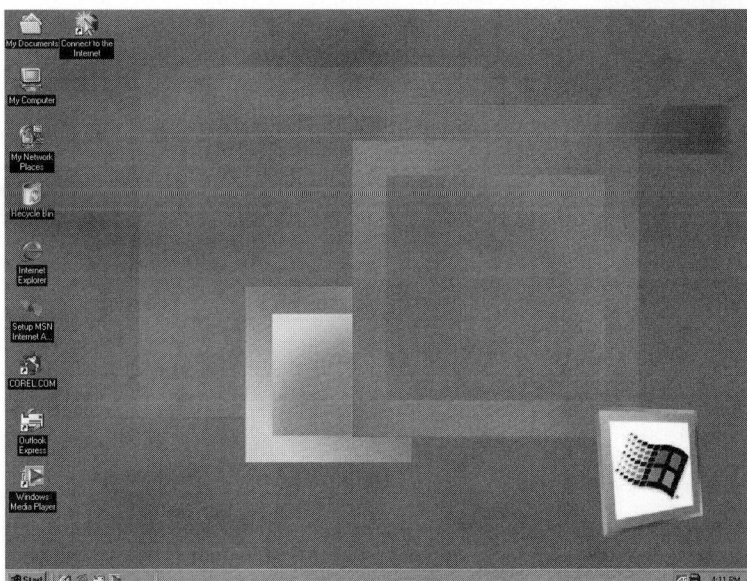

Figure 2-1: Windows Me Desktop

PROCEDURE - 2

The *Start* button at the bottom-left corner of the screen allows access to programs and applications available within Windows Me. The Taskbar, just to the right of the *Start* button, is used to display the applications currently open. Clicking on the *Start* button will produce a menu that can be used to start programs, open documents, change system settings, get help, search for items on the computer, and more. These options are accessed through the *Run*, *Help*, *Search*, *Settings*, *Documents*, and *Programs* options. An additional option at the bottom of the menu is used to shut the computer down in various ways. When Windows Me is shut down, it will automatically close all open applications and check the system for errors.

The menu items with arrows indicate submenus, which can be viewed by placing the mouse cursor on the specific menu item. To open a selected item, simply click on it, and its window will appear on the screen. Each time a program is started or a window is opened, a corresponding button appears on the Taskbar. To switch between applications, simply click on the desired program button to make it the active window.

The *Documents* entry displays a list of the most recently-opened documents. The *Settings* entry displays options for configuring different parts of the system. The Search utility is used to locate folders, files, web pages, businesses on the Internet, and people from your address book or various online services. The Help file system provides information about many Windows Me functions and operations. The *Run* option is used to start programs or open folders from a command line. The *Shut Down* option exits the system, restarts the computer, or logs the user off. The Programs submenu, depicted in Figure 2-2, has several options, including *Accessories*, *Start Up*, *Internet Explorer*, *Outlook Express*, and *Windows Media Player*.

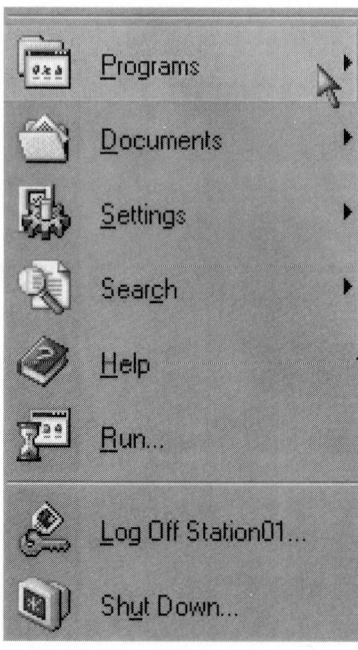

Figure 2-2: Start Menu

Operating System Technology

PROCEDURE

1. **Boot the computer to Windows Me**
   ____a. Turn on the computer and select **Windows Millennium** from the OS selection menu.

2. **Explore the Windows Me environment**
   ____a. Click on the **Start** button.
   ____b. List the *Start* menu options in Table 2-1.
   ____c. Position the mouse pointer on **Programs**.
   ____d. List the available *Programs* menu options in Table 2-2.
   ____e. Position the mouse pointer on **Accessories**.
   ____f. List the available *Accessory* menu options in Table 2-3.

   NOTE: You may have to click on the arrow at the bottom of these submenus to expand their viewing area, depending on how many options you have available to choose from.

   ____g. Click on the **Start** button to close the *Start* menu.

3. **Start an application**
   ____a. Click on the **Start** button.
   ____b. Move to **Programs/Accessories**, and click on the **WordPad** option.

   NOTE: This is a simple word processor for writing and editing letters and documents.

10 - LAB GROUP 1

PROCEDURE - 2

4. **Manipulate an application window**
   ___a. Click-and-hold the left mouse button on the **title bar** at the top of the *WordPad* window, as shown in Figure 2-3.

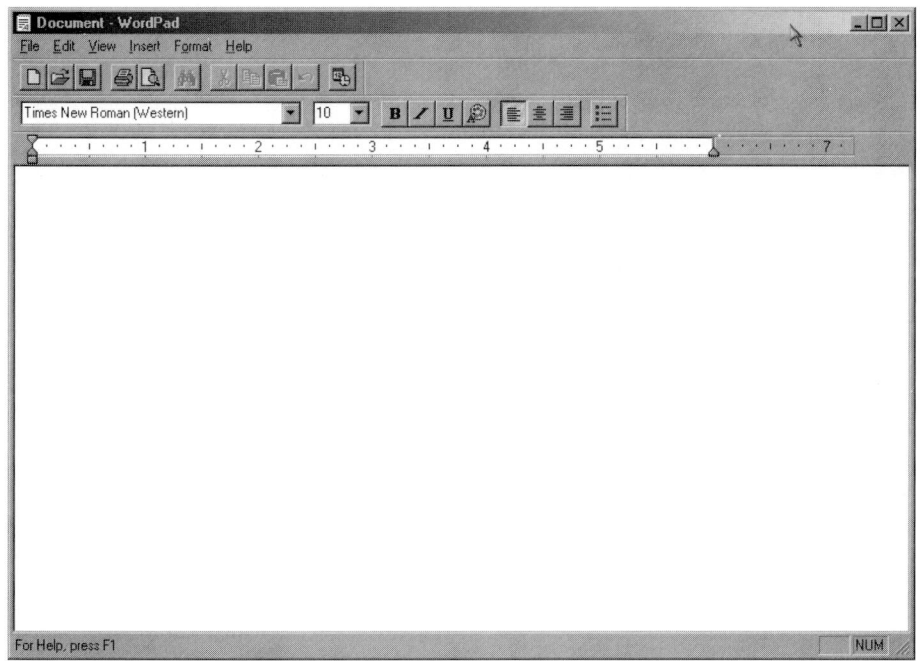

Figure 2-3: WordPad Application

___b. Move the mouse so that the window is approximately centered on the screen.
___c. Release the mouse button.
___d. Move the mouse pointer back and forth over the right edge of the window, so that the cursor turns into a two-way arrow.
___e. Click on the right edge of the window, drag it to the right side of your screen, and release the button.
___f. Move the cursor back and forth over the left side of the window, so that it turns into a two-way arrow.
___g. Click on the left edge of the window, drag it to the center of your screen, and release the button.
___h. Close the *WordPad* program by clicking on the X in the upper-right corner of the window, as shown in Figure 2-4.

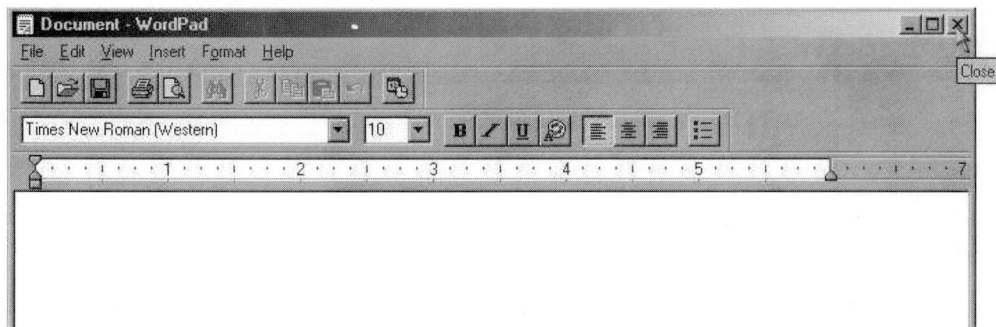

Figure 2-4: The Close Button

PROCEDURE - 2

5. **Start multiple applications**
   ___a. Click on the **Start** button.
   ___b. Select the **Programs** option from the *Start* menu.
   ___c. Move to the **Accessories** entry.
   ___d. Click on the **Notepad** entry to open its window.
   ___e. Repeat steps a through c, clicking on the **WordPad** option to open its window.
   ___f. Repeat steps a through c, clicking on the **Paint** option to open its window.

6. **Minimize/maximize various windows**
   ___a. Click on the dash in the upper-right corner of the *Paint* window as pictured in Figure 2-5.

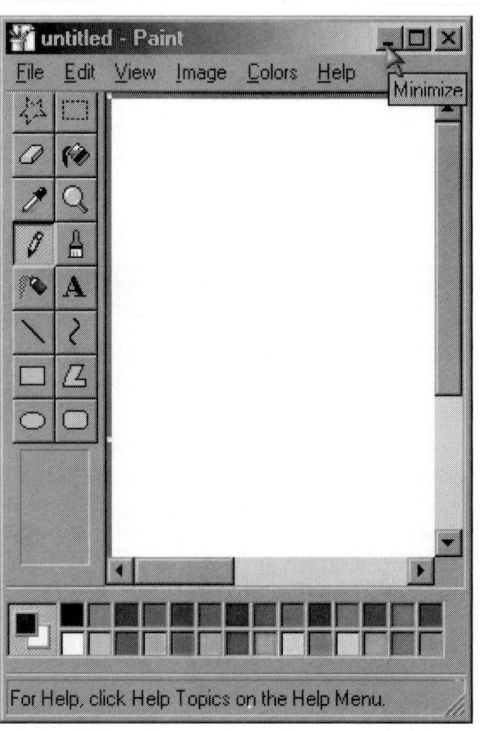

Figure 2-5: Paint Program

NOTE: The window minimizes, and the button representing the application remains on the Taskbar.

___b. Click on the dash in the upper-right corner of the *WordPad* window.

NOTE: The window minimizes to the Taskbar button.

___c. Click on the square in the upper-right corner of the *Notepad* window.

NOTE: The window will maximize to fill the screen.

___d. Click on the double box in the upper-right corner.

NOTE: The window will minimize or return to about half size.

___e. Click on the dash in the upper-right corner to minimize the window to the Taskbar.
___f. Click on the **Notepad** button on the Taskbar to restore the window to the screen. Then, repeat this step for the *WordPad* and *Paint* application windows.

PROCEDURE - 2

7. **Switch between applications**
   - a. Click on the **Notepad title bar** to activate the *Notepad* application and move it to the foreground.
   - b. Click on the **WordPad title bar** to make it the currently active window.
   - c. Click on the **Paint title bar** to make it the currently active window.

NOTE: You may need to click on Paint on the Taskbar.

8. **Arrange the application icons**
   - a. Click on the dash in the upper-right corner of each program's title bar to minimize it to the Taskbar.
   - b. Move the cursor to the **My Computer** icon.
   - c. Click-and-hold the left mouse button to drag the icon to the center of the screen.
   - d. Release the left mouse button.
   - e. Right-click any empty spot on the screen to open the pop-up menu list.
   - f. Move the cursor to the **Arrange Icons** entry, and click on the **Auto Arrange** option.
   - g. Click on each application icon in the Taskbar to restore it to the screen.
   - h. Right-click the title bar of the *Notepad* to open the task list.

NOTE: From here you can move, size, minimize, maximize, or close an application window.

   - i. Close each application by using the task list's **Close** option or by clicking on the **X** button in the upper-left corner of each window.

My Computer

This window contains the Control Panel and icons for the floppy-disk drive, hard drives, and CD-ROM drive. Whenever drives are added to the system, they will appear here. The Control Panel allows you to customize the desktop, among many other things, and it will be discussed in detail later in this procedure.

Windows Explorer

The Windows Explorer utility is used to manage files and disks. It enables the user to copy, move, and delete files on any of the system's drives. The *Windows Explorer* screen is divided into two parts: The left side displays a directory tree, containing all the directories and subdirectories of the system's available drives, and the right side shows the files of the selected directory or subdirectory. A Status Bar at the bottom of the screen shows the number of files and number of bytes the subdirectory consumes. An example of this is illustrated in Figure 2-6 on the next page.

Multiple directories can be displayed on the same screen with the Windows Explorer. This feature makes it easy to perform file operations by simply opening another window. The new window is identical to the first, including its drive icons, and will normally appear directly on top of the first. By resizing each window to fill the top and bottom of the screen respectively, both windows can be accessed with equal ease.

PROCEDURE - 2

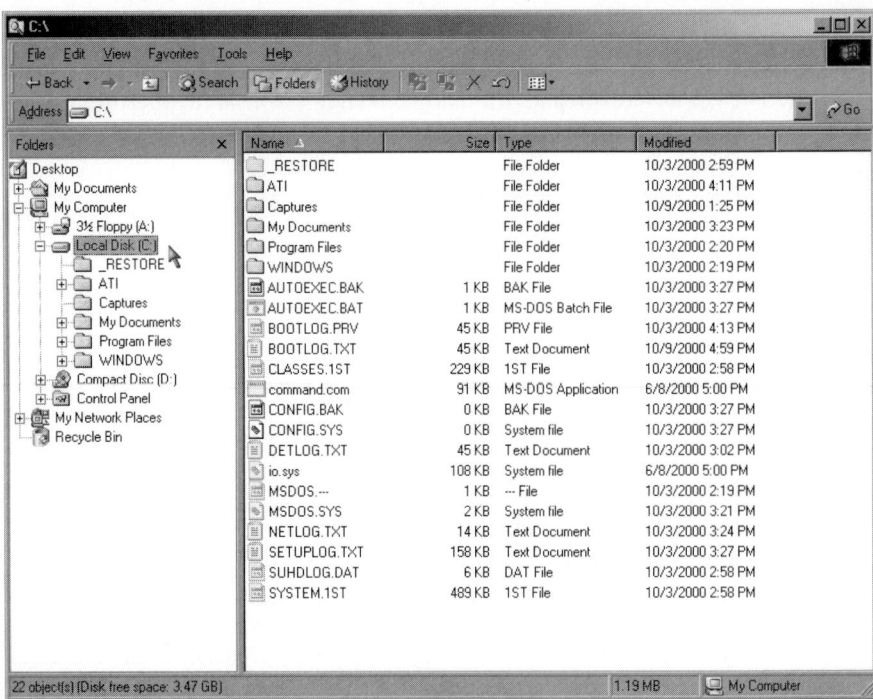

Figure 2-6: Windows Explorer

1. **Open Windows Explorer**
   ___a. Navigate the path *Start/Programs/Accessories/Windows Explorer*.
   ___b. Double-click **My Computer** in the left portion of the screen.
   ___c. Double-click on **Local Disk (C:)**.
   ___d. Record the number of objects in the current directory in Table 2-4a.
   ___e. Record the total free drive space on the current drive in Table 2-4b.

2. **Change directories**
   ___a. Click on the **WINDOWS** folder.

   NOTE: If a Warning screen appears in the right pane of Windows Explorer, simply click on the 'View the entire contents of this folder' link to continue.

   ___b. Record the number of objects in this directory in Table 2-4e.
   ___c. Right-click the Windows directory and choose **Properties**.
   ___d. Record the number of files that are in the Windows directory in Table 2-4f.
   ___e. Click on **OK** to close the *Windows Properties* window.

3. **Create a directory named Students under C:**
   ___a. Click on the **C: drive** icon to highlight it.
   ___b. Select the **File** option from the menu bar.
   ___c. Move the cursor to the **New** option and click on **Folder**.
   ___d. Type the word **Students** in the highlighted folder name box, next to the folder displayed in the right half of the *Windows Explorer* window.
   ___e. Press the ENTER key.

4. **Create a directory under Students using your three initials as the directory (subdirectory) name**
   ___a. On the left side of the screen, click on the **C:\STUDENTS** folder to highlight it.
   ___b. Select the **File** option from the menu bar.
   ___c. Move the cursor to the **New** option, and click on **Folder**.

14 - LAB GROUP 1

PROCEDURE - 2

    ___d.   Type your three initials in the highlighted folder name box, next to the folder displayed in the right half of the *Windows Explorer* window. This is your personal directory.
    ___e.   Press the **ENTER** key.

5. Expand the directory tree to show the subdirectory again
    ___a.   Double-click the **STUDENTS** folder.

6. Hide the subdirectory that uses your initials
    ___a.   Click on the minus sign (-) next to the *C:* folder.
    ___b.   Click on the plus sign (+) next to the *C:\STUDENTS* folder.

Moving Folders Around

When a file is moved, it is copied from one directory or disk to another without leaving a version at the source. Unlike a copy operation, the source file is erased in a move. To copy a file to a different drive, the file can simply be dragged. However, to copy a file to a different directory on the same drive, it must be selected with a right-click, held, dragged, and released. The desired operation is then selected from the options list. To move a file to the same disk, drag the file from the file contents window and drop it at the destination directory on the left side. To move a file to a different drive, right-click and drag it as described above.

Multiple files can be selected for move and copy operations. To select multiple adjacent files, click on the first file folder, press the shift key, and click on the last file. All of the files between the first and last files will be highlighted. To select non-adjacent files for file operations, press the *CTRL* key and click on each file name. Once the multiple files are selected, right-click, hold, and drag them to the desired location and select *Move*, *Copy*, *Cancel*, or *Delete*.

1. Move the personal directory you created earlier to the Windows directory
    ___a.   Click-and-hold the pointer over your personal directory folder.
    ___b.   Drag the folder icon to the *WINDOWS* folder and release.
    ___c.   Double-click the **WINDOWS** folder to open it (if it doesn't automatically open) and verify the folder has been moved there.

2. Copy your personal directory from the Windows directory back to the C:\Students directory
    ___a.   Right-click-and-hold the pointer over your personal directory folder.
    ___b.   Drag the folder to the *STUDENTS* folder and release the mouse button.
    ___c.   Click on the **Copy Here** option.

3. Delete the copy of your personal directory that is under the Windows directory
    ___a.   Click on the **C:\WINDOWS\XXX** folder to highlight it (*XXX* being your initials).
    ___b.   Press the **DELETE** key on the keyboard.
    ___c.   Click on **Yes** to verify sending the folder to the Recycle Bin.
    ___d.   Close the Windows Explorer program.

4. Open the Windows Explorer
    ___a.   Click on **Start**, then **Run**, and type **Explorer**, and click on **OK**.

PROCEDURE - 2

5. **Display file information**
   ___a. Expand My Computer and C:.
   ___b. Click on the **WINDOWS** folder.
   ___c. Click on the **View** option in the menu bar.
   ___d. Click on the **Details** option in the pull-down menu list.

6. **Sort the files under Windows by type**
   ___a. Click on the **WINDOWS** folder, if necessary.
   ___b. Click on the **View** option.
   ___c. Move the cursor to *Arrange Icons*, and then click on the **By Type** option.
   ___d. Scroll down the *WINDOWS* folder until you see text documents.
   ___e. Record the number of Text Document files in Table 2-5.

7. **Search for files**
   ___a. Click on the **C: drive** icon.
   ___b. Select the **Search** button from the toolbar as shown in Figure 2-7.

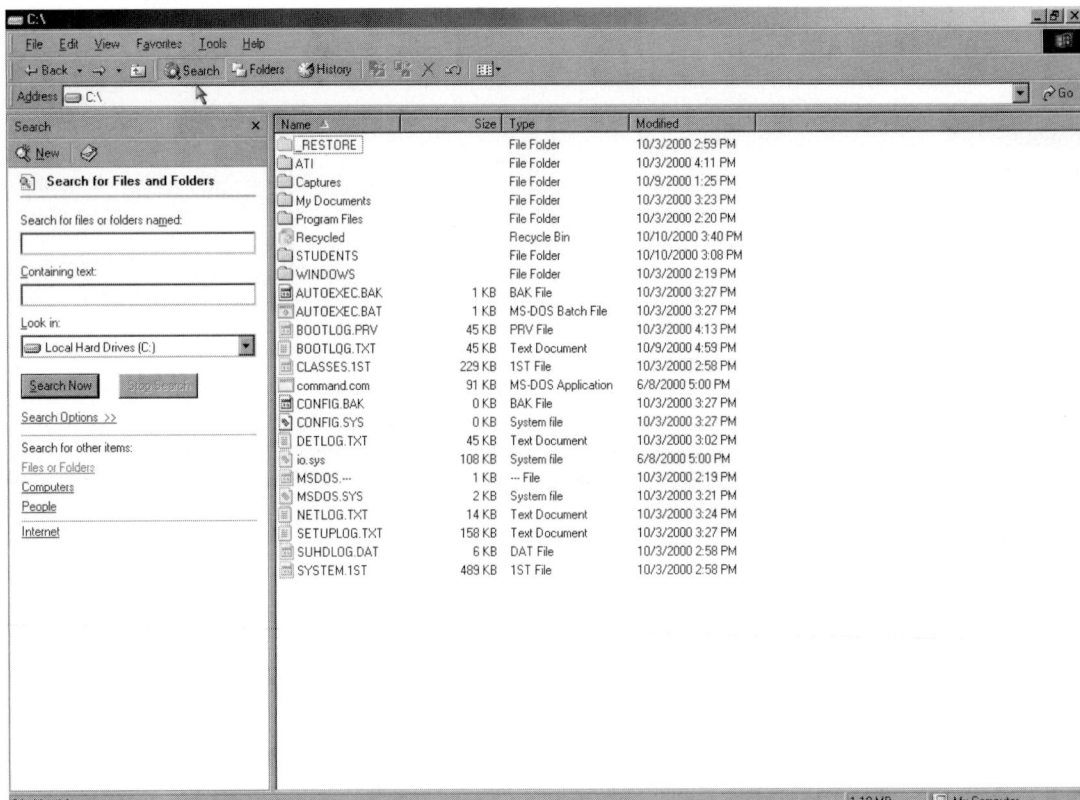

Figure 2-7: Windows Explorer Search View

   ___c. In the left section of the window under *Search for files or folders named*, type ***.txt**.
   ___d. Click on **Search Now** to confirm the selection.
   ___e. Record the number of .txt files in Table 2-6.
   ___f. Click on the **X** in the upper-right corner of the *Search* window to close the Search pane.

NOTE: To restore your folders window click on the Folders button on the button bar.

PROCEDURE - 2

8. **Randomly select files under the WINDOWS folder**
   ___a. Make sure that your personal directory folder is visible on the left side of the screen. If not, double-click the **STUDENTS** folder.
   ___b. Click on the **WINDOWS** folder to highlight it.
   ___c. Click on the first file with a Text Document extension.
   ___d. Press-and-hold the **CTRL** key.
   ___e. Move the cursor to the next file with a Text Document extension, and click on it.
   ___f. Repeat step e for the next two text files.
   ___g. Release the **CTRL** key.

9. **Move the selected files to your personal folder**
   ___a. Move the pointer over one of the highlighted files in the list.
   ___b. Click-and-hold the mouse button while you drag the files to your personal directory.
   ___c. Release the mouse button over your directory folder to drop the files in a new location.

10. **Select all the files under your personal folder**
    ___a. Click on your personal directory folder.
    ___b. Select the first file in the list and click on it.
    ___c. Press-and-hold the **SHIFT** key.
    ___d. Choose the last file.
    ___e. Release the **SHIFT** key.

11. **Copy the files from your personal directory back to the WINDOWS folder**
    ___a. Press-and-hold the **CTRL** key and click on the first file. This will un-highlight the first file.
    ___b. Release the **CTRL** key.
    ___c. Press-and-hold the **CTRL** key and click on the first file. This will highlight the file.
    ___d. Release the **CTRL** key.
    ___e. Right-click and hold the mouse button over the highlighted files and drag them to the *WINDOWS* folder.
    ___f. Release the mouse button over the *WINDOWS directory* folder.
    ___g. On the resultant context menu click on **Copy Here** to copy the files to the *WINDOWS* folder.

12. **Rename the first file in your personal folder to MYFILE**
    ___a. Click on your personal directory folder.
    ___b. Click on the first file in the list.
    ___c. Click on the **File** option in the menu bar.
    ___d. Click on the **Rename** option in the drop-down menu list.
    ___e. Type **Myfile.txt** in the box that appears next to the file selected.
    ___f. Click anywhere on an open portion of the screen.

13. **Delete all the files under your personal folder**
    ___a. Click on your personal directory folder.
    ___b. Click on the first file in the list.
    ___c. Hold down the **SHIFT** key and click on the last file in the list.
    ___d. Release the *SHIFT* key and press the **DELETE** key.
    ___e. Click on the **Yes** button to confirm sending these files to the Recycle Bin.

PROCEDURE - 2

Formatting a Blank Floppy Disk

Windows Explorer can be used to perform other DOS-like functions, such as formatting diskettes. When formatting, the format window will display several options, as shown in Figure 2-8. There are two disk capacities, two format types, and labeling options to choose from. When the disk has been formatted, a summary screen appears providing a detailed report on the format results.

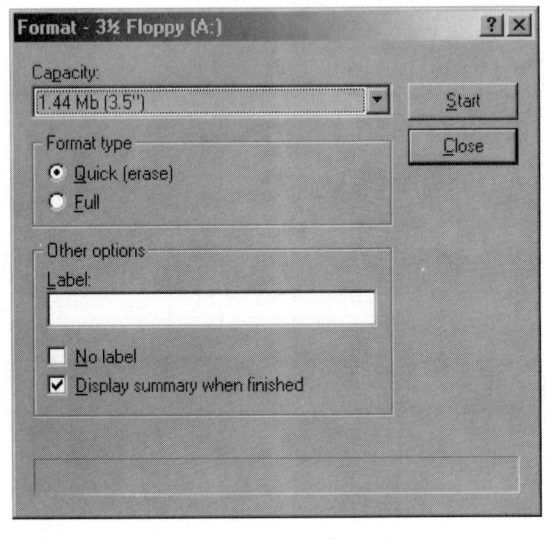

Figure 2-8: Format Window

1. **Format a blank floppy disk**
   - ___ a. Insert the blank disk into the floppy drive.
   - ___ b. Right-click the floppy (**A:**) drive.
   - ___ c. Select the **Format** option from the menu.
   - ___ d. Move to the *Capacity* box and click on it.
   - ___ e. Select the **1.44 MB** option.
   - ___ f. Click on the **Start** button.
   - ___ g. After the procedure is complete, record the total bytes available on the disk in Table 2-7.

   NOTE: *This information is obtained from the format results.*

   - ___ h. Close the *Summary* and *Format* windows by clicking on **Close** in each window.

2. **Copy files from the C: drive to the newly formatted floppy disk**
   - ___ a. Highlight the *Windows* directory.
   - ___ b. Scroll down to where you see the text files ending with .txt.
   - ___ c. Right-click on the first text file in the list and drag it to the floppy (A:) drive.
   - ___ d. Release the right mouse button and choose **Copy Here**.

3. **Change drives**
   - ___ a. Place the student work disk in drive A:.
   - ___ b. Move the cursor to the A: drive branch in the directory tree, and click on it.
   - ___ c. Record the number of objects in the current directory in Table 2-4c.
   - ___ d. Record the total free space on the current drive in Table 2-4d.

4. **Label the disk with your initials**
   - ___ a. Click on the **A: drive** icon.
   - ___ b. Select the **File** option from the list.
   - ___ c. Click on the **Properties** option in the drop-down menu list.
   - ___ d. Type your three initials in the *Label* dialog box.
   - ___ e. Click on the **OK** button.

5. **Close the Windows Explorer**
   - ___ a. Click on the **X** at the upper-right corner of the *Windows Explorer* window.

PROCEDURE - 2

The Control Panel

The Windows Me Control Panel, shown in Figure 2-9, allows the user to customize the desktop and configure many of the system's settings. The Control Panel can be accessed through the desktop's *My Computer* icon, or by clicking on the *Start* button and choosing *Settings*. The customization of the desktop includes setting screen colors and selecting wallpaper. Wallpaper is the pattern that shows behind the various application windows. Other Control Panel options include changing display settings or fonts and establishing *Regional Settings* and *Sound* options. The Control Panel is used to specify how the mouse, keyboard, joystick, modem, and multimedia hardware respond. The Control Panel is also useful in assigning printers and ports for operation.

Figure 2-9: Control Panel

The Control Panel's utilities can be used to add and remove hardware and programs. The *Add New Hardware* and *Add/Remove Programs* options are used to further configure the operation of Windows. The *Add New Hardware* option is used to set up the computer's ports and interrupts so that hardware options do not conflict with each other. The *Add/Remove Programs* option can be used to install and uninstall most of the programs that one would ever install on the computer.

1. **Open the Control Panel**
   ___a. Double-click the **My Computer** icon.
   ___b. Double-click the **Control Panel** icon.
   ___c. Click on the **Maximize** button in the upper-right corner of the *Control Panel* window.

2. **Change the Date and Time**
   ___a. Double-click the Control Panel's **Date/Time** icon.
   ___b. Click on the **Time zone** menu and make sure it's set for your location.
   ___c. Click on the **OK** button to accept the changes.

WINDOWS ME NAVIGATING - 19

PROCEDURE - 2

3. **Change Screen Colors**
   - ___ a. Double-click the Control Panel's **Display** icon.
   - ___ b. Click on the **Appearance** tab.
   - ___ c. Click on the arrow beside the *Scheme* box.
   - ___ d. Scroll down to move through the standard color options available.
   - ___ e. Choose the Windows Standard color scheme by clicking on it.
   - ___ f. Click on the **OK** button to close the *Display Properties* window.

4. **Choosing a Sound effect Scheme**
   - ___ a. Double-click the **Sounds and Multimedia** icon in the Control Panel.
   - ___ b. Click on the arrow beside the *Scheme* box.
   - ___ c. Choose **Windows Default** as the sound theme by clicking on it.
   - ___ d. Click on **No** on the *Save Scheme* window.
   - ___ e. Click on **OK** to save the settings.
   - ___ f. Click on the **X** button at the right corner of the title bar to close the Control Panel.

Windows Setup

Windows Setup is used to add new applications after Windows Me has been installed. Setup can be accessed by double-clicking the Control Panel's *Add/Remove Programs* icon. Configuration changes can be made by clicking on the *Windows Setup* tab. To add or remove a component, click on the box next to it. The *Details* option will display additional information about the selection. To install a new Windows Me application, check the box next to the option and click on the *Apply* button. The system will search the available drives for applications, and then install them. The *Add/Remove* option can also be used to remove nonessential Windows components. This is particularly helpful when the hard drive becomes full. Removing these items can free up about 12 megabytes.

Some manufacturers include a proprietary setup program for their Windows Me applications. These drivers can be installed through the *Run* option from the *Start* menu. This will produce a dialog box that can be used to enter the path of the setup program.

1. **Open Windows Setup**
   - ___ a. Double-click the **My Computer** icon.
   - ___ b. Double-click the **Control Panel** icon.
   - ___ c. Double-click the **Add/Remove Programs** icon.
   - ___ d. Click on the **Windows Setup** tab.
   - ___ e. Record the number of Component options in Table 2-8.

2. **Search for new applications**
   - ___ a. Click in the box beside the *Accessibility options* entry to select that application.
   - ___ b. Click on the **Apply** button.

   NOTE: Windows Me will search the available drives for software related to the application, and install it if it has not already been installed.

   - ___ c. Insert the disk, if requested by the system.
   - ___ d. Reboot the computer when prompted.

3. **Close the Control Panel**
   - ___ a. Click on the **Cancel** button to close the window.
   - ___ b. Click on the **Close** button (**X**) in the upper-right corner of the *Control Panel* window.

PROCEDURE - 2

4. **Exit Windows Me**
   ___a. Click on the **Start** button at the bottom of the screen.
   ___b. Click on the **Shut Down** option.
   ___c. Select the **Shut down** option in the drop-down menu.
   ___d. Click on the **OK** button.
   ___e. Turn off the computer system if it doesn't have the automatic power off capability.

TABLES

Table 2-1

Start Menu Options	

Table 2-2

Programs Menu Options	

WINDOWS ME NAVIGATING - 21

PROCEDURE - 2

Table 2-3

	Accessory Menu Options	

Table 2-4

Table 2-4a:	
Table 2-4b:	
Table 2-4c:	
Table 2-4d:	
Table 2-4e:	
Table 2-4f:	

Table 2-5

Number of Text Document Files:	

Table 2-6

Number of .txt Files Search:	

Table 2-7

Total Bytes Available:	

PROCEDURE - 2

Table 2-8

Number of Component Options:	

LAB QUESTIONS

Feedback

1. Describe the function of the X box in a *Windows Me* window.

2. List the items normally found under the My Computer icon.

3. Which Windows Me utility is similar to the File Manager in previous versions of Windows?

4. If the user wants to perform a DOS operation in Windows Me, describe how this can be accomplished.

5. In the event that a file is mistakenly deleted from a directory, what action can be performed in Windows Me to get it back?

6. Describe what occurs when the user clicks the right mouse button in an open area of the screen.

LAB PROCEDURE 3

Windows Me Command Prompt Navigating

OBJECTIVES

1. Use the DIR command.
2. Manipulate directories and files.
3. Change file attributes.
4. Use the MEM command.

Operating System Technology

RESOURCES

1. PC-compatible desktop/tower computer system—Customer-supplied desktop/tower hardware system **OR** Marcraft MC-8000 Computer Hardware Trainer **OR** suitable PC hardware trainer running Windows Millennium Edition

DISCUSSION

In hard drive–based systems it is common to organize related programs and data into areas called directories. This makes files easier to find and work with, since modern hard drives are capable of holding vast amounts of information. Most directories can hold up to 512 directories or filename entries.

It would be difficult to work with directories if you did not know which one you were working in. The DOS prompt can be set up to display which directory is currently being used. This directory is referred to as the current, or working directory (e.g., C:\DOS\forms would indicate that you were working with programs located in the directory named forms, which is a subdirectory of the directory named DOS). The first back slash represents the root directory on the C: hard drive. When looking at a directory listing, the presence of two dots (..) near the top identify it as a subdirectory. These dots indicate the presence of a parent directory above the subdirectory that you are currently looking at. A single dot (.) is displayed at the top of the listing to represent the current directory. The format for using DOS commands is:

COMMAND

COMMAND (space) location

COMMAND (space) SOURCE location (space) DESTINATION location

The first example applies to DOS commands that occur in a default location, such as obtaining a listing of the files on the current disk drive. The second example illustrates how single-location DOS operations, such as formatting a diskette in a particular disk drive, are specified. The final example illustrates how DOS operations that involve a source and a final destination, such as moving a file from one place to another, are entered.

PROCEDURE - 3

Placing one or more software switches at the end of the basic command can modify many DOS commands. A switch is added to the command by adding a space, a forward-slash (/), and a single letter:

COMMAND (space) option /switch

Common DOS command switches include /P for page, /W for wide format, and /S for system. Different switches are used to modify different DOS commands.

The following is a list of some basic DOS commands that you should know in the event that Windows can't boot up.

DIR: The Directory command gives a listing of the files and directories that are in the current directory from which the DIR command is typed. It also lists the size of the individual files, how many bytes the files take up, and how many megabytes of free disk space are left on the hard drive.

MD: Creates a new directory in an indicated spot in the directory tree structure.

CD: Changes the location of the active directory to a position specified with the command.

DELTREE: Removes a selected directory and all the files and subdirectories below it.

COPY: The file copy command copies a specified file or group of files from one place (disk or directory) to another.

XCOPY: This command copies all the files in a directory, along with any subdirectories and their files. This command is particularly useful for copying files and directories between disks with different formats (e.g., from a 1.2 MB disk to a 1.44 MB disk).

ATTRIB: Changes file attributes such as Read-only (+R or -R), Archive (+A or -A), System (+S or -S), and Hidden (+H or -H). The + and - signs are to add or subtract the attribute from the file.

DEL: This command allows the user to remove unwanted files from the disk when typed in at the DOS prompt.

VER: If the current DOS version is not known, typing this command at the DOS prompt will display it on the screen.

EDIT: This command allows you to edit the contents of many types of files as well as create files.

MEM: This command shows you where your memory is being used.

Operating System Technology

PROCEDURE

1. **Boot the computer to Windows Me**
   ____ a. Turn on the computer and select Windows Millennium Edition from the OS selection menu.

2. **Verify the operating system's version and view a directory listing of the current directory with the VER and DIR commands**
   ____ a. Navigate the path *Start/Programs/Accessories/MS-DOS Prompt*.
   ____ b. At the command prompt, type **VER**.
   ____ c. In Table 3-1, enter the operating system name and version number from the screen.
   ____ d. At the command prompt type **DIR** and press **ENTER** and a listing similar to that shown in Figure 3-1 on the next page scrolls.

NOTE: Notice that some files scrolled by without pausing so that you couldn't see what they were. To be able to see everything in the listing, we need to have a way of controlling the output to the screen so that we can see all of the filenames.

26 - LAB GROUP 1

PROCEDURE - 3

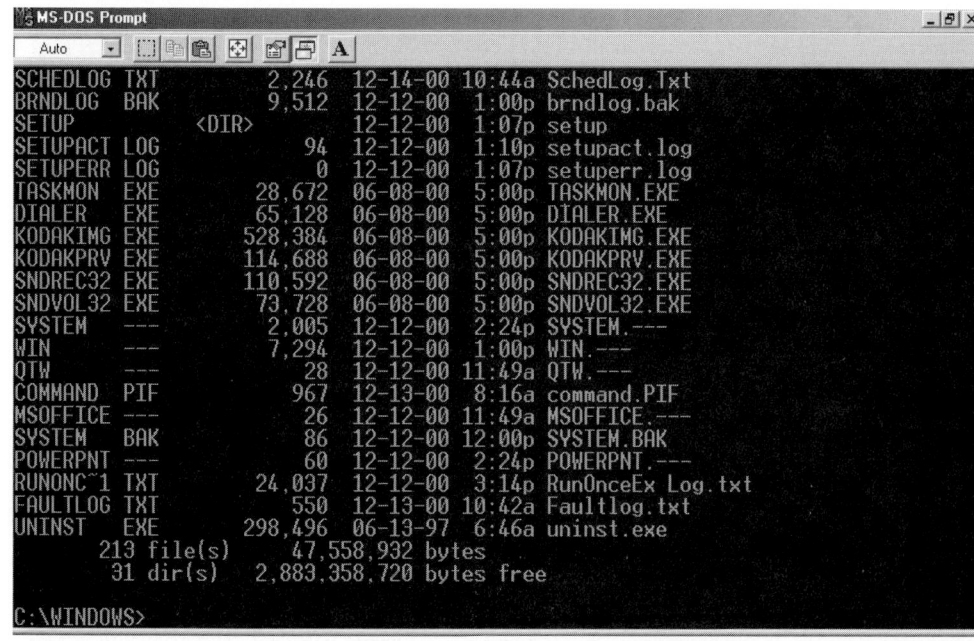

Figure 3-1: MS-DOS Prompt Window – DIR Command

3. **Modify the view of the directory listing using various switches**
   ___a. At the command prompt, type **DIR /p** and press **ENTER**.
   ___b. Press any key to continue viewing the directory listing.
   ___c. Repeat step b until the end of the directory listing is reached.
   ___d. In Table 3-2, enter the amount of files and directories (dir) in the current directory.
   ___e. At the command prompt type **DIR /w** and press **ENTER**, and a listing similar to that shown in Figure 3-2 scrolls.

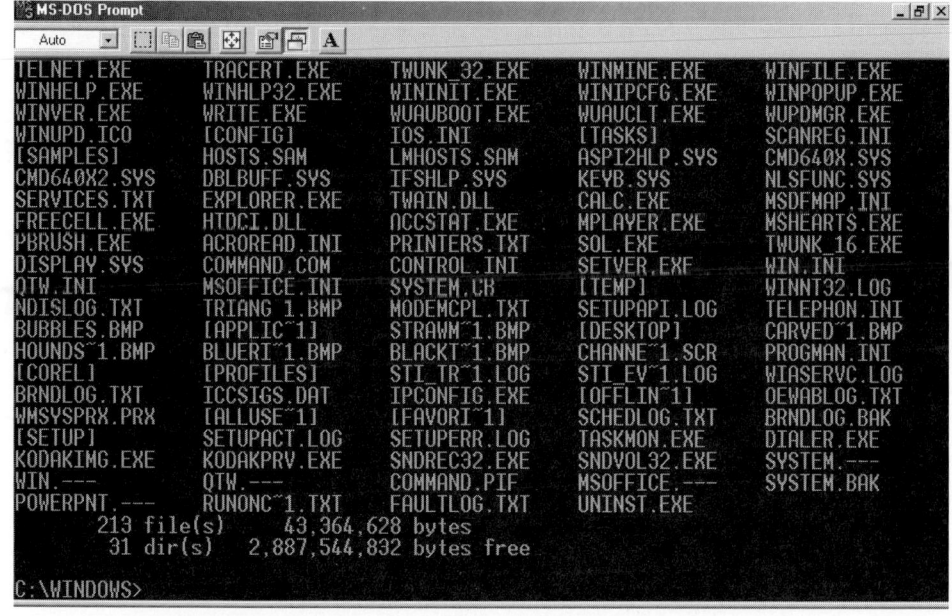

Figure 3-2: MS-DOS Prompt Window – DIR /w Command

   ___f. At the command prompt, type **DIR /w /p** and press **ENTER**.
   ___g. Continue to press any key until the end of the listing is reached.

WINDOWS ME COMMAND PROMPT NAVIGATING - 27

PROCEDURE - 3

4. **Make a directory and change the current directory to the new directory using MD and CD**
   ___ a. Change from the C:\Windows directory to the root directory (C:\) by typing **CD..** and then pressing **ENTER** at the command prompt.
   ___ b. Create a new directory with your first name and last initial in the root directory by typing **MD** "**yourname**" and pressing **ENTER** at the command prompt as shown in Figure 3-3.

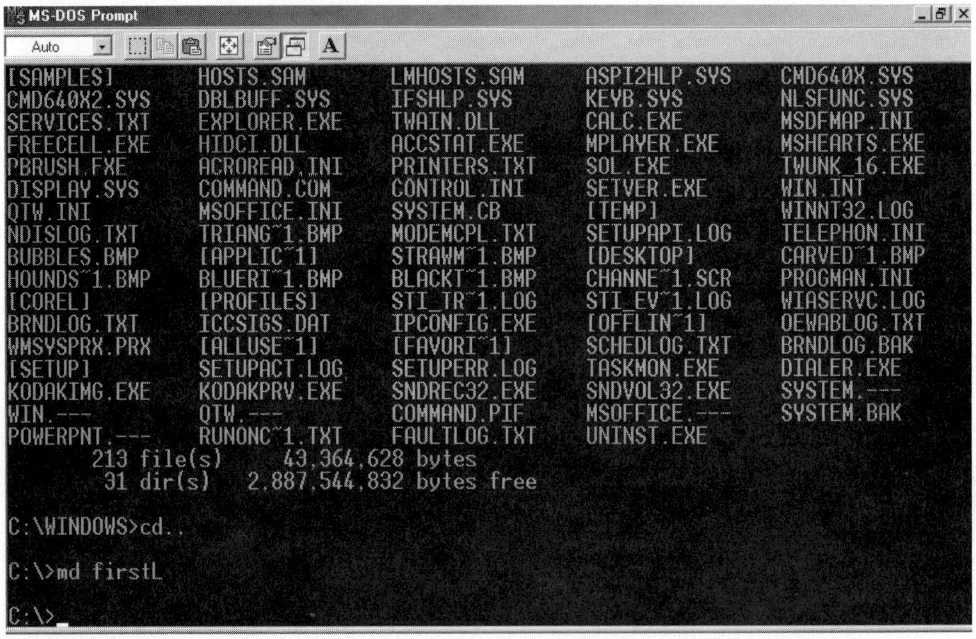

Figure 3-3: MS-DOS Prompt Window – Making a Directory Command

   ___ c. Verify that the new directory was created by typing **DIR /w /p** and pressing **ENTER** at the command prompt.
   ___ d. Change the current directory to your new directory by typing **CD** "**yourname**" and pressing **ENTER** at the command prompt. You should now have a window that looks similar to Figure 3-4.

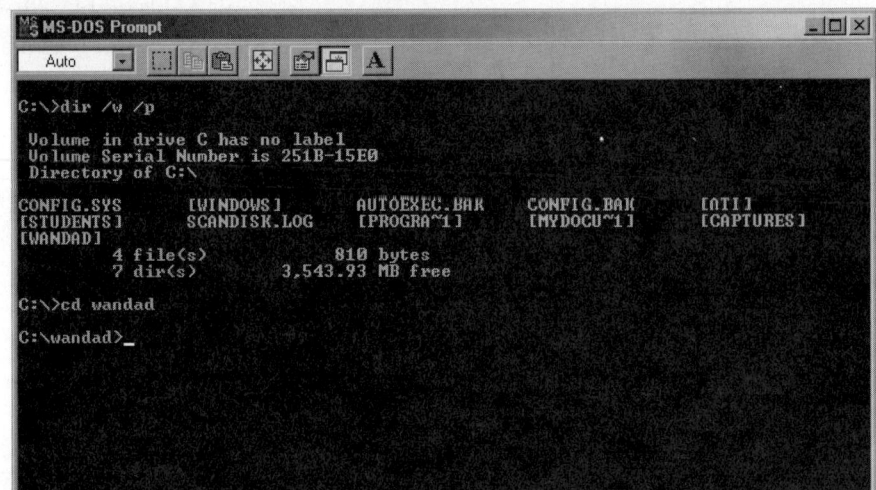

Figure 3-4: MS-DOS Prompt Window – Change Directory Command

5. **Copy files and directories to new locations using COPY and XCOPY commands**
   ___ a. Copy all the files in the *C:\My Documents\My Pictures* directory to your new directory by typing **COPY C:\MYDOCU~1\MYPICT~1** and pressing **ENTER** at the command prompt.

PROCEDURE - 3

NOTE: DOS does not understand filenames that are longer than 8 characters with a 3 character extension. Windows 9x and Windows Millennium, however, do understand long filenames. Any file or directory names that are longer than 8 characters will automatically be truncated in DOS by shortening the name and using the tilde (~) and usually the number 1 afterward.

____ b. In Table 3-3, enter the number of files that were copied to your directory.
____ c. Verify that the files were copied to your directory by typing **DIR** and pressing **ENTER** at the command prompt.
____ d. Copy the directory *C:\My Documents\My Music* and its content to your directory by typing **XCOPY C:\MYDOCU~1\ /E** and pressing **ENTER**.

NOTE: The above XCOPY command will also copy any subdirectories and replace the files that were copied in Step 5a.

____ e. Type **DIR** and press **ENTER** to verify that the files and their directory were transferred.
____ f. At the command prompt, type **CD MYMUSI~1** and press **ENTER**.
____ g. Type **DIR** to verify that the files were copied.
____ h. Type **CD..** and press **ENTER** to switch to your directory.

6. **Delete files and remove directories using the DEL and DELTREE commands**
   ____ a. Delete the file called SAMPLE.JPG from your directory on the hard drive by typing **DEL SAMPLE.JPG** and pressing **ENTER** at the command prompt.
   ____ b. Verify that the file is removable by typing **DIR** and viewing the remaining content of your directory.
   ____ c. Delete the "My Music" directory and all its content by typing **DELTREE MYMUSI~1** and pressing **ENTER**.
   ____ d. When asked to confirm the removal of this directory and its content, press the **Y** key and then **ENTER**, as shown in Figure 3-5.
   ____ e. Type **DIR** and press **ENTER** to verify the deletion of the directory.
   ____ f. Delete all of the remaining files in your directory by typing **DEL *.*** and pressing **ENTER** at the command prompt.
   ____ g. When asked to confirm the deletion of all the files in the directory, press the **Y** key and then **ENTER**.
   ____ h. Repeat Steps c-e for MYPICT~!.
   ____ i. At the command prompt, type **DIR** and press **ENTER** to confirm that the files have been deleted.

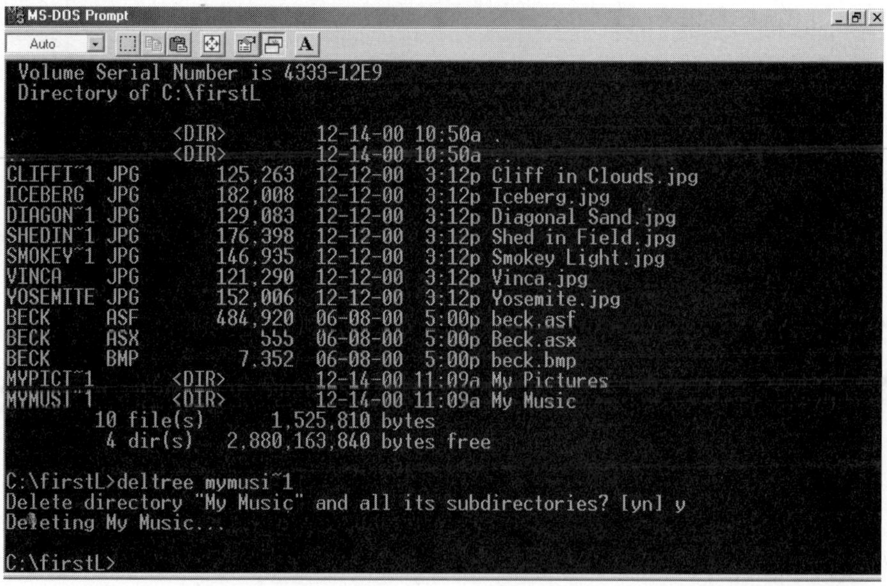

Figure 3-5: MS-DOS Prompt Window – Confirming the Deleting of a Directory

*NOTE: Typing DEL *.* in any directory will cause the operating system to permanently remove every file that is in the current directory, so do not use *.* unless you intend to remove all files.*

7. **Change file attributes of files to make them hidden or not, read only or not, and system files or not, using the ATTRIB command.**
   ____ a. At the command prompt, type **CD..** and press **ENTER** to return to the root directory.

PROCEDURE - 3

___ b. View a directory listing of the root directory using the **DIR** command.
___ c. In Table 3-4 enter the amount of files and directories in the root directory.
___ d. Type **ATTRIB MSDOS.SYS** to see what attributes this file has.

NOTE: S=System, H=Hidden, and R=Read Only

___ e. Remove the system and hidden attributes from the file by typing **ATTRIB -s -h MSDOS.SYS** and pressing **ENTER**.
___ f. Type **DIR** at the command prompt and see that MSDOS.SYS is now visible, and the amount of files in this directory has changed from what you entered in Table 3-4.
___ g. Copy MSDOS.SYS to another location as a backup by typing **COPY MSDOS.SYS C:\"yourname"** (yourname being the name of the directory you made in the previous steps) and pressing **ENTER**, as shown in Figure 3-6.

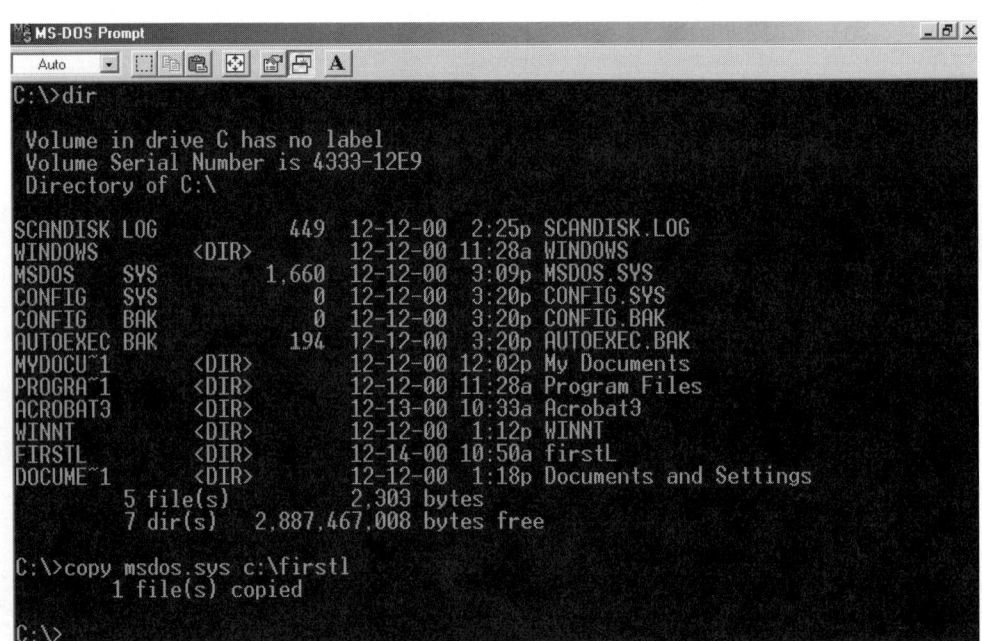

Figure 3-6: MS-DOS Prompt Window – Copying a File

___ h. Try deleting the MSDOS.SYS file now by typing **DEL MSDOS.SYS** and pressing **ENTER**.
___ i. In Table 3-5, document the results.
___ j. Remove the Read Only attribute from MSDOS.SYS by typing **ATTRIB -R MSDOS.SYS** and pressing **ENTER**.
___ k. Now repeat Step h above.
___ l. Type **DIR** and see if the file is still there.
___ m. Copy MSDOS.SYS from your directory back to the root directory by typing **COPY C:\yourname\MSDOS.SYS** and pressing **ENTER**.
___ n. View the directory listing to verify that the file is now back.
___ o. Reset the file's attributes by typing **ATTRIB +R MSDOS.SYS** and pressing **ENTER**.
___ p. Try to delete the file again by typing **DEL MSDOS.SYS** and pressing **ENTER**.
___ q. Reset the file's other two attributes by typing **ATTRIB +S +H MSDOS.SYS** and pressing **ENTER**.
___ r. Check the directory listing to verify that the file is hidden again.

PROCEDURE - 3

8. **View how the system is using the different segments of memory by using the MEM command**
   ___a. At the command prompt, type **MEM** and press **ENTER**.
   ___b. In Table 3-6, fill in all the information from the screen in the appropriate spot on the table.
   ___c. Show memory usage by program classification by typing **MEM /C /P** and pressing **ENTER**.
   ___d. In Table 3-7, list the name of each program module and its Total Memory Usage.
   ___e. Close the *MS-DOS Prompt* windows by typing **EXIT**, and pressing the **ENTER** key.

TABLES

Table 3-1

DOS VER Command	
Operating System:	
Version Number:	

Table 3-2

Current Directory Listing	
Number of Directories:	
Number of Files:	

Table 3-3

Number of Files Copied to Your Directory:	

Table 3-4

Listing of Root Directory	
Number of Files:	
Number of Directories:	

Table 3-5

PROCEDURE - 3

Table 3-6

Memory Type	Total	Used	Free
------------------------------	------------------	------------------	------------------
Conventional			
Upper			
Reserved			
Extended (XMS)			
------------------------------	------------------	------------------	------------------
Total memory			
Total under 1 MB			
Total Expanded (EMS)			
Free Expanded (EMS)			
Largest executable program size			
Largest free upper memory block			
MS-DOS is resident in the upper memory area.			

PROCEDURE - 3

Table 3-7

Name	Total	Conventional	Upper Memory
------------------	------------------	------------------	------------------

LAB QUESTIONS

1. How does XCOPY differ from COPY?

2. What command would you use to verify the amount of free space on a drive?

3. What command would you use to delete the directory that you created and all of the files it contained?

4. What command would you use to view the memory usage per program file?

5. What switch would you use in conjunction with the DIR command to get the screen to pause?

6. What command would you use to find out the version of the operating system?

7. What command would you use to change the current directory to another directory?

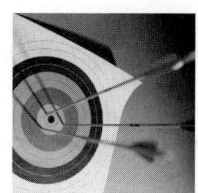

Feedback

LAB PROCEDURE 4

Advanced Windows Me

OBJECTIVES

1. Create the Windows Edition Millennium Startup disk.
2. Investigate the file structure of the Windows Millennium Edition operating system.
3. Boot to a Windows Me Startup disk.
4. Manipulate the system's Registry files.
5. Use the Registry Editor to change registry settings.

Operating System Technology

RESOURCES

1. PC-compatible desktop/tower computer system — Customer-supplied desktop/tower hardware system **OR** Marcraft MC-8000 Computer Hardware Trainer **OR** suitable PC hardware trainer with Windows Millennium Edition installed
2. Blank formatted floppy disk

DISCUSSION

In Windows Me and Windows 9x, many of the functions previously performed by the various INI files in Windows 3.x have been shifted to a central area called the *Registry*. The operating system uses the Registry to store and confirm configuration information. During startup, the system checks the Registry to find out what is installed and how it is configured. Information in the Registry can be manipulated through a utility called the *Registry Editor*.

In the following procedure, you will create a clean Startup disk for troubleshooting problems that arise when Windows becomes corrupt. In addition, you will use the Windows Me Registry Editor to manipulate system settings.

You will also review the standard procedure for restoring the Registry after changes have been made to it. This is particularly important if changes occur that prevent the operating system from restarting. The final portion of the procedure will restore the Registry to the state it was in the last time Windows Me successfully started.

Using the Registry Editor and changing settings within the Registry would take several extensive lab procedures to master. However, the steps of this procedure will adequately introduce you to the Registry, how it is accessed, and how to work with it normally. Further investigation of the Registry and its editing tool is recommended.

PROCEDURE - 4

Operating System Technology

PROCEDURE

Creating a Startup Disk

Since Windows Me does not start up through DOS, it could be very difficult to gain access to the system if Windows becomes disabled. Therefore, it is helpful to have a clean Startup disk to troubleshoot Windows Me–related problems. In the event that the Windows program becomes non-functional, it will be necessary to use the Startup disk you create to restore the system to proper operation.

When creating a floppy Startup disk, Windows Me transfers a number of diagnostic files to it. These utilities are particularly helpful in getting a Windows Me machine operational again. Since there is no path to DOS except through Windows, this disk provides one of the few tools for the technician to service a down machine with this operating system.

1. **Boot the computer to Windows Me**
   - ___a. Turn on the computer and select Windows Millennium Edition from the OS selection menu.

2. **Create the emergency Startup disk**
   - ___a. Navigate the path *Start/Settings/Control Panel* and double-click the **Add/Remove Programs** icon to open the *Add/Remove Programs Properties* window.
   - ___b. Select the **Startup Disk** tab.
   - ___c. Click on the **Create Disk** button, and insert a floppy disk into the A: drive.
   - ___d. When prompted, click on **OK** to begin making the Startup disk.
   - ___e. Click on the **OK** button when the operation is complete.

3. **Examine the Startup disk**
   - ___a. Close the *Control Panel* window.
   - ___b. Navigate the path *Start/Programs/Accessories* and select **Windows Explorer**.
   - ___c. Expand My Computer and click on the 3 1/2-inch floppy A: drive.
   - ___d. List the files created on the Startup disk in Table 4-1.
   - ___e. Label the disk as an Emergency Startup disk.
   - ___f. Close the *Windows Explorer* window.

4. **Examine the *CONFIG.SYS* file on the Startup disk**
   - ___a. Navigate the path *Start/Programs/Accessories* and select **Notepad**.
   - ___b. In the menu bar, click on the **File** menu and select **Open**.
   - ___c. Click on the down arrow to open the *Look In* drop-down menu and select the **3 ½-inch floppy (A:) drive**.
   - ___d. Click on the down arrow to open the *File of type* drop-down menu and select **All Files (*.*)**.
   - ___e. Double-click the **CONFIG.SYS** file and then record each of the subheadings in Table 4-2.

5. **Examine the *AUTOEXEC.BAT* file on the boot disk**
   - ___a. In the menu bar, click the File menu and select Open.
   - ___b. Click on the down arrow to open the *Look In* drop-down menu and select the **3 ½-inch floppy (A:) drive**.

   NOTE: *The file of type drop-down menu will automatically have All Files (*.*) selected unless Notepad has been closed between Step 4 and Step 5.*

   - ___c. Double-click the **AUTOEXEC.BAT** file and examine its content.

36 - LAB GROUP 1

PROCEDURE - 4

___d. Close the *Notepad* utility and then shut down the computer.

Booting to the Windows Me Startup Disk

When the operating system is not functioning properly, it is often difficult to correct the problem from within the operating system itself. Even if the system has not locked up, it is usually best to attempt any fixes by booting to the operating system on an Emergency Startup disk. This will allow you to directly manipulate many of the files on the system.

1. **Boot to the Startup disk**
   ___a. Place the Windows Me Startup disk you created into the floppy (A:) drive.
   ___b. Turn on the computer.
   ___c. Hold down the **SHIFT** and **F5** keys to boot to the MS-DOS prompt.

2. **Examine the file structure of your hard disk**
   ___a. At the A:\> prompt, type **c:** and press the **ENTER** key to change to the *C:\ root* directory.
   ___b. At the C:\> prompt, type **dir /a /p** and press the **ENTER** key to list all the files and subdirectories in the root directory.

   NOTE: *The /a switch causes all system and hidden files to also be displayed. The /p switch causes the list to display one screen at a time while pausing.*

   ___c. As you scroll through the list, record the number of files and directories shown at the bottom of the list in Table 4-3.
   ___d. Remove the Startup disk and press the **Reset** button on the front panel of the computer to restart your computer.
   ___e. Choose **Windows Millennium** from the OS menu.

Using RegEdit

To begin the procedure you must save a copy of the Registry keys, so that they can be restored to the previous settings. Please note that it is important to observe this procedure exactly. Also, most changes will not take effect until Windows is exited and restarted.

1. **Start the RegEdit function**
   ___a. From the *Start* menu, select **Run** and type **regedit** in the *Open* test box.
   ___b. Click on the **OK** button to open the *Registry Editor*.

The RegEdit screen will appear, similar to that shown in Figure 4-1, where the Registry's main keys are depicted.

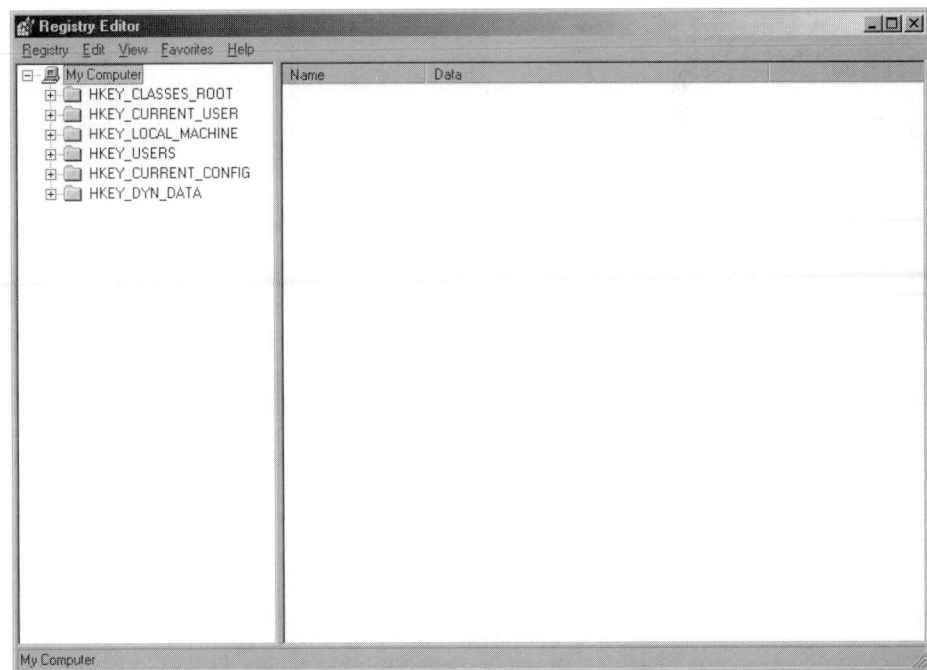

Figure 4-1: Registry Editor

ADVANCED WINDOWS ME - 37

PROCEDURE - 4

RegEdit Screen

Keys and subkeys have nodes assigned to them. Normally, the node will have a + sign if it has not been expanded. To expand the node, simply click on the plus (+) sign. The node will change to a minus (-) sign, and the structure of the node will be expanded to show the subkeys directly below it. To collapse the structure, click on the minus sign.

When a subkey is selected, a Value Entry will appear in the window on the right side of the screen. There are three parts to the Value Entry — the type of data (as denoted by the symbol in the icon), the name of the value, and the value setting. The value can be one of two types — binary data signified by 0s and 1s in the icon, or human-readable character strings signified by an "ab" character pair in the icon.

1. **Export the Registry to a backup disk**
    - ___a. In the menu bar, click on the **Registry menu** and then select **Export Registry**.
    - ___b. Click on the radio button next to **All** to select it.
    - ___c. Click on the down arrow to open the **Save in** drop-down menu and select the **C:** drive.
    - ___d. In the *File name* text box, type **regback** and then click on the **Save** button to begin the exporting process.
    - ___e. Navigate the *Start/Programs/Accessories* path and select **Windows Explorer**.
    - ___f. Click on the plus (+) sign next to *My Computer* to expand the directory tree.
    - ___g. Highlight the **C:** drive on the left side of the window, and then scroll through the list of files on the right to verify that the backup field *regback.reg* is there.
    - ___h. Close *Windows Explorer* by clicking on the **X** button in the upper right corner of the window

    NOTE: Normally you wouldn't back up the Registry to the computer that the Registry belongs to. You wouldn't be able to successfully back up the Registry if you couldn't access the contents of that computer to restore the Registry. The size of the backed up Registry is much larger than a floppy disk can hold and without the computers networked at this time, there isn't much else to do. This will however make you familiar with backing up the Registry.

2. **Review the method for restoring the Registry after changes**
    - ___a. From within the *Registry Editor* window, click on the **Help** menu in the menu bar and select **Help Topics**.
    - ___b. In the left window pane, click on **Restore the registry** to bring the help file on this subject into view in the right window pane.
    - ___c. Record the steps shown in the right window pane for restoring the Registry in Table 4-4.
    - ___d. Click on the **X** in the upper-right corner to close the *Registry Editor Help* window.

HKEY_CLASSES_ROOT

The HKEY_CLASSES_ROOT key contains information that defines certain software settings.

1. **Examine several Windows Me file type definitions**
    - ___a. Double-click on the **HKEY_CLASSES_ROOT key**.
    - ___b. Scroll down through the *File Type* listing, and click on the **ani** entry.
    - ___c. Record the type of data this file extension represents, from under the *Data* column on the right, in Table 4-5a.
    - ___d. Repeat Steps b and c for the **avi**, **bmp**, and **jpeg** file types.
    - ___e. Record the definitions from Step d in Table 4-5b through d.

PROCEDURE - 4

HKEY_LOCAL_MACHINE

The HKEY_LOCAL_MACHINE key contains specific hardware and software settings information about the local system.

1. **Examine the content of the HKEY_LOCAL_MACHINE key**
   ___a.   Double-click the **HKEY_LOCAL_MACHINE** key.
   ___b.   Double-click the **CONFIG** folder.
   ___c.   Double-click the **0001** and **DISPLAY** folders.
   ___d.   Select the **FONTS** folder, and record the font types currently available for the monitor in Table 4-6.
   ___e.   Select the **SETTINGS** folder for the Display.
   ___f.   Record the Setting values for the monitor display in Table 4-7.

2. **Examine the system's configuration settings in the HKEY_LOCAL_MACHINE key**
   ___a.   Move to and open the **System/Current Control Set/Control/Print/Printers subkey**.
   ___b.   List any installed printer drivers in Table 4-8.
   ___c.   Close all extended subkeys by clicking on their minus (-) signs.
   ___d.   Close the *Registry* window

HKEY_CURRENT_USER

The HKEY_CURRENT_USER key contains information about all of the users that are currently logged on the system. It points to the HKEY_USERS key. In this section of the procedure, the interrelationships between the Control Panel and the HKEY_CURRENT_USER and HKEY_USERS keys will be demonstrated.

1. **Check the color settings in the Control Panel**
   ___a.   Double-click the **My Computer** icon on the desktop.
   ___b.   Double-click the **Control Panel** icon.
   ___c.   Double-click the **Display** icon.
   ___d.   Click on the **Appearance** tab.
   ___e.   Click on the down arrow to open the *Item* drop-down menu and select **Active Title**.
   ___f.   Click on the **1st Color** button.
   ___g.   Click on the **Other** button at the bottom of the color swatches.
   ___h.   Record the color values for red, green, and blue in Table 4-9a through c.
   ___i.   Using the position site finder inside the palette, and the Luminance arrow to the right of the palette, change the color to what is shown in Figure 4-2.

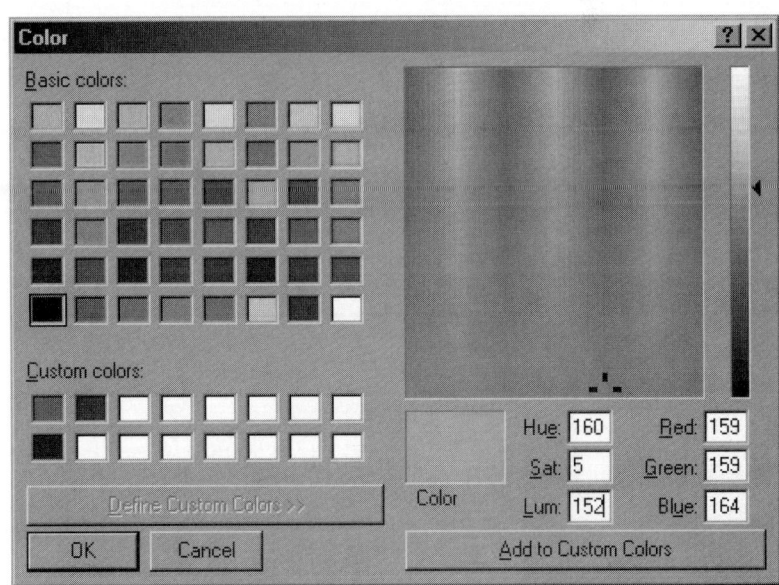

Figure 4-2: Windows Display Color Palette

PROCEDURE - 4

  ___j. Record the final red, blue, and green color values in Table 4-9d through f.
  ___k. Click on two **OK** buttons to return to the *Control Panel* window.
  ___l. Close the Control Panel.
  ___m. Close the *My Computer* window.

2. **Examine the Control Panel settings in the HKEY_CURRENT_USER key**
    ___a. Open the Registry and double-click the **HKEY_CURRENT_USER** key.
    ___b. Double-click the **CONTROL PANEL** folder.
    ___c. Click on the **COLORS** folder.
    ___d. Record the color values for the Active Title in Table 4-9g.

3. **Examine the Control Panel settings in the HKEY_USERS key**
    ___a. Scroll down to the **HKEY_USERS key** and double-click on it.
    ___b. Double-click the **DEFAULT** folder.
    ___c. Double-click the **CONTROL PANEL** folder.
    ___d. Click on the **COLORS** folder.
    ___e. Record the color values for the Active Title in Table 4-9h.

Adjusting Color Values

1. **Compare the change to the definition keys**
    ___a. Navigate to *HKEY_CURRENT_USER/Control Panel* and click on the **COLORS** folder.
    ___b. Record the color values for the Active Title in Table 4-9i.
    ___c. Navigate back to the *HKEY_USERS/Default/Control Panel* and click on the **COLORS** folder.
    ___d. Record the color values for the Active Title in Table 4-9j.

2. **Review the devices controlled by the CONTROL PANEL folder**
    ___a. Move to the **CONTROL PANEL** folder in the HKEY_CURRENT_USER key and select it.
    ___b. List the system devices found under the Control Panel in Table 4-10.

3. **Close the Registry Editor**

PROCEDURE - 4

TABLES

Table 4-1

Files Created on Startup Disk		

Table 4-2

Subheadings in CONFIG.SYS File		

Table 4-3

Number of Files and Directories in C:\ Root Directory	
Files:	
Directories:	

ADVANCED WINDOWS ME - 41

PROCEDURE - 4

Table 4-4

	Steps for Restoring the Registry
1.	
2.	
3.	
4.	
5.	

Table 4-5

	Windows Me File Type Definitions
a. ani	
b. avi	
c. bmp	
d. jpeg	

Table 4-6

Available Font Types

PROCEDURE - 4

Table 4-7

Display Setting Values			
Setting	Value	Setting	Value

Table 4-8

Installed Printers	

Table 4-9

Color Settings of Active Title			
Table	Value	Table	Value
4-9a		4-9f	
4-9b		4-9g	
4-9c		4-9h	
4-9d		4-9i	
4-9e		4-9j	

ADVANCED WINDOWS ME - 43

PROCEDURE - 4

Table 4-10

System Devices Under Control Panel	

Feedback

LAB QUESTIONS

To answer some of these questions, it will be necessary to have the tools on the display screen.

1. Where in Windows did you go to create the Startup disk?
2. What would you use the Setup disk for?
3. Which tool is used to place restrictions on different parts of the system?
4. Where is the screen's color information found in the Registry?
5. What are the three parts of a subkey value entry?
6. How is a key or subkey entry expanded?

LAB PROCEDURE 5

Windows 2000 Navigation

OBJECTIVES

1. Understand directory structure.
2. Create a Notepad document.
3. Cut, copy, paste, and rename files.
4. Search for files.
5. Change Windows Explorer views.
6. Modify folder options.
7. Use Control Panel.
8. Configure appearance.

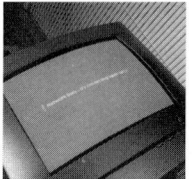

Operating System Technology

RESOURCES

1. PC-compatible desktop/tower computer system — Customer-supplied desktop/tower hardware system **OR** Marcraft MC-8000 Computer Hardware Trainer **OR** suitable PC hardware trainer with Windows 2000 Professional installed

DISCUSSION

It is important to know how to use the interface of Windows 2000. At first glance it may look similar to the Windows 9x environment, but the operation of Windows 2000 is somewhat different. This lab will familiarize you with some of the basic commands associated with navigating Windows 2000. You will learn how to change the appearance of windows, a few basic Control Panel settings, and folder options.

PROCEDURE

1. **Navigation and directory structure**
   ___ a. Boot the computer to Windows 2000.
   ___ b. Move your mouse to the bottom left of the screen and click on **Start**.
   ___ c. Follow the path *Start/Programs/Accessories/Windows Explorer*, similar to Figure 5-1. Click on the down arrows if necessary.

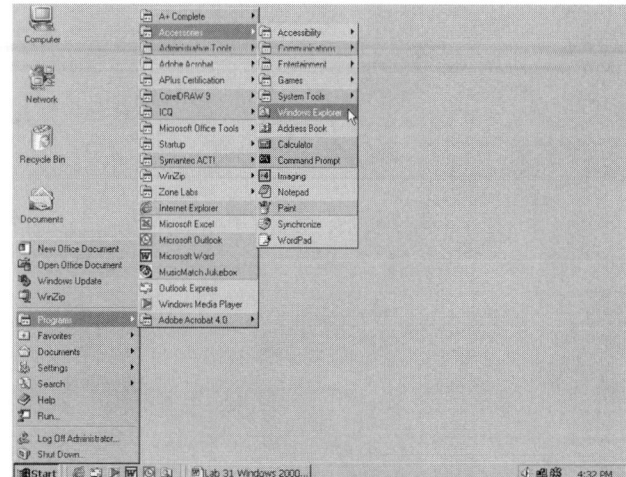

Figure 5-1: The Desktop and Start Menu

WINDOWS 2000 NAVIGATION - 45

PROCEDURE - 5

___ d. The file system on the computer is organized into a group of folders. Double-click through the path *My Computer/C:/WINNT*. On the right-hand window pane you can see the content of that folder.

NOTE: If the configuration is such that you do not see the folder's content, it will be necessary to click on the "Show Files" link to view the folder's content.

___ e. Click on the (**C:**) drive and then click on **File/New/Folder**, as shown in Figure 5-2.

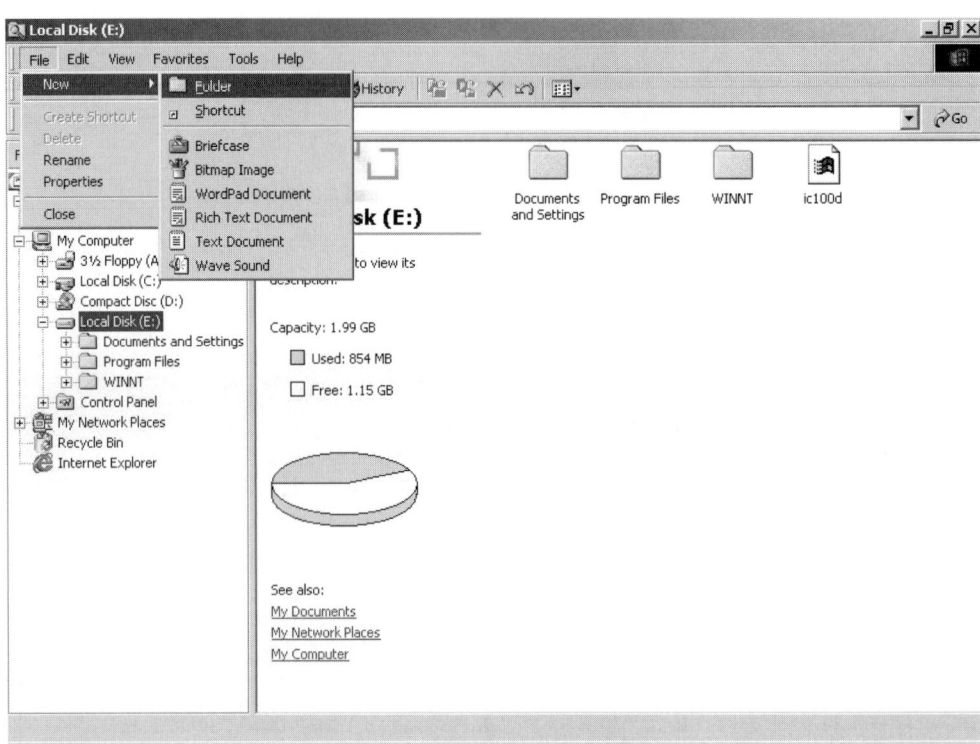

Figure 5-2:
Windows Explorer

___ f. Type **YourInitials** for the name of the folder and press **ENTER**.
___ g. Move the folder into the *WINNT* folder by clicking and holding the mouse, dragging the folder on top of the folder, and releasing the mouse.
___ h. Close Windows Explorer by clicking on the "**X**" in the top right of the window.
___ i. On the desktop, double-click on **My Computer**.
___ j. Right-click the (**C:**) drive, and click on **Properties**. Record the free space in Table 5-1.
___ k. Click on **OK** for *Local Disk (C:) Properties*.
___ l. Open the (**C:**) drive by double-clicking on the icon. Open the *WINNT* Folder.
___ m. Look for the *YOURINITIALS* folder you just created. Right-click on it and select **Delete**.
___ n. When you are asked to confirm, click on **Yes**.
___ o. Close all open windows.

2. **Create a Notepad document**
___ a. Open *Notepad* by navigating the path *Start/Programs/Accessories/Notepad*. This simple text-edit program will now start.
___ b. Maximize the program by clicking on the center button in the top right of the title bar.
___ c. Type **This is a test** in the document. Click on **File/Save**.
___ d. Type **YourName.txt** for the filename.
___ e. Select the menu to the right of *Save in:*

PROCEDURE - 5

___f.   Select Local Disk (**C:**). The window should look similar to Figure 5-3.

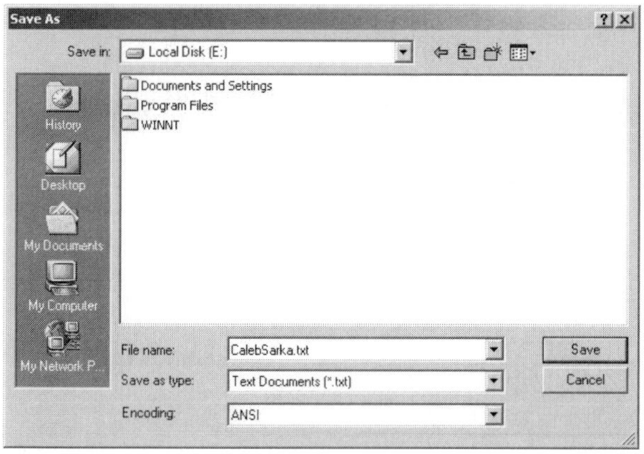

Figure 5-3: Save Dialog

___g.   Click on **Save**.
___h.   Close *Notepad*.

3. Create a shortcut

NOTE: In the following procedures, if the My Computer window opens in a full-sized window or maximized, you will not be able to see your desktop. If so, click on the "square" button at the right corner of the title bar to restore it to its previous size. You can then resize the window, if necessary, to see the desktop.

___a.   Open *My Computer*. Double-click on **C:**
___b.   Look for the file *YourName.txt*. Right-drag it to the desktop and choose **Create Shortcuts Here**, as shown in Figure 5-4.
___c.   You have just created a shortcut to the text file.

NOTE: This is a convenient way of accessing programs and files. Double-clicking a shortcut will open the file or program that is referenced.

___d.   Close any open windows.

Figure 5-4: Right-Drag Options

4. Cut, copy, paste, and rename files
___a.   Right-click the **Shortcut to YourName.txt** and click on **Copy**.
___b.   Go through the path *My Computer/(C:)*. Right-click in any blank space, and click on **Paste**.

NOTE: This Copy/Paste method can be used for duplicating any file, program or shortcut to any folder or location within the Windows realm.

___c.   Right-click the shortcut you just made and click on **Rename**.
___d.   Type **YourName2 Shortcut** and press the **ENTER** key on the keyboard.
___e.   Right-click the shortcut you just renamed and choose **Cut**.
___f.   Right-click the desktop and choose **Paste**.
___g.   Delete the two shortcuts (*Shortcut to YourName.txt* and *Shortcut to YourName2*) from the desktop by clicking on the first, holding the **CTRL** key on the keyboard, and clicking on the second.
___h.   Release the **CTRL** key, and right-click on one and choose **Delete**.
___i.   Choose **Yes** to confirm the deletion of the two files.

NOTE: Notice that you are only deleting shortcuts to the file, not the actual "YourName.txt" file.

PROCEDURE - 5

___j. Right-click the **Recycle Bin** on the desktop, choose **Empty Recycle Bin**, and confirm by clicking on **Yes** when prompted.
___k. Close all open windows.

5. **Search for files**
   ___a. Navigate the path *Start/Search/For Files or Folders*.
   ___b. Type **YourName.txt** into the *Search for files or folders named:* field.
   ___c. Choose **Look In Local Disk (C:)** as in Figure 5-5.

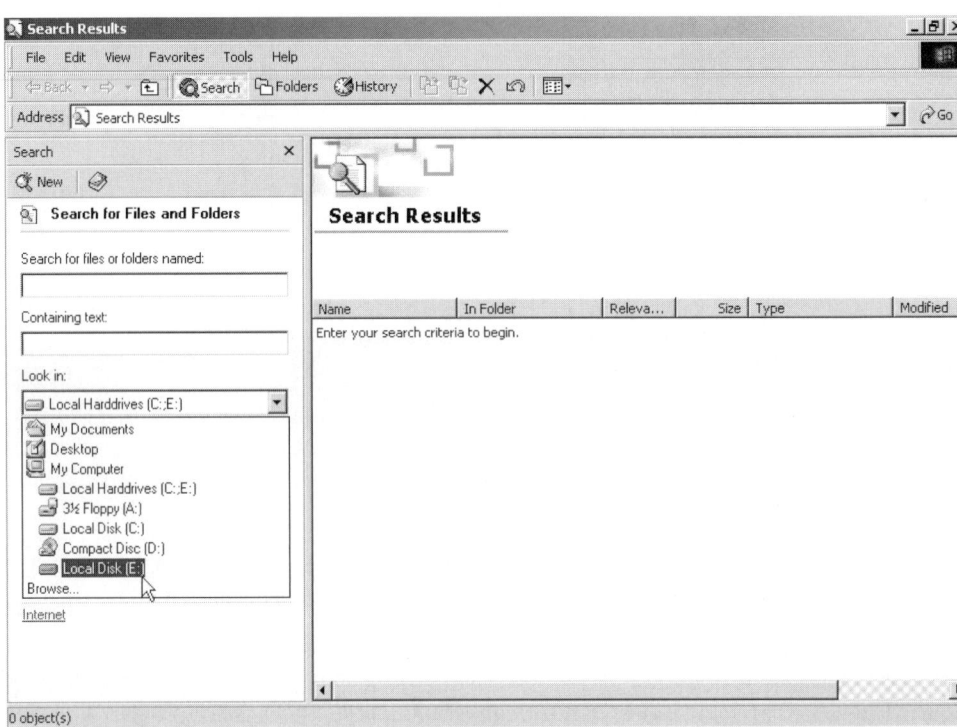

Figure 5-5: Search for Files and Folders

   ___d. Click on **Search Now**.
   ___e. You should see the file "YourName.txt" appear in the right-hand window pane. Notice the information you can see about the file.
   ___f. You may need to use the scroll bar in the bottom of the window to see additional information about the file. Record the desired information in Table 5-2.

NOTE: You can now manipulate the file found in the same manner as using Windows Explorer.

   ___g. Delete *test.txt* by right-clicking on the file's icon and choosing **Delete**. Choose **Yes** when prompted.

NOTE: Delete the actual file, not the shortcut, in the RECENT folder.

   ___h. Close all open windows.

6. **Windows Explorer views**
   ___a. Open *My Computer*.
   ___b. Navigate the path *C:\WINNT*. If necessary click on **Show files** on the left-hand column.
   ___c. Click on the **View** menu. Record the item with a "dot" in Table 5-3.

PROCEDURE - 5

___ d. Change your view to **Details**. Observe the window. It should look similar to Figure 5-6.

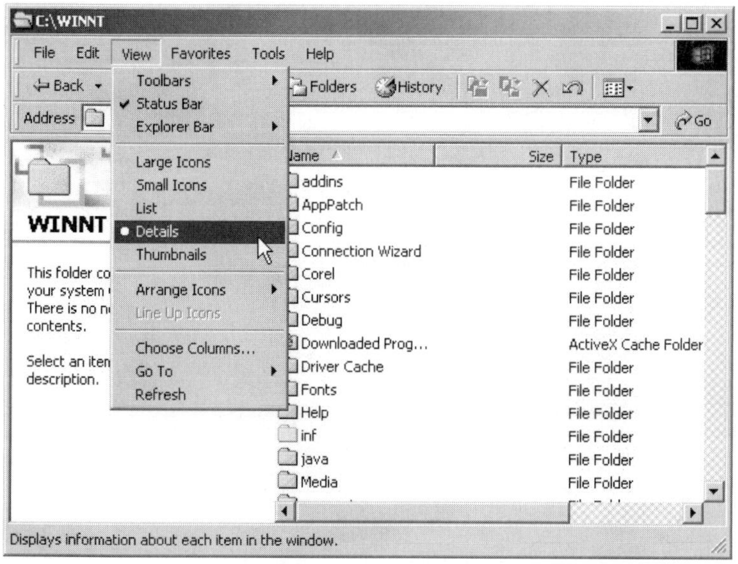

Figure 5-6: Details View

___ e. Look for the *Windows Explorer* application. Record its size in Table 5-4.
___ f. Change your view to **Thumbnails**.
___ g. Right-click on a blank space in the folder and choose **Arrange Icons/By Type**.
___ h. Scroll down to find a bitmap image and double-click on your selection. Record the filename in Table 5-5.
___ i. An image-editing program such as *Paint* should open. Observe it and close the program.
___ j. Now change your view of the *WINNT* folder to **Large Icons**, **Small Icons**, and **List** in turn. Observe the differences in each.
___ k. Close all windows.

7. **Folder Options**
   ___ a. Open *My Computer*.
   ___ b. Click on **Tools/Folder Options**. In this window you can change settings on browsing local items, file types, and offline file configurations.
   ___ c. Click on the **View** tab. The window should look similar to Figure 5-7.
   ___ d. Scroll down and verify that *Show My Documents on the Desktop* is checked. Click on **Apply**.
   ___ e. Click on **OK**.
   ___ f. Now uncheck the same item in the *Folder Options* window. Record your observations in Table 5-6.
   ___ g. Recheck the item.
   ___ h. Click on **OK** and close all windows.

8. **Basic Control Panel**
   ___ a. Open the Control Panel using the path *Start/Settings/Control Panel*.
   ___ b. Record how many objects exist in Table 5-7.
   ___ c. Double-click the **Mouse** icon.
   ___ d. Click on the **Motion** tab.
   ___ e. Increase the speed to **Fast**, and move the mouse.
   ___ f. Decrease the speed to **Minimum**, and move the mouse.

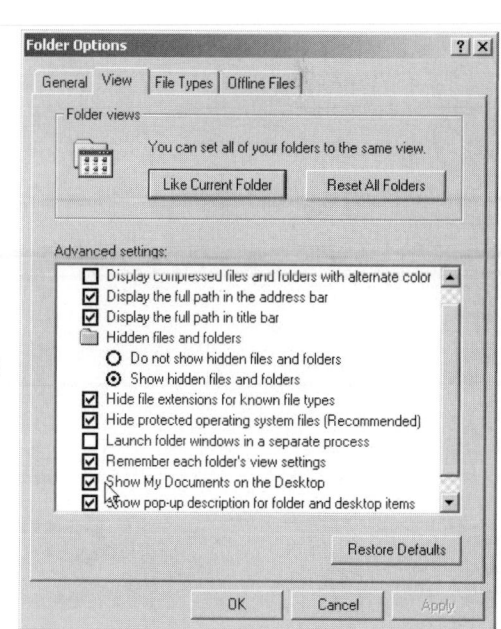

Figure 5-7: Folder Options View

WINDOWS 2000 NAVIGATION - 49

PROCEDURE - 5

    ___g.   Change the speed back to **Normal** and click on **OK**.
    ___h.   In Control Panel double-click the **Keyboard** icon.
    ___i.   Change the Cursor blink rate to its *fastest* setting. Observe the cursor on the left.
    ___j.   Change the Cursor blink rate to its *slowest* setting. Observe the cursor on the left.
    ___k.   Click on **Cancel** and close all open windows.

9. **Windows appearance**
    ___a.   Right-click on the desktop and click on **Properties**. In this window you can change settings for your background, screen saver, windows colors, screen effects, and display adapter settings.
    ___b.   Click on the **Appearance** tab.
    ___c.   Choose the **Brick** scheme and click on **Apply**.
    ___d.   Choose **3D Objects** under the item drop-down menu.
    ___e.   Follow the path *Color/Other*.
    ___f.   Click on a color of your choice as in Figure 5-8, and then click on **OK**.

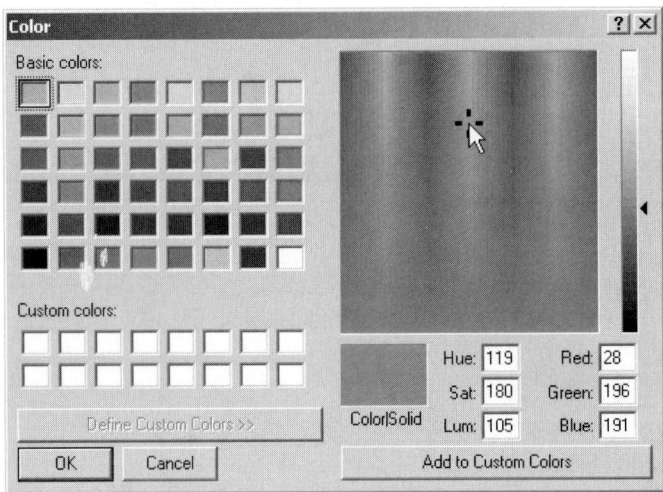

Figure 5-8: Color Palette

    ___g.   Click on **Apply**. Record the color you chose in Table 5-8.
    ___h.   Change the *Scheme* back to **Windows Standard** and click on **OK**.

TABLES

Table 5-1

Hard Drive Free Space:	

PROCEDURE - 5

Table 5-2

In Folder:	
Size:	
Type:	
Modified:	

Table 5-3

View Item with a "Dot":	

Table 5-4

Size of Explorer Application:	

Table 5-5

Bitmap Image Filename:	

Table 5-6

Table 5-7

Table 5-8

PROCEDURE - 5

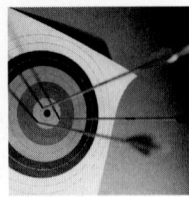

Feedback

LAB QUESTIONS

1. How are the Start menu and file system organized?
2. What is the mouse operation used for moving a folder?
3. What is the method used in this lab for creating a shortcut?
4. What are four common operations for file manipulation?
5. How is the file search window similar to Windows Explorer?
6. What is the Folder Options window used for?
7. What is the Display Properties window used for?
8. What is the "Thumbnails" view?
9. What are the two areas of the Control Panel used in this lab?
10. What are the 3D objects?

LAB PROCEDURE 6

Windows 2000 Administrative Tools

OBJECTIVES

1. View Component Services (COM+).
2. View Data Sources (ODBC).
3. View Event Viewer.
4. View Local Security Policy.
5. Use a Performance Counter.
6. View Services.
7. View Telnet Server Administration.

Operating
System
Technology

RESOURCES

1. PC-compatible desktop/tower computer system — Customer-supplied desktop/tower hardware system **OR** Marcraft MC-8000 Computer Hardware Trainer **OR** suitable PC hardware trainer with Windows 2000 installed

DISCUSSION

COM+ is a set of services based on extensions of Microsoft Transaction Server (MTS) and the Component Object Model (COM). The idea of COM applications is not at all new. It's simply the term used to refer to groups of COM components developed to work together. A COM application example is Microsoft Excel, which consists of a primary executable and accompanying application extension DLLs for spell checking, Visual Basic functionality, and so on. Some of what differentiates a COM+ application is written into the component code, and some is defined through the Component Services administrative tool.

COM+ is a part of the Microsoft Management Console (MMC). MMC does not perform administrative functions, but works with tools that do. MMC can be used to create, save, and open administrative tools (called MMC consoles) that manage the hardware, software, and network components of your Windows system. MMC is a feature of Windows 2000, Windows NT, Windows 95, and Windows 98. The Component Services Console Tree can use the console tree of the Component Services administrative tool to view the applications, components, and security roles.

PROCEDURE - 6

Operating System Technology

PROCEDURE

1. **Component Services**
   ___a. Boot the computer to Windows 2000.
   ___b. Navigate the path *Start/Settings/Control Panel*.
   ___c. Double-click **Administrative Tools**. The window should look similar to Figure 6-1.

Figure 6-1: Administrative Tools

   ___d. You should now see the shortcuts to the eight administrative tools provided in Windows 2000. Double-click **Component Services**.

   NOTE: You may need to maximize the window and resize the window pane.

   ___e. Expand the *Component Services* icon that appears by clicking on the plus (+) sign next to the *Component Services* icon.
   ___f. Click on the plus (+) sign next to the *Computers* icon.
   ___g. Then click on the plus (+) sign next to the *My Computer* icon.
   ___h. Expand the *COM+ APPLICATIONS* Folder. This corresponds to the applications installed on this computer. You can change the properties of an application by right-clicking the application and then clicking on **Properties**.
   ___i. Record the three items that appear in Table 6-1.
   ___j. Expand the *Distributed Transaction Coordinator*. This contains the Transaction List, which displays current transactions in which the computer is participating. It also contains Transaction Statistics.
   ___k. Click on the **Transaction Statistics**. In the right-hand window pane, information such as performance, types, speed, and maximum and minimum response time for the transactions in which a computer participates is displayed. The window should look similar to Figure 6-2 on the next page.

54 - LAB GROUP 1

PROCEDURE - 6

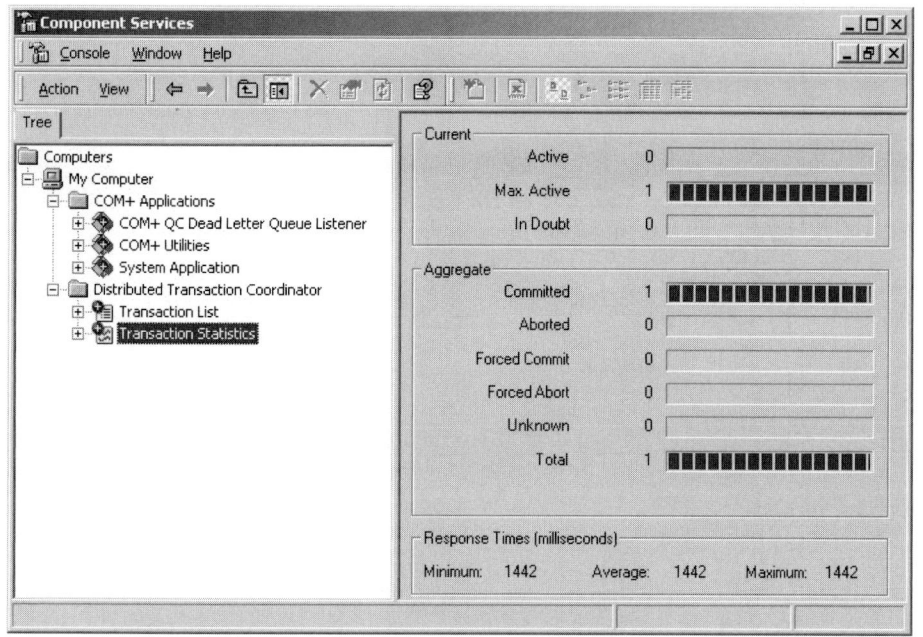

Figure 6-2: Component Services

___1. Close the *Component Services* window.

2. Data sources

Open Database Connectivity (ODBC) can be used to access data from a variety of database management systems. An ODBC driver allows ODBC-enabled programs to get information from ODBC data sources. DSN stands for Data Source Name.

___a. From the *ADMINISTRATIVE TOOLS* folder double-click **Data Sources (ODBC)**.
___b. The window that opens will look similar to Figure 6-3.

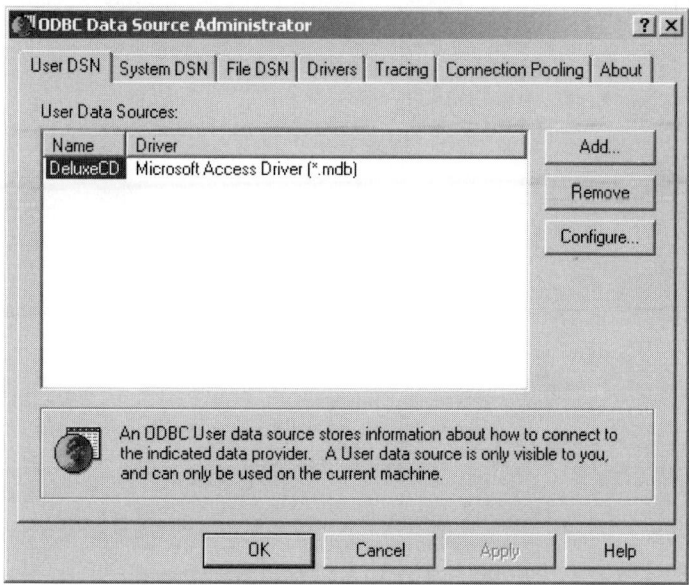

Figure 6-3: ODBC

WINDOWS 2000 ADMINISTRATIVE TOOLS - 55

PROCEDURE - 6

___ c. Read the explanation at the bottom of the window. Click on the **System DSN** tab.
___ d. Record the explanation about a System DSN from the bottom of the window in Table 6-2.
___ e. Click on the **File DSN** tab. This area of ODBC allows a connection to a specific database file.
___ f. Click on the **Drivers** tab. Count how many drivers are installed; you may need to scroll down.
___ g. Record the number of drivers in Table 6-3.
___ h. Click on the **Tracing** tab. Read its description in the bottom of the window.
___ i. Click on the **Connection Pooling** tab. Read its description in the bottom of the window.
___ j. Click on the **About** tab. Record its description in Table 6-4.
___ k. Close the ODBC Data Source Administrator.

3. Event Viewer

Event viewer is a useful tool for diagnosing hardware, software, and system problems with Windows. When an error occurs it will usually be logged for later viewing in Event Viewer. If log warnings show that a disk driver can only read or write to a sector after several retries, the sector is likely to go bad eventually. Logs can also confirm problems with software. If a program crashes, a program event log can provide a record of activity leading up to the event.

___ a. From the *ADMINISTRATIVE TOOLS* folder double-click on **Event Viewer.**
___ b. The window should look similar to Figure 6-4. There are three areas of Event Viewer: Application Log, Security Log, and System Log.

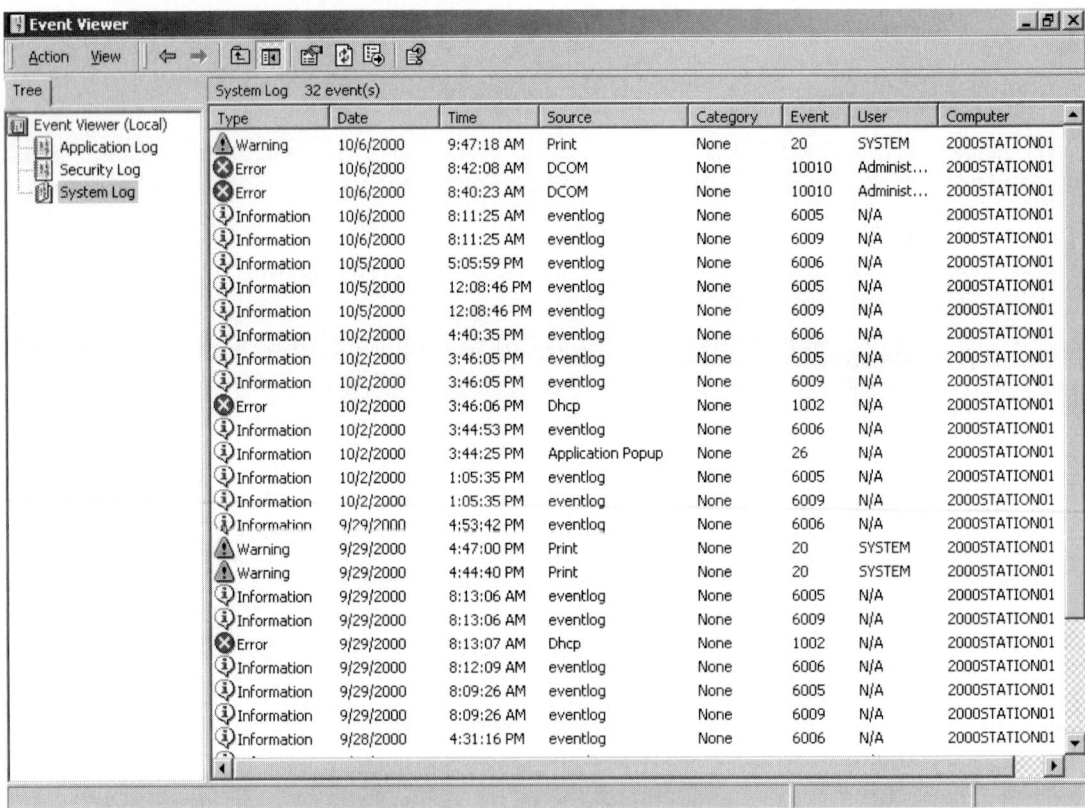

Figure 6-4: Event Viewer

___ c. The System Log is highlighted by default. Items are sorted by latest date first in the right-hand window pane. There are three types of events: Warnings, Errors, and Information. Look at the first item in the list. Record the required information in Table 6-5.

PROCEDURE - 6

___d. Click on the **Application Log** and view any information that it contains. This area records any errors or information that applications encounter with Windows.

___e. Click on the **Security Log**.

___f. Record how many events appear in Table 6-6. Here Windows will monitor and record actions that are viewed as security violations.

___g. Close *Event Viewer*.

4. **Local Security Settings**

Local Security Settings is used to configure security policies for the local computer. These settings include the Password policy, Account Lockout policy, Audit policy, IP Security policy, user rights assignments, recovery agents for encrypted data, and other security options. Local Security Policy is only available on Windows 2000 computers that are not domain controllers. If the computer is a member of a domain, these settings may be overridden by policies received from the domain.

___a. From the *ADMINISTRATIVE TOOLS* folder double-click **Local Security Policy**.

___b. The window should look similar to Figure 6-5.

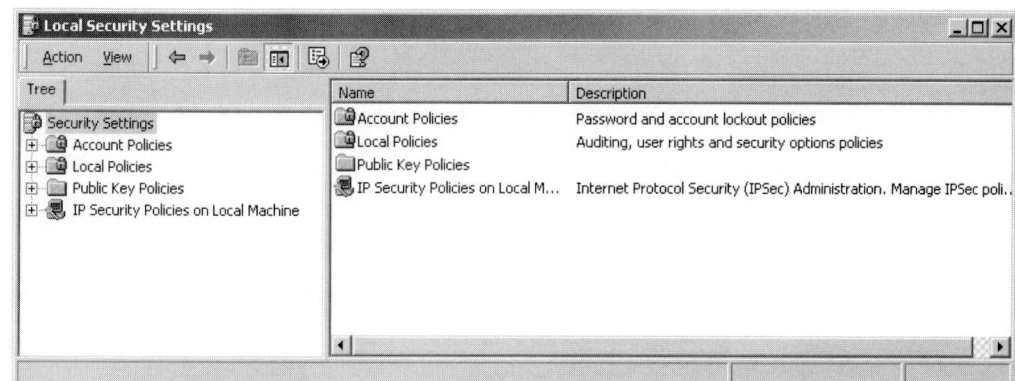

Figure 6-5: Local Security Settings

___c. Expand **Account Policies**.

___d. Click on **Password Policy**.

___e. Record the Maximum password age in Table 6-7. The Maximum password age is the time a password will remain the same until the user is prompted to change it.

___f. Expand **Local Policies**.

___g. Click on **User Rights Assignment**.

___h. View the right-hand window pane and scroll down to "*Shut down the system*".

___i. Double-click on **Shut down the System**, and a window similar to Figure 6-6 appears.

___j. The users that have rights to this operation will be listed. From this window you can add and delete users assigned to shut down the system. Record the users assigned to this task in Table 6-8.

___k. Click on **OK**.

___l. Click on **Security Options** under *Local Policies*.

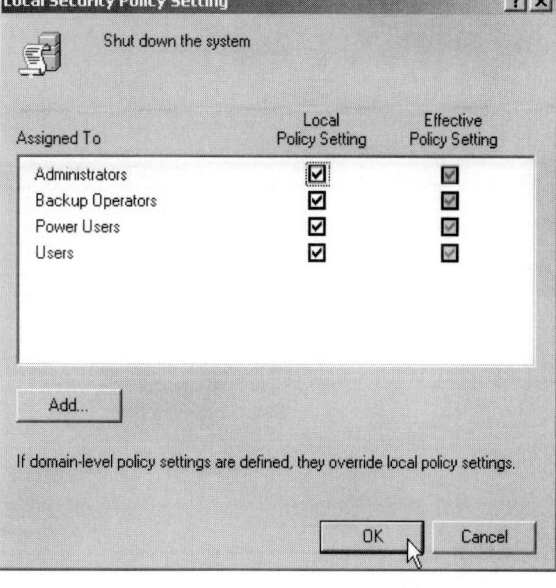

Figure 6-6: Local Security Policy Setting

PROCEDURE - 6

___ m. Record the first policy that is listed in Table 6-9.
___ n. Click on **IP Security Policies** on Local Machine.
___ o. Record the three policies in Table 6-10.
___ p. Close *Local Security Settings*.

5. Performance

The performance console collects and displays real-time data about memory, disk, processor, network, and other activity in a graph, histogram, or report form.

___ a. From the *ADMINISTRATIVE TOOLS* folder double-click **Performance**.

NOTE: Notice that the System Monitor is selected on the left-hand window pane by default. There are no graphs selected by default.

___ b. Click on the large plus (+) button above the graph in the right-hand window pane to add a computer.
___ c. By default the performance object is set to *Processor* and the counter selected is *% Processor Time*.
___ d. Click on **Add**.
___ e. Click on **Close**.
___ f. You are now monitoring how much the processor is used in terms of time. Start a few programs like *Internet Explorer* and *Notepad* and then close them.
___ g. Observe the changes in the chart. The window will look similar to Figure 6-7.

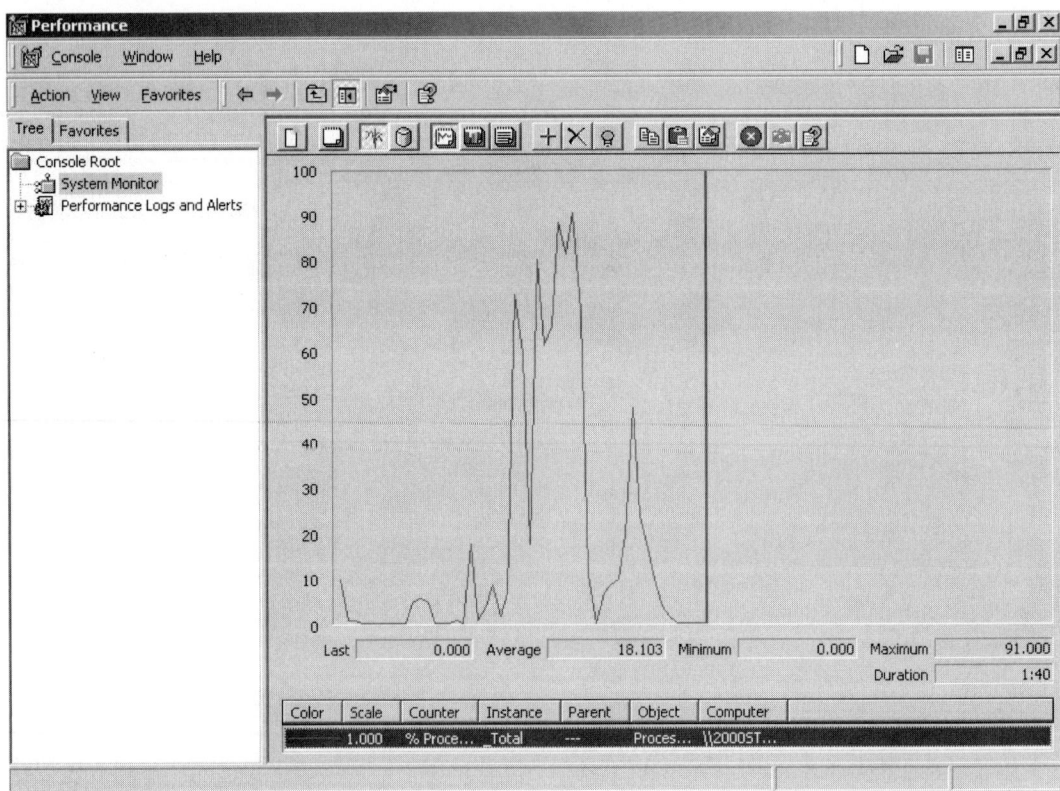

Figure 6-7: Performance Charting

___ h. Notice the key at the bottom of the window. It shows the color of the line, scale, and other information about the chart.

58 - LAB GROUP 1

PROCEDURE - 6

___ i. As before, click on the (+) button.

NOTE: You can add more than one graph on the same chart. When you add another line to the chart, the Performance console will automatically choose an available color for the graph.

___ j. This time select **Memory for the Performance object**. You may need to scroll the drop-down menu.
___ k. Select **% Committed Bytes In Use** as the counter. You may need to scroll up in the list.
___ l. The window should look similar to Figure 6-8.

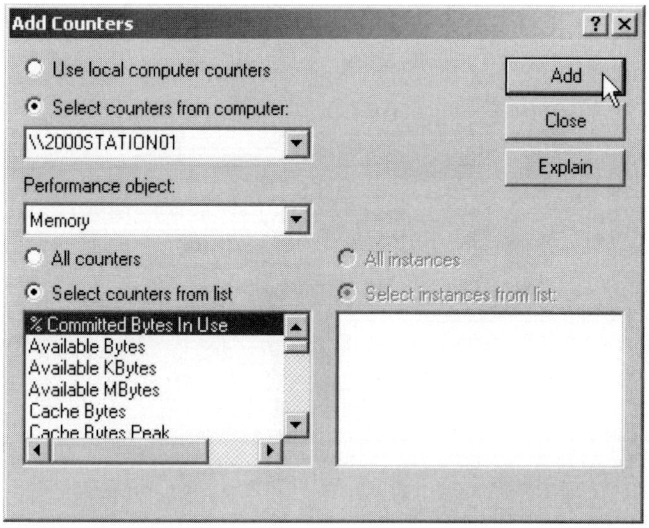

Figure 6-8: Add a Counter

___ m. Click on **Add**.
___ n. Click on **Close**.
___ o. Record the Color of the % Processor Time and % Committed Bytes In Use lines in Table 6-11.
___ p. As before, start a program, but this time do not close it, just minimize it.
___ q. Record your observations of the % Committed Bytes In Use line in Table 6-12.
___ r. Close *Performance* and any other programs you have started in this step, but do not close the *Administrative Tools* window.

6. **Services**

The Services console is used to manage the services on your computer, set recovery actions to take place if a service fails, and create custom names and descriptions for services so that you can easily identify them.

___ a. From the *ADMINISTRATIVE TOOLS* folder double-click **Services**.
    These are services listed on the right-hand window pane.

NOTE: From this window you can see all the services that are running, either by default from Windows 2000 or from installed programs that add a service.

___ b. Double-click the **Alerter Service**. From this window you change the properties for starting the service, add an action when the service fails, or change its Log On properties.
___ c. Read its Description and click on **Cancel**. You can see the status of the service; it will be either Started or blank (implying stopped).
___ d. Count how many services have been started and record this in Table 6-13.
___ e. Close *Services*.

WINDOWS 2000 ADMINISTRATIVE TOOLS - 59

PROCEDURE - 6

7. Telnet Server Administration

Telnet is a service that allows you to "telephone-net" into another computer. Originally it was designed to view information on a remote computer (hundreds of miles away) as if you were sitting at that computer. Today we just use the Internet for this type of long distance communication, but telnet can still be a useful tool. The Telnet Server is built into Windows 2000 to allow remote computers access through a telnet client. The client can be invoked by typing "telnet" from the command line.

___a. From the *ADMINISTRATIVE TOOLS* folder double-click on **Telnet Server Administration**. You will see a window similar to Figure 6-9.

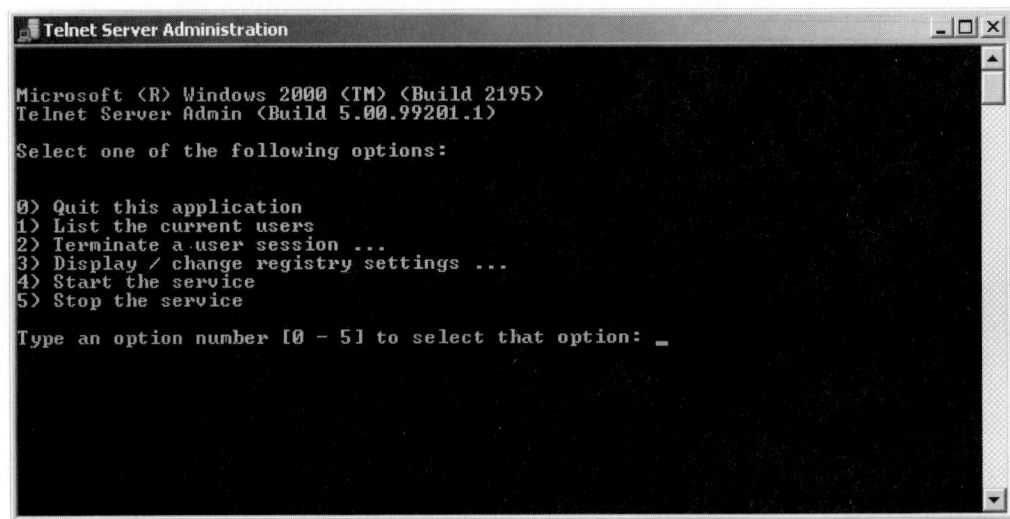

Figure 6-9: Telnet Server Administration Window

___b. Type **4** and press **ENTER** to start the service.

NOTE: After the service has started, other computers connected on the LAN can connect to the computer via the command prompt. A remote computer can connect by typing "telnet" and the IP address of a computer with the Telnet Server running.

___c. Stop the telnet service by typing **5** and pressing **ENTER**.
___d. Enter **0** to quit the *Telnet Server Administration*.
___e. Close all open windows, and shut down the computer.

TABLES

Table 6-1

Com+ Applications Folder:	

60 - LAB GROUP 1

PROCEDURE - 6

Table 6-2

System DSN Explanation:	

Table 6-3

Number of ODBC Drivers:	

Table 6-4

ODBC About Description:	

Table 6-5

Event Viewer System Log - First Event	
Type:	
Date:	
Source:	

Table 6-6

Security Log Events:	

Table 6-7

Maximum Password Age:	

Table 6-8

Users Assigned to Shut Down the System:	

WINDOWS 2000 ADMINISTRATIVE TOOLS - 61

PROCEDURE - 6

Table 6-9

First Listed Policy:	

Table 6-10

IP Security Policies:	

Table 6-11

	Colors
% Processor Time:	
% Committed Bytes in Use:	

Table 6-12

Table 6-13

Number of Services Started:	

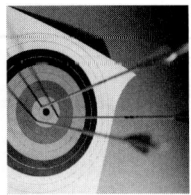

Feedback

LAB QUESTIONS

1. How many items did you have in the Application Log of Event Viewer?
2. How can Event Viewer be useful?
3. What is an automatic feature of the Performance console?
4. Which option in Telnet Server Administration starts the service?
5. How would you navigate to view all the services that are running?

LAB PROCEDURE 7

Windows 2000 Computer Management

OBJECTIVES

1. View various areas of Computer Management.
2. Use Task Manager.

Operating System Technology

RESOURCES

1. PC-compatible desktop/tower computer system — Customer-supplied desktop/tower hardware system **OR** Marcraft MC-8000 Computer Hardware Trainer **OR** suitable PC hardware trainer running Windows 2000

DISCUSSION

Windows Computer Management provides access to administration tools for managing disks as well as local and remote computers. Some of the tools included are Event Viewer, System Information, Performance Logs and Alerts, Shared Folders, Device Manager, Local Users and Groups, and Disk Defragmenter. These can be useful tools for viewing the hardware and software components of your computer.

PROCEDURE

1. **Start Computer Management**
   a. Boot the computer to Windows 2000.
   b. Open Computer Management through the path *Start/Settings/Control Panel*. Double-click on **Administrative Tools** and double-click on **Computer Management**. The window will look similar to Figure 7-1.
   c. Click on **Event Viewer**. Notice the contents in the right-hand window pane. This is the same Event Viewer that you have used in previous labs.

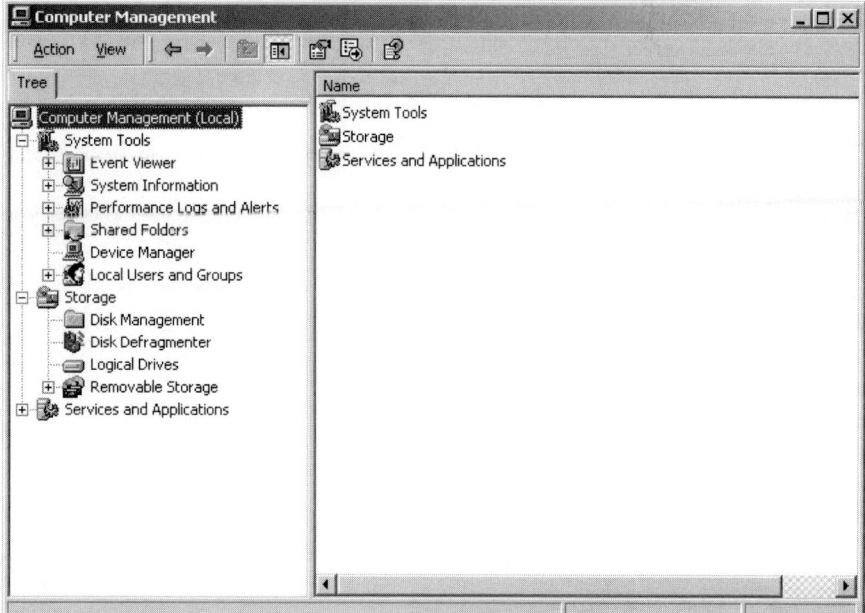

Figure 7-1: Computer Management

PROCEDURE - 7

2. **System Information**
    - a. Click on **System Information**. If you have used "msinfo32" in Windows 98 or Me this will look familiar. From this menu you can view properties of your hardware resources and components, software environment, and Internet Explorer settings.
    - b. Expand *System Information* and click on **System Summary**.
    - c. Record the required fields in Table 7-1.
    - d. Click on **Hardware Resources** and expand the folder.
    - e. From this window you can view properties such as I/O Address Ranges, Memory Ranges, and device IRQ settings. Click on **I/O**. Record one of the Address Ranges of the PCI bus in Table 7-2.
    - f. Click on **IRQs** and record the IRQ of the keyboard in Table 7-3.
    - g. Expand **Components** under *System Information*.
    - h. Click on **Display**. Record the required fields in Table 7-4.
    - i. Expand the *PORTS* folder and select **Serial**.
    - j. View the information displayed. Record the COM1 Baud Rate in Table 7-5.
    - k. Select **Parallel** and view the information displayed.
    - l. Expand **Software Environment** under *System Information*.
    - m. Select the **DRIVERS** folder and view the information displayed.
    - n. Select **Startup Programs**. This area can be useful for optimizing system performance. If your system is running slower than normal you may have unnecessary programs running.
    - o. Collapse System Information by clicking on the minus (-) sign next to its icon.

3. **Performance Logs and Alerts**
    - a. From *Computer Management* expand **Performance Logs and Alerts**.
    - b. You will see three areas: Counter Logs, Trace Logs, and Alerts. These logs can be initialized from the Performance area of Administrative tools. Collapse Performance Logs and Alerts.

4. **Shared Folders**
    - a. From *Computer Management* expand **Shared Folders**.
    - b. Click on the **Shares Icon**. From this window you can see all the folders that are shared from your computer.
    - c. Click on **Shares**. Record the Shared Folders in Table 7-6.
    - d. Click on **Sessions**. From this area you can view any remote users attached to your computer.
    - e. Click on **Open Files**. From this area you can view which files are being accessed over the network. Record any open files in Table 7-7.
    - f. Collapse *Shared Folders*.

5. **Device Manager**
    - a. From Computer Management click on **Device Manager**. The window should look similar to Figure 7-2.
    - b. This area can perform the same functions as Device Manager in Windows 98 or 95. This is a useful tool for viewing any conflicts or hardware setup problems with various components on the computer. Expand **Mice and other pointing devices**.

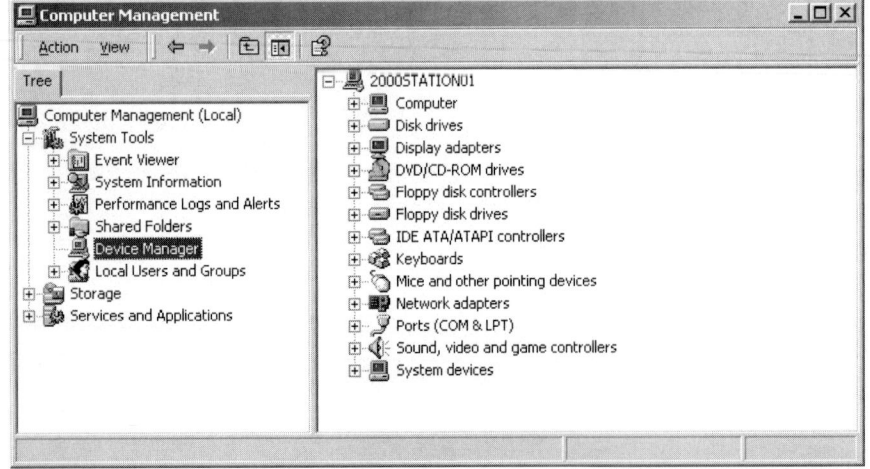

Figure 7-2: Device Manager

64 - LAB GROUP 1

PROCEDURE - 7

    c.   Record any items listed in Table 7-8.
    d.   Click on the **View** menu and select **Devices by connection**. From this view you can see a hierarchical structure of connections to the computer.
    e.   Click on the **View** menu and select **Resources by type**.
    f.   Expand the **Interrupt request (IRQ)** list.
    g.   Look for the keyboard and double-click on its icon.
    h.   You will see a properties window appear, it will look similar to Figure 7-3. Click on the **Resources** tab.
    i.   From this window you can view the I/O range and IRQ of the device. Record the Input/Output Range(s) of the keyboard in Table 7-9.
    j.   Click on **Cancel**.

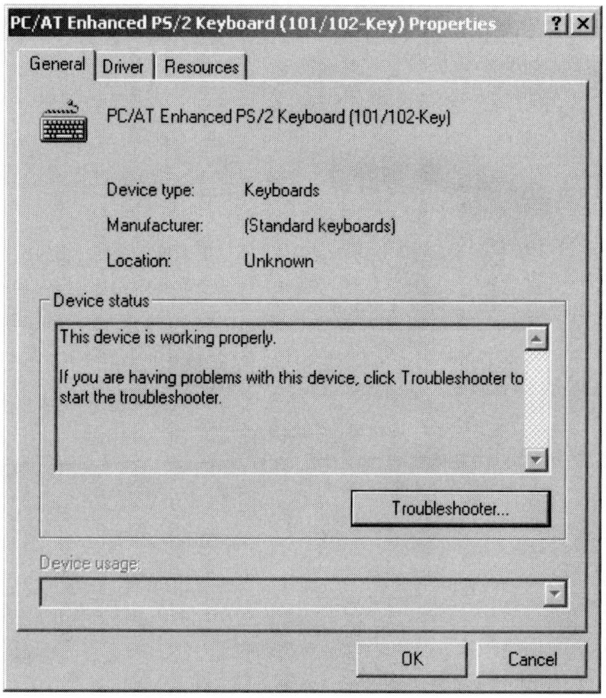

6. **Local Users and Groups**
    a.   From *Computer Management* double-click the **Local Users and Groups** icon to expand it.
    b.   Click on **Users**.
    c.   By default two users are set up by Windows: Administrator and Guest. Guest is disabled by default. Double-click on **Guest**.
    d.   You will see a window similar to Figure 7-4. The account is disabled by default. *Uncheck Account* is disabled.

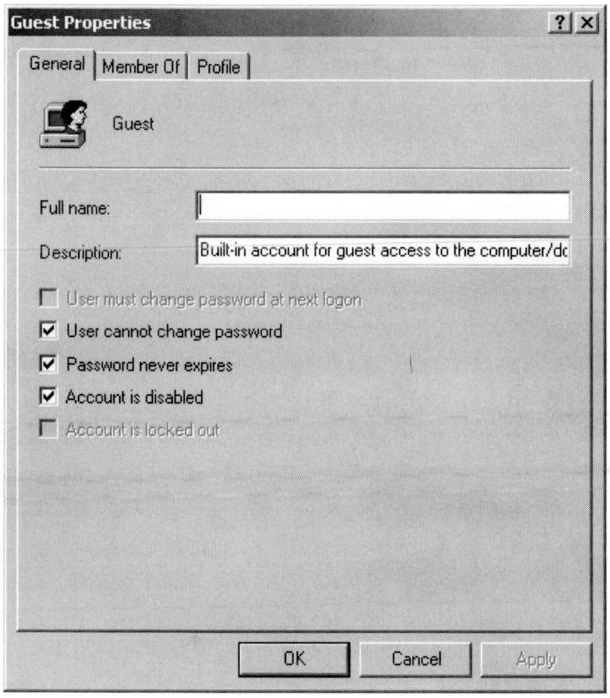

Figure 7-3: Keyboard Properties

Figure 7-4: Guest User Properties

    e.   Click on **OK**.
    f.   Click in a blank space in the window.
    g.   Click on the **Action** menu and **Select New** user.
    h.   From this window you can create a new user to log on the computer. They can log on locally or over the network. Click on **Close**.

WINDOWS 2000 COMPUTER MANAGEMENT

PROCEDURE - 7

    ___i.   Click on **Groups** and record the description of Administrators in Table 7-10.

NOTE: You may need to double-click the icon next to the name to view the user's properties.

    ___j.   Collapse *Local Users and Groups*.

7. **Storage**
   - ___a.   From *Computer Management* expand **Storage**.
   - ___b.   Click on **Disk Management**.
   - ___c.   From this window you can view partitioning information, similar to the fdisk command in DOS.
   - ___d.   Record the file system of (C:) in Table 7-11.
   - ___e.   Click on **Disk Defragmenter**. Disk Defragmenter moves the pieces of each file or folder to one location on the volume, so that each occupies a single, contiguous space on the disk drive. Regular defragmentation will improve system performance.
   - ___f.   Click on **Volume (C:)**.
   - ___g.   Click on the **Analyze** button.
   - ___h.   In a moment the *Analysis Complete* dialog will appear. Click on **View Report**.
   - ___i.   Read the *Most fragmented files* section and click on **Close**.
   - ___j.   The window should look similar to Figure 7-5. Depending on system speed and percent fragmented the defrag may take from 5-60 minutes. If time permits, click on **Defragment**.

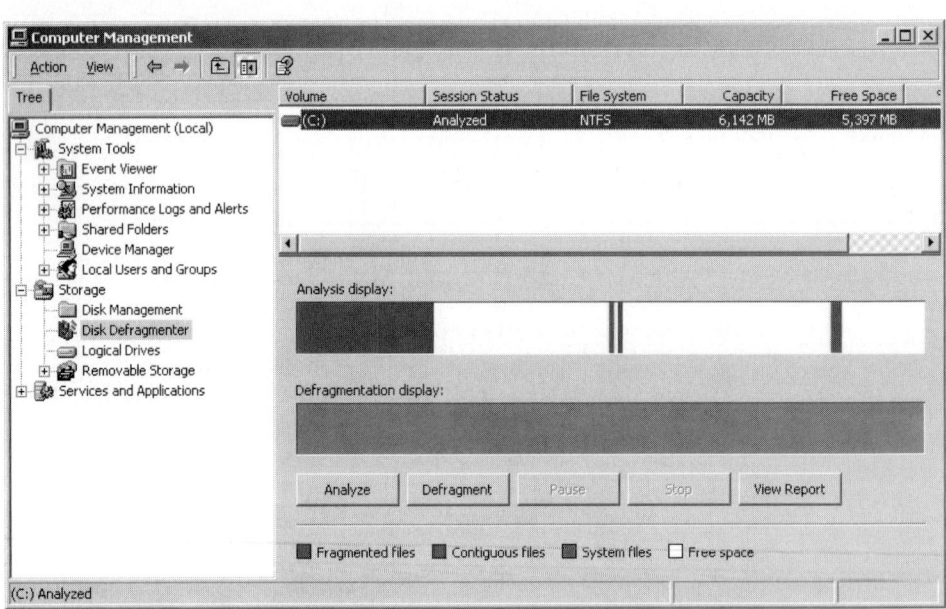

Figure 7-5:
Disk Defragmenter

- ___k.   Click on **Logical Drives**.
- ___l.   You will see A:, C:, D:, and any other physical drives installed on your computer. You can double-click on each one and view its properties.
- ___m.   Expand **Removable Storage**. From this area you can manage backup devices on the computer.

8. **Services and Applications**
   - ___a.   From *Computer Management* expand Services and Applications.
   - ___b.   Click on **Services**. As you have seen before, these are the services running on the computer.
   - ___c.   Expand **Indexing Service**. This Service indexes all the files and folders on the computer for easy searching. Record any catalog items in Table 7-12.
   - ___d.   Close *Computer Management* and all windows.

PROCEDURE - 7

9. **Task Manager**
   ___a. From the Windows 2000 desktop press **CTRL+ALT+DELETE** on the keyboard.
   ___b. Click on the **Task Manager** button.
   ___c. Click on the **Applications** tab. If you have any applications running, such as Microsoft *Word* or *Internet Explorer*, you can view their status and end them if necessary.
   ___d. Click on the **Processes** tab. This displays all services, applications, and other processes running on the system. Record how many processes are running in Table 7-13.
   ___e. Click on **View/Select Columns**. The window will look similar to Figure 7-6.
   ___f. From this window you can add columns that display advanced information about a process. Select all the columns by clicking in the box to the left of each name and placing a check mark.
   ___g. Click on **OK**. You can now view more information about a specific process. You may need to use the horizontal scroll bar.
   ___h. Look at the *System Idle Process* and record its Memory Usage in Table 7-14.
   ___i. Click on the **Performance** tab.
   ___j. From this tab you can view a graphical representation of CPU Usage and Memory Usage. Record the value for Total Physical Memory (K) in Table 7-15.
   ___k. Close *Task Manager*.
   ___l. Close all open windows, and shut down the computer.

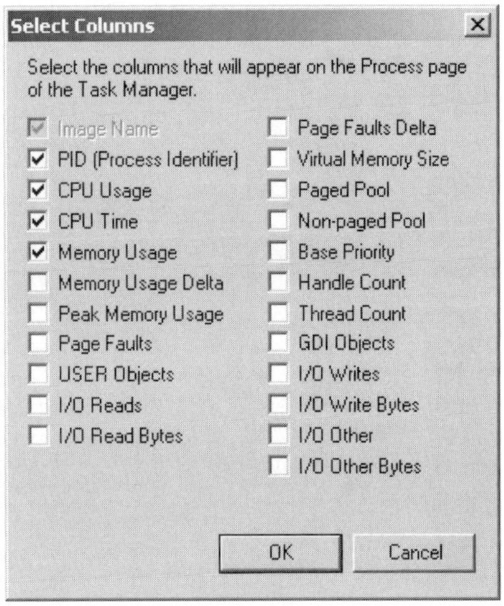

Figure 7-6: Select Columns

TABLES

Table 7-1

System Information - System Summary	
OS Name:	
Version:	
Total Physical Memory:	
Available Physical Memory:	

Table 7-2

Sample PCI Bus Address Range:	

PROCEDURE - 7

Table 7-3

Keyboard IRQ:	

Table 7-4

Display Information	
Adapter Name:	
Adapter Type:	
Resolution:	
Bits / Pixels:	

Table 7-5

COM1 Baud Rate:	

Table 7-6

Shared Folders	

Table 7-7

Open Files:	

Table 7-8

Items Listed in Mice and Other Pointing Devices:	

Table 7-9

Keyboard Input / Output Ranges:	

PROCEDURE - 7

Table 7-10

Administrators Description:	

Table 7-11

File System of (C:):	

Table 7-12

Indexing Service Catalogs:	

Table 7-13

Processes Running on System:	

Table 7-14

System Idle Process Memory Usage:	

Table 7-15

Total Physical Memory:	

LAB QUESTIONS

1. What can System Information be used for?

2. How can you view all the shared folders of the system?

3. What can Device Manager be used for?

4. What default users are set up by Windows?

5. What does Disk Defragmenter do?

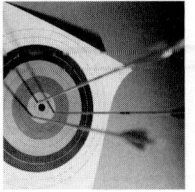

Feedback

LAB PROCEDURE 8

Windows XP Navigating

OBJECTIVES

1. Explore the Start menu.
2. Use My Computer.
3. Add a program to the Quick Launch toolbar.
4. Remove a program from the Start menu.
5. Add a program to the Start menu.
6. Customize the Start menu.
7. Change the Taskbar view to Classic view.

Operating System Technology

RESOURCES

1. PC-compatible desktop/tower computer system — Customer-supplied desktop/tower hardware system **OR** Marcraft MC-8000 Computer Hardware Trainer **OR** suitable PC hardware trainer running Windows XP Professional

DISCUSSION

Windows XP looks significantly different than either Windows Me or Windows 2000. In Figure 8-1 you can see that the desktop now is missing the icons for *My Computer*, *Network Neighborhood*, and *My Documents*. The only icon that is still there is the *Recycle Bin*, which has moved to the bottom right by default. In the lab we will show you where to locate these icons. We will also show you how to add the programs that you use frequently to the Quick Launch toolbar and *Start* menu for quick access without cluttering up your desktop. The last thing to show you is how to change the operation of the *Start* menu back to the way it operates in Windows 2000.

Figure 8-1: The Windows XP Desktop

PROCEDURE - 8

Operating System Technology

PROCEDURE

1. **Navigate to My Computer from the Windows XP Start menu**
   ___ a. Boot the computer into Windows XP.
   ___ b. Click on the **Start** button with your mouse. Figure 8-2 shows the *XP Start* menu.
   ___ c. Click on the **My Computer** icon.
   ___ d. My Computer in XP is arranged according to device type as shown in Figure 8-3.

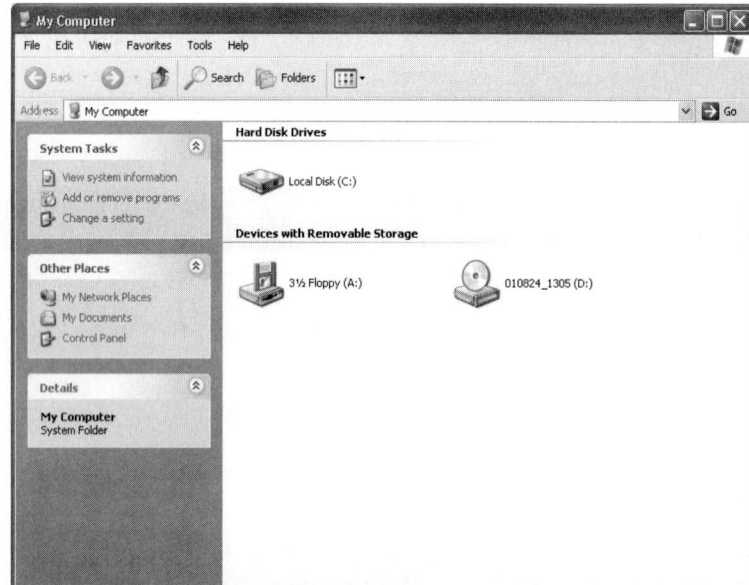

Figure 8-2: The Windows XP Start Menu

Figure 8-3: My Computer in Windows XP

___ e. Notice the links on the left side of *My Computer*. You can quickly open useful programs or folders by single-clicking on any of these links, just as if you were in Internet Explorer.
___ f. Click on **System Tasks** and the links located below that heading, then hide them.
___ g. Click on **System Tasks** again to bring the links back.
___ h. Click on **View system information**. This brings up the *System Properties* box, as in Figure 8-4, which is identical to the *System Information* icon located in the Control Panel.
___ i. Close the *Systems Properties* box by clicking on the **X** on the upper-right corner.

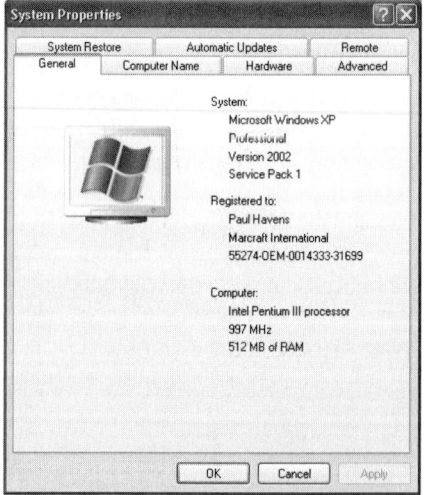

Figure 8-4: The Systems Properties Dialog Box

72 - LAB GROUP 1

PROCEDURE - 8

___ j. Click on **Change a setting** to change the view to Control Panel, as in Figure 8-5.

___ k. Click on **Back** in the upper-left corner to return to *My Computer*.

___ l. Click on **Start**, and then hover the mouse over the *All Programs* arrow, as in Figure 8-6. This will open up the *Programs Menu* that is similar to the *Programs* menu in Window Me and Windows 2000. This is used the same way, so we won't go into the functionality of this *Programs Menu*.

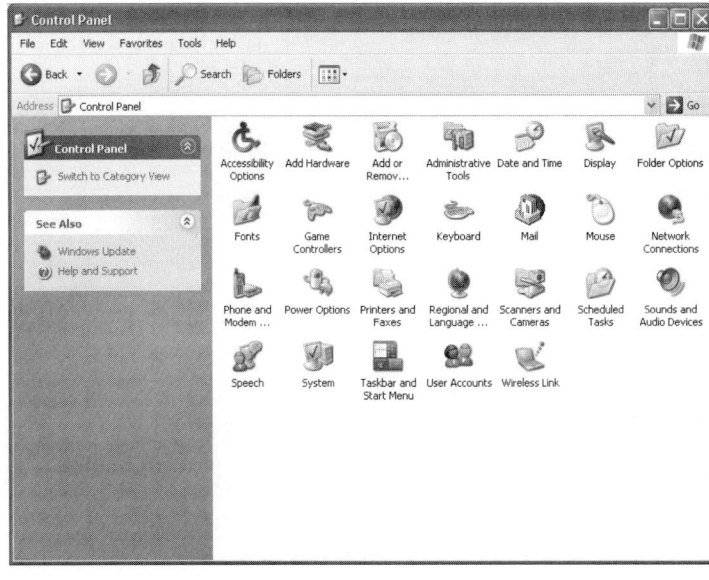

Figure 8-5: The Control Panel

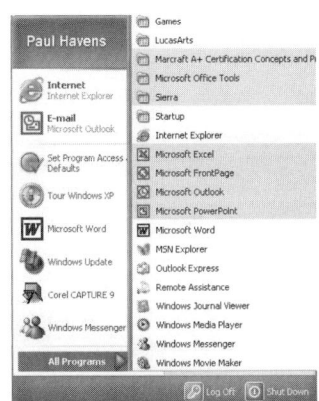

Figure 8-6: The Windows XP All Programs Menu

___ m. Click on the desktop to exit from the *Start* menu.

2. Add programs to the Quick Launch toolbar

___ a. Let's make sure that the computer is using the Quick Launch toolbar. Right-click on the Taskbar on the bottom of the screen. Make sure not to click on an area where a program is running. You should get the menu shown in Figure 8-7.

Figure 8-7: The Taskbar Menu

WINDOWS XP NAVIGATING - 73

PROCEDURE - 8

___ b. Hover the mouse over the word **Toolbars**, then make sure that the Quick Launch toolbar is checked as in Figure 8-8. If it is not checked, click on it.

Figure 8-8: Enabling the Quick Launch Toolbar

___ c. Right-click on the Taskbar on the bottom and click on **Lock the Taskbar** to unlock it. This will give you the ability to move items in the Taskbar.
___ d. Click on the second set of dots to widen the Quick Launch toolbar, as in Figure 8-9.

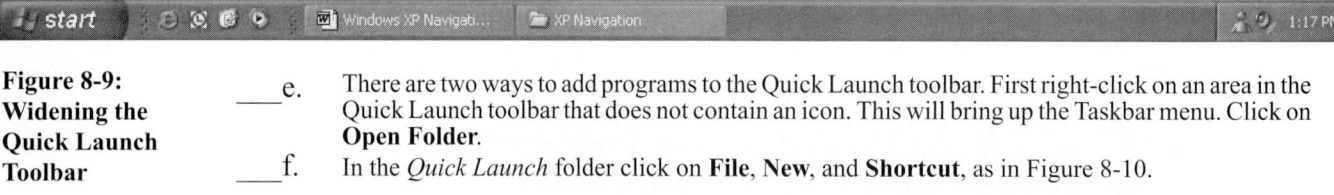

Figure 8-9: Widening the Quick Launch Toolbar

___ e. There are two ways to add programs to the Quick Launch toolbar. First right-click on an area in the Quick Launch toolbar that does not contain an icon. This will bring up the Taskbar menu. Click on **Open Folder**.
___ f. In the *Quick Launch* folder click on **File**, **New**, and **Shortcut**, as in Figure 8-10.

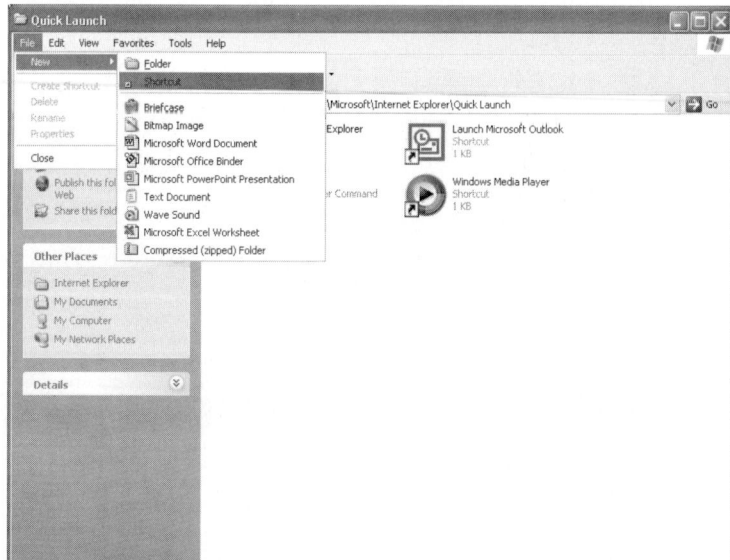

Figure 8-10: Adding Shortcuts to Quick Launch Folder

74 - LAB GROUP 1

PROCEDURE - 8

___g. This will bring up the Create Shortcut wizard seen in Figure 8-11. If you know the complete path to the program you could type it in the box. We will use the other method. Click on **Browse** to bring up the *Browse for Folder* dialog box.

___h. Click on the + next to My Computer, C Drive, Program Files, and Messenger to get to the *msmsgs* icon shown in Figure 8-12.

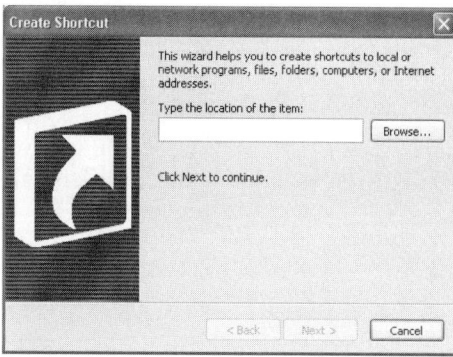

Figure 8-11: The Create Shortcut Dialog Box

Figure 8-12: Locate Program for Quick Launch Toolbar

___i. Click on **OK**.

___j. You will now see the path and program typed into the *Create Shortcut* dialog box. Click on **Next**.

___k. You need to type in a name for the program; by default the file name is in the box. Just type **Microsoft Messenger** to replace the file name in the box.

___l. Click on **Finish**.

___m. Your *Quick Launch* folder should now have a Microsoft Messenger Shortcut Icon in it as shown in Figure 8-13.

___n. Close the *Quick Launch* folder by clicking on the **X** in the upper-right corner.

___o. Notice the *Messenger* icon in the Quick Launch toolbar. Hover the mouse over the icon. You should see the Microsoft Messenger name appear above the icon.

___p. Now right-click on the Taskbar and click on **Lock the Taskbar** to lock it.

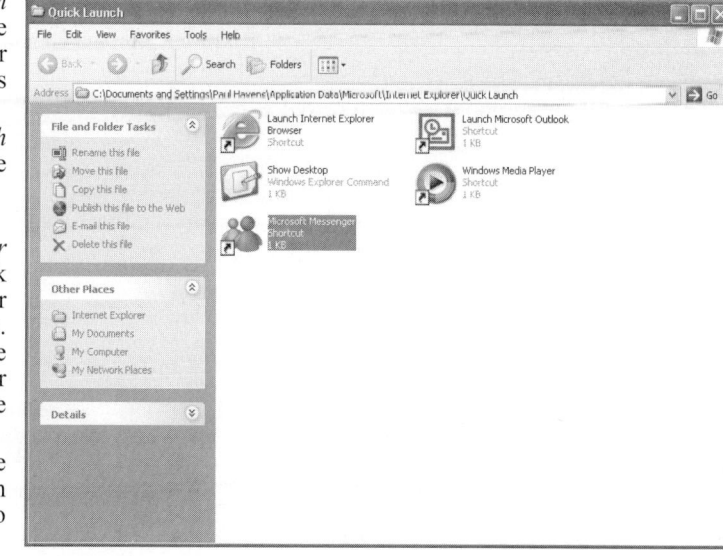

Figure 8-13: Microsoft Messenger Icon Added to Folder

WINDOWS XP NAVIGATING - 75

PROCEDURE - 8

___q. Notice that the Taskbar is locked wherever you had the dots positioned. Take the time to unlock the Taskbar and position the dots in an area where all the icons can be visible, but there isn't a lot of extra space, and then lock the Taskbar.

___r. Another way to add icons to the Quick Launch toolbar is to drag the programs into the toolbar. Click on **Start**.

___s. Click on **All Programs**, then **Accessories** as in Figure 8-14.

Figure 8-14: The Accessories Menu

___t. When clicking on the **Calculator** icon you need to right-click and hold-and-drag the icon down to the Quick Launch toolbar, then release the right mouse button.

___u. A menu will display similar to Figure 8-15; select **Copy Here**. This will keep the shortcut in the *Programs* menu and create an additional one on the Quick Launch toolbar.

___v. Let's test the shortcut by clicking on the **Calculator** icon. The calculator should display.

___w. Click on the **X** to close Calculator.

___x. We will now delete the icons in the Quick Launch toolbar. Right-click on the **Calculator** icon and select **Delete** from the menu as shown in Figure 8-16.

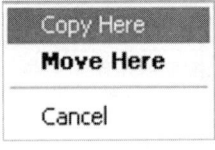

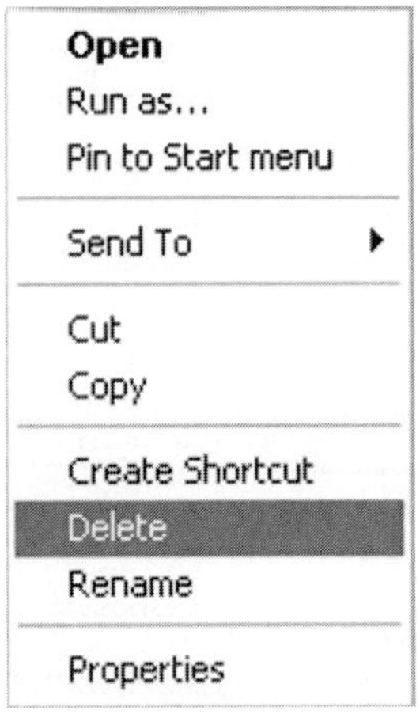

Figure 8-15: Right-Drag Options

Figure 8-16: Deleting a Shortcut from the Quick Launch Toolbar

76 - LAB GROUP 1

PROCEDURE - 8

___y. You will get the *Confirm File Delete* dialog box. Click on **Yes** to send the Calculator shortcut to the Recycle Bin.

___z. Repeat Steps x and y for the *MSN messenger* icon. Notice that the dialog box changed for MSN messenger; this is because we are deleting a shortcut instead of an actual file.

3. Customize the Start menu

___a. Click on **Start**.

___b. Right-click on **Tour Windows XP** and select **Remove from This List** as in Figure 8-17.

___c. Notice that the icon is now gone. We will now replace the icon.

___d. This menu displays the programs most used to replace the icon we need to run the Windows XP Tour. Click on **All Programs**, **Accessories**, and **Tour Windows XP**.

___e. When the *Tour Windows XP* dialog box comes up, click on **Cancel**.

___f. Click on **Start**. You will now see the *Tour Windows XP* icon back on the left-hand side as in Figure 8-18.

Figure 8-17: Removing Icon from Start Menu

Figure 8-18: The Start Menu

___g. For further customization right-click on the **Start** menu and select **Properties**.

___h. The *Taskbar and Start Menu Properties* dialog box comes up as in Figure 8-19.

___i. Click on **Customize** to the right of *Start* menu.

___j. Click on **Small Icons** to select it.

___k. Now click on the **Advanced** tab at the top.

___l. On this tab, you can select which folder and options you want to have on the *Start* menu and how to display them. Record all 15 main options in Table 8-1 (do not include the *how to display* options).

___m. Click on **OK**.

Figure 8-19: Start Menu Properties

WINDOWS XP NAVIGATING - 77

PROCEDURE - 8

____ n. Click on **Start**. The menu should now have small icons as in Figure 8-20. Notice the small icons for the programs underneath the logon name.

____ o. Right-click on the **Start** button and click on **Properties**.

____ p. Click on **Customize**.

____ q. Change the icons back to the large size and click on **OK**.

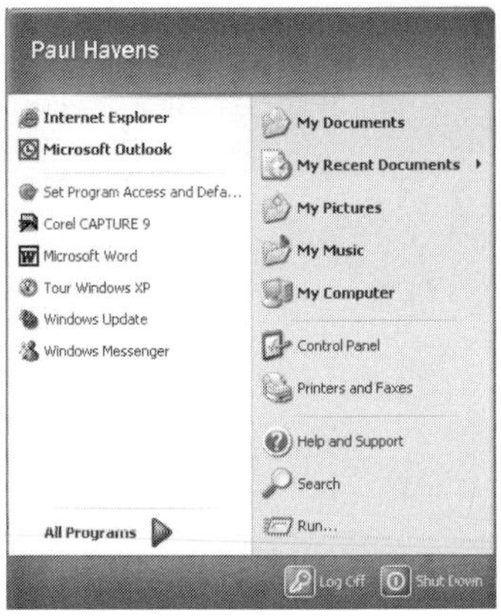

4. Customize the Taskbar

____ a. Click on the **Taskbar** tab at the top of the *Taskbar and Start Menu Properties* box as shown in Figure 8-21.

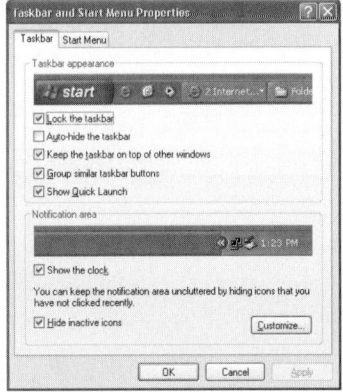

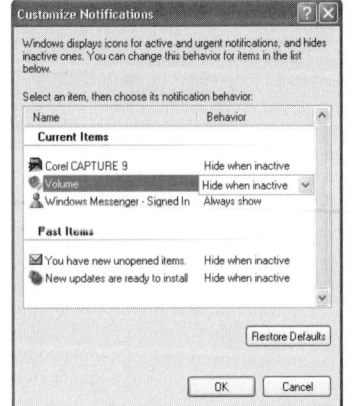

Figure 8-21: Taskbar Properties

Figure 8-20: Start Menu with Small Icons

____ b. Notice the options at the top. We have done *Lock the taskbar* and *Show Quick Launch* by using the right-click menu on the Taskbar.

____ c. Click on **Group similar taskbar buttons** to uncheck it. Notice the Internet Explorer Taskbar item and how it changes.

____ d. Click on **OK**.

____ e. Now click on the **Internet Explorer** icon on the Quick Launch toolbar four times and launch four different Internet Explorer windows.

____ f. Notice how each has its own *Taskbar* button.

____ g. Now right-click on the **Start** menu and select **Properties**.

____ h. Click on the **Taskbar** tab at the top.

____ i. Now click on **Group similar taskbar buttons** and click on **Apply**. Explain what happens to the Internet Explorer buttons in Table 8-2.

____ j. The customizable part on the bottom lets you add or remove the clock from the bottom right corner. It also lets you choose which icons you want to display or hide.

____ k. Click on **Customize**.

____ l. Figure 8-22 shows an example of the customizable options. Click on the **volume** icon and change it to *Hide when inactive*. Click on **OK**.

____ m. The bottom right corner should now have an arrow as in Figure 8-23. Click on the arrow to see the *Volume* icon.

____ n. Click on **Customize** and change the *Volume* icon to *Always show* and click on **OK**. The *Volume* icon should reappear in the corner.

Figure 8-22: Customize Notifications Window

Figure 8-23: Hidden Icons Symbol

78 - LAB GROUP 1

PROCEDURE - 8

5. **Change the Start menu to the classic Windows 2000 display**
   ___a. Click on the **Start Menu** tab inside the *Taskbar and Start Menu Properties* box.
   ___b. Select **Classic Start** menu.
   ___c. Click on **OK**.
   ___d. Click on the **Start** button.
   ___e. Describe how the *Start* menu changes in Table 8-3.
   ___f. Right-click on the **Start** button and select **Properties**.
   ___g. Select **Start Menu** and click on **OK**.

TABLES

Table 8-1

PROCEDURE - 8

Table 8-2

Table 8-3

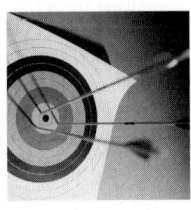

Feedback

LAB QUESTIONS

1. How do you get to My Computer in Windows XP?
2. How do you scroll to installed programs in Windows XP?
3. Name two ways to add programs to the Quick Launch toolbar.
4. How do you get to My Computer in Windows XP?
5. How do you change the Start menu back to the classic Start menu?

LAB PROCEDURE 9

Windows XP Control Panel

OBJECTIVES

1. Explore Control Panel using Category View.
2. Switch to Classic View.

Operating
System
Technology

RESOURCES

1. PC-compatible desktop/tower computer system — Customer-supplied desktop/tower hardware system **OR** Marcraft MC-8000 Computer Hardware Trainer **OR** suitable PC hardware trainer running Windows XP Professional

DISCUSSION

In Windows XP the Control Panel has changed to Category View. In this lab procedure we will show you how to use the categories to get tasks accomplished. We will also show you how to switch the view back to the Classic View. Most technicians use this view because they know what they are looking for, whereas the Category View is useful for non-technical users. The final thing we will show you is how to use the system restore function to keep your computer backed up.

PROCEDURE

1. **Use the Category View in Control Panel**
   ___ a. Click on **Start/Control Panel**.
   ___ b. Control Panel should display as in Figure 9-1. (If Control Panel displays in the Classic View you may have to click on Category View in the upper-left corner.)

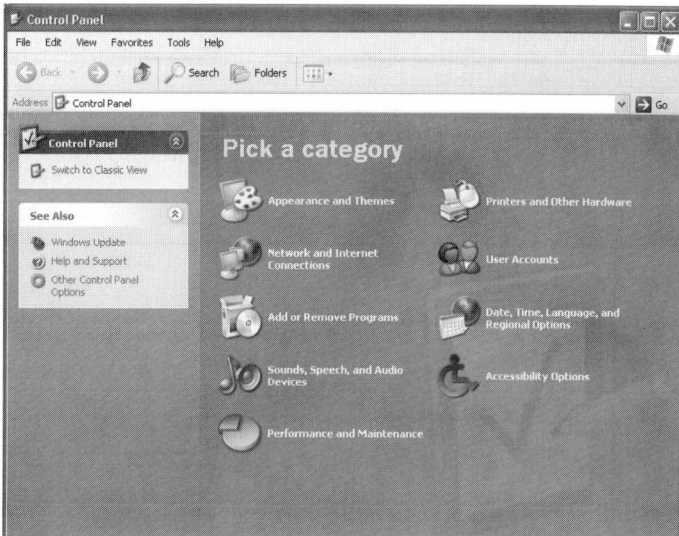

Figure 9-1: Control Panel: Category View

WINDOWS XP CONTROL PANEL - 81

PROCEDURE - 9

____ c. Click on **Appearance and Themes**.

Here is where you would change the theme, background, screen saver, and screen resolution by clicking on the different tasks. You can also click on the normal Control Panel icons at the bottom of the window as shown in Figure 9-2. We will not explain all the tasks from here on out, but will go through each category.

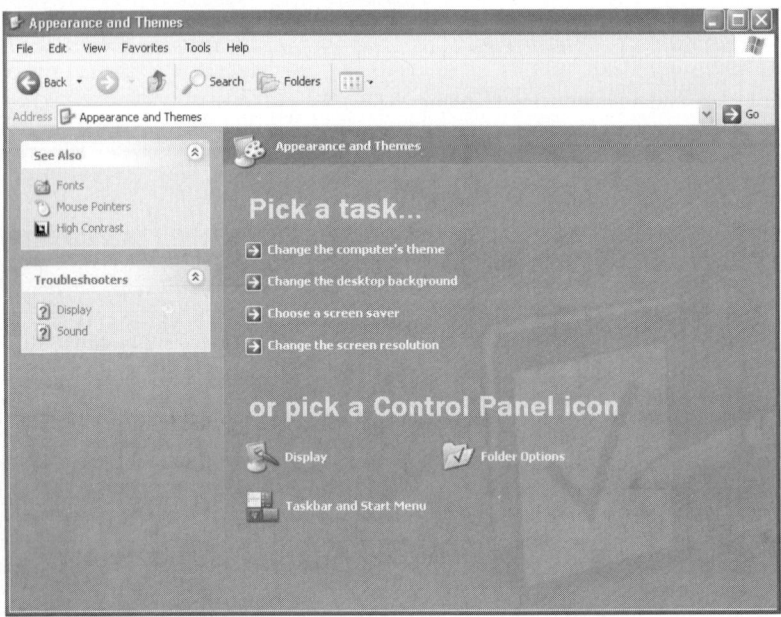

**Figure 9-2:
Appearance and
Themes Category**

____ d. Click on the **Up** button.
____ e. Click on **Printers and other hardware**.
____ f. Record all the tasks that can be accomplished here in Table 9-1.
____ g. Click on the **Up** button.
____ h. Click on **Network and Internet Connections**.
____ i. Record the tasks that can be accomplished here in Table 9-2.
____ j. Click on the **Up** button.
____ k. Click on **User Accounts**.
____ l. A *User Accounts* dialog box comes up as in Figure 9-3. Click on the **X** to close the box.

Figure 9-3: User Accounts

82 - LAB GROUP 1

PROCEDURE - 9

Table 9-4

Table 9-5

Table 9-6

Table 9-7

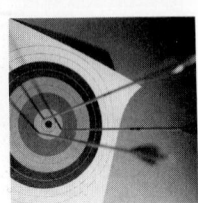

Feedback

LAB QUESTIONS

1. How do you access the Control Panel in Windows XP?
2. How do you change views from Classic View to Category View?
3. Which category is where users can change the theme, background, screen saver, and screen resolution?
4. How do you change views from Category View to Classic View?
5. How many Control Panel category icons are located in the Control Panel window in Category View?

PROCEDURE

___m. In Tables 9-3 through 9-7, record the tasks that can be accomplished in each remaining category.

NOTE: Some icons do not bring up another category screen. They run programs such as User Accounts. Simply explain which program these icons run.

2. **Switch the view to Classic Control Panel view**
   ___a. Click on **Switch to Classic View** on the upper-left side of the *Control Panel* window.
   ___b. This will switch it to the Classic View as in Figure 9-4. Click on **Switch to Category View** to change it back.

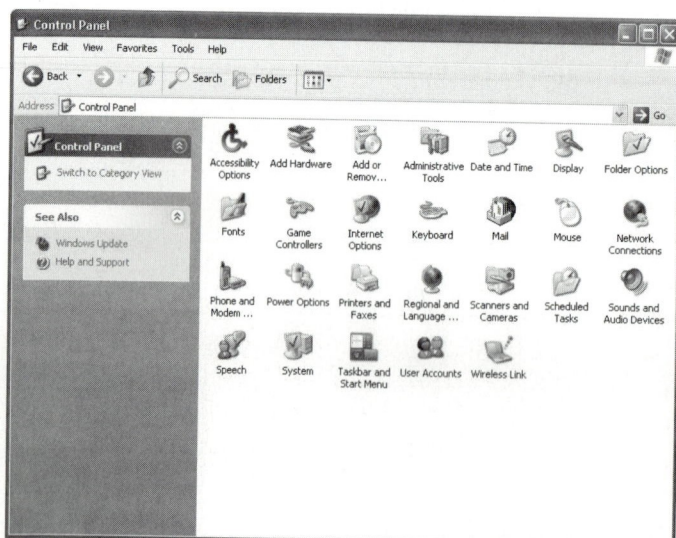

Figure 9-4: Classic Control Panel

___c. Click on the **X** in Control Panel to close it.

TABLES

Table 9-1

Table 9-2

Table 9-3

WINDOWS XP CONTROL PANEL - 83

LAB PROCEDURE 10

Windows 2000 Plug-and-Play

OBJECTIVES

1. Remove network adapter.
2. Install network adapter with Plug-and-Play.
3. Remove modem.
4. Install modem with Plug-and-Play.

Operating
System
Technology

RESOURCES

1. PC-compatible desktop/tower computer system — Customer-supplied desktop/tower hardware system **OR** Marcraft MC-8000 Computer Hardware Trainer **OR** suitable PC hardware trainer with Windows 2000 installed
2. A Windows 2000 Plug-and-Play network adapter installed
3. A Windows 2000 Plug-and-Play modem installed
4. Network connection (optional)

DISCUSSION

The performance of Plug-and-Play (PnP) has improved with easy installation of PnP hardware in new systems. Windows 2000 doesn't require that you restart the computer as much as with previous operating systems. If a device is not PnP-compatible you may be able to install it manually through *Add/Remove Hardware* in the Control Panel. You may need the drivers provided by the manufacturer unless Windows has them already. In this lab you will install a PnP modem and network adapter with Windows 2000.

PROCEDURE

1. **View network adapter in Device Manager**
   ___ a. Boot to the Windows 2000 desktop.
   ___ b. Right-click on **My Computer** and select **Properties**.
   ___ c. Click on the **Hardware** tab and click on **Device Manager**.
   ___ d. You will see a list of device types attached to the computer.
   ___ e. Look for the section called *Network adapters* and expand it by clicking on the plus (+) sign next to the icon.

PROCEDURE - 10

___f. The window should look similar to Figure 10-1. Record the name of the network adapter in Table 10-1.

**Figure 10-1:
Network Card in Device Manager**

___g. Right-click on the network adapter and click on **Uninstall**.
___h. You will be prompted to *Confirm Device Removal*. Click on **OK**.

2. **Remove network adapter**
   ___a. Close all windows and shut down the computer.
   ___b. Open the computer case.
   ___c. Remove any external cables from the network card.
   ___d. Remove the mounting screw of the network adapter.
   ___e. Gently pull the adapter out of its expansion slot and set the adapter and screw aside.

3. **View hardware changes**
   ___a. Turn on the computer and boot to the Windows 2000 desktop.
   ___b. Right-click on **My Computer** and select **Properties**.
   ___c. Click on the **Hardware** tab and click on **Device Manager**.
   ___d. Record your observations in Table 10-2.
   ___e. Close all windows and shut down the computer.

4. **Add network adapter**
   ___a. Gently insert the network card back into the available expansion slot.
   ___b. Add the mounting screw of the network adapter.
   ___c. Plug in any external cables that you removed previously.
   ___d. Turn the computer on and boot to the Windows 2000 desktop.
   ___e. The network adapter will install automatically. You may not see any dialog windows. Navigate to **Device Manager** as in previous steps.
   ___f. Record your observations in Table 10-3.
   ___g. If you are connected to a LAN double-click on **My Network Places** from the desktop.
   ___h. Double-click **Computers Near Me**. If you are connected you should see other computers in the window.

PROCEDURE - 10

5. **An alternative approach**
   ___a. From Device Manager right-click on the network adapter and choose **Uninstall**.
   ___b. Confirm the *Device Removal* by clicking on **OK**.
   ___c. Right-click the top icon (the computer name STATION01, for example) and choose **Scan for hardware changes** as in Figure 10-2.

Figure 10-2: Scan for Hardware Changes

   ___d. The computer should detect an Ethernet adapter. You will see a window similar to Figure 10-3. The words "Ethernet controller" will change to the specific name of the network adapter.
   ___e. Notice that the adapter is now installed in Device Manager. Close all windows.

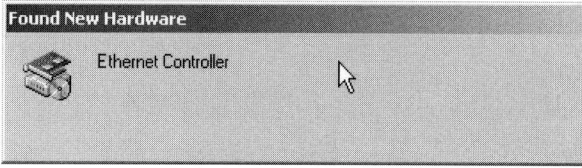

Figure 10-3: Found New Hardware

6. Repeat Steps 1 through 4 with the Plug-and-Play modem

7. **Test the modem**
   ___a. Navigate to **Device Manager**.
   ___b. Look for the modem and right-click on its icon. Click on **Properties**.
   ___c. Click on the **Diagnostics** tab.
   ___d. Click on the **Query Modem** button. If the modem is installed the computer will communicate with the modem. Responses to commands will appear in the window, similar to Figure 10-4.
   ___e. Close all open windows.
   ___f. Shut down the computer.

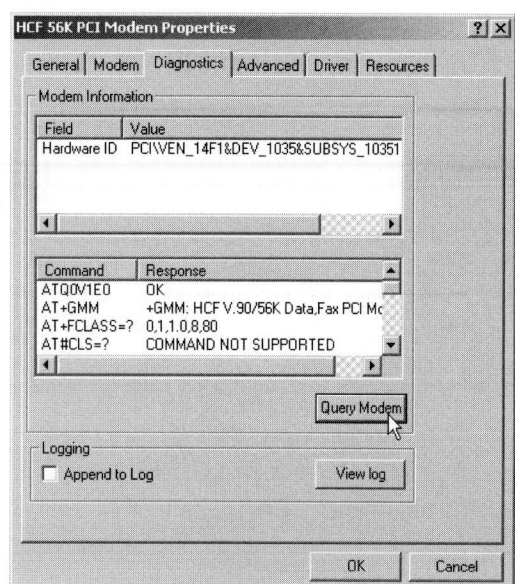

Figure 10-4: Sample Modem Query

WINDOWS 2000 PLUG-AND-PLAY - 87

PROCEDURE - 10

TABLES

Table 10-1

Network Adapter:	

Table 10-2

Observations After Removal:	

Table 10-3

Observations After Adding:	

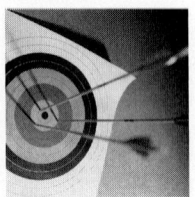

Feedback

LAB QUESTIONS

1. What does PnP stand for?
2. Why can PnP be useful?
3. What is an alternative way of installing a non-PnP device?
4. Will you see any dialog windows when installing a PnP device?
5. How can you scan for hardware changes while the computer is running?

LAB PROCEDURE 11

Windows XP Plug-and-Play

OBJECTIVES

1. Remove Network Interface Card (NIC).
2. Install NIC with Plug-and-Play capabilities.
3. Remove modem.
4. Install modem with Plug-and-Play capabilities.

Operating System Technology

RESOURCES

1. PC-compatible desktop/tower computer system—Customer-supplied desktop/tower hardware system **OR** Marcraft MC-8000 Computer Hardware Trainer **OR** suitable PC hardware trainer with a Plug-and-Play modem and NIC installed under Windows XP

DISCUSSION

This procedure is very similar to procedure 11. We wanted to show you how the Plug-and-Play installations have improved with each Windows operating system. In this procedure we will again have you remove the network adapter and modem and reinstall them. This lab should go very fast since you have already performed this task.

PROCEDURE

1. **Remove Network Interface Card (NIC)**
   ___ a. Boot to the Windows XP desktop.
   ___ b. Press and hold the **Windows** key (located next to the left ALT key) then press the **Pause** key (upper-right keyboard next to the 10 key). This should bring up the *System Properties* box.
   ___ c. Click on the **Hardware** tab.
   ___ d. Click on **Device Manager**.
   ___ e. Click on the + next to *Modems* and *Network Adapters* as in Figure 11-1.
   ___ f. Record the devices in Tables 11-1 and 11-2.
   ___ g. Right-click on the network card and select **Uninstall**.
   ___ h. In the *Confirm Device Removal* dialog box click on **OK**.
   ___ i. Now click on **Start** and **Shut Down**.

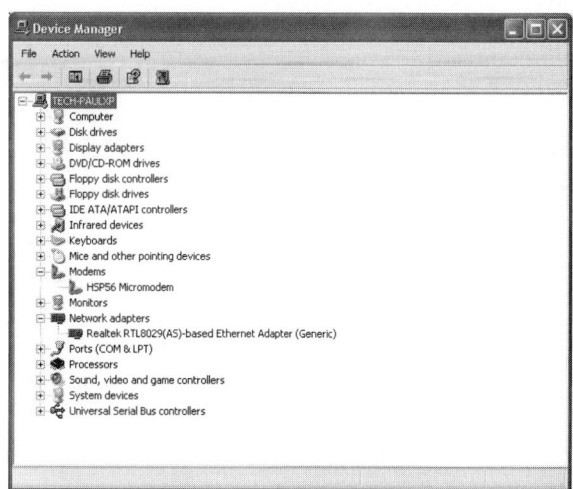

Figure 11-1: XP Device Manager

PROCEDURE - 11

    ___j.   Select **Shut Down** and click on **OK** to turn off the computer.
    ___k.   After unplugging the computer, remove the network interface card from the computer.
    ___l.   Boot up the computer into Windows XP.
    ___m.   Press the **Windows** key + **Pause** key to bring up System Properties.
    ___n.   Click on **Hardware** then **Device Manager**.
    ___o.   Notice that the network adapter is not installed.
    ___p.   Now click on **Start/Shutdown** and select **Shut Down**.

> **WARNING**
>
> On ATX machines you must make sure to unplug the computer to prevent damage to the computer. ATX machines have a 5-volt supply to the motherboard even when off.

2. **Install NIC with Plug-and-Play capabilities**
    ___a.   Install the network card into the trainer.
    ___b.   Make sure to connect the network cable and fasten the screw.
    ___c.   Boot the computer to Windows XP desktop.

NOTE: There should not have been any Found New Hardware dialog boxes. Since the hardware was already installed it still exists in Windows XP and will install the software automatically.

    ___d.   Press the **Windows Key** + **Pause** to bring up System Properties.
    ___e.   Click on the **Hardware** tab, then **Device Manager**.
    ___f.   The network card should now be in Device Manager again.
    ___g.   Make sure it matches what you recorded in Table 11-1.

3. **Repeat Steps 1 and 2 for the modem**

TABLES

Table 11-1

Network Adapter:	

Table 11-2

Modem:	

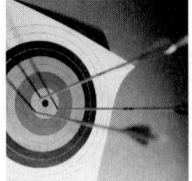

Feedback

LAB QUESTIONS

1. How do you remove drivers in Windows XP?

2. Why must you unplug ATX computers before removing or installing adapter cards?

3. What is the key combination used to bring up System Properties?

4. Do any dialog boxes appear when installing previously installed hardware in Windows XP?

5. Is there usually any interaction between the user and the operating system when installing Plug-and-Play devices?

LAB PROCEDURE 12

Windows Me Printers

OBJECTIVES

1. Print a test page.
2. View CMOS parallel port settings.
3. Print a CMOS screen.
4. Install a printer in Windows Me.
5. Explore Windows printer properties.
6. Print a test page on the printer.

Operating System Technology

RESOURCES

1. PC-compatible desktop/tower computer system — Customer-supplied desktop/tower hardware system **OR** Marcraft MC-8000 Computer Hardware Trainer **OR** suitable PC hardware trainer with Windows Me installed
2. A printer with documentation
3. Manufacturer's printer drivers (optional)
4. Printer power cable
5. Printer interface cable

DISCUSSION

This lab is very general in nature because printer settings vary greatly between manufacturers and printer models. Most printers have a parallel port interface. Some have USB, SCSI, serial port, and possibly infrared interfaces with the computer. We will explore some of the CMOS settings regarding parallel ports that connect to printers. You will print a test page without the computer and use PRINT SCREEN to print some basic text. You will also install a printer with Windows Me, explore the properties of the printer, and print a test page.

PROCEDURE

1. **Test page**
    ___ a. Plug in the power cable to the printer.
    ___ b. Plug in the parallel cable to the printer and the computer.
    ___ c. Turn on the printer.

PROCEDURE - 12

    ___d.   Consult your printer's documentation on how to print a test page and do so. This is usually accomplished by pressing a combination of the printer's buttons.

2. Parallel port mode
    ___a.   Boot the computer and press **DELETE** or whatever key is used to enter setup.
    ___b.   Use the **ARROW** keys to select **Integrated Peripherals** and press **ENTER**.
    ___c.   Scroll down with the ARROW keys to "Parallel Port Mode".
    ___d.   Press the **PAGE UP**, **PAGE DOWN**, **+**, or **-** keys to view all the options available.
    ___e.   These parallel port modes could possibly support printers that have EPP or ECP communication features. Record your different parallel port modes in Table 12-1.
    ___f.   Change the settings back to their default.
    ___g.   Press **ESC** to return to the main *CMOS* screen.

3. Print screen
    ___a.   Make sure that the printer is on and connected to the computer.
    ___b.   Press the **PRINT SCREEN** key. Depending on your BIOS version you may need to press **PRINT SCREEN** several times or press **SHIFT + PRINT SCREEN**.
    ___c.   Verify that the screen has printed.
    ___d.   Press **ESC** to exit CMOS Setup. Select **Yes** to quit without saving. Press **ENTER**.
    ___e.   Turn off the computer and the printer.

4. Install printer in Windows
    ___a.   Obtain the manufacturer and model of the printer and record them in Table 12-2.
    ___b.   Boot to the Windows Millennium Edition desktop.
    ___c.   Navigate the *Start/Settings/Printers* path.
    ___d.   In the window that opens, double-click on **Add Printer**.
    ___e.   The *Add Printer Wizard* will appear; click on **Next**.
    ___f.   The *Local printer* and *Network printer* options will appear as in Figure 12-1. Verify that *Local printer* is selected. Click on **Next**.
    ___g.   Referring to Table 12-2, scroll down the "Manufacturers:" list, as shown in Figure 12-2, and click on the appropriate manufacturer for your printer. Scroll down the "Printers:" list and select the appropriate model of your printer. Click on **Next**.

NOTE: If your printer is not listed, insert the CD provided by the manufacturer, click on Have Disk, specify the location, click on OK, and follow the prompts to install the printer.

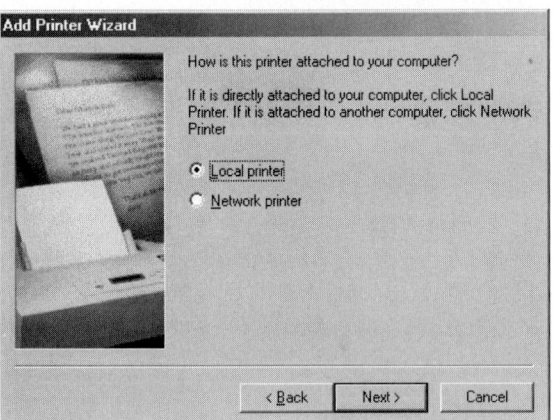

Figure 12-1: Add Printer Wizard

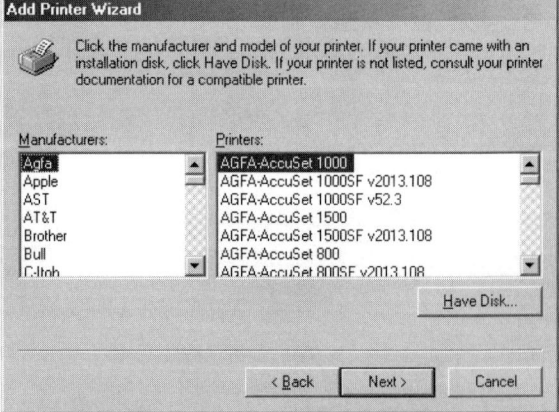

Figure 12-2: Printer Selection

92 - LAB GROUP 1

PROCEDURE - 12

___h. Click on **LPT1** (unless otherwise directed by your instructor) from the list that appears. This is the port that is typically used on a computer for printing. Click on **Next**.

___i. You will be prompted to specify a name for the printer. Use the default and click on **Next**.

___j. You will be prompted to print a test page. Select **No**. Click on **Finish**.

___k. After files are copied, verify that the printer now appears in the *PRINTERS* folder. It should look similar to Figure 12-3.

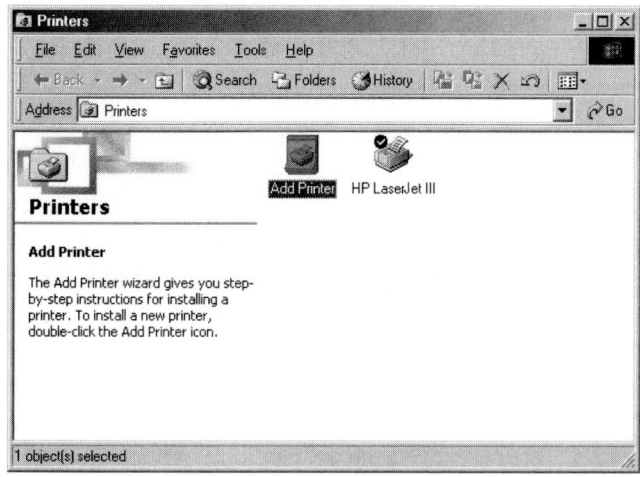

Figure 12-3: Printers Folder

5. **View Printer Properties and test page**

___a. Double-click on the printer you have just installed.

___b. A window similar to Figure 12-4 will appear. Click on **Printer/Properties**.

___c. The properties of the printer will now open to the *General* tab. From this tab you can change the name, location, comments, and printing preferences of the printer. Click on the **Print Test Page** button.

___d. A window similar to Figure 12-5 will appear. Verify that the test page has printed correctly and click on **Yes**.

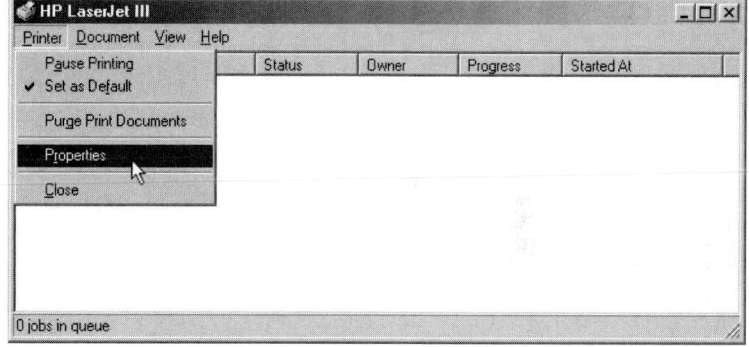

Figure 12-4: The Printer Window

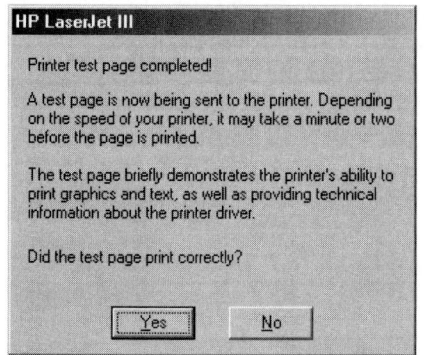

Figure 12-5: Test Page Dialog

___e. On the test page that has printed look for the "Driver name:" information. Record the name of the driver in Table 12-3.

___f. Click on the **Details** tab. This shows information about the communication ports available on your computer. From this window you can Add, Delete, and Configure ports. Record the printer port that your printer is connected to in Table 12-4.

___g. Click on the **Graphics** tab. From this tab you can change the printer's resolution and intensity.

WINDOWS ME PRINTERS - 93

PROCEDURE - 12

___ h. Click on the **Fonts** tab. From this window you can view the fonts supported by your printer. Record the first two fonts listed in Table 12-5.

___ i. Click on the **Device Options** tab. It may look similar to Figure 12-6. The settings in this window are specific to your printer. You can change various printer memory settings from this window.

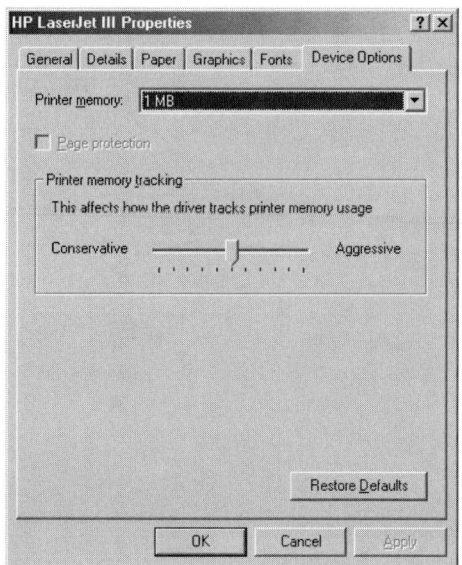

Figure 12-6: Device Options

___ j. Click on **OK** and close all open windows.
___ k. Shut down the computer.

TABLES

Table 12-1

Parallel Port Modes			

Table 12-2

Printer	
Manufacturer:	
Model:	

PROCEDURE - 12

Table 12-3

Printer Driver Name:	

Table 12-4

Printer Port that Printer is Connected to:	

Table 12-5

Fonts Tab:	

LAB QUESTIONS

1. Did you install a local or network printer?

2. On what port is the printer installed?

3. Did you share the printer?

4. What can you do from the Graphics tab?

5. What are some possible settings from the Device Options tab?

6. What did you have to do to print a test page with your printer?

7. What was your specific procedure for printing the screen?

8. What key is used to enter setup on your system?

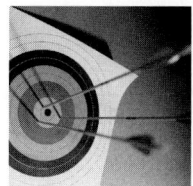

Feedback

LAB PROCEDURE 13

Windows 2000 Printers

OBJECTIVES

1. Install a printer.
2. Explore printer properties.
3. Print a test page on the printer.

Operating System Technology

RESOURCES

1. PC-compatible desktop/tower computer system — Customer-supplied desktop/tower hardware system **OR** Marcraft MC-8000 Computer Hardware Trainer **OR** suitable PC hardware trainer with Windows 2000 installed
2. A printer connected to the computer with power turned on
3. Manufacturer's printer drivers (optional)

DISCUSSION

This lab will help you install a printer with Windows 2000. The procedure for installing the drivers may vary depending on the model of your printer. You will then explore the properties of the printer and print a test page.

PROCEDURE

1. **Install printer**
   - a. Boot to the Windows 2000 desktop.
   - b. Navigate the *Start/Settings/Printers* path.
   - c. In the window that opens double-click on **Add Printer**.
   - d. The *Add Printer Wizard* will appear. Click on **Next**.
   - e. The *Local printer* and *Network printer* options will appear as in Figure 13-1. Verify that *Local printer* and *Automatically detect and install my Plug and Play printer* are selected. Click on **Next**.
   - f. If Windows is unable to detect a Plug-and-Play printer, click on **Next** to install the printer manually.

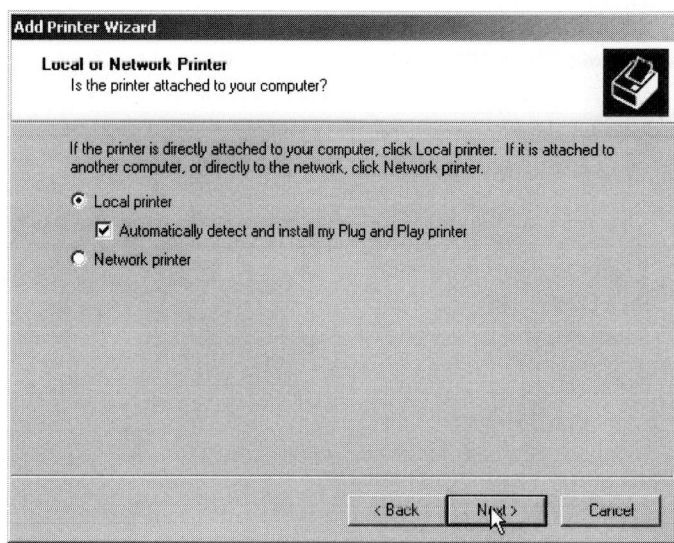

Figure 13-1: Add Printer Wizard

WINDOWS 2000 PRINTERS - 97

PROCEDURE - 13

___ g. Click on **LPT1** (unless otherwise directed by your instructor) from the list that appears. This is the port that is typically used on a computer for printing. Click on **Next**.

___ h. Referring to Figure 13-2, scroll down the "*Manufacturers:*" list to click on the appropriate manufacturer for your printer. Scroll down the "*Printers:*" list and select the appropriate model of your printer. If your printer is not listed, insert the CD provided by the manufacturer, click on **Have Disk**, specify the location, click on **OK**, and follow the prompts to install the printer.

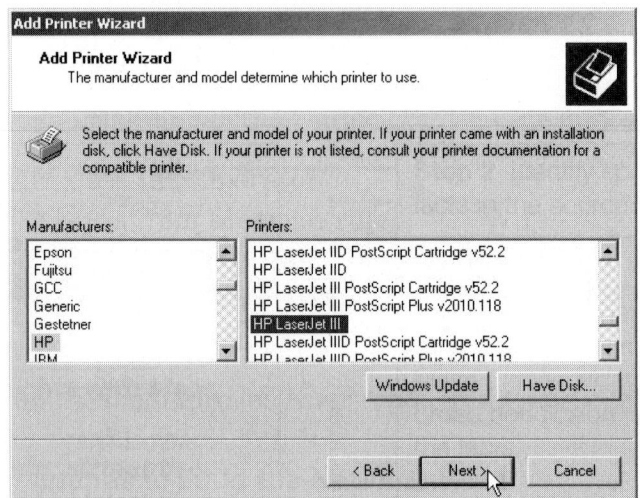

**Figure 13-2:
Printer Selection**

Figure 13-3: Completing the Add Printer Wizard

___ i. Record the manufacturer and model of the printer in Table 13-1. Click on **Next**.

___ j. You will be prompted to specify a name for the printer. Use the default and click on **Next**.

___ k. Choose **Do not share this printer**. This will be used in a later procedure. Click on **Next.**

___ l. You will be prompted to print a test page; select **No**. Click on **Next**.

___ m. You will see a window similar to Figure 13-3. Verify the information and click on **Finish**.

___ n. After files are copied verify that the printer now appears in the *PRINTERS* folder.

2. **View Printer Properties and test page**

___ a. Double-click the printer you have just installed.

___ b. A window similar to Figure 13-4 will appear. Click on **Printer/Properties**.

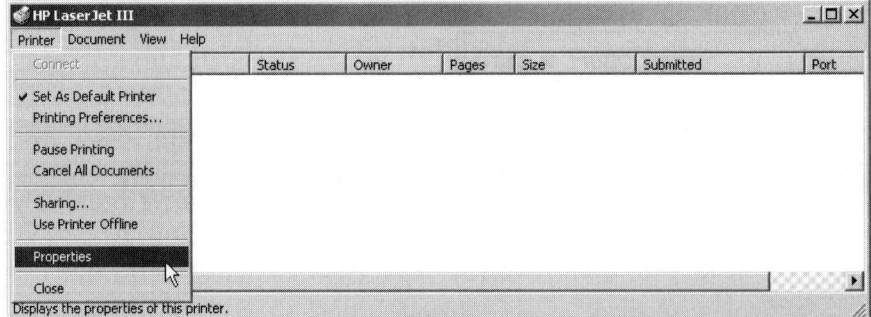

**Figure 13-4:
The Printer Window**

98 - LAB GROUP 1

PROCEDURE - 13

___c. The properties of the printer will now open to the *General* tab. From this tab you can change the name, location, comments, and printing preferences of the printer. Click on the **Print Test Page** button.

___d. A window similar to Figure 13-5 will appear. Verify that the test page has printed correctly and click on **OK**.

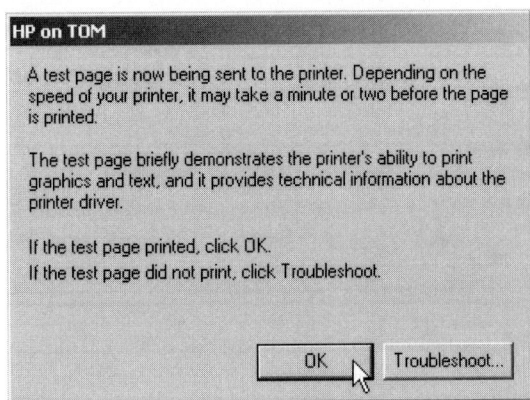

Figure 13-5: Test Page Dialog

___e. On the test page that has printed look for the "*Driver name:*" information. Record the name of the driver in Table 13-2.

___f. Click on the **Ports** tab. This shows information about the communication ports available on your computer. From this window you can Add, Delete, and Configure ports.

___g. Click on the **Advanced** tab. From this tab you can change the printer's availability schedule, spool settings, defaults, print processing format, and separator page settings.

___h. Click on the **Security** tab. From this window you change access privileges from users on your computer.

___i. Click on the **Device Settings** tab. It may look similar to Figure 13-6. The settings in this window are specific to your printer. You can change various paper and cartridge settings from this window.

___j. Click on **OK** and close all open windows.

___k. Shut down the computer.

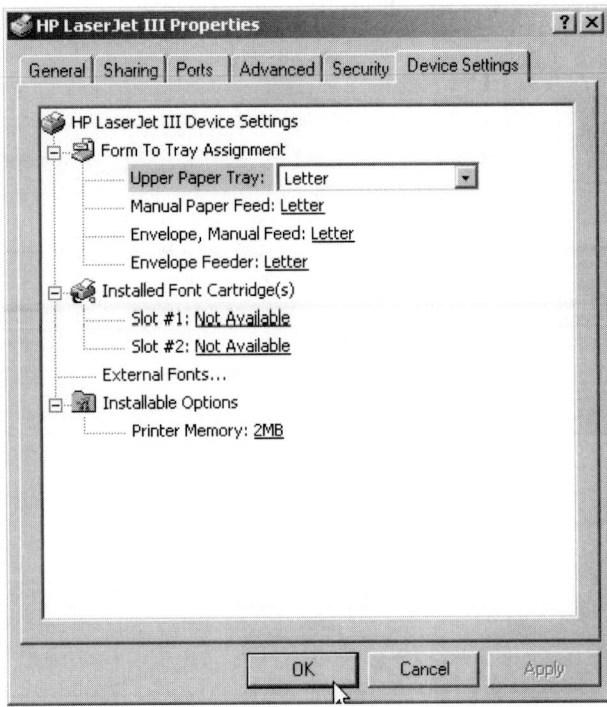

Figure 13-6: Device Settings

WINDOWS 2000 PRINTERS - 99

PROCEDURE - 13

TABLES

Table 13-1

Printer	
Manufacturer:	
Model:	

Table 13-2

Printer Driver Name:	

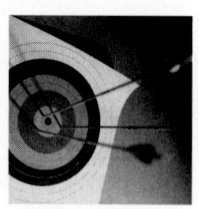

Feedback

LAB QUESTIONS

1. Did you install a local printer or a network printer?
2. On what port is the printer installed?
3. Did you share the printer?
4. What can you do from the Advanced tab?
5. What are some possible settings from the Device Settings tab?

LAB PROCEDURE 14

Installing Printers in Windows XP

OBJECTIVES

1. Install a printer.
2. Share a printer.
3. Install a network printer.
4. Uninstall a network printer.

Operating
System
Technology

RESOURCES

1. PC-compatible desktop/tower computer system — Customer-supplied desktop/tower hardware system **OR** Marcraft MC-8000 Computer Hardware Trainer **OR** suitable PC hardware trainer running Windows XP Professional
2. A printer connected to the printer locally
3. A shared network printer
4. Print drivers if necessary

DISCUSSION

In this lab we will install a printer locally on the machine. We will also install a network printer and print a test page. In Windows XP, connecting to a network printer becomes almost automatic. We use a Hewlett-Packard LaserJet 1100 printer. The results may vary with different printers.

PROCEDURE

1. **Install a printer on the parallel port**
    ___ a. Boot the computer into Windows XP.
    ___ b. Plug the printer into the trainer's parallel port, LPT1.
    ___ c. Now plug in the printer and turn it on.
    ___ d. In the Taskbar a message will appear that new hardware is found, and that Windows is installing the drivers; then it will finally say the hardware is installed and ready for use. No user interaction is necessary if the driver is available either locally or at the Windows Update site; the computer just fetches the driver automatically.
    ___ e. Click on **Start**.

PROCEDURE - 14

    ___f.   Click on **Printers and Faxes**. The *Printers and Faxes* window will appear as in Figure 14-1.

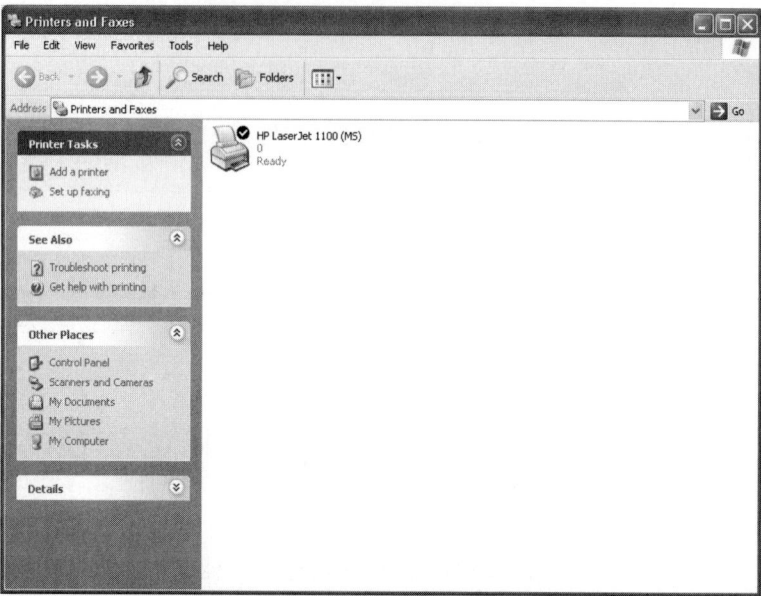

Figure 14-1: XP Printers and Faxes

    ___g.   Right-click on the newly installed printer and select **Properties**.
    ___h.   The printer's *Properties* box will come up as in Figure 14-2.

Figure 14-2: XP Printer Properties Box

2. **Share a printer in Windows XP**
   ___a.   Click on the **Sharing** tab.
   ___b.   Select **Share this printer**.
   ___c.   Share the printer with the name of Marcraft.
   ___d.   Click on **OK**.
   ___e.   Close the printer's *Properties* box by clicking on the **X**.

3. **Connect to a network printer in Windows XP**
   ___a.   Now click on **Start** and then click on **Printers and Faxes**.
   ___b.   On the left side click on the words **Add a printer**.

PROCEDURE - 14

Figure 14-3: Add Printer Wizard

___ c. The Add Printer Wizard comes up as in Figure 14-3. It states that if you have a Plug-and-Play printer you do not need to use this wizard. Since we are installing a network printer click on **Next**.

___ d. The *Local or Network Printer* dialog box comes up as in Figure 14-4, select **A network printer** if it is not already selected and click on **Next**.

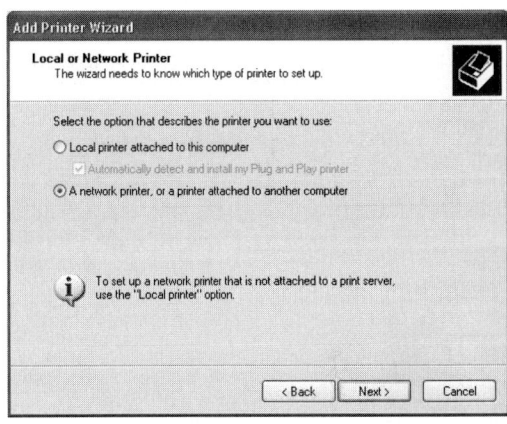

Figure 14-4: Local or Network Printer Dialog Box

___ e. The *Specify a Printer* dialog box comes up. Make sure to click on **Connect to this printer** and click on **Next** to browse for the printer.

___ f. The *Browse for Printer* box comes up as in Figure 14-5. Double-click the computer of the workstation next to you or a specific computer as specified by your Instructor. This will expand it to the printer name shared on it.

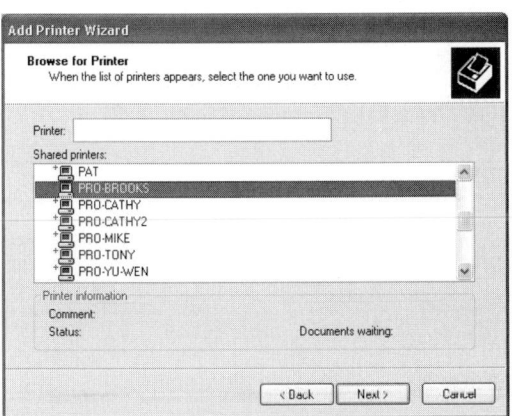

Figure 14-5: Browse for Printer Dialog Box

___ g. Double-click on the **Printer share name**. In this lab procedure it should be *Marcraft*.

___ h. The *Default Printer* dialog box opens up as in Figure 14-6. Select no to not have this printer be the default printer. Click on **Next**.

___ i. A *Completing the Add Printer Wizard* dialog box comes up. Click on **Finish**.

___ j. Your *Printers and Faxes* window should still be open. Verify that the printer is installed. Record the name of the network printer in Table 14-1.

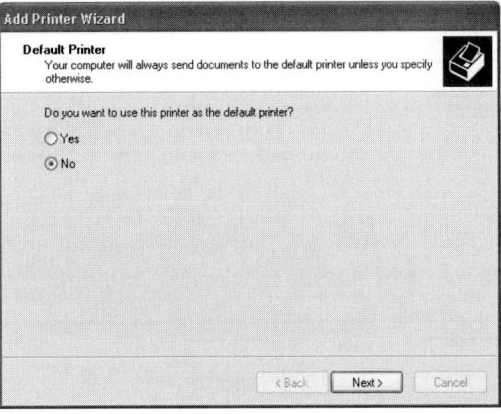

Figure 14-6: Default Printer Dialog Box

PROCEDURE - 14

4. **Uninstall a printer in Windows XP**
   ___a. Right-click on the network printer and select **Delete**.
   ___b. A *Printers* dialog box comes up asking you if you are sure you want to remove your connection to the printer on the server. Click on **Yes**.

TABLES

Table 14-1

Name of Printer:	

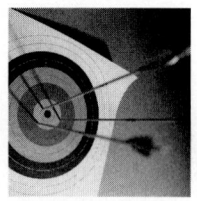

Feedback

LAB QUESTIONS

1. How do you install a local Plug-and-Play printer in Windows XP?

2. How do you share a printer on a network in Windows XP?

3. How do you get to the Add Printer Wizard in Windows XP?

4. When adding a network printer how do you browse the network for available printers?

5. How does a network printer display in the Printers and Faxes window?

LAB GROUP 2

SYSTEM ADMINISTRATION TOOLS

LAB PROCEDURE 15

Windows Me System Information

OBJECTIVES

1. View various areas of System Information.
2. Tour Microsoft's new Help and Support interface.
3. Use the Tools menu to run programs to enhance or repair your system.

Operating System Technology

RESOURCES

1. PC-compatible desktop/tower computer system — Customer-supplied desktop/tower hardware system **OR** Marcraft MC-8000 Computer Hardware Trainer **OR** suitable PC hardware trainer running Windows Me or Windows 98

DISCUSSION

Windows 98 and Windows Millennium Edition are equipped with a powerful set of tools to assist users with various troubleshooting tasks.

PROCEDURE

1. **Boot the computer to Windows Me**
   ___a. Turn on the computer and select **Windows Me** from the OS selection menu.

2. **Tour Windows Me Help and Support Information tool**
   ___a. Navigate the path *Start/Programs/Accessories/System Tools* and then select **System Information** to open the *MS Help and Support* window.
   ___b. In Table 15-1, list the subtopics underneath *System Summary* from the left window pane.

3. **View Hardware Resources**
   ___a. Double-click the **HARDWARE RESOURCES** directory in order to expand it.
   ___b. Click the **IRQs subtopic** under *HARDWARE RESOURCES* to show the settings in the right pane.
   ___c. In Table 15-2, list the resources' IRQs and device names.

4. **View Components**
   ___a. Double-click the **COMPONENTS** directory to expand it.
   ___b. Click on the **DISPLAY** subcomponent and record the adapter name, adapter type, resolution, and bits/pixel in Table 15-3.
   ___c. Double-click the **PORTS** subcomponent and choose **Serial**.
   ___d. In Table 15-4, list the baud rate for COM1.

PROCEDURE - 15

5. **View the Software Environment**
   ___a. Double-click the **SOFTWARE ENVIRONMENT** directory to expand it.
   ___b. Click on the **DRIVERS** subcomponent and view the drivers that are listed in the right pane.
   ___c. Subsequently click on each subcomponent underneath the *SOFTWARE ENVIRONMENT* directory to become familiar with the types of information available here.
   ___d. Click on the **STARTUP PROGRAMS** subcomponent.

   NOTE: This subsection can be helpful when troubleshooting boot problems and when optimizing your system. It is also a good place to check if your computer is running unnecessary programs at startup.

6. **View Internet Explorer's subcomponent information**
   ___a. Double-click the **INTERNET EXPLORER** directory to expand it.
   ___b. In Table 15-5, list all of the subcomponents that are listed under the Internet Explorer.

Viewing the Tools that are Available in the Tools Menu

You can use System Restore to undo harmful changes to your computer and restore its settings and performance. System Restore returns your computer to an earlier time (called a restore point) without losing recent work, such as saved documents, e-mail, or history and favorites lists.

Your computer automatically creates restore points (called system checkpoints), but you can also use System Restore to create your own. This is useful if you are about to make a major change to your system, such as installing a new program or changing your Registry.

1. **Use System Restore to create a restore point for your computer**
   ___a. In the menu bar click on the **Tools** menu and select **System Restore**.
   ___b. Click on the radio button next to *Create a restore point* and click on **Next** to continue.
   ___c. In the *System Restore* window, shown in Figure 15-1, give your restore point a descriptive name. I recommend using the date in the name. Type today's date with the word Restore at the end of the name (for example, 12-01-01Restore)
   ___d. Click on the **Next** button to continue.
   ___e. Click on **OK** to close the *Confirm New Restore Point* window.

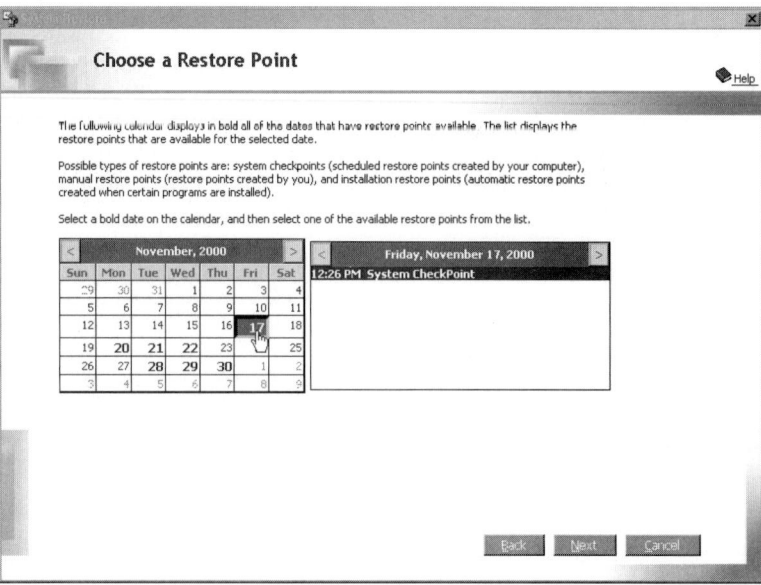

Figure 15-1:
System Restore Window

108 - LAB GROUP 2

PROCEDURE - 15

2. **Use System Restore to return your system to an earlier state**
   ___ a. Click on the **Tools** menu and select **System Restore**.
   ___ b. With *Restore my computer to an earlier time* checked, click on **Next** to continue.
   ___ c. Select a bold date in the calendar as far back as you can to restore your system to. In our example, we went back to the previous month.
   ___ d. Highlight a *System CheckPoint* listing on the right, as shown in Figure 15-2, and click on **Next** to continue.
   ___ e. Make sure all programs are closed, except the *Help* and *Support* windows, and click on **OK** to continue.
   ___ f. Verify the date and time of the restore point and enter it into Table 15-6.
   ___ g. Click on **Next** to begin the restoration process.
   ___ h. The computer will automatically reboot itself to a *Restoration status* window.
   ___ i. Verify that the restoration was completed successfully, and click on **OK**.

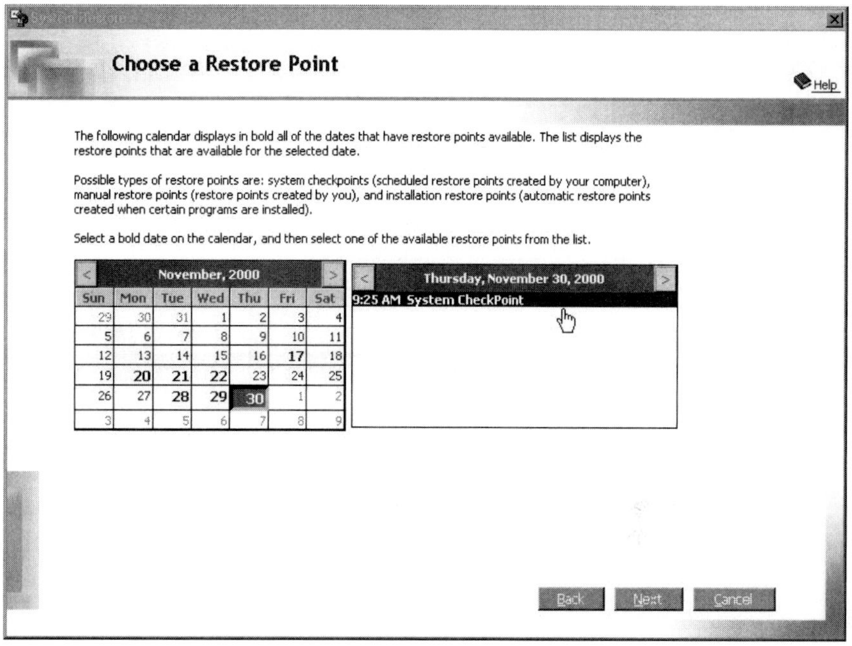

   Figure 15-2: System Restore Window

3. **Work with the System Configuration Utility (SCU)**
   ___ a. From within the *Microsoft Help and Support* interface, click on the **Tools** menu and select **System Configuration Utility**.
   ___ b. On the *General* tab, click on the **Advanced** button.
   ___ c. In Table 15-7, list the optional Settings that are under the *Advanced Troubleshooting Settings*.

NOTE: It is recommended that only advanced users and system administrators change these settings. It is always a good idea to keep track of the changes that you've made.

   ___ d. Click on **Cancel** to exit the *Advanced Troubleshooting* window.
   ___ e. Click on the **Startup** tab to show a list of all programs that load during the boot process.
   ___ f. In Table 15-8, list everything that loads on your specific computer at startup.
   ___ g. On the *General* tab, click on the radio button next to *Selective startup*.
   ___ h. In Table 15-9 list the selections for startup.
   ___ i. Click on the radio button next to *Diagnostic startup*, and click on **OK** to shut the SCU.
   ___ j. When prompted to restart your computer, select **Yes**.
   ___ k. In Table 15-10, list the boot options from the screen.
   ___ l. Allow Windows to boot to the default (Normal).
   ___ m. Shut down the computer.

PROCEDURE - 15

TABLES

Table 15-1

System Summary Subtopics:	

Table 15-2

Resources	
IRQ No.	Device Name

PROCEDURE - 15

Table 15-3

Display Subcomponents	
Adapter Name:	
Adapter Type:	
Resolution:	
Bits/Pixel:	

Table 15-4

COM1 Baud Rate:	

Table 15-5

Internet Explorer Subcomponents:	

Table 15-6

Restore Point	
Date:	
Time:	

PROCEDURE - 15

Table 15-7

Optional Settings Under Advanced Troubleshooting Settings:	

Table 15-8

Specific Programs Loaded at Startup	

PROCEDURE - 15

Table 15-9

General Program Selections Loaded at Startup:	

Table 15-10

Diagnostic Startup Boot Options:	

LAB QUESTIONS

1. Is the same IRQ listed for multiple devices?

2. Which utility within System Information allows you to return your computer to the same state it was in and to choose how far back to change it back to?

3. What is System Information used for?

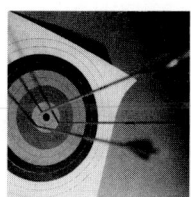

Feedback

LAB PROCEDURE 16

Windows Me Disk Management

OBJECTIVES

1. Use ScanDisk.
2. Defrag your system.
3. Use files archived to a folder.

Operating System Technology

RESOURCES

1. PC-compatible desktop/tower computer system — Customer-supplied desktop/tower hardware system **OR** Marcraft MC-8000 Computer Hardware Trainer **OR** suitable PC hardware trainer with Windows Me installed

DISCUSSION

This lab discusses some common disk management procedures. ScanDisk is a utility that runs automatically at the beginning of Windows Setup, before running disk defragmentation, and when Windows detects an improper shutdown of the operating system. Windows runs the application in a default configuration, where only the data is scanned and fixed automatically. You can also set ScanDisk to check for hard disk errors, and repair them either automatically or by prompting you first.

Disk fragmentation is a leading cause of poor computer performance. Fragmentation occurs when the data on the hard drive is constantly changing because of reads and writes. When some data is removed from a section of the hard drive (because you uninstalled a program, for example) it leaves a hole. That blank spot on the disk between the other data will be filled by the next program files that need to be stored. The problem occurs when the new program is larger than the empty spot on the disk can hold. So part of the program is stored there, and the rest is carried on down to the next available spot. When programs are broken up and stored here and there instead of directly in order, the hard drive is forced to work more, which slows it down dramatically. The Windows Defragmenter utility not only takes all of the programs and puts them back in order, but it goes by the rate of access to each program and puts the ones that you use the most nearest the front of the hard drive, thus increasing access speeds. Disk defragmentation should be done at least once a month, and more often if you do a lot of adding/removing programs.

One more very important part of disk management is backing up your important data on such storage media as CD-R, high-capacity floppy, tape drive, DVD-R, or another hard drive. Windows 98 has a backup utility that can be used for one file or the entire hard drive. Windows Millennium Edition uses compressed folders and archiving to accomplish this task. Compressed folders make it easy to organize or archive projects, folders, and files. Just drag a file onto a compressed folder to compress it, and drag the file out of the compressed folder to extract it. You can also extract all of the files or folders in a compressed folder by using the Extract wizard.

In this lab you will scan your hard drive for errors, defrag your hard drive, create a compressed folder, add a text document to the compressed folder as a backup, and extract the archived document from the compressed folder.

PROCEDURE - 16

Operating System Technology

PROCEDURE

1. **Run the ScanDisk utility**
   a. Boot the computer to Windows Me.
   b. From the desktop, navigate the path *Start/Programs/Accessories/System Tools* and then select **ScanDisk** from the *System Tools* menu.
   c. In the *ScanDisk* window, check the settings *Thorough* and *Automatically fix errors* as shown in Figure 16-1.

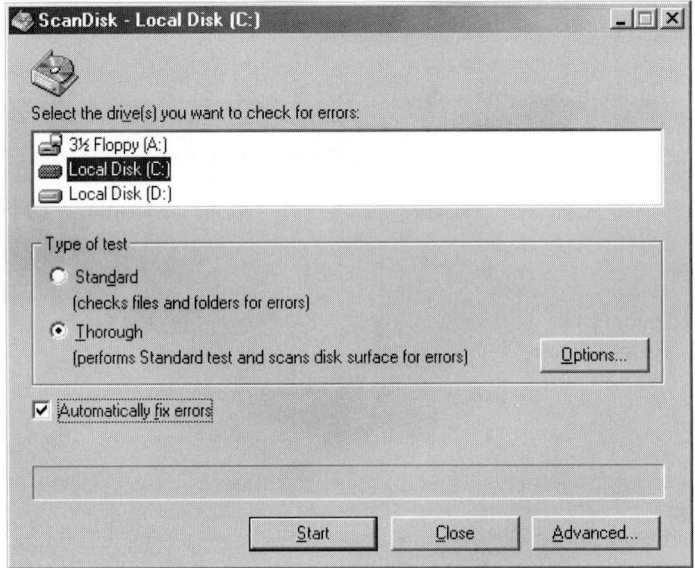

Figure 16-1: ScanDisk Window

   d. Click on the **Advanced** button and in Table 16-1 list the five different settings sections shown in the *Advanced* window.
   e. Click on **Cancel** to close the *Advanced* window.
   f. With the **C:** drive highlighted in the drive selection window, click on the **Start** button to begin scanning the hard drive.
   g. Once ScanDisk is done, in Table 16-2, record the total disk space, the number of bad sectors, and the size of each allocation unit from the *ScanDisk Results* window.
   h. Click on **Close** twice to close the *ScanDisk Results* window and the *ScanDisk Properties* window.

2. **Defragment the hard drive**
   a. From the desktop, navigate the path *Start/Programs/Accessories/System Tools* and then select **Disk Defragmenter** from the *System Tools* menu.
   b. Click on the **Settings** button and in the *Disk Defragmenter Settings* window, make sure *Rearrange program files* and *Check the drive for errors* are checked, as shown in Figure 16-2.
   c. Click on the **OK** button to return to the *Select Drive* window.

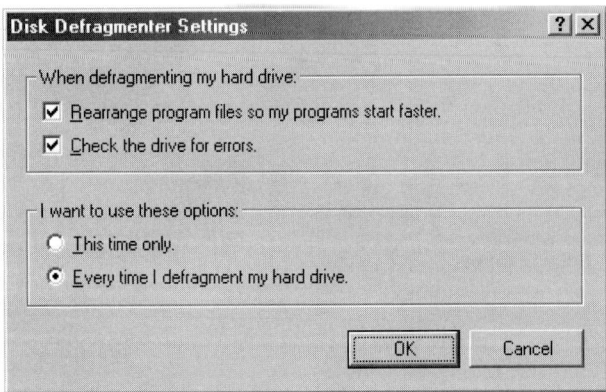

Figure 16-2: Disk Defragmenter Settings

116 - LAB GROUP 2

PROCEDURE - 16

    d. With the C:\ drive selected for the defragmentation, click on the **OK** button to begin disk defragmentation.
    e. Click on the **Show Details** button and watch the defragmentation process.
    f. Click on the **Legend** button in the lower-right portion of the screen to bring up the *Defrag Legend* dialog. The *Defrag Legend* should be similar to that shown in Figure 16-3.
    g. In Table 16-3, list the color of the Unoptimized data that belongs at beginning of the drive, the Optimized (defragmented) data, and the Data that's currently being written.
    h. Close th*e Defrag Legend* by clicking on the **Close** button.
    i. When defragmentation is complete, click on **Yes** to exit the program.

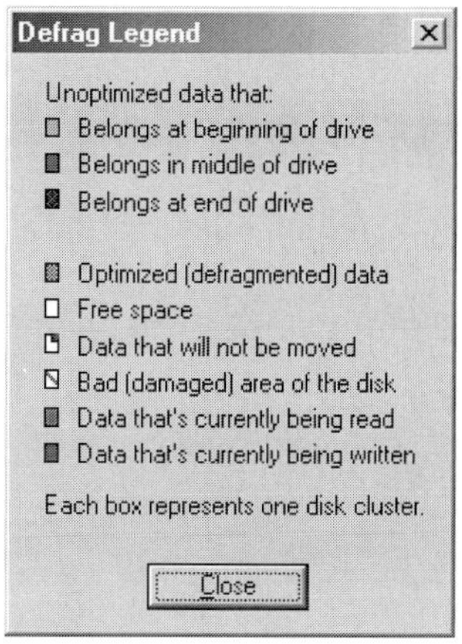

3. **Install Compressed Folders**
    a. From within the Control Panel, click on **Add/Remove Programs**.
    b. Click on the **Windows Setup** tab.
    c. Click on **System Tools** and then the **Details** button.
    d. Place a checkmark in the box next to *Compressed Folders* and click on **OK**.
    e. Click on **Apply** to install the compressed folders.
    f. Click on **Yes** to reboot the computer.

Figure 16-3: Defrag Legend

4. **Create a compressed folder**
    a. On the desktop, double-click **My Computer**.
    b. Double-click the **C:** drive.
    c. Double-click **My Documents**.
    d. On the *File* menu, point to **New**, and then click on **Compressed Folder**, as shown in Figure 16-4.

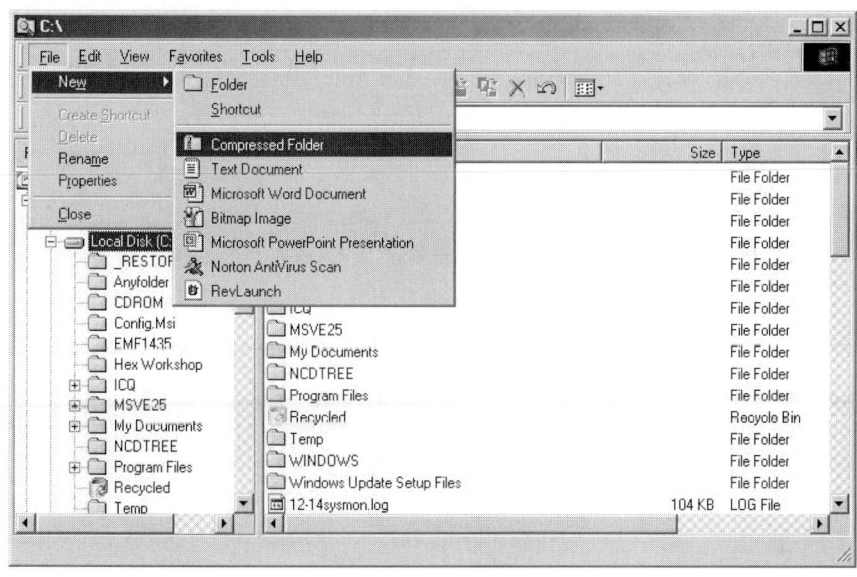

Figure 16-4: Compressed Folder Option

    e. Type **YourName.zip**, YourName being you and your partner's first and last names, as the name for the new folder, and then press **ENTER**.

5. **Create a file**
    a. In the left pane, click on the **MY DOCUMENTS** folder.
    b. Create a *WordPad* document by clicking on **File/New/text document**.
    c. Type **YourName.txt** as the name of the document.
    d. Close all windows.

PROCEDURE - 16

6. **Add a file to the compressed folder for archiving**
   ___a.   Open Windows Explorer.
   ___b.   Click on the **My Documents** subdirectory.
   ___c.   Right-click the file "*YourName.txt*" and hold down the right mouse button.
   ___d.   Drag the file to the compressed folder named *YOURNAME.ZIP* and release the right mouse button.
   ___e.   Select **Copy Here** from the menu.
   ___f.   Enter the compressed folder by clicking on the **View** menu and selecting **Details**.

7. **Extract a file from a compressed folder**
   ___a.   From within Windows Explorer, double-click the compressed folder **YOURNAME.ZIP**. Your window should look similar to Figure 16-5.

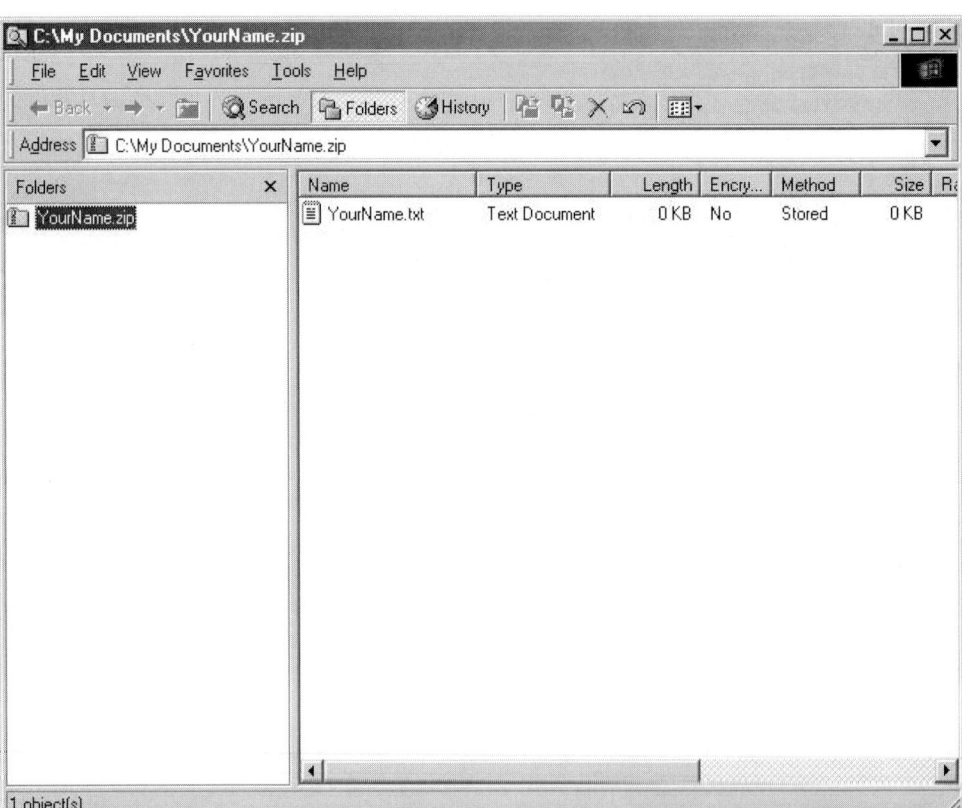

Figure 16-5: Your Compressed Folder

   ___b.   Right-click the file "*YourName.txt*" and drag it to the *MY PICTURES* folder located within the *MY DOCUMENTS* folder.
   ___c.   Release the mouse button and select **Copy Here** to extract the file to the specific location.
   ___d.   Close all open windows, and shut down the computer.

PROCEDURE - 16

TABLES

Table 16-1

The Five Settings in the ScanDisk Advanced Section:	

Table 16-2

ScanDisk Results	
Total Disk Space:	
Number of Bad Sectors:	
Size of Each Allocation Unit:	

Table 16-3

Select Colors From Defrag Legend	
Unoptimized data that belongs at beginning of drive:	
Optimized (defragmented) data:	
Data that's currently being written:	

PROCEDURE - 16

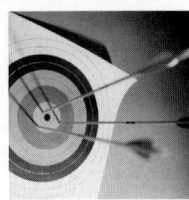

Feedback

LAB QUESTIONS

1. List the different types of storage media that can be managed in Windows Me.

2. What is one of the leading causes for a computer system slowing down?

3. In Windows Me, where is the ScanDisk utility located?

4. By what ratio was the file compressed in this procedure?

5. Using the methods in this lab, can you encrypt and compress a file at the same time?

LAB PROCEDURE 17

Windows 2000 Accessories

OBJECTIVES

1. Learn about Power Options.
2. Learn about Accessibility Options.
3. Learn about Regional Options.
4. Learn about Sounds and Multimedia.

Operating System Technology

RESOURCES

1. PC-compatible desktop/tower computer system — Customer-supplied desktop/tower hardware system **OR** Marcraft MC-8000 Computer Hardware Trainer **OR** suitable PC hardware trainer with Windows 2000 installed
2. Sound card and speakers

DISCUSSION

This lab will explore some of the various system customizing options in Windows 2000. The Power Options are useful if the system is on a laptop. These features can be used to turn off the monitor and hard disks to conserve energy and battery life. Accessibility Options can be used to help people with audio and visual impairments by making sounds at various keyboard events and showing visual alerts. Regional Options can change language and various country specific settings on the computer. You can change the default sounds for different events.

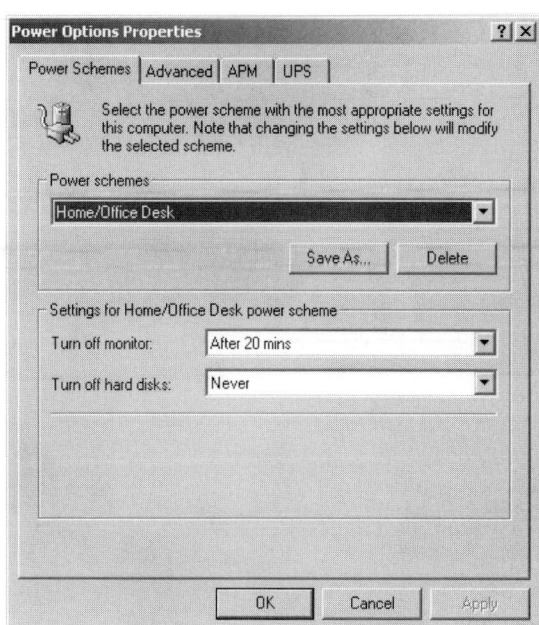

Figure 17-1: Power Options

PROCEDURE

1. **Power Options**
   ___ a. Boot to the Windows 2000 desktop.
   ___ b. Navigate the path *Start/Settings/Control Panel*.
   ___ c. Double-click on **Power Options**. You will see a window similar to Figure 17-1.

PROCEDURE - 17

    ___d.   Record your *Turn off monitor* and *Turn off hard disks* settings in Table 17-1.
    ___e.   Change the *Turn off monitor* setting to **After 1 min** and click on **Apply**.
    ___f.   Do not move the mouse or press any keys for one minute and record your observations in Table 17-2.
    ___g.   Move the mouse and change the *Turn off monitor* setting back to its original state.
    ___h.   Click on **OK** for the *Power Options* properties.

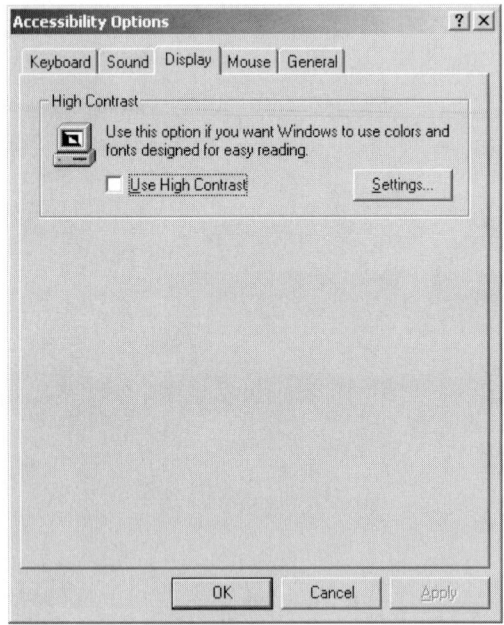

Figure 17-2: Accessibility Contrast Options

2. **Accessibility Options**
    ___a.   From the Windows 2000 Control Panel double-click on **Accessibility Options**.
    ___b.   Click on the **Display** tab. You will see a window similar to Figure 17-2.
    ___c.   Select **Use High Contrast**. Click on **Apply**.
    ___d.   Record your observations in Table 17-3.
    ___e.   Uncheck *High Contrast* and click on **Apply** to restore the display to its original state. You may need to resize the Taskbar by dragging the edge down to its original position.
    ___f.   In *Accessibility Options* click on the **Mouse** tab.
    ___g.   Select **Use MouseKeys**. Click on **Apply**.
    ___h.   Look at the keyboard and verify that the num lock light is on. If it is not, press the **NUM LOCK** key.
    ___i.   There are arrow keys on the numeric keypad on the right-hand side of the keyboard. Up is 8, down is 2, left is 4, and right is 6. Press up and record your observations in Table 17-4.
    ___j.   Uncheck *Use MouseKeys* and click on **Apply** to restore the option back to its original state.
    ___k.   Click on **OK** to close the *Accessibility Options* window.

3. **Regional Options**
    ___a.   From the Windows 2000 Control Panel double-click on **Regional Options**. You will see a window similar to Figure 17-3.

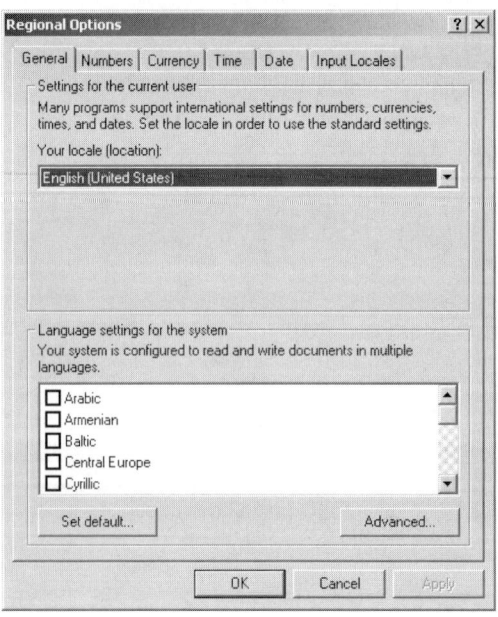

Figure 17-3: Regional Options

PROCEDURE - 17

    ___b.   Under the *General* tab record your locale in Table 17-5.
    ___c.   Under the *Numbers* tab record the digit grouping in Table 17-5.
    ___d.   Under the *Currency* tab record the currency symbol in Table 17-5.
    ___e.   Under the *Time* tab record the time format in Table 17-5.
    ___f.   Under the *Date* tab record the date separator in Table 17-5.
    ___g.   Under the *Input Locales* record the uppermost input language in Table 17-5.
    ___h.   Click on **OK** to close the *Regional Options* window.

4.   **Sounds and Multimedia**
    ___a.   From the Windows 2000 Control Panel, double-click on **Sounds and Multimedia**. You will see a window similar to Figure 17-4.

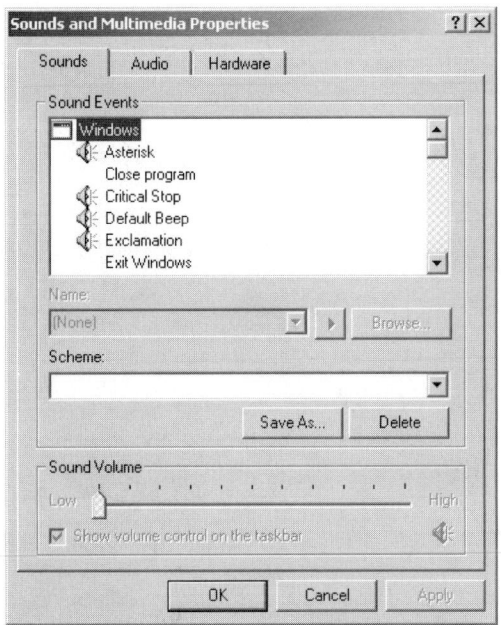

Figure 17-4: Sound and Multimedia Properties

    ___b.   Click on the **Asterisk** event.
    ___c.   Record the "Name:" in Table 17-6. This is the name of the sound file that Windows plays when the corresponding event has occurred.
    ___d.   If you have a sound card and speakers, press the play button and you will hear the sound.
    ___e.   Click on the **Audio** tab. Record the preferred device for sound playback in Table 17-7.
    ___f.   Click on the **Advanced** tab under sound playback.
    ___g.   Record the speaker setup in Table 17-8.
    ___h.   Click on **OK** to close the *Advanced* window.
    ___i.   Click on the **Hardware** tab.
    ___j.   Record the number of devices listed in Table 17-9.
    ___k.   Browse for the CD-ROM in the device listing and double-click on it.
    ___l.   Record the name of the window that appears in Table 17-10.
    ___m.   Click on **OK** to close the window that you just opened.
    ___n.   Click on **OK** to close the *Sound and Multimedia Properties*.
    ___o.   Close the Control Panel.
    ___p.   Shut down the computer.

PROCEDURE - 17

TABLES

Table 17-1

Power Options Properties	
Turn off monitor:	
Turn off hard disks:	

Table 17-2

Observations After One Minute:	

Table 17-3

Display Observations:	

Table 17-4

Observations of Use MouseKeys:	

Table 17-5

Regional Options	
Your Locale:	
Digit Grouping:	
Currency Symbol:	
Time Format:	
Date Separator:	
Input Language:	

PROCEDURE - 17

Table 17-6

"Asterisk Event" Sound File Name:	

Table 17-7

Preferred Device for Sound Playback:	

Table 17-8

Speaker Setup:	

Table 17-9

Number of Hardware Devices:	

Table 17-10

Name of Window:	

LAB QUESTIONS

1. What two settings are available for a power scheme?

2. What features of accessibility were demonstrated in this lab?

3. Where would you go to change the language of the system?

4. The Regional Options/Date feature does what?

5. What is one way to change the hardware settings of an audio card in Windows 2000?

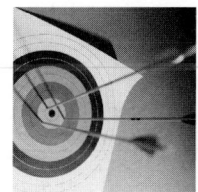

Feedback

LAB PROCEDURE 18

Windows 2000 Disk Management

OBJECTIVES

1. Use Disk Cleanup.
2. Back up a file.
3. Restore a backup.
4. Compress a file.
5. Encrypt a file.

Troubleshooting

RESOURCES

1. PC-compatible desktop/tower computer system — Customer-supplied desktop/tower hardware system **OR** Marcraft MC-8000 Computer Hardware Trainer **OR** suitable PC hardware trainer with Windows 2000 installed
2. A blank 1.44 MB floppy disk

DISCUSSION

This lab will discuss some common disk management procedures. You can use storage media such as a CD-R, high-capacity floppy, tape drive, DVD-R, or secondary hard drive. Windows has a backup utility that can be used to schedule backups of your files. It is a good practice to clean unnecessary files off your hard drive. Windows has a utility called Disk Cleanup that can delete some of these files for you. Windows has a built-in file compression utility, but there are many third-party utilities available as well. For security reasons you may need to encrypt your files. The Encrypting File System (EFS) included with Microsoft Windows 2000 is based on public-key encryption. Each file is encrypted using a randomly generated file encryption key. Each file has a unique file encryption key, making it safe to rename. If you move a file from an encrypted folder to an unencrypted folder on the same drive, the file remains encrypted. If you copy an unencrypted file into an encrypted folder, the file remains unencrypted. You don't have to decrypt a file to open it and use it. EFS automatically detects an encrypted file and locates a user's file encryption key from the system's key store to open the file. In this lab you will create, back up, restore, compress, and encrypt a WordPad Document.

PROCEDURE

1. **Disk Cleanup**
   ___ a. Boot the computer into Windows 2000.
   ___ b. Navigate the path *Start/Programs/Accessories/System Tools* and select **Disk Cleanup**.

PROCEDURE - 18

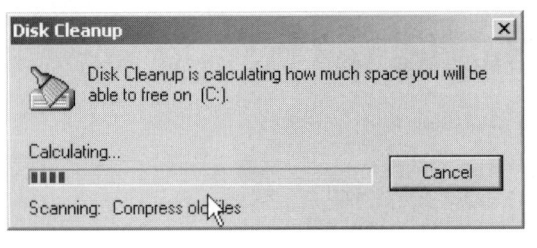

Figure 18-1: Calculating Cleanup Space

___c. When prompted to select the drive to clean up, select the **C: Drive** and click on **OK**. You will see a window similar to Figure 18-1 calculating the space to clean up.

___d. After the calculation has completed, record the entries in "Files to delete:" that have a check mark in Table 18-1.

___e. Select **Recycle Bin** and **Temporary files** by clicking in the box to the left of their respective icons. A check mark will appear.

___f. Click on the **More Options** tab. You will see two areas: Windows components and Installed programs.

___g. Click on the **Clean up** button under *Windows Components*. You will see a window similar to Figure 18-2.

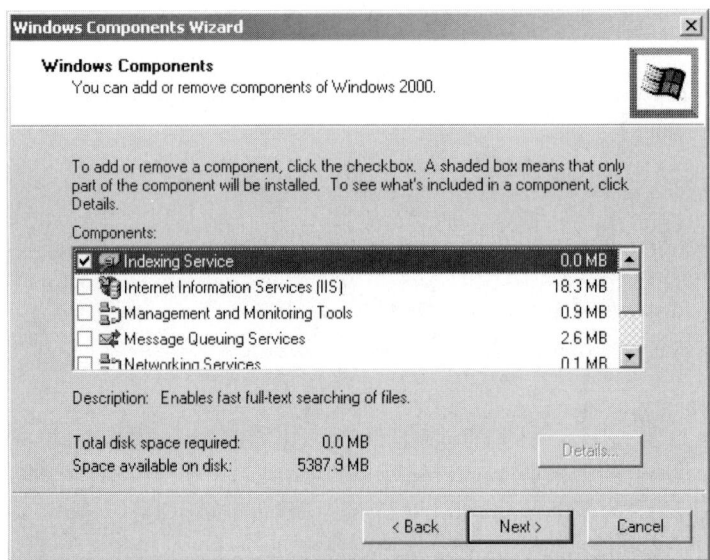

Figure 18-2: Add/Remove Windows Components

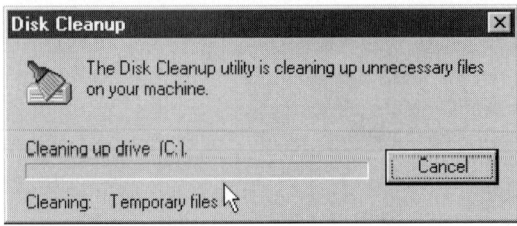

Figure 18-3: Cleaning Up Files

NOTE: You can check or uncheck items from this window to add or remove Windows components. This window can also be accessed through Control Panel/Add/Remove Programs.

___h. Click on **Cancel**.
___i. Click on **OK** to close the *Disk Cleanup* window for C:.
___j. Confirm the "Are you sure" question by clicking on **Yes**. You will see a window similar to Figure 18-3.
___k. When the cleanup has completed close all windows.

2. **Create a file**
   ___a. From the Windows 2000 desktop double-click on **My Documents**.
   ___b. Create a *WordPad* Document by clicking on **File/New/WordPad Document**.
   ___c. Type **YourName** as the name of the document.
   ___d. Close all windows.

PROCEDURE - 18

3. **Backup**
   ___ a. Navigate the path *Start/Accessories/System Tools/* and then select **Backup** from the *System Tools* menu. You will see the *Welcome* screen.
   ___ b. Click on the **Backup** tab. You will see a window similar to Figure 18-4. From this area you can select drives or folders to back up on one of the media types.

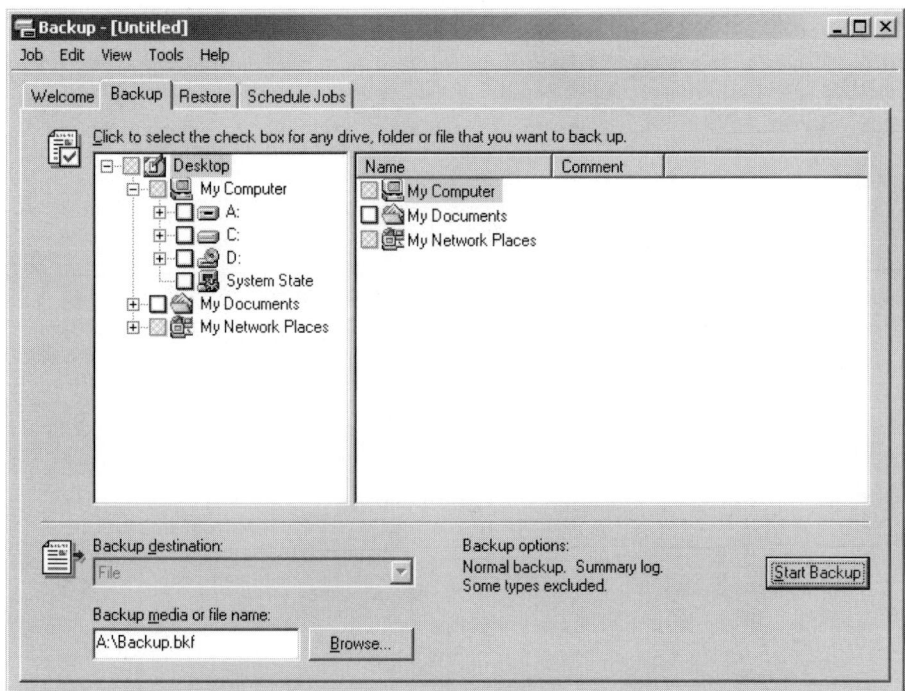

Figure 18-4: Select Items to Back Up

   ___ c. In the left pane, click on **System State** to highlight it, but do not place a checkmark in the box next to it.
   ___ d. Record the items that appear in the right-hand window pane in Table 18-2.
   ___ e. Click on the **MY DOCUMENTS** folder and put a checkmark in the box next to the icon.

NOTE: You will be able to do this backup on a floppy as long as the MY DOCUMENTS folder is small enough.

   ___ f. Record the drive and filename of the backup (in the bottom left of the window) in Table 18-3.
   ___ g. Insert a blank floppy into the floppy drive.
   ___ h. Click on the **Start Backup** button. You will see a window similar to Figure 18-5.
   ___ i. Enter "**your name**" for the Backup description.
   ___ j. Enter "**your name**" for the label to identify the media if it is overwritten.
   ___ k. Click on the **Start Backup** button. You will see a *Backup Progress* window.
   ___ l. When the backup has completed, click on **Close**.
   ___ m. Close the *Backup* window.

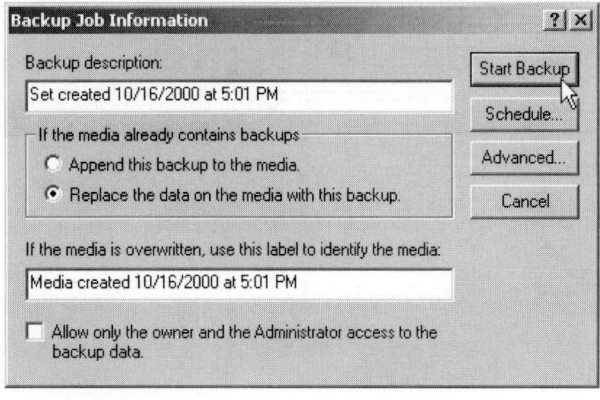

Figure 18-5: Backup Job Information

PROCEDURE - 18

4. **Delete a file**
   ___a. From the Windows 2000 desktop double-click the **My Documents** icon.
   ___b. Right-click on the document that you created earlier and select **Delete**.
   ___c. Confirm by clicking on **Yes**.
   ___d. Close all windows.

5. **Restore the backup**
   ___a. Open the *Windows Backup* utility by navigating the path *Start/Programs/Accessories/System Tools/* and then selecting **Backup**. You will see the **Welcome** screen.
   ___b. Click on the **Restore** tab.
   ___c. In the right window pane, double-click **File** to expand it.
   ___d. Expand the backup with Your Name on it by double-clicking it.
   ___e. Place a check mark next to the C: drive to restore the files that were backed up.
   ___f. Click on the **Start Restore** button.
   ___g. Confirm restoration by clicking on **OK**. You will see a window similar to Figure 18-6.
   ___h. Make sure the source file to back up has the correct filename and path, and click on **OK**.
   ___i. After the restore has completed, click on **Close**.
   ___j. Close all windows.

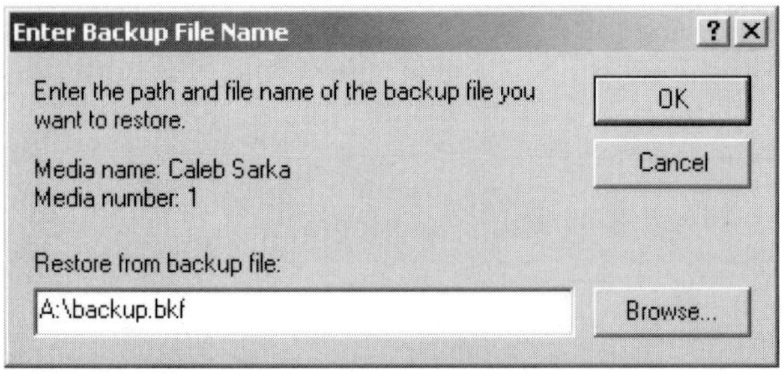

Figure 18-6: Confirm Restoration Dialog

6. **Test the restoration**
   ___a. From the Windows 2000 desktop double-click on **My Documents**.
   ___b. Record your observations about the files in this folder in Table 18-4.

NOTE: The remainder of this lab can be performed only if you have an NTFS partition on your hard disk. Consult your instructor before performing Steps 7 and 8 below.

7. **Compress a file**
   ___a. From the Windows 2000 desktop double-click on **My Documents**.
   ___b. Double-click on your *WordPad* document that was just restored.
   ___c. To add some size to the file, enter 10 lines of the character **X** with the keyboard. (You can hold down the key for one line, and copy and paste the rest.)
   ___d. Close the document. When prompted, click on **Yes** to save the changes.
   ___e. Right-click on the document and choose **Properties**.
   ___f. Record its "Size on disk" in Table 18-5.
   ___g. Click on the **Advanced** button. You will see a window similar to Figure 18-7.
   ___h. Select **Compress contents to save disk space**. Click on **OK**.
   ___i. Click on the **Apply** button.
   ___j. Record the new "Size on disk" in Table 18-6.

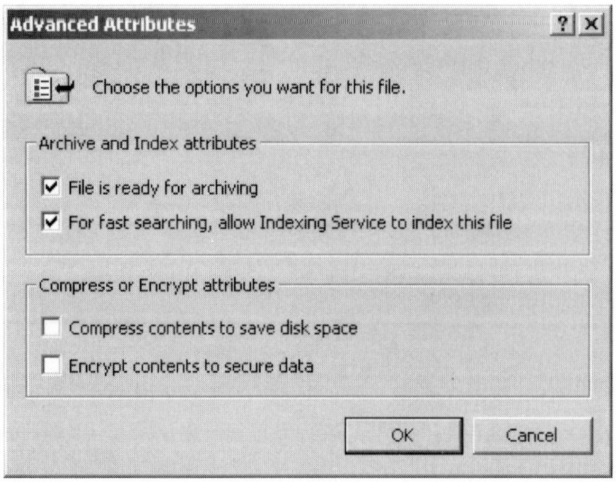

Figure 18-7: Advanced Attributes

PROCEDURE - 18

8. **Encrypt a file**
   ___ a. From the properties of the document click on the **Advanced** button again.
   ___ b. Select **Encrypt contents to secure data**, which will turn the compression option off.
   ___ c. Click on **OK** to close the *Advanced Attributes* window.
   ___ d. Click on **OK** to close the *File Properties* window. You will see a window similar to Figure 18-8.

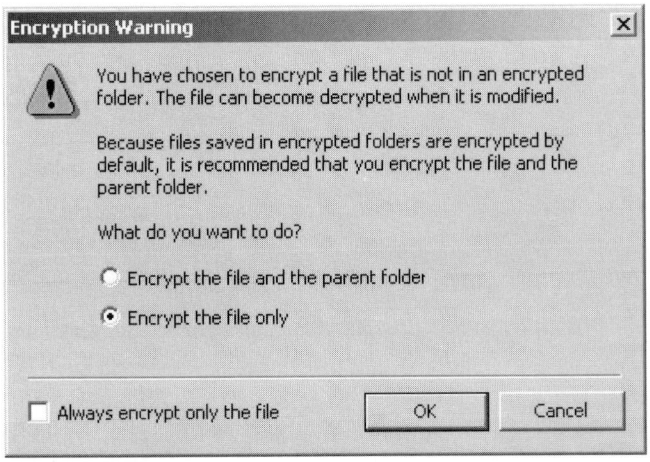

   Figure 18-8: Encryption Warning

   ___ e. Click on the radio button next to *Encrypt the file and the parent folder* to select it and click on **OK**.
   ___ f. While the file is selected you will see "Attributes: Encrypted" in the right-hand portion of the *My Documents* window.
   ___ g. Close all open windows, and shut down the computer.

TABLES

Table 18-1

Files to Delete:	

Table 18-2

System State (right-hand pane):	

WINDOWS 2000 DISK MANAGEMENT - 131

PROCEDURE - 18

Table 18-3

Backup Drive and Filename:	

Table 18-4

Observation About Files:	

Table 18-5

File Size on Disk:	

Table 18-6

New File Size on Disk:	

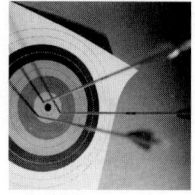

Feedback

LAB QUESTIONS

1. What are some storage medias?
2. What does EFS stand for?
3. What are two ways to access Add/Remove Windows components?
4. By what ratio was a file compressed in this procedure?
5. Using the methods in this lab, can you encrypt and compress a file at the same time?

LAB PROCEDURE 19

Windows 2000 Registry

OBJECTIVES

1. Use RegEdit to change a string.
2. Export the Registry and view its size.

Troubleshooting

RESOURCES

1. PC-compatible desktop/tower computer system — Customer-supplied desktop/tower hardware system **OR** Marcraft MC-8000 Computer Hardware Trainer **OR** suitable PC hardware trainer with Windows 2000 installed

DISCUSSION

Windows 2000 stores its configuration information in a database called the Registry. The Registry contains information for users, system hardware, software, and other settings. For example, to run a program at startup you could add the string "programname.exe" to the key "*HKEY_LOCAL_MACHINE\Software\Microsoft\Windows\CurrentVersion\Run*." Windows constantly references the Registry during its operation. Incorrectly editing the Registry may severely damage your system. If you do damage your system, you may be able to repair the Registry or restore it to the same version you were using when you last successfully started your computer. You may resort to reinstalling Windows if the system is damaged beyond repair, but you may lose any changes that have been made in the Registry. The Registry is organized hierarchically as a tree made up of keys, subkeys, hives, and value entries. There are three types of values: String, Binary, and DWORD. Two Registry editors are included with Windows 2000: REGEDT32 and REGEDIT. In RegEdit the keys have icons similar to the folder icons in windows. With Regedt32 you can set the security for Registry keys. Also, in Regedt32 you can view or edit the value data types REG_EXPAND_SZ and REG_MULTI_SZ. With both RegEdit and RegEdt32 you can edit the Registry of another computer on the network if you have administrative rights and the Remote Registry Service is running on the other computer. In this lab we will use RegEdit to change some basic colors on the computer. We will be editing the string "*My Computer\HKEY_USERS\45 CHARACTER\Control Panel\Colors\Menu*", where 45 CHARACTER is a unique identification number assigned to the user. There should be only one registered user on the computer, the Administrator. The Menu string is 212 208 200 (Gray) by default. In this Registry string there are three numbers that each range from 0 to 255. They represent a value in their respective colors: red, green, and blue. Four basic colors are listed in Figure 19-1 as an example.

Figure 19-1: Basic Colors

RED	GREEN	BLUE	RESULTS
0	0	255	All blue in color
0	255	0	All green in color
255	0	0	All red in color
212	208	200	The default Windows gray

PROCEDURE - 19

Troubleshooting

PROCEDURE

1. **Edit a string**
   ___ a. Boot to the Windows 2000 desktop.
   ___ b. Start Microsoft Registry Editor by clicking on **Start/Run**. Type **regedit** and click on **OK**.
   ___ c. You will see a window similar to Figure 19-2. Expand HKEY_USERS by clicking on the plus (+) sign next to its icon.

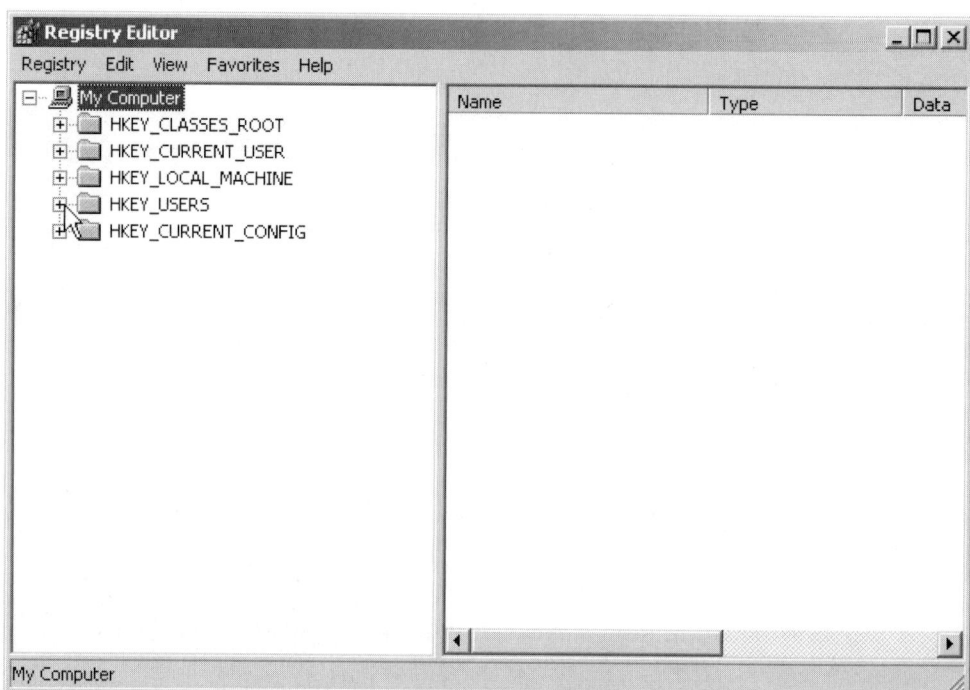

Figure 19-2: RegEdit.exe

   ___ d. Expand the 45 CHARACTER key. It could be s-1-5-127520070-1808537768-1060284298-500, for example.
   ___ e. Expand the CONTROL PANEL key.
   ___ f. Click on the **COLORS** key.
   ___ g. In the right-hand window pane look for the string value *Menu* and record its "type" in Table 19-1.
   ___ h. Double-click the *Menu* string. Your screen should look similar to Figure 19-3.
   ___ i. Record the "Value data" in Table 19-2.
   ___ j. Enter **0 255 0** for the Value data, and click on **OK**.
   ___ k. Close the Registry Editor and restart the computer.

134 - LAB GROUP 2

PROCEDURE - 19

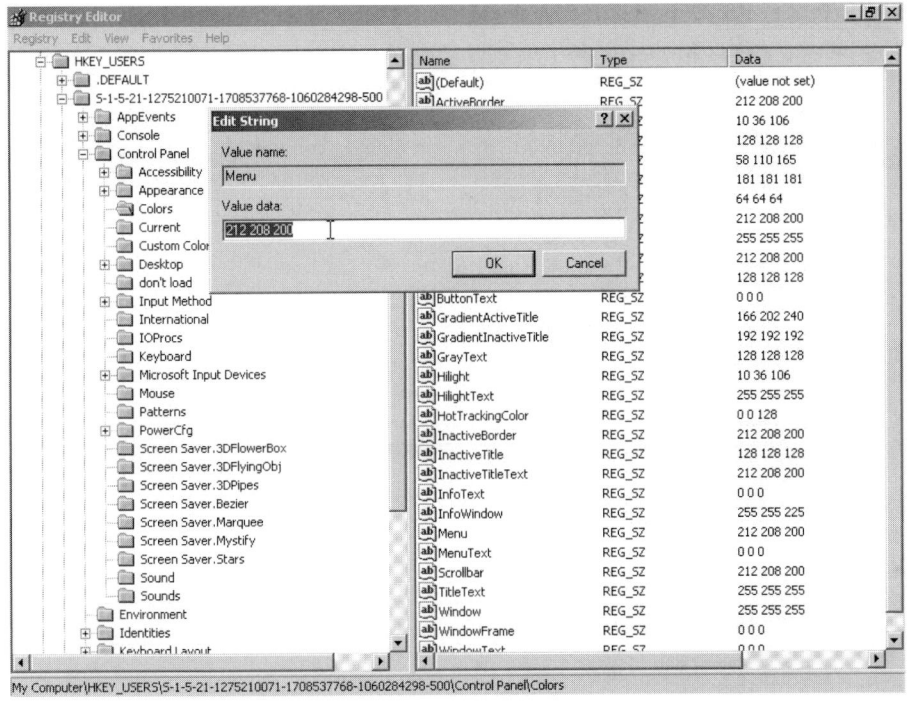

Figure 19-3: Editing a String

2. **View the results**

   ___ a. Once the computer has restarted to Windows, click on the **Start** menu.
   ___ b. Record your observations in Table 19-3.
   ___ c. Right-click the desktop and select **Properties**.
   ___ d. Click on the **Appearance** tab.
   ___ e. Under the *Item:* drop-down menu select **Menu**.
   ___ f. To the right of the drop-down menu is a field called **Color**. Click on it and then click on **Other**.
   ___ g. You will see a window similar to Figure 19-4. Record the Red, Green, and Blue values in Table 19-4.
   ___ h. Enter **212** for the Red value.
   ___ i. Enter **208** for the Green value.
   ___ j. Enter **200** for the Blue value.
   ___ k. Click on **OK** to close the *Color* box.
   ___ l. Click on **OK** to close the *Display Properties* window.
   ___ m. Restart the computer.

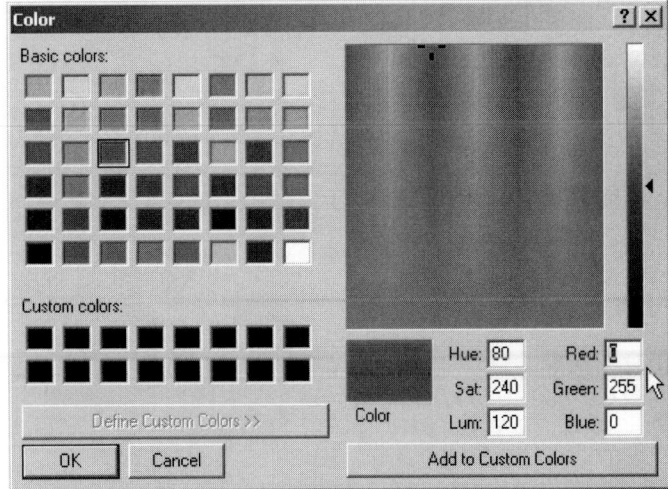

Figure 19-4: Menu Color Properties

3. **View Registry string value**

   ___ a. Once the computer has restarted, start the Registry Editor and browse to the *Menu* string as in Steps 1a-f.
   ___ b. Double-click the *Menu* string as before.
   ___ c. Record your observations about the value of the string in Table 19-5.
   ___ d. Close the *Edit String* window.

WINDOWS 2000 REGISTRY - 135

PROCEDURE - 19

4. **Export Registry**
   ___a. In the menu bar, click on the **Registry** menu and then select **Export Registry**. You will see a window similar to Figure 19-5.

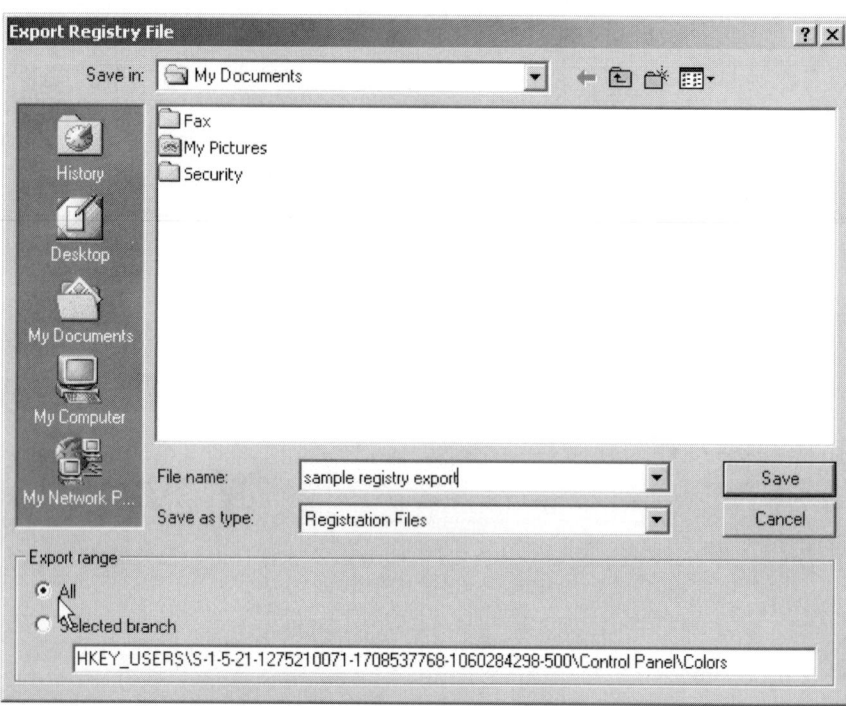

Figure 30-5:
Export Registry File

   ___b. Under *Export* range click on the **All** radio button.
   ___c. In the *Save in* box confirm that the default location is *MY DOCUMENTS*. If it is not, change the default location to **MY DOCUMENTS**.
   ___d. In the *File name* box enter **sample registry export** for the filename and click on **Save**.
   ___e. After a few moments the Registry files will be exported to MY DOCUMENTS. Close the Registry Editor.
   ___f. From the Windows desktop, double-click the **My Documents** icon.
   ___g. Right-click the "sample registry export" and click on **Properties**.
   ___h. Enter its size in Table 19-6.
   ___i. Close all windows.

TABLES

Table 19-1

"Menu" Key Type String:	

Table 19-2

Menu "Value Data":	

PROCEDURE - 19

Table 19-3

Reboot Observation with New Value Data:	

Table 19-4

Color Palette Values		
Red	Green	Blue

Table 19-5

Reboot Observation with Restored Value Data:	

Table 19-6

File Size of Sample Registry Export:	

LAB QUESTIONS

1. What are three things that the Registry keeps track of?

2. If you damage the Registry beyond repair, what may you have to do?

3. What advantages does RegEdt32 offer?

4. What is the correlation between the Red, Green, and Blue values of the Menu color and the Registry string that you changed?

5. What conclusions can you make about the correlation between Windows' operation and its Registry?

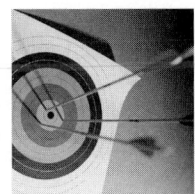

Feedback

LAB PROCEDURE 20

Windows Me Safe Mode

OBJECTIVES

1. Examine the features of the Startup Menu.
2. Boot to Windows Millennium with troubleshooting.
3. Boot to Safe Mode in Windows Me.

Troubleshooting

RESOURCES

1. PC-compatible desktop/tower computer system — Customer-supplied desktop/tower hardware system **OR** Marcraft MC-8000 Computer Hardware Trainer **OR** suitable PC hardware trainer with CD-ROM drive and printer installed
2. Windows Millennium Edition installed

DISCUSSION

When troubleshooting a system that is having problems, the Startup Menu can be very helpful. This menu can bring up a DOS prompt, enabling you to edit, move, delete, or rename files. The Startup Menu also allows you to reboot your system in several different modes. These involve such procedures as bootup display and recording, and limiting bootup programs in order to eliminate system, application, and driver conflicts.

The Windows Me Startup Menu, shown in Figure 20-1, can be accessed by using the Windows Me Startup Disk, or by holding down the *F8* key (or *CTRL* key) after the RAM memory test is complete. This menu offers *Normal mode*, *Logged mode*, *Safe mode* and *Step-by-step confirmation* options. Using the Startup disk, you have the above options and the option to boot to a command prompt.

In *Normal mode*, the system simply tries to restart as it normally would, loading all its normal Startup and Registry files.

The *Logged mode* option also attempts to start the system in *Normal mode*, but keeps an error log file that contains the steps performed and the outcome. The text file C:\BOOTLOG.TXT can be read with any text editor such as *Notepad*, or can be printed out on a working system.

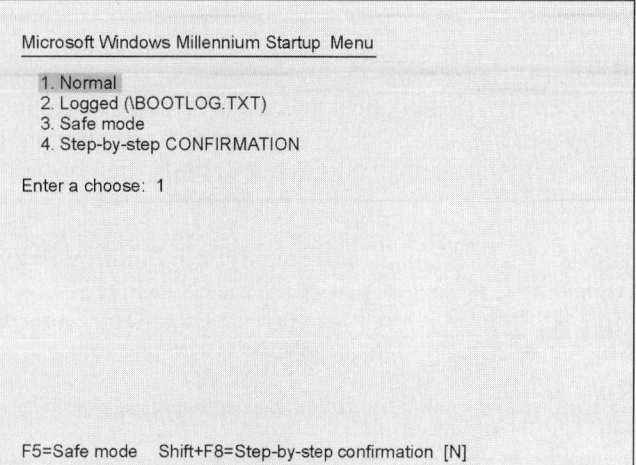

Figure 20-1: Windows Me Startup Menu

WINDOWS ME SAFE MODE - 139

PROCEDURE - 20

If Windows Millennium Edition or 98 determines that a problem has occurred that prevents the system from starting, it will attempt to enter *Safe Mode* at the next startup. *Safe Mode* bypasses several startup files including CONFIG.SYS, AUTOEXEC.BAT, and the Registry, as well as the [Boot] and [386eb\nh] sections of the SYSTEM.INI file. In this mode, the keyboard, mouse, and standard VGA drivers are active. *Safe Mode* can also be accessed by pressing the *SHIFT+F8* key during startup.

The *Step-by-Step Confirmation mode* displays each startup command, line by line, and waits for a confirmation or skip order from the keyboard before moving ahead. This can help you to isolate and avoid an offending startup command so that it can be replaced or removed.

The *Command Prompt mode* will bring up a DOS command-line prompt. This mode will allow you to use DOS commands in order to make, delete, move, copy, rename, and edit files.

Troubleshooting

PROCEDURE

NOTE: This lab requires the Windows Millennium Edition operating system. For dual-boot systems, select Windows Millennium Edition when prompted in each of the following procedures.

1. **Boot to the Startup Menu**
   ___a. Turn on the power to the system.
   ___b. After the RAM memory test finishes counting up, press and hold the **CTRL** key until the Startup Menu appears.

2. **Boot the system to Logged mode**
   ___a. Type **2** to choose the second option, and then press the **ENTER** key.

3. **Read the boot log**
   ___a. Navigate the path *Start/Programs/Accessories*, and then click on the **Windows Explorer** icon from the *Accessories* menu.
   ___b. In the Folders pane on the left, click on the icon for **C:**.
   ___c. In the menu bar, click on the **Tools** menu, the **Folder Options** menu, then select the **View** tab.
   ___d. Select **Show hidden files and folders**, and click on the **OK** button.
   ___e. Back in Windows Explorer, under the Contents pane on the right, locate and double-click the **Bootlog.txt** file.
   ___f. Examine the contents of this file.
   ___g. Close all open windows.

4. **Boot the system to Step-by-Step mode**
   ___a. Click on the **Start** button and then click on **Shut Down**.
   ___b. Select **Restart**, and then click on the **OK** button.
   ___c. After selecting the Windows Me operating system bootup, press and hold the **CTRL** key down.
   ___d. Select the *Step-by-Step mode* from the screen by pressing the **DOWN ARROW** key until the **Step-by-Step Confirmation** is highlighted.
   ___e. Press the **ENTER** key.
   ___f. Press the **ENTER** key or the **Y** key to confirm the use of the startup steps and say **Yes** to all the steps.

NOTE: To skip a command line, press the ESC key or the N key.

5. **Boot the system to Safe Mode**
   ___a. Click on the **Start** button and then click on **Shut Down**.
   ___b. Select **Restart**, then click on the **OK** button.

140 - LAB GROUP 2

PROCEDURE - 20

  ___c. Select the Windows Millennium Edition operating system, and then press the **ENTER** key.
  ___d. Immediately press the **F5** key.
  ___e. Close the *Help and Support* window once Windows finishes rebooting.

6. **Attempt to access the CD-ROM drive and the printer**
  ___a. Double-click the **My Computer** icon.
  ___b. Attempt to locate the CD-ROM drive. Your window will look similar to Figure 20-2.
  ___c. Double-click the **C: hard drive** icon.
  ___d. Locate and double-click the **BOOTLOG.TXT** file.
  ___e. In the menu bar, click on the **File** menu and then select **Print**, as shown in Figure 20-3.
  ___f. In Table 20-1, list what happens when you click on **Print**.
  ___g. In the menu bar click on the **File** menu then **Exit** to close the *BOOTLOG.TXT* window.
  ___h. Close all windows.
  ___i. Double-click the **My Computer** icon.
  ___j. Double-click the **Control Panel folder** icon.
  ___k. Double-click the **System** icon.

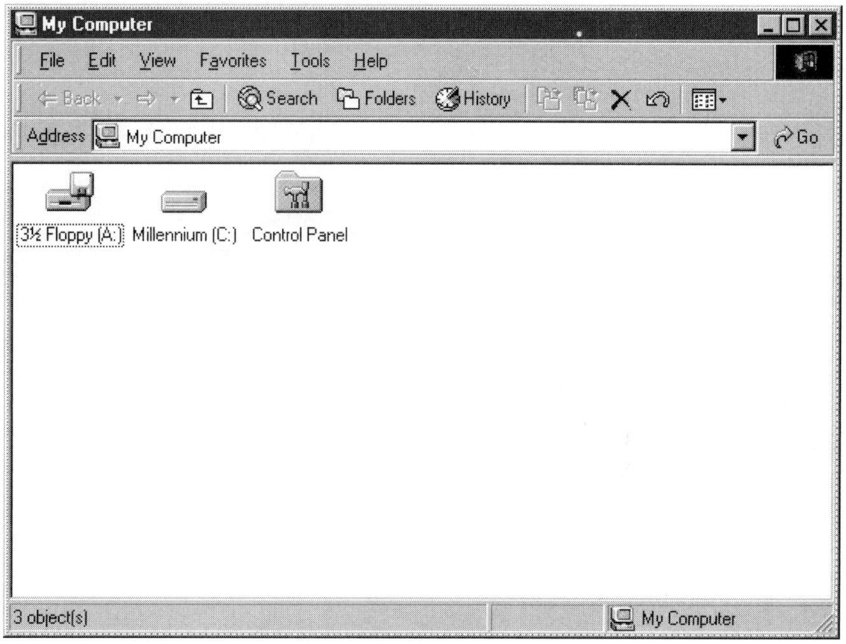

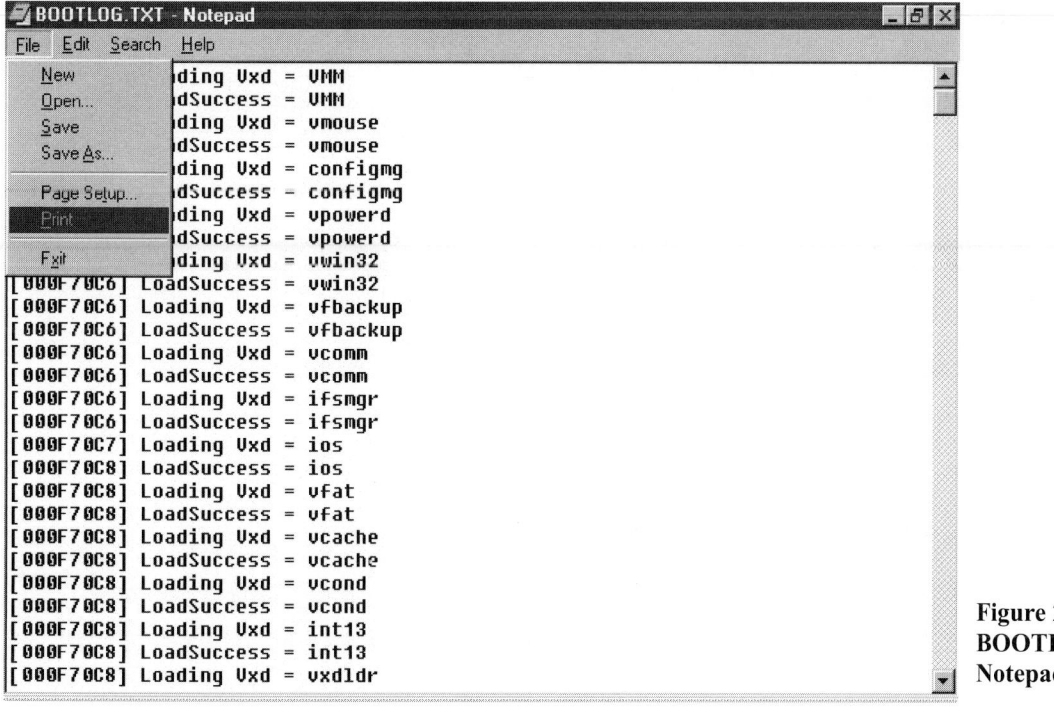

Figure 20-2: My Computer Window

Figure 20-3: BOOTLOG.TXT Notepad Window

WINDOWS ME SAFE MODE - 141

PROCEDURE - 20

___ l. Click on the **Device Manager** tab.
___ m. Click on the plus (+) sign to the left of the *CD-ROM* icon, and then select the CD-ROM driver to highlight it.
___ n. Click on the **Properties** button.
___ o. Record the device status, as shown in Figure 20-4, in Table 20-2, and then click on the **Cancel** button.
___ p. Click on the plus (+) sign to the left of the **Ports** icon, and then select the **Printer Port (LPT1)** to highlight it.
___ q. Click on the **Properties** button.
___ r. Record the device status of the Printer Port (LPT1) in Table 20-3, then click on the **Cancel** button.
___ s. Close all open windows and shut down Windows and the computer.

Figure 20-4: CD-ROM Properties Page

TABLES

Table 20-1

Table 20-2

Device Status:	

Table 20-3

Device Status Printer Port (LPT1):	

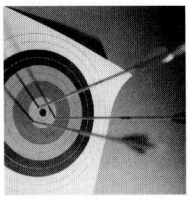

Feedback

LAB QUESTIONS

1. Name one application that will run in Safe Mode.

2. What text file can you update from the Startup Menu?

3. Will a Network Interface Card (NIC) operate while in Safe Mode?

4. If your computer crashes during startup, what mode will it enter on restart?

LAB PROCEDURE 21

Windows Me Setup Log Files

OBJECTIVES

1. Locate log files in Windows Me.
2. Create and examine the log file BOOTLOG.TXT.
3. Examine the log file DETLOG.TXT.
4. Examine the log file NETLOG.TXT.
5. Examine the log file SETUPLOG.TXT.

Troubleshooting

RESOURCES

1. PC-compatible desktop/tower computer system — Customer-supplied desktop/tower hardware system **OR** Marcraft MC-8000 Computer Hardware Trainer **OR** suitable PC hardware trainer
2. Windows Millennium Edition installed on hard drive

DISCUSSION

The Windows Me operating system maintains a number of log files that track system performance and can be used to assess system failures. These log files are SETUPLOG.TXT, NETLOG.TXT, and DETLOG.TXT and are stored in the system's root directory. All three are text files that can be viewed with a text editor such as WordPad and can be printed out. These filenames are indicative of the types of information they log. During a Logged mode startup, the system will attempt to boot in Normal mode, but will keep an error log file called BOOTLOG.TXT (Bootup Log) that tracks the events of the startup procedure and the outcome of those events. Similarly, the SETUPLOG.TXT (Installation and Setup Log) file tracks the events of the Installation and/or Setup process. The DETLOG.TXT (Detection Log) file monitors the presence of detected hardware devices and identifies the parameters for them. Likewise, the NETLOG.TXT (Network Log) file monitors the installation and configuration of your network connection.

> **WARNING**
>
> Unless specifically instructed to do so, do not save any changes to the information contained in these four files.

WINDOWS ME SETUP LOG FILES - 143

PROCEDURE - 21

Troubleshooting

PROCEDURE

BOOTLOG.TXT

The BOOTLOG.TXT file contains the sequence of events conducted during the system startup, and is located in the root directory (C:\). A boot log can be created by pressing the *SHIFT + F8* keys during startup, or by starting Windows Me at the command prompt using the Windows Me Startup disk.

1. **Create a BOOTLOG.TXT file at startup**
   ___a. Turn on the power to the system.
   ___b. Select **Windows Millennium** and press the **ENTER** key.
   ___c. Press and hold down the CTRL key.
   ___d. Press the **DOWN ARROW** key to highlight **2. Logged (\BOOTLOG.TXT)**, and press the **ENTER** key.

2. **Locate the log files with the Search tool**
   ___a. Navigate the path *Start\Search*, and then select **Files or Folders**.
   ___b. Make certain that the **C: drive** is selected in the *Look in* box.
   ___c. In the *Named* box, type ***log.txt**, and click on the **Search Now** button. Your window will look similar to Figure 21-1.

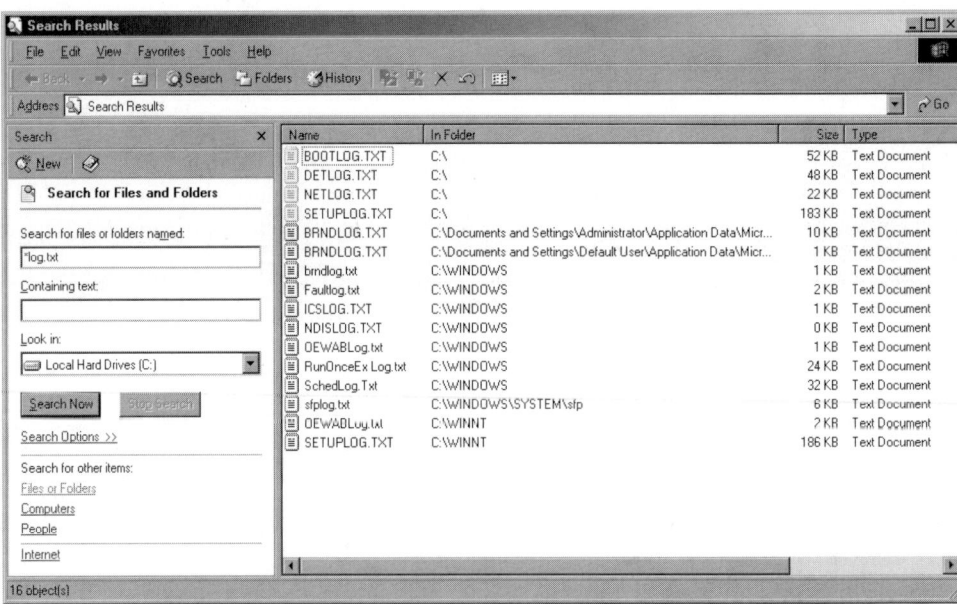

Figure 21-1:
Search Results

   ___d. In the *Listing Display* window, click on the **Name** column button, and then click on the **In Folder** column button.
   ___e. Record the information for the first four files in Table 21-1.

NOTE: You may need to use the horizontal scroll bar at the bottom of the window to see all of the information for the first four *log.txt files.

144 - LAB GROUP 2

PROCEDURE - 21

3. **Open and examine the BOOTLOG.TXT file**
   ___a. Double-click the **Bootlog.Txt** file icon to open the file in *Notepad*.
   ___b. Click on the **Maximize** button to expand the *Notepad* window, as shown in Figure 21-2.

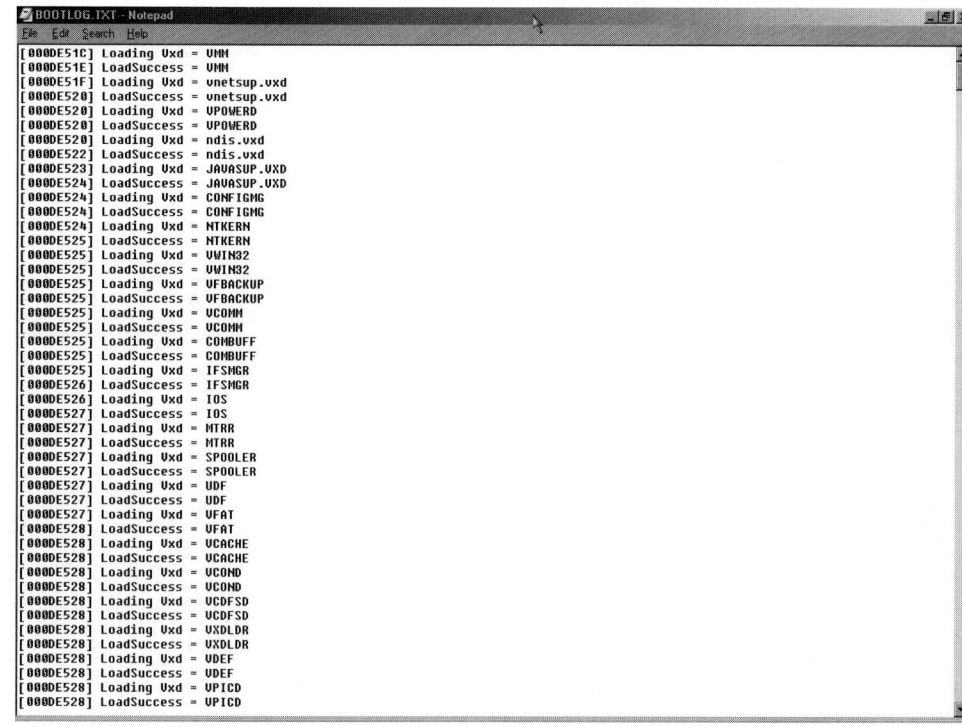

Figure 21-2: BOOTLOG.TXT File

In the first group, the system loads the VxD drivers. These drivers are shown to be successfully loaded by a line beginning "Loading Vxd=", followed by a line reading "LoadSuccess=".

   ___c. Record the names of the first and last VxD drivers to be loaded, and record whether or not they loaded successfully in Table 21-2.

The next group can be checked to verify if the system-critical VxD drivers have been initialized. These drivers are shown to be successfully initialized by a line beginning "SYSCRITINIT=", followed by a line reading "SYSCRITINITSUCCESS=".

   ___d. Record the names of the first and last VxD drivers to be initialized, and record whether or not they were initialized successfully in Table 21-3.

The next group shows the initialization of the VxD device drivers. These devices are shown to be successfully initialized by a line beginning "DEVICEINIT=", followed by a line reading "DEVICEINITSUCCESS=".

   ___e. Record the names of the first and second devices to be initialized, and record whether or not they were initialized successfully in Table 21-4.

The next group, which may be found inside the device initialization group, shows the dynamic loading and initialization of the system device drivers. These devices are shown to be successfully initialized by a line beginning "Dynamic load device" followed by a line reading "Dynamic init device", then "Dynamic init success", and finally "Dynamic load success".

___f. Record the names of the first and second devices to be dynamically loaded and initialized, and record whether or not the process was done successfully in Table 21-5.

The next group confirms the initialization of the system VxDs. These devices are shown to be successfully initialized by a line beginning "INITCOMPLETE=", followed by a line reading

"INITCOMPLETESUCCESS=".

___g. Record the names of the first and last VxD initializations to be confirmed, and record whether or not they were performed successfully in Table 21-6.

The final section begins with the line "Initializing KERNEL". This describes the loading of the various parts of the operating system kernel and its support drivers. These steps are shown to be successful by a line beginning "LoadStart=", followed by a line reading "LoadSuccess=".

___h. Record the names of the first and last kernel parts to be loaded, and record whether or not they were loaded successfully in Table 21-7.

DETLOG.TXT

The DETLOG.TXT file is stored in the system's root directory (C:\) and is used in the recovery after an operating system crash. DETLOG.TXT can be edited or created in two different ways. First, it is created after a normal hardware setup. Second, it can be created or edited after a failed hardware setup. When a system crashes during the hardware detection portion of the startup procedure, a temporary DETCRASH.LOG (Detect Crash) log file is created. The file contains information about the detection module that was running when the crash occurred. DETCRASH.LOG is a binary file and cannot be read directly. However, a text version of this file is created and named DETLOG.TXT, as shown in Figure 21-3.

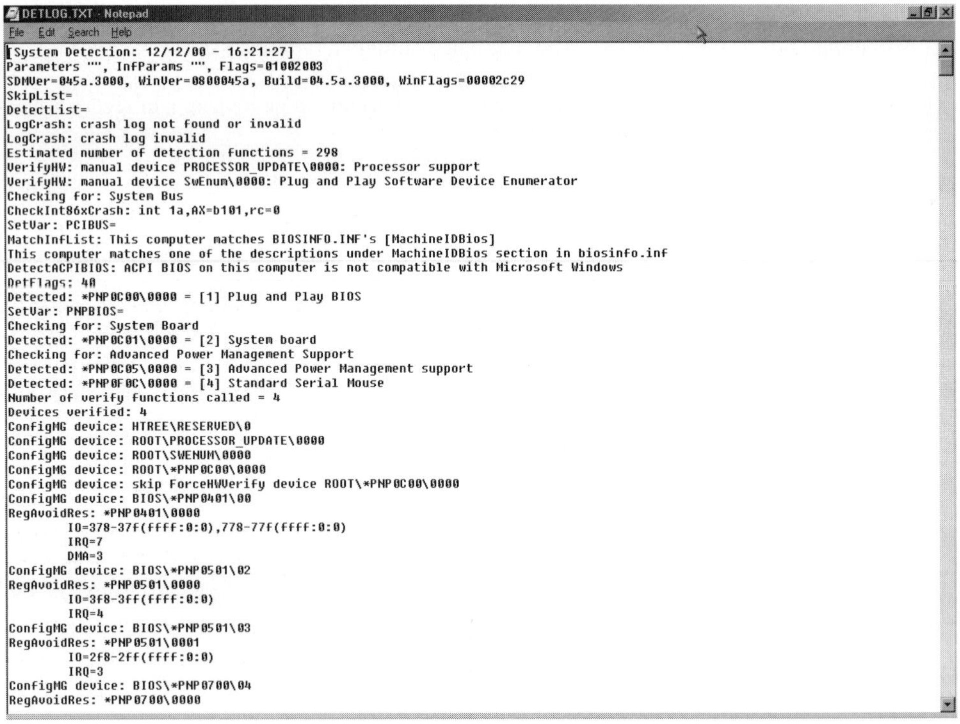


```
[System Detection: 12/12/00 - 16:21:27]
Parameters "", InfParams "", Flags=01002003
SDMVer=045a.3000, WinVer=0800045a, Build=04.5a.3000, WinFlags=00002c29
SkipList=
DetectList=
LogCrash: crash log not found or invalid
LogCrash: crash log invalid
Estimated number of detection functions = 298
VerifyHW: manual device PROCESSOR_UPDATE\0000: Processor support
VerifyHW: manual device SwEnum\0000: Plug and Play Software Device Enumerator
Checking for: System Bus
CheckInt86xCrash: int 1a,AX=b101,rc=0
SetVar: PCIBUS=
MatchInfList: This computer matches BIOSINFO.INF's [MachineIDBios]
This computer matches one of the descriptions under MachineIDBios section in biosinfo.inf
DetectACPIBIOS: ACPI BIOS on this computer is not compatible with Microsoft Windows
DetFlags: 40
Detected: *PNP0C00\0000 = [1] Plug and Play BIOS
SetVar: PNPBIOS=
Checking for: System Board
Detected: *PNP0C01\0000 = [2] System board
Checking for: Advanced Power Management Support
Detected: *PNP0C05\0000 = [3] Advanced Power Management support
Detected: *PNP0F0C\0000 = [4] Standard Serial Mouse
Number of verify functions called = 4
Devices verified: 4
ConfigMG device: HTREE\RESERVED\0
ConfigMG device: ROOT\PROCESSOR_UPDATE\0000
ConfigMG device: ROOT\SWENUM\0000
ConfigMG device: ROOT\*PNP0C00\0000
ConfigMG device: skip ForceHWVerify device ROOT\*PNP0C00\0000
ConfigMG device: BIOS\*PNP0401\00
RegAvoidRes: *PNP0401\0000
        IO=378-37f(ffff:0:0),778-77f(ffff:0:0)
        IRQ=7
        DMA=3
ConfigMG device: BIOS\*PNP0501\02
RegAvoidRes: *PNP0501\0000
        IO=3f8-3ff(ffff:0:0)
        IRQ=4
ConfigMG device: BIOS\*PNP0501\03
RegAvoidRes: *PNP0501\0001
        IO=2f8-2ff(ffff:0:0)
        IRQ=3
ConfigMG device: BIOS\*PNP0700\04
RegAvoidRes: *PNP0700\0000
```

Figure 21-3: DETLOG.TXT File

PROCEDURE - 21

1. **Open and examine the DETLOG.TXT file**
   ___ a. In the menu bar, click on the **File** menu and then select **Open**.
   ___ b. In the *Open* window, scroll to the right and then double-click **DETLOG.TXT**.

NOTE: If the file is not visible, type DETLOG.TXT in the File name box and be sure that you are looking at Local Disk (C:\), and click on the Open button.

   ___ c. If *DETLOG.TXT* is too large for *Notepad* to open, you will be asked to use *WordPad* to read it.
   ___ d. Record the information of the first line in Table 21-8.
   ___ e. In Table 21-9, record the first item to be checked, which begins with "Checking for".
   ___ f. Record the number of functions called, and the number of devices detected/verified in Table 21-10.

NETLOG.TXT

The NETLOG.TXT file is stored in the system's root directory (C:\) and is used in the troubleshooting of network problems. This file, as shown in Figure 21-4, is created at the installation of a Network Interface Card (NIC) and its accompanying software setup.

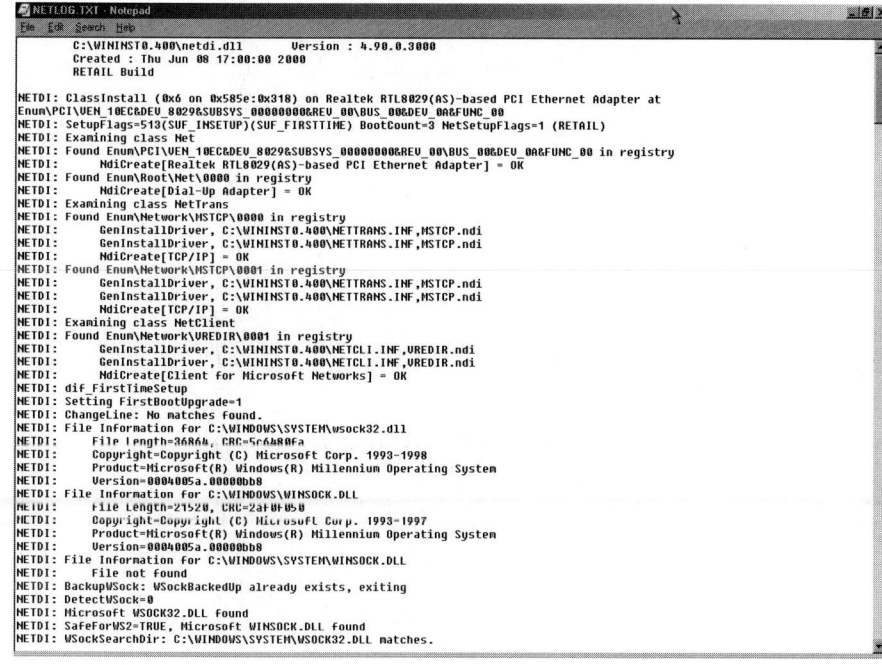

Figure 21-4: NETLOG.TXT File

1. **Open and examine the NETLOG.TXT file**
   ___ a. Open the **NETLOG.TXT** file from drive C: in *Notepad* in the same manner as in Step 1a above.
   ___ b. Click on the **Maximize** button to expand the *Notepad* window.
   ___ c. In Table 21-11 record the first three devices listed, which are identified by "NdiCreate" at the beginning of the lines.

NOTE: The device is enclosed inside a set of square brackets, [ ], or a set of parentheses, ( ).

   ___ d. Close the *NETLOG.TXT* file *Notepad* window.

PROCEDURE - 21

SETUPLOG.TXT

The SETUPLOG.TXT file holds setup information that was established during the installation process. The file is stored in the system's root directory (C:\) and is used in safe recovery situations. Entries are added to the file as they occur in the setup process, as shown in Figure 21-5. Therefore, the file can be read to determine what action was being taken when a setup failure occurred.

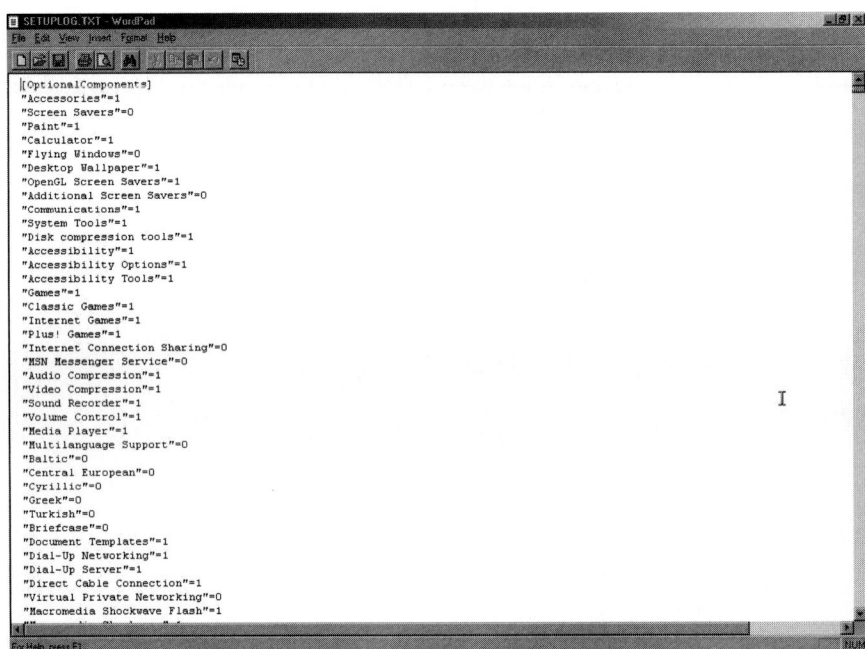

Figure 21-5:
SETUPLOG.TXT File

1. **Open and examine the SETUPLOG.TXT file**
   ___a. Open the **SETUPLOG.TXT** from drive C: in the same manner as in Step 1a above.
   ___b. Click on the **Maximize** button to expand the *Notepad* window.
   ___c. Record the name of the first section in Table 21-12.
   ___d. Record the name of the last section in Table 21-13.
   ___e. Close the *SETUPLOG.TXT* file *Notepad* window.

2. **Exit the Notepad program and turn off the computer**

TABLES

Table 21-1

Search Results of *log.txt Search:	

PROCEDURE - 21

Table 21-2

First Group Drivers Load Status:		
Which One	Driver	Status

Table 21-3

System-Critical Drivers Load Status:		
Which One	Critical Driver	Status

Table 21-4

Device Drivers Load Status:		
Which One	Device Driver	Status

Table 21-5

Dynamically Loaded & Device Initialization Load Status:		
Which One	Device	Status

Table 21-6

Initialization of System VxD Device Load Status:		
Which One	Device	Status

Table 21-7

Initialization of Kernel Driver and Load Status:		
Which One	Kernel Driver	Status

WINDOWS ME SETUP LOG FILES

PROCEDURE - 21

Table 21-8

1st Line of DETLOG.TXT File

Table 21-9

"Checking For":	

Table 21-10

Functions Called:	
Devices Detected/Verified:	

Table 21-11

NdiCreate Items:	

Table 21-12

Name of First Section [SETUPLOG.TXT]:

Table 21-13

Name of Last Section [SETUPLOG.TXT]:

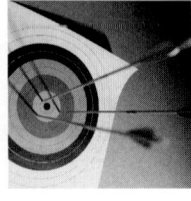

Feedback

LAB QUESTIONS

1. How do you tell if a VxD device driver has initialized correctly?

2. What file monitors the use of the file VMM.VXD?

3. Was a screen saver loaded at installation? (0=no, 1=yes)

4. What is the NETLOG.TXT file used for?

LAB PROCEDURE 22

Windows 2000/XP Startup Modes

OBJECTIVES

1. Restart and try various startup options.

RESOURCES

1. PC-compatible desktop/tower computer system — Customer-supplied desktop/tower hardware system **OR** Marcraft MC-8000 Computer Hardware Trainer **OR** suitable PC hardware trainer with Windows 2000 or Windows XP installed
2. A PS2 mouse
3. A LAN connection

Troubleshooting

DISCUSSION

In this lab we will explore different startup options that appear when pressing the *F8* key at startup. These options can be useful for troubleshooting system problems. The Windows Advanced Options Menu includes the following default options:

- Safe Mode
- Safe Mode with Networking
- Safe Mode with Command Prompt
- Enable Boot Logging
- Enable VGA Mode
- Last Known Good Configuration (your most recent setting that worked)
- Directory Services Restore Mode (Windows domain controllers only)
- Debugging Mode
- Boot Normally (Windows 2000 only)
- Start Windows Normally (Windows XP only)
- Reboot (Windows XP only)
- Return to OS Choices Menu (Windows XP only)

Safe Mode will start Windows with a minimal set of drivers used to run Windows, including mouse, monitor, keyboard, hard drive, base video, and default system services. You can enter Safe Mode with Networking or Safe Mode with Command Prompt by selecting the appropriate mode. VGA mode is useful when you have installed a video driver and have configured it incorrectly. If the computer starts with a blank screen or you see random lines all over the screen, you may choose VGA mode to start Windows.

PROCEDURE - 22

This mode will start the computer with the base video settings (640 X 480, 256 Colors). Boot Logging starts Windows and logs services that load or do not load to C:\winnt\ntbtlog.txt. Last Known Good Configuration starts Windows using the Registry information saved at the last proper shutdown. Directory Services Restore is used for Windows domain server systems. Debugging Mode starts Windows and sends debug information through the serial port to another computer. In Hardware Profiles you can change Windows startup to select a designated profile. Hardware Profiles can be useful for saving hardware-specific information when transporting a hard drive between two computers. One can do this without the need to reinstall all the devices on each system at every startup.

This procedure is compatible with both Windows 2000 and Windows XP. There are subtle differences, however, and you might want to do this procedure in both Windows 2000 and Windows XP.

PROCEDURE

Troubleshooting

1. **Safe Mode**
   - a. Turn on the computer (restart if it is already on) and boot to Windows 2000 or Windows XP.
   - b. When the screen displays the text "*Starting Windows, For Troubleshooting and Advanced Startup Options for Windows 2000, press F8*", press the **F8** key on the keyboard. (This is not displayed in Windows XP; you just keep pressing the **F8** key over and over again until you get the Advanced Options Menu.)
   - c. You will see the Advanced Options Menu. Safe Mode is selected by default. Press **ENTER**.
   - d. Once Windows starts you will see an information window about Safe Mode. Click on **OK**.
   - e. Right-click the desktop and select **Properties** from the drop-down menu to open the *Display Properties* window, and click on the **Settings** tab.
   - f. While in Safe Mode, Windows gives limited options on many things. Click on the **Colors** drop-down menu. Record your observations in Table 22-1.
   - g. Click on the **Cancel** button.
   - h. From the desktop, double-click the **My Network Places** icon.
   - i. Double-click on **Entire Network**.
   - j. Double-click on **Microsoft Windows Network**.
   - k. You will see a dialog window similar to Figure 22-1. During Safe Mode, you cannot view the network. Click on the **OK** button.
   - l. Close all windows and restart.

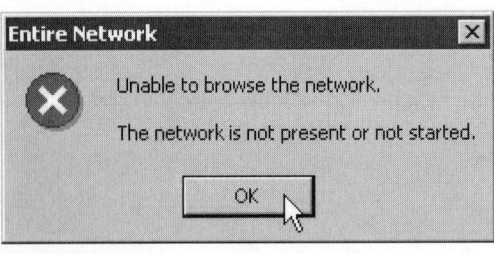
Figure 22-1: Unable to Browse Network Dialog

2. **Safe Mode with Networking**
   - a. When the computer has restarted, boot the computer to Windows 2000 and press the **F8** key as before.
   - b. From the *Windows 2000 Advanced Options Menu* scroll down by pressing the **DOWN ARROW** on the keyboard. Select Safe Mode with Networking and press **ENTER**.
   - c. Once Windows starts you will see an information window about Safe Mode. Click on **OK**.
   - d. From the desktop, double-click the **My Network Places** icon.
   - e. Double-click on **Entire Network**.
   - f. Double-click on **Microsoft Windows Network**.
   - g. You should see your workgroup in the window. Double-click on it and record your observations in Table 22-2.
   - h. Close all windows and restart.

PROCEDURE - 22

3. **Safe Mode with Command Prompt**
   - a. When the computer has restarted, boot the computer to Windows 2000 and press the **F8** key as before.
   - b. From the *Windows 2000 Advanced Options Menu* scroll down and select **Safe Mode with Command Prompt**. Press **ENTER**.
   - c. The operating system will boot to a command prompt. (C:\>). Type **dir** and press **ENTER** to view the contents of the drive.
   - d. Record the amount of bytes free in Table 22-3.
   - e. Type **explorer** and press **ENTER**. This will start the Windows Explorer.
   - f. You will receive the Safe Mode message. Click on **OK**.
   - g. Drag the title bar of cmd.exe (the command prompt) to the right.
   - h. Record the changes to the operating environment as a result of typing **explorer** in Table 22-4.
   - i. In the command line type **exit** and press **ENTER**.
   - j. Click on the **Start** menu and select **Shut Down**.
   - k. Select **Restart** from the drop-down menu and click on **OK**.

4. **Boot Normally**
   - a. When the computer has restarted, boot the computer to Windows 2000 and press **F8** as before.
   - b. From the *Windows Advanced Options Menu* scroll down and select **Boot Normally in Windows 2000** or **Start Windows Normally** in Windows XP. Press the **ENTER** key.
   - c. Use Windows Explorer to delete the file *c:\WINNT\ntbtlog.txt* in Windows 2000 and *c:\Windows\ntbtlog.txt* in Windows XP. You may need to click on **Show files** if you cannot view the contents of the *System* folder.
   - d. You have just deleted the boot log text file that Windows uses to log activity when *Enable Boot Logging startup* is selected. Close all windows and restart the computer.

5. **Boot Logging**
   - a. When the computer has restarted, boot the computer to Windows 2000 and press **F8** as before.
   - b. From the *Windows 2000 Advanced Options Menu* scroll down and select **Enable Boot Logging**. Press **ENTER**. Windows will now create a boot log file (*C:\WINNT\ntbtlog.txt*) to record its activity at startup.
   - c. Once Windows has started you can view the contents of the logged file. From the desktop double-click on **My Computer**.
   - d. Double-click on **(C:)**.
   - e. Double-click on **WINNT** (Win2K) or **Windows** (WinXP).
   - f. Click on **Show files** if necessary. Its hyperlink is located on the left-hand portion of the window.
   - g. Scroll down and double click on **ntbtlog**.
   - h. *Notepad* will open the file. The window will appear similar to Figure 22-2. You can now view the boot log that contains all loaded and not-loaded drivers. Record the date that appears on the first line of the file in Table 22-5.
   - i. Scroll down and view the contents of the file.
   - j. Close all windows and restart the computer.

PROCEDURE - 22

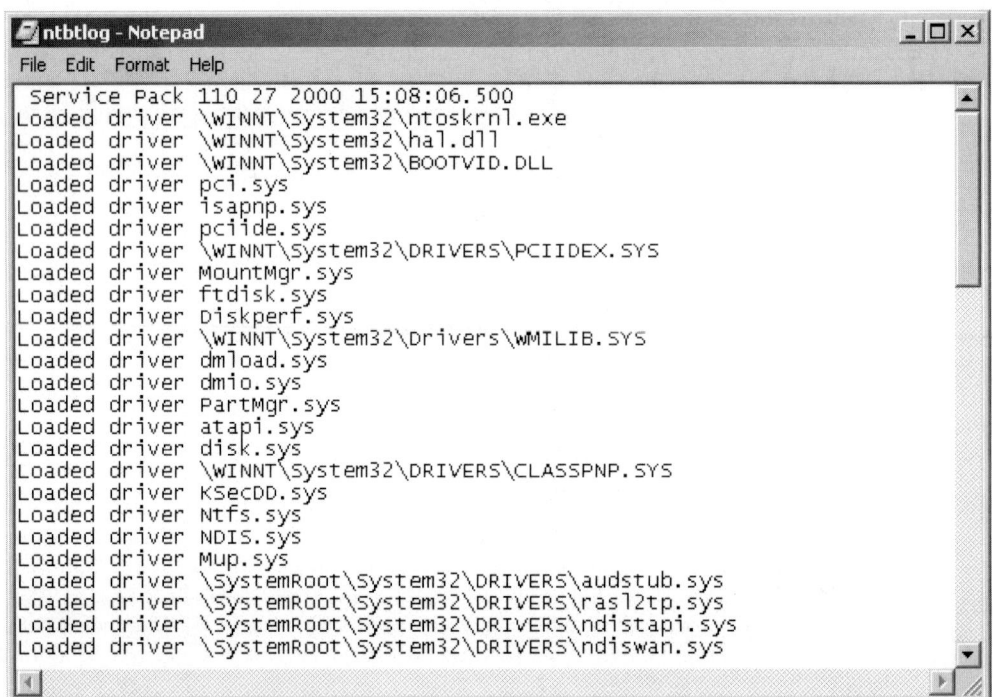

Figure 22-2: NT Boot Log

6. **VGA Mode**
   ___a. When the computer has restarted, boot the computer to Windows 2000 and press **F8** as before.
   ___b. From the *Windows 2000 Advanced Options Menu* scroll down and select **Enable VGA Mode**. Press **ENTER**.
   ___c. When Windows has started, right-click the desktop and click on **Properties**.
   ___d. Click on the **Settings** tab.
   ___e. Record the settings for Colors and Screen area in Table 22-6.
   ___f. Close all windows and restart the computer.

7. **Last Known Good Configuration**
   ___a. When the computer has restarted, boot the computer to Windows 2000 and press **F8** as before.
   ___b. From the Windows 2000 Advanced Options Menu scroll down and select **Last Known Good Configuration**. Press **ENTER**.
   ___c. If you have made hardware profiles previously in Windows you can select them and boot to them. Press **L** to switch to the Last Known Good configuration.
   ___d. Profile 1 should be selected. Press **ENTER**. If you pressed *D* your options would change to the default configuration.

8. **Hardware Profiles**
   ___a. When Windows has started, right-click on **My Computer** and select **Properties**.
   ___b. Click on the **Hardware** tab.
   ___c. Click on the **Hardware Profiles** button.
   ___d. A window similar to Figure 22-3 will appear. From this window you can add and delete hardware profiles. Click on **Cancel**.
   ___e. Close all windows and shut down the computer.

PROCEDURE - 22

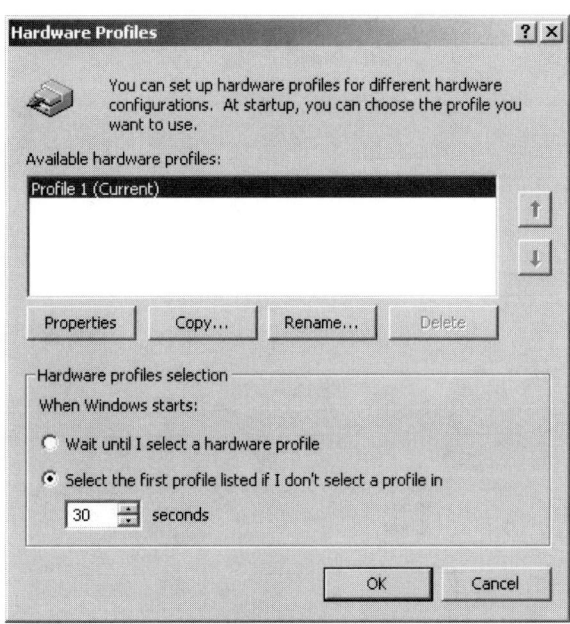

Figure 22-3:
Hardware
Profiles

TABLES

Table 22-1

Colors Drop-down Menu Observations

Table 22-2

Network Observations:	

Table 22-3

Bytes Free on C:\ at Command Prompt

Table 22-4

Operating Environment Changes Observations

PROCEDURE - 22

Table 22-5

Boot Log Date:	

Table 22-6

Display Colors:	
Display Screen Area:	

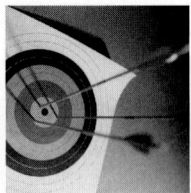

Feedback

LAB QUESTIONS

1. How many startup options are included with Windows 2000 by default?

2. What does Safe Mode do?

3. When can VGA mode be useful?

4. How would you access the Start menu when in Safe Mode with Command Prompt?

5. Under what circumstances could Hardware Profiles be useful?

LAB PROCEDURE 23

Windows XP System Restore

OBJECTIVES

1. Set up drive space to be used by System Restore.
2. Restore your computer from an existing restore point.

Troubleshooting

RESOURCES

1. PC-compatible desktop/tower computer system — Customer-supplied desktop/tower hardware system **OR** Marcraft MC-8000 Computer Hardware Trainer **OR** suitable PC hardware trainer running Windows XP Professional

DISCUSSION

System Restore automatically tracks changes to your computer at specific intervals to create restore points. Restore points can be scheduled or manually created. They also are automatically created before any changes are made to the system configuration. These restore points only back up system and program files.

System Restore, by default, is set up to monitor and restore all partitions on all drives in your system. It also monitors all installations of all applications or drivers that users install through normal delivery mechanisms like CD-ROMs, floppy drives, and so on. If you accidentally delete a monitored program file (such as .exe or .dll files) or they have become corrupted, you can restore your computer to a state that existed before those changes occurred.

System Restore does not lose your personal files or passwords. It does not restore any files located in the *My Documents* folder. It does not restore any files with common data file name extensions, such as .doc or .xls. To keep your personal data files completely safe from System Restore writing over them, save them in the *My Documents* folder.

If a program was installed after the restore point that you are restoring, the program will most likely be uninstalled. Data files that were created with that program will not be lost; however, you will have to reinstall the program to use the data files.

PROCEDURE

1. **Set up the amount of drive space to be used by System Restore**
   ___ a. Open **System Restore** by navigating the *Start\All Programs\Accessories\System Tools\System Restore* path, as shown in Figure 23-1.

PROCEDURE - 23

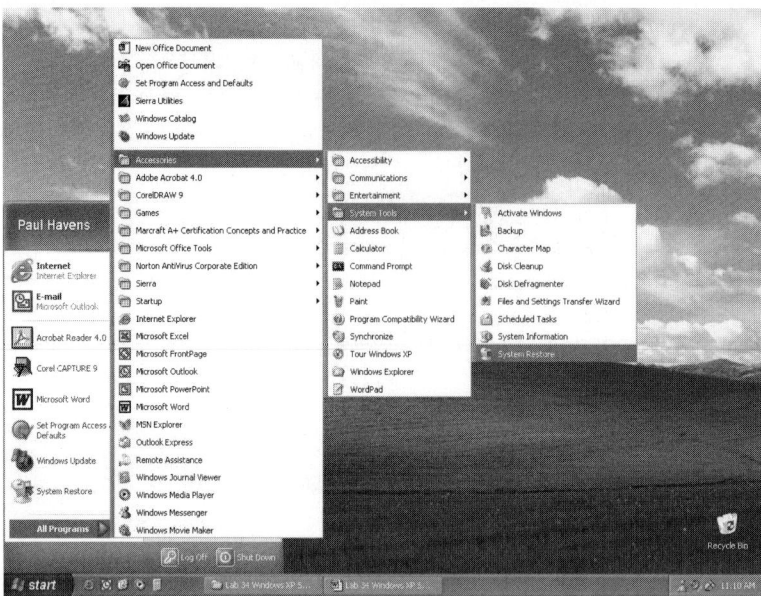

Figure 23-1: Opening System Restore

___ b. The *Welcome to System Restore* screen will appear, as shown in Figure 23-2.

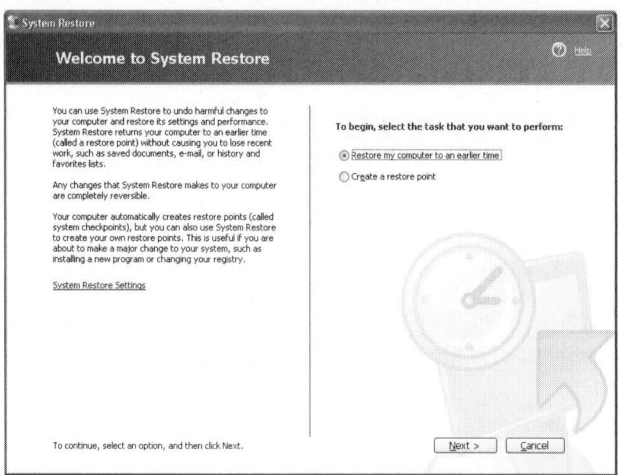

Figure 23-2: System Restore Welcome Screen

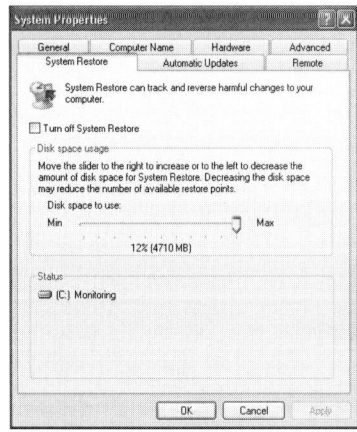

___ c. The *Welcome* screen contains a brief explanation of the System Restore utility, an area to select whether you wish to *Restore my computer to an earlier time*, or *Create a restore point*. On the left-hand side is a link to the *Advanced* settings for System Restore. Click on **System Restore Settings**. In a single hard drive system, you will receive a Properties page like the one in Figure 23-3. (In multiple-drive systems, the page will offer options for obtaining the status of the different drives.)

Figure 23-3: System Properties/System Restore Tab

158 - LAB GROUP 2

PROCEDURE - 23

___d. Notice the check box at the top of the screen. Turning off System Restore disables the function on all drives. Leave the box cleared. For computers with a single drive skip to Step e. Highlight drive C from the list and click on the **Settings** button. The *System Restore* settings for the selected drive are displayed.

___e. You may move the slider to increase or decrease the amount of disk space allocated for the Restore Points. Click on **OK** to close the *Drive Settings* dialog box (multiple drives only), then click on **OK** to close the *System Properties* screen.

2. **Restore your system from an existing Restore Point**

___a. Make sure *Restore my system to an earlier time* is selected and click on **Next** to continue. The *Select a Restore Point* wizard opens, as shown in Figure 23-4. Notice that there is a calendar on the left side of the wizard. The dates displayed in bold contain restore points that you may use to restore your system to that date.

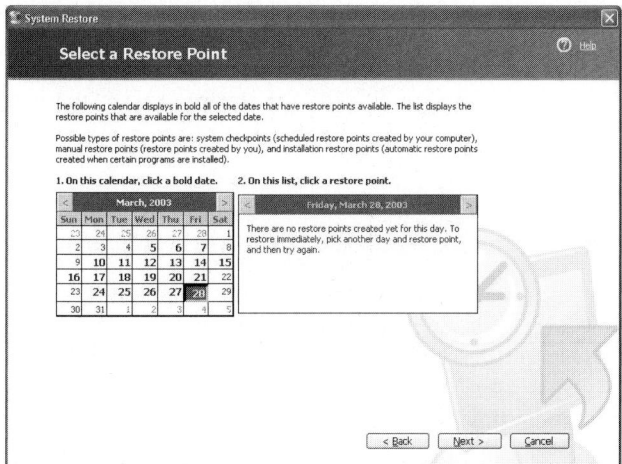

Figure 23-4: Select a Restore Point Wizard

___b. Choose the closest date to the current day with a valid restore point and click on it once.

___c. Notice that the right side changes to what was done for the computer to create the restore point. In Figure 23-5 the restore point created on March 26, 2003 had multiple restore points created and each one has a time associated with it. For yours it should have one checkpoint and display a system checkpoint with the time. If there are multiple restore points on that day, select the one latest in the day and click on **Next**.

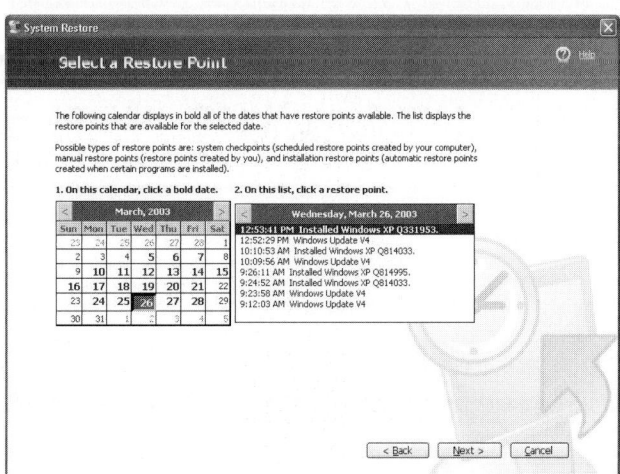

Figure 23-5: Restore Point Date with Multiple Restore Points

PROCEDURE - 23

___d. Clicking on **Next** will cause the *Confirm Restore Point Selection* screen to appear, as shown in Figure 23-6. This screen provides the date and time of the restore point being used.

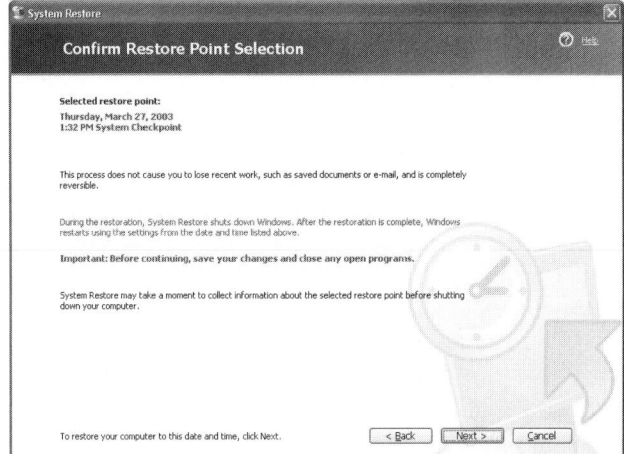

Figure 23-6: Restore Point Confirmation Screen

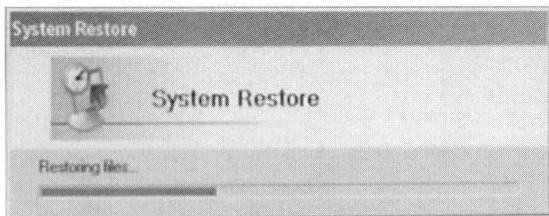

Figure 23-7: System Restore Process

___e. Click on **Next** to begin the restore process.
___f. The wizard collects some information about the system and then logs off. It then starts the restore process as shown in Figure 23-7.
___g. After the restore process is finished, the system will be restarted, and then the desktop appears and the System Restore wizard displays the results as shown in Figure 23-8. If the restore process failed, you would be advised to choose another Restore Point, and try again.

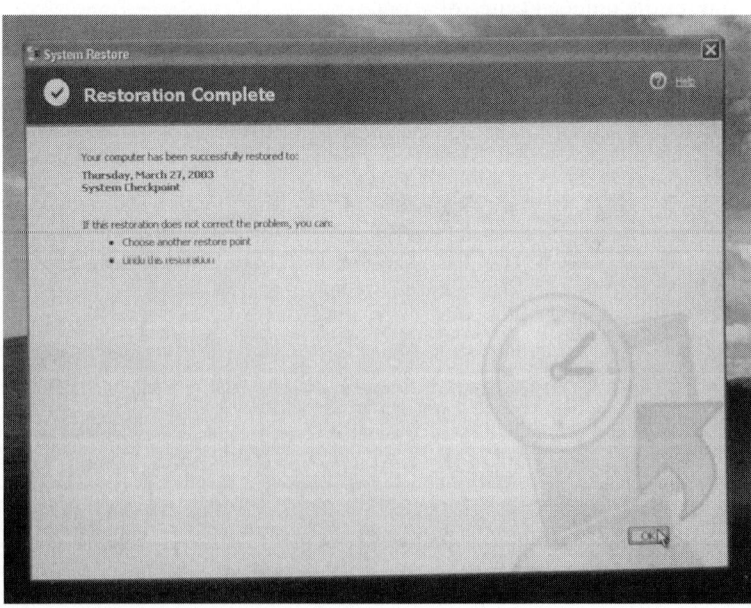

Figure 23-8: System Restore Results Screen

160 - LAB GROUP 2

PROCEDURE - 23

3. **Create a system restore point**
   ___a. We will now manually create a system restore point. Open the System Restore wizard from the *Start* menu as before. This time select **Create a Restore Point** and click on **Next** to continue.
   ___b. You will be asked to provide a name for the restore point. The name you choose should be representative of the purpose of the point, such as "New Driver" or the current date. For this lab we will enter the date. Enter the current date in the *Restore point description* text box, as shown in Figure 23-9, and click on **Create** to continue.

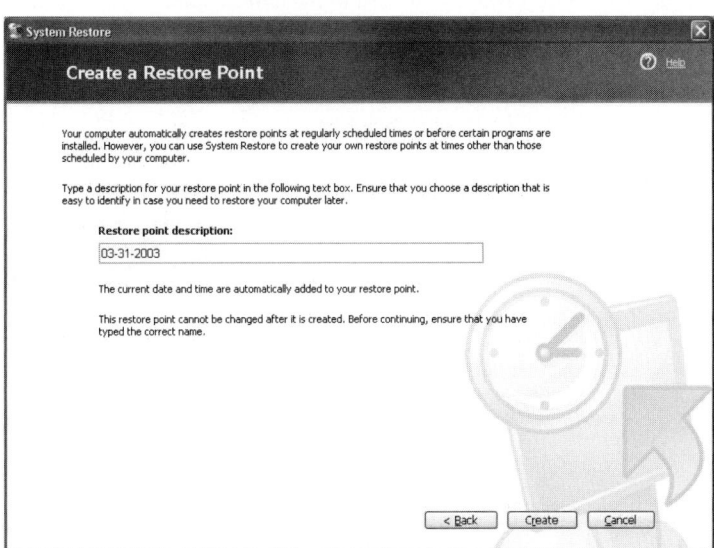

Figure 23-9: Restore Point Description

   ___c. The system will create the restore point, and when done will display confirmation that the point has been created, as shown in Figure 23-10. Click on **Home** when finished to return to the *Welcome to System Restore* screen.

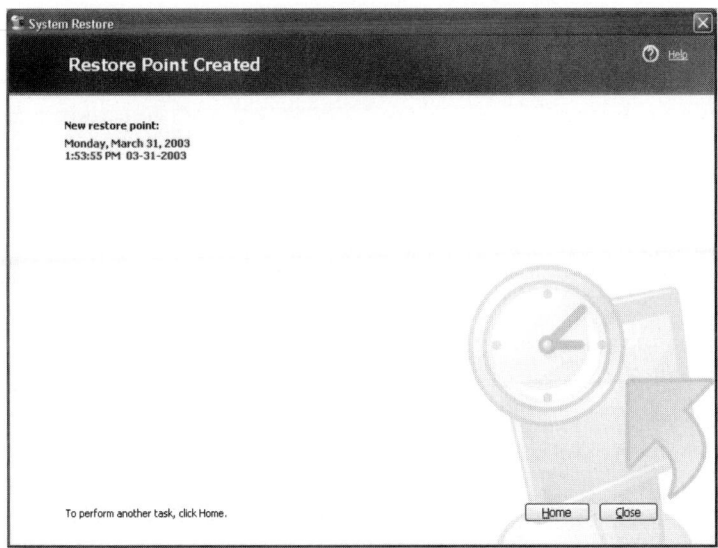

Figure 23-10: Restore Point has been Created

PROCEDURE - 23

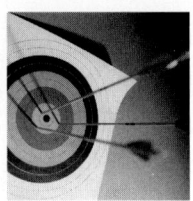

Feedback

LAB QUESTIONS

1. What does System Restore monitor by default in a system restore point?
2. How do you adjust the amount of disk space allocated to System Restore?
3. Is it possible to turn off System Restore?
4. What do you use to restore the system to an earlier restore point?
5. What do you use to create a system restore point?

LAB PROCEDURE 24

Windows 2000 Virus Protection

OBJECTIVES

1. Manually scan the C: drive for viruses.

Troubleshooting

RESOURCES

1. PC-compatible desktop/tower computer system — Customer-supplied desktop/tower hardware system **OR** Marcraft MC-8000 Computer Hardware Trainer **OR** suitable PC hardware trainer with Windows 2000 installed
2. Anti-virus package - McAfee VirusScan utility **OR** other user supplied anti-virus utility

DISCUSSION

Viruses can harm the operation of your system. When visiting questionable web sites, or opening infected e-mail, you may get a virus that causes your system to operate strangely. Viruses can delete documents, system files, or other files on your computer. They can be spread to other users through e-mail, the Internet, or any other electronic means of communication. It is important to rid the computer of any viruses and perform preventive maintenance on your system. It is also important to have the latest .DAT files, which define the known viruses, because new viruses appear every day. McAfee can also update its files on your computer directly from their web site. This lab will help you to use McAfee VirusScan to scan the hard drive on your computer.

PROCEDURE

1. **Manual scan for viruses**
   - a. Boot to the Windows 2000 desktop.
   - b. Double-click the **McAfee VirusScan Central Shortcut** on the desktop.
   - c. If you are prompted to perform a scan because one has not been preformed before, click on **No**.
   - d. You will now see a window similar to Figure 24-1. Click on the **Scan** button.
   - e. Highlight **Local Disk (C:)**.
   - f. Click on the **Settings** button.

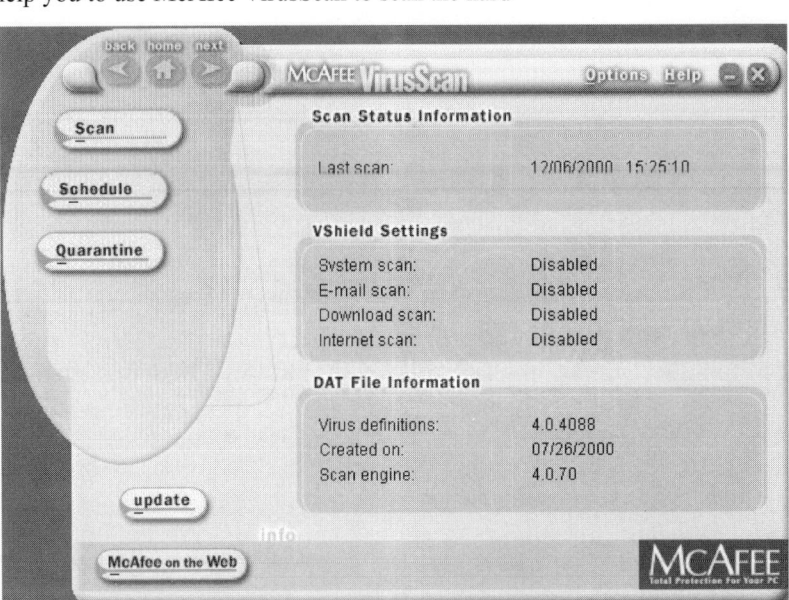

Figure 24-1: McAfee VirusScan

PROCEDURE - 24

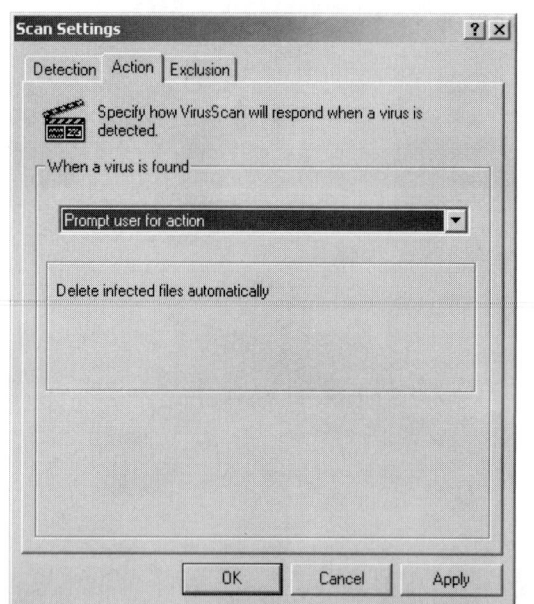

Figure 24-2:
Scan Settings

____ g. Record the items selected under "What to scan" in Table 24-1.
____ h. Click on the **All files** radio button.
____ i. Click on the **Action** tab. You will see a window similar to Figure 24-2.
____ j. Click on the down arrow to open the "*When a virus is found*" menu so that it expands and record the options in Table 24-2.
____ k. Click on the **Exclusion** tab.
____ l. From this window you can add or remove folders to be excluded during a scan. Record the item that is excluded in Table 24-3.
____ m. Click on **OK** to close the *Scan Settings* window.
____ n. Click on the **Activity Log** button. You will see a window similar to Figure 24-3.
____ o. Click on the **Log Settings** button.
____ p. Record the Items under "Enable logging for" in Table 24-4.
____ q. Click on **OK** to close the *Log Settings* window.

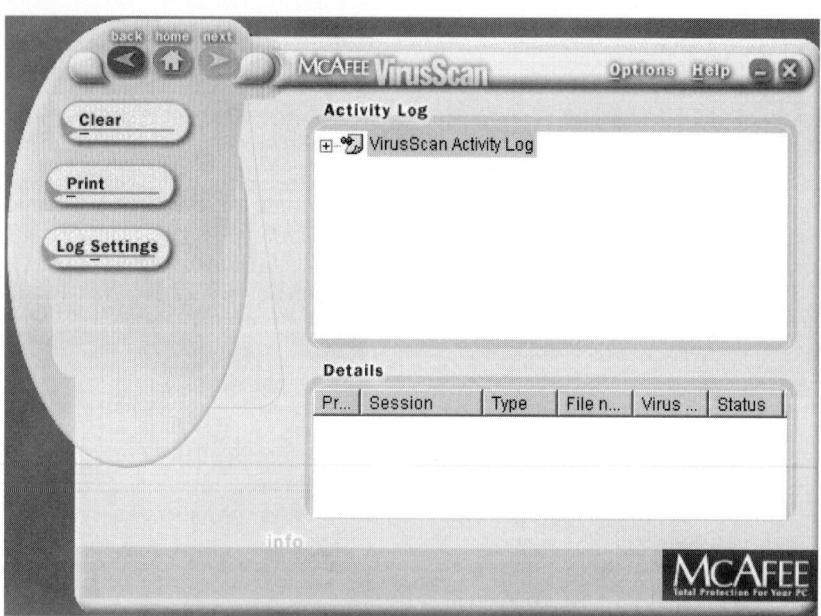

Figure 24-3:
Activity Log

____ r. Click on the **VirusScan Activity Log** and then expand it by clicking on the + sign next to the icon.
____ s. Click on the **VirusScan Log**, if it exists, to highlight it.
____ t. Click on the **Clear** button.
____ u. Click on the **Back** button in the upper-left portion of the window to return to the previous scan window.
____ v. Click on the **Scan Now** button and the virus scan will begin. It may take several minutes.
____ w. Record your observations of the bottom of the window in Table 24-5. What do you think it is showing?

164 - LAB GROUP 2

PROCEDURE - 24

2. **View results**
   ___ a. If any viruses are detected you should choose to delete the file affected.
   ___ b. Immediately after the scan is finished a window similar to Figure 24-4 will open. Click on **OK** to the result window.
   ___ c. Click on the **Activity Log** button.
   ___ d. Expand the **VirusScan Activity Log**.
   ___ e. Expand the **VirusScan Log**.
   ___ f. You will see an item with the current date and time of the scan you just performed. Expand the item.
   ___ g. Click on **Scan Settings**.
   ___ h. Under the *Details* window you can see various information about the scan. Record the required values in Table 24-6.
   ___ i. Click on **Scan Summary** and record the required details in Table 24-7.
   ___ j. Close the *McAfee VirusScan* window.

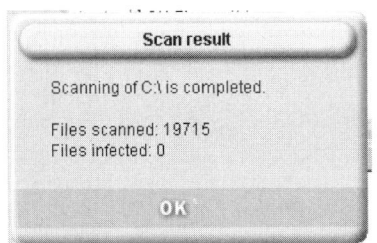

Figure 24-4: Scan Results

3. **VirusScan Console**
   ___ a. In the System Tray there is an icon that looks like a magnifying glass. This is the **VirusScan Console**. Double-click on it. You will see a window similar to Figure 24-5.

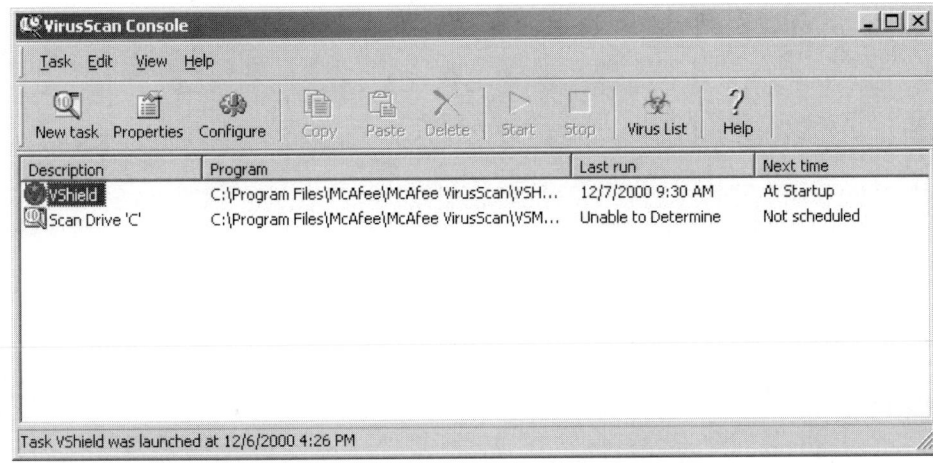

Figure 24-5: VirusScan Console

   ___ b. Double-click on **Scan Drive 'C'**.
   ___ c. Click on the **Schedule** tab. You can specify when an automatic scan should take place from this window.
   ___ d. Click on **Enable** and record the options to run in Table 24-8.
   ___ e. Click on **Cancel** and Close the *VirusScan Console* window.

4. **Virus Shield**
   ___ a. In the system tray there is an icon that looks like a V inside a shield. It may have a red circle with a slash in front of it. This is the **Virus Shield**. It can be made to monitor actions during normal operation. Double-click on it.
   ___ b. If the System Scan is disabled; enable it.
   ___ c. Press **CTRL+ALT+DELETE** and click on **Task Manager**.
   ___ d. Click on the **Performance** tab.

WINDOWS 2000 VIRUS PROTECTION - 165

PROCEDURE - 24

___ e. Arrange your screen so that you can see the Memory Usage of Task Manager and System Scan Status at the same time. The screen should look similar to Figure 24-6.

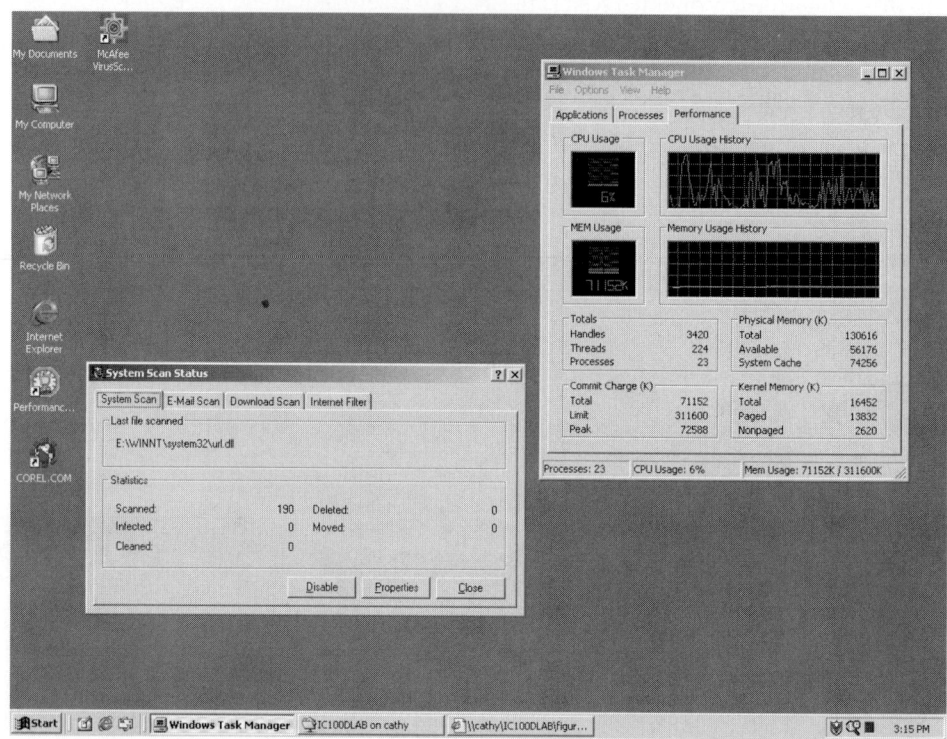

**Figure 24-6:
View Both Windows at Once**

___ f. Click on the **Disable** button and then the Enable button in System Scan and record the differences of memory usage in Table 24-9.

NOTE: We already know that programs take up system resources when they're running. This program also scans every file that is accessed.

___ g. Test this by opening a program like *Internet Explorer* and looking at the Last file scanned and the Scanned statistics for the number of files scanned.
___ h. Record the names of the other three tabs of the *System Scan Status* window in Table 24-10.
___ i. Disable **System Scan**, close all open windows, and shut down the computer.

TABLES

Table 24-1

What to Scan:	

166 - LAB GROUP 2

PROCEDURE - 24

Table 24-2

"When a Virus is found" Options:	

Table 24-3

Excluded Item:	

Table 24-4

"Enable logging for":	

Table 24-5

Scan Observations

Table 24-6

Details Window - Required Values	
Scan Engine Version:	
Scan Item 1:	
Scan All Files	

PROCEDURE - 24

Table 24-7

Scan Summary Details	
Virus in Memory:	
Files Infected:	

Table 24-8

Schedule Options:		

Table 24-9

Differences	
Memory Used During Disable:	
Memory Used During Enable:	

Table 24-10

System Scan Tabs:	

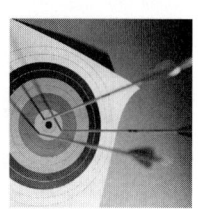

Feedback

LAB QUESTIONS

1. Approximately how many files did you scan for viruses?

2. What other drives were available in "Where & What" when doing a scan of drive C:?

3. Where would you view the date and time of your last scan?

4. Where would you go to have the C: drive scanned once a day?

5. Why is it important to have the latest virus .DAT files?

LAB GROUP 3
NETWORK MANAGEMENT

LAB PROCEDURE 25

Windows Me Dial-Up Access

OBJECTIVES

1. Install Dial-Up Networking.
2. Establish a connection to another computer, using Dial-Up Networking via modem.

Networking

RESOURCES

1. PC-compatible desktop/tower computer system — Customer-supplied desktop/tower hardware system **OR** Marcraft MC-8000 Computer Hardware Trainer **OR** suitable PC hardware trainer with Windows Millennium Edition installed
2. Modem installed
3. ISP dial-up account

DISCUSSION

If your Windows Me installation is new, the necessary IP and DNS information will need to be set up. If the installation is an upgrade of an earlier operating system that already had established communication settings, Windows Me will attempt to detect these settings, and install them as the default settings.

In a dial-up environment, the dialing information and parameters are set up through the *Start* menu. Simply click on *Start\Settings* and select the *Dial-Up Networking* entry. This should produce the *Dial-Up Networking* window. Select the *Make New Connection* icon.

There are basically two types of Internet connection schemes to deal with. The first is a dial-up installation involving a local modem and the telephone system. The second is a remote connection through a local area network. Currently, the fastest speed for an analog is 56K.

From this point, the connection wizard will prompt you for information about the modem type, COM port selection, ISP dial-up telephone number, and the country. Entering this information will produce a My Connection icon in the Dial-Up Networking window. Click on the new icon to set up the appropriate Internet information. Clicking on the *Properties* button and selecting the *Networking* tab brings you to *Advanced* options. Clicking on the *TCP/IP Settings* button allows you to input ISP-provided DNS information as shown in Figure 25-1. Normally, the *Server assigned IP address* option is selected. This allows the Dynamic Host Configuration Protocol (DHCP) server at the ISP to dynamically assign IP addresses to your system using one of its allotted IP addresses. In most cases, an ISP would not be willing to service a normal account with a static IP address. When this option is selected, the given IP is assigned to your system even when it is not being used. Therefore, the ISP cannot use that IP for any other account even though it is not busy.

PROCEDURE - 25

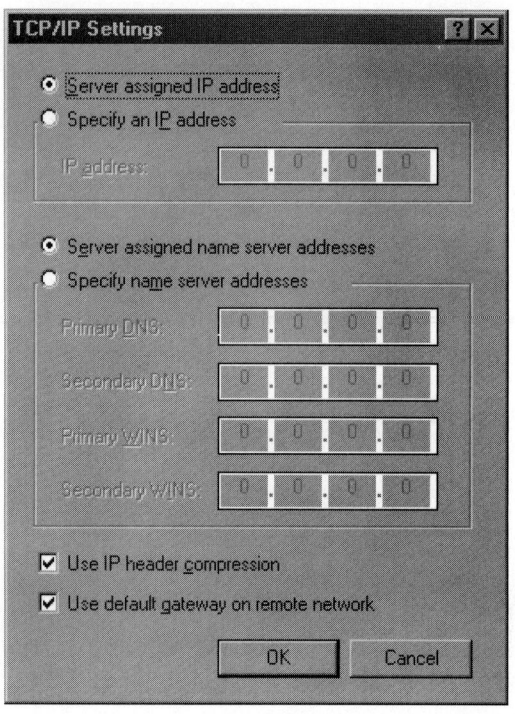

Figure 25-1: Establishing Internet Properties

If the Internet connection is made through a LAN system, the communication information is entered through the Control Panel's *Network* icon. The network administrator will need to supply Windows Me with the computer's DNS information from the local network router installation. In most cases, the network server communicates with the ISP as described for the dial-up network installation above. However, within a LAN-based system, the router software assigns each node on the network a static IP address, as shown in Figure 25-2.

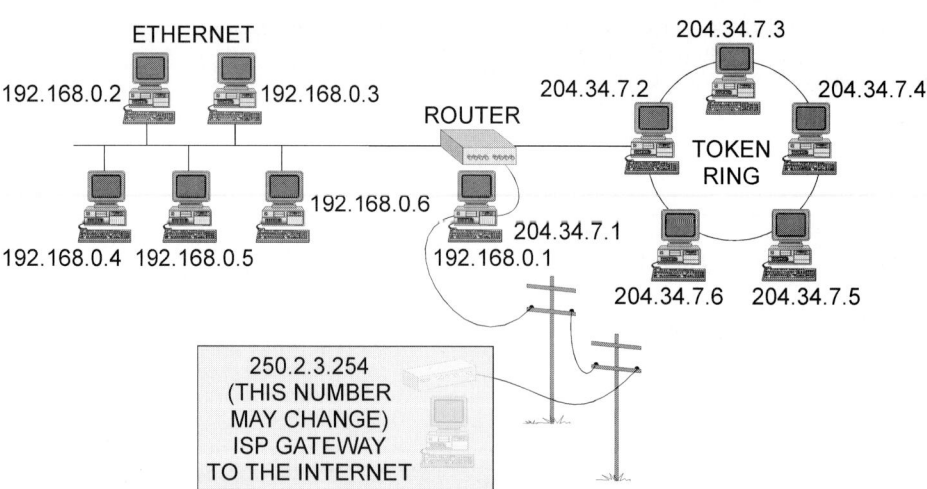

Figure 25-2: Local IP Addresses in a LAN System

172 - LAB GROUP 3

PROCEDURE - 25

PROCEDURE

Networking

Configure the Dial-Up Networking Feature

1. **Boot the computer to Windows Millennium Edition**
   ___a. Turn on the computer and select **Windows Me** from the OS selection menu.

2. **Set up Dial-Up Networking to connect to the Internet**

   NOTE: If your computer already has the Dial-Up Networking installed, proceed to Step 2j.

   ___a. Navigate the path *Start/Settings/Control Panel/* and double-click the **Add/Remove Programs** icon to open the *Add/Remove Programs* window.
   ___b. Click the **Windows Setup table**.
   ___c. In the *Components* box, select **Communications**.
   ___d. Click on the **Details** button.
   ___e. In the *Components* window, check the check box next to **Dial-Up Networking** to select it.
   ___f. Click on the **OK** button twice, and follow the instructions.
   ___g. Restart the computer.
   ___h. Close the *Control Panel* window.
   ___i. Navigate the path *Start/Setting* and select **Dial-Up Networking** from the menu.
   ___j. Double-click on **Make New Connection**.
   ___k. In the *Make New Connection* screen, enter the name of your Internet Service Provider (ISP) in the *Type* window.

3. **Check the Windows Me modem configuration**
   ___a. Click on the **Configure** button.
   ___b. Set the *Maximum speed value* to the highest setting available.
   ___c. Click on the **Connection** tab, and record the modem connection preferences information in Table 25-1.
   ___d. Click on the **Port Settings** button.
   ___e. Set the *Receive Buffer speed* setting to **Maximum**.
   ___f. Set the *Transmit Buffer speed* setting to **High**.

   The Receive Buffer speed is set above the Transmit Buffer speed, otherwise the modem will try to transmit as fast as it receives, and will end up filling the buffer. This will slow down the operation of the connection.

   ___g. Click on the **OK** button to return to the *Connection* window.
   ___h. Click on the **Advanced** button.
   ___i. Record the Hardware and Software flow control settings in Table 25-2.

   This is also where you would add any extra settings you want to have for your modem. An example is M0, which usually turns the volume on your modem off so that your computer is silent when connecting to the Internet.

   ___j. Click on **OK** to return to the *Modem Preferences* window.

WINDOWS ME DIAL-UP ACCESS - 173

PROCEDURE - 25

4. **Set up the ISP dial-up connection information**
    - a. Click on **OK** again to return to the *Make New Connection* window.
    - b. Click on **Next** to advance to the phone number entry page.
    - c. Type in the phone number of your ISP (provided by your instructor) and click on **Next**.
    - d. Click on the **Finish** button to produce an icon in the *Dial-Up Networking* window similar to the one shown in Figure 25-3.

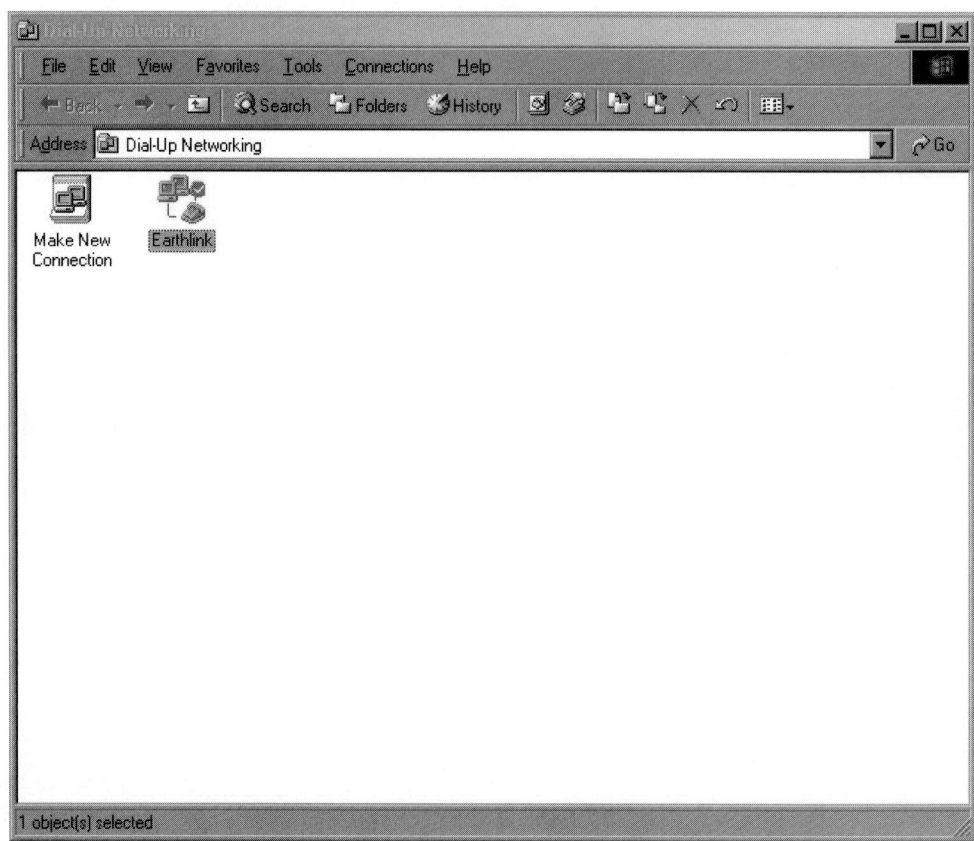

Figure 25-3: Dial-Up Networking Window

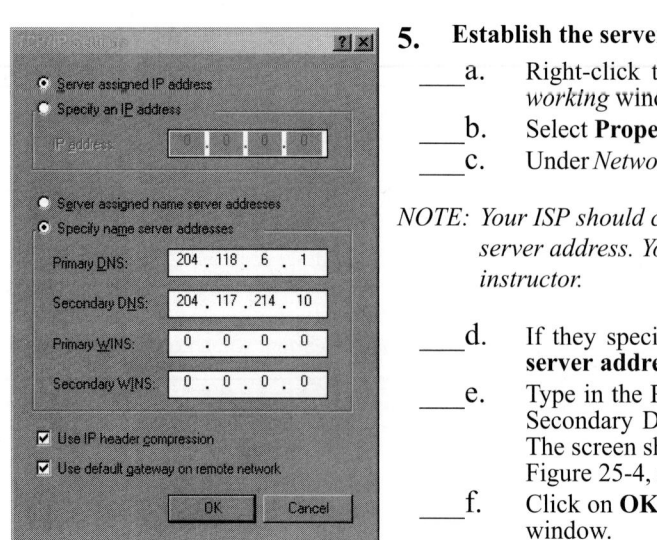

Figure 25-4: Editing a String

5. **Establish the server address for the connection**
    - a. Right-click the icon just created in the *Dial-Up Networking* window.
    - b. Select **Properties** from the list.
    - c. Under *Networking*, click on the **TCP/IP Settings** button.

    NOTE: *Your ISP should connect to the Internet through a specific server address. You'll need to get this information from your instructor.*

    - d. If they specify an address click on the **Specify name server addresses** radio button to mark it.
    - e. Type in the Primary DNS (Domain Name Service) and Secondary DNS address provided to you by your ISP. The screen should be similar to the one depicted in Figure 25-4, except for your ISP addresses.
    - f. Click on **OK** twice to return to the *Dial-Up Networking* window.

174 - LAB GROUP 3

PROCEDURE - 25

6. **Connect to the Internet**
   ___a. Double-click the icon of the new connection.
   ___b. Enter the User name and Password supplied by your instructor (from the ISP).
   ___c. Click on **Connect**.

You should hear the modem dialing (unless you specified M0). A *Connecting To* window should appear, displaying the status of the modem. The duration time is continually updated. If an Internet browser was already set up, the *Connected To* window would minimize to the Taskbar. The system is now connected to the Internet.

7. **Shut down the computer**

TABLES

Table 25-1

Modem Connection Preferences	
Data Bits:	
Parity:	
Stop Bits:	

Table 25-2

Hardware and Software Flow Control Settings:	

LAB QUESTIONS

1. Describe the information that must be obtained from the ISP when setting up a dial-up networking account.

2. What type of protocol was selected for connecting to the Internet?

3. What is a DNS address?

4. What type of server is used to dynamically assign IP addresses?

5. What is the current maximum speed of an analog modem?

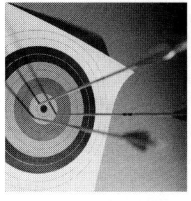

Feedback

LAB PROCEDURE 26

Windows Me Network Operations

OBJECTIVES

1. Set up File and Print Sharing.
2. Share drives, folders, and files.
3. Set up drive mapping to a folder on another computer.
4. Connect to a shared network resource.
5. Add a Network Place.

Networking

RESOURCES

1. Two PC-compatible desktop/tower computer systems — Customer-supplied desktop/tower hardware systems **OR** Marcraft MC-8000 Computer Hardware Trainers **OR** suitable PC hardware trainers with 64 MB RAM
2. Windows Me operating system (installed)
3. Network Interface Card (installed)
4. Working network connection

DISCUSSION

While most networks currently in use consist of client workstations connected to network servers, many networks consist of 50 or fewer computers connected together in a simple peer-to-peer network. In peer-to-peer networks, all workstations operate as both clients (who request services) and servers (who provide services). In a typical situation, ten computers are networked using 100BaseT Ethernet (IEEE 802.3) running the TCP/IP protocol, allowing all users on the network the ability to access files on each of the other computers. This sharing of files is the primary function of most peer-to-peer networks.

Two types of sharing are available on Windows 9x/Me workstations — share-level and user-level. Share-level access control means that a user may be required to supply a password to access a shared folder. User-level access control means that access is granted to a single user or group of users and on a server-based LAN. User-level access control will not be covered by this lab procedure.

You may share drives or folders through the properties window for each item. You can grant full access to other users, read-only access, or you may limit access by requiring a password. The item selected for sharing can be made quite specific. You can share a single subfolder and deny access to anything else in a full directory, or you can grant access to a full directory and choose which specific subdirectories will not be shared. This flexibility allows the user a significant amount of control over network sharing.

PROCEDURE - 26

Sharing can be made easier by mapping a drive over the network. A user can map a drive on another computer so that it can be accessed through a new drive icon listed in Windows Explorer, instead of having to navigate there each time you wish to use a network resource. You simply double-click on the mapped drive icon and it opens.

The mapping process can be made even easier by using the Add Network Place wizard to create an icon that will be mapped to a specific drive or folder on another network workstation. This icon will not appear as a drive icon, but instead will be listed as a network icon under My Network Places. A Network Place can be a shared folder, a web folder on the Internet, or even an FTP site.

Networking

PROCEDURE

1. **Set up File and Print Sharing**
    ___a. Boot your computer to the Windows Me desktop.
    ___b. Navigate the path *Start/Settings/Control Panel* and then double-click the **Network** icon to open it.
    ___c. Click on the **File and Print Sharing** button in the *Network Configuration* window as shown in Figure 26-1.

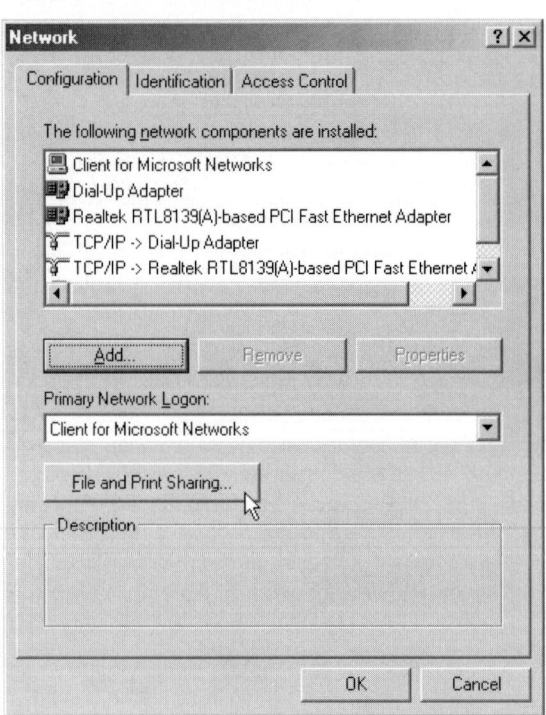

Figure 26-1: The Network Control Panel

    ___d. Click on the check box **I want to be able to give others access to my files** to select it.
    ___e. Click on the check box **I want to be able to allow others to print to my printer(s)** to select it.
    ___f. Click on the **OK** button.
    ___g. Click on the **Identification** tab.
    ___h. Record the listed Computer Name in Table 26-1.
    ___i. Click on the **OK** button to close the *Network* window.
    ___j. Click on the **Yes** button to restart your computer.

PROCEDURE - 26

2. **Share your C: drive with the local network**
   ___a. Double-click the **My Computer** icon, and then locate and examine the icon for your C: drive.
   ___b. Right-click the **Local Disk (C:)** icon and select **Sharing** from the pop-up menu.
   ___c. Click on the radio button next to **Shared As** to enable read-only sharing of this logical drive.
   ___d. Click on the **OK** button to accept the changes and close the window.
   ___e. Examine the Local Disk (C:) icon and record the change in appearance of this icon in Table 26-2.

3. **Share folders with other users on the network**
   ___a. Open Windows Explorer.
   ___b. Click on the plus sign (+) next to **My Computer** to expand the directory.
   ___c. Double-click on **Local Disk (C:)** to expand the directory tree.
   ___d. With the C: drive highlighted, click on the **File** menu, and select **New**, and then **Folder**.
   ___e. Type the Computer Name you recorded in Table 26-1, and then press the **ENTER** key.
   ___f. Right-click your new folder and select **Sharing** from the pop-up menu.
   ___g. Click on the radio button next to **Shared As**, as shown in Figure 26-2, to enable read-only sharing of this folder.

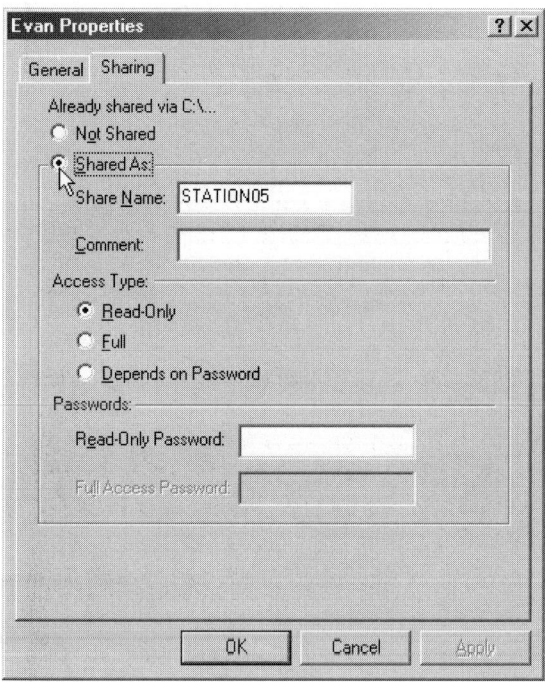

Figure 26-2: The Sharing Properties Tab

   ___h. Click on the **OK** button to save your settings, and then close the *Properties* window for your folder.

NOTE: A shared folder is identified in the same manner as a shared drive, with a hand holding the folder icon.

4. **Set Full access permission for a shared folder**
   ___a. Double-click your new folder to open it.
   ___b. Click on the **File** menu, and select **New**, and then **Folder** from the menu.
   ___c. Type in your first name and press the **ENTER** key.
   ___d. Right-click your new folder and select **Sharing** from the pop-up menu.

PROCEDURE - 26

    ___e.   Click on the radio button next to **Shared As** to enable read-only sharing of this hard drive.
    ___f.   In Table 26-3, record the options listed under Access Type.
    ___g.   Click on the radio button next to **Full** to enable read, write, and execute permission for all guest users.

NOTE: Entering a password in the Full Access Password box will force any user who attempts to access your shared folder to enter the appropriate password before access is granted.

    ___h.   Click on the **OK** button, save your settings, and close the window.

5. **Set password-controlled access for a shared folder**
    ___a.   Double-click on your new folder to open it.
    ___b.   Click on the **File** menu, and select **New**, and then **Folder** from the menu.
    ___c.   Type in your last name and press the **ENTER** key.
    ___d.   Right-click your new folder and select **Sharing** from the pop-up menu.
    ___e.   Click on the radio button next to **Shared As** to enable read-only sharing of this hard drive.
    ___f.   Click on the radio button next to **Depends on Password** to enable read, write, and execute permission for all guest users.
    ___g.   Place your cursor in the box next to *Read-Only Password* and type **marcraft**, as shown in Figure 26-3.

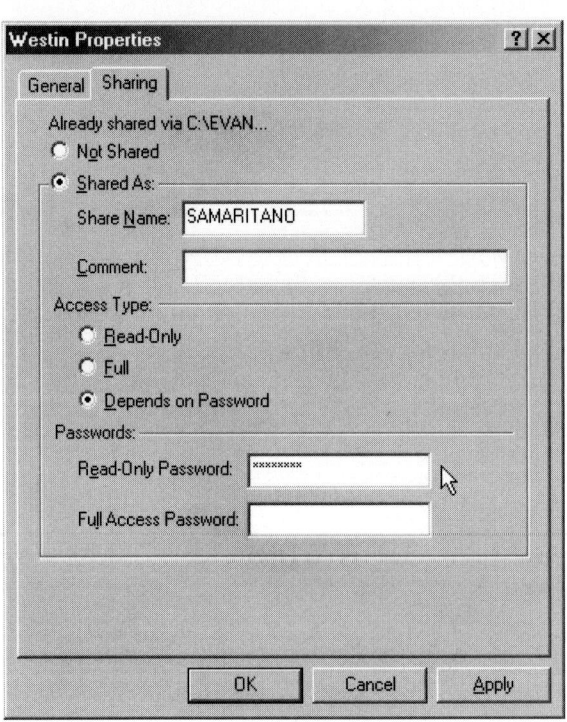

Figure 26-3: The Password is Displayed

NOTE: The password won't be displayed as regular alphabetic text for security purposes.

    ___h.   Place your cursor in the box next to *Full Access Password* and type **aplus**.
    ___i.   Click on the **Apply** button and a *Password Confirmation* window will appear.
    ___j.   Enter the Read-Only Password and the Full Access Password exactly as you did in Steps g and h above, and click on the **OK** button to continue.
    ___k.   Click on the **OK** button, save your settings, and close the window.

PROCEDURE - 26

6. **Create a text file to be shared across the network**
   ___a. Navigate the path *Start/Programs/Accessories* and select **Notepad**.
   ___b. Type your first and last name on line one and your Computer Name on the next line, and then close *Notepad*.
   ___c. When prompted to save the changes, click on the **Yes** button.
   ___d. In the *Save As* window, open the drop-down menu next to *Save in* and select the **Local Disk [C:] drive**.
   ___e. Navigate to your password-protected shared folder with your last name as shown in Figure 26-4.

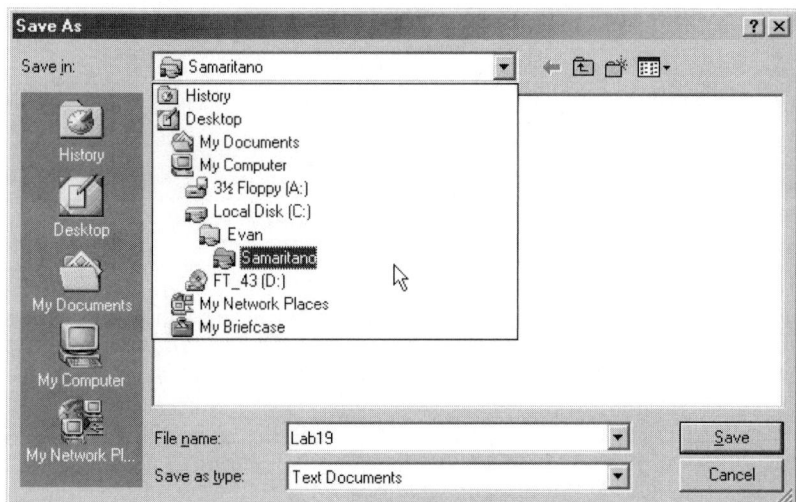

Figure 26-4: Save the File to Your Protected Folder

   ___f. Click in the *File name* box and type **Lab34**, then click on the **Save** button.

7. **Map a network drive in Windows Explorer**
   ___a. Bring Windows Explorer to the front by clicking on the button in the Taskbar.
   ___b. Click on the **Tools** menu and select **Map Network Drive**.

NOTE: The Map Network Drive window will show the next available drive letter for your system.

   ___c. Click in the *Path* box and type ***computer_name*\C**, where *computer_name* is the name of the other workstation.
   ___d. Click to select the check box next to **Reconnect at logon**, in order to re-create the mapped drive every time you restart your computer, as shown in Figure 26-5.
   ___e. Click on the **OK** button to save your settings and close the *Map Network Drive* window.
   ___f. Close the new *Windows Explorer* window that appears for the newly mapped drive.

NOTE: In the Folders windows at the left of the Windows Explorer window, a new drive icon should have appeared just above the CONTROL PANEL folder. This is the icon that you mapped the drive to and will be labeled "C on 'computer_name' (E:)". If it doesn't appear in a few seconds, press the F5 key to refresh the screen. If it still does not appear, then the drive has not been successfully mapped.

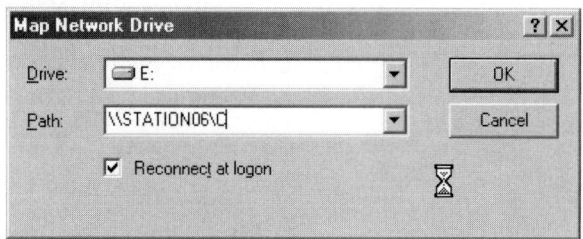

Figure 26-5: The Map Network Drive Window

PROCEDURE - 26

8. **Repeat these procedures on another network workstation**
   ___a. Change to another workstation on the network, and then boot to the Windows Me desktop.
   ___b. Repeat Step 1: Set up File and Print Sharing.
   ___c. Repeat Step 2: Share your C: drive with the local network.
   ___d. Repeat Step 3: Share folders with other users on the network.
   ___e. Repeat Step 4: Set Full access permission for a shared folder.
   ___f. Repeat Step 5: Set password-controlled access for a shared folder.

   NOTE: Use a fellow student's name, or make up a name for these new shared folders. Use the read-only and full passwords from Step 5 (makes it easier to remember).

   ___g. Repeat Step 6: Create a text file to be shared across the network.
   ___h. Repeat Step 7: Map a network drive in Windows Explorer.
   ___i. Return to your original workstation.

9. **Copy files and folders to and from another computer on the network**
   ___a. In Windows Explorer, navigate to the folder labeled *COMPUTER_NAME*.
   ___b. Click on the folder with your last name to highlight it.
   ___c. Click on the **Edit** menu and select **Copy** from the menu.
   ___d. In the *Folders* window to the left, scroll down to the drive that you just mapped to, and then click on it to highlight it.
   ___e. Click on the **Edit** menu again and select **Paste** from the menu to copy the folder to the other computer.
   ___f. In the right window, locate and double-click the folder labeled with the name of the other computer (COMPUTER_NAME) in order to highlight it.
   ___g. On the right side, right-click the text file without releasing the mouse button, and drag the file to your folder labeled COMPUTER_NAME on your computer.
   ___h. Release the mouse button and choose **Copy Here** to copy the file to the other computer.
   ___i. Scroll down to the other computer (under the mapped drive), and then click on your folder labeled with the other last name to highlight it.
   ___j. Click on the **Edit** menu and choose **Copy**.
   ___k. Scroll up to the Local Disk [C:] directory on your computer, and double-click the folder labeled **COMPUTER_NAME**.
   ___l. Click on the **Edit** menu and choose **Paste** to copy the folder to your C:*computer_name* directory.
   ___m. Close Windows Explorer.

10. **Add a Network Place in Windows Millennium Edition**
    ___a. On the desktop, double-click the **My Network Places** icon.
    ___b. In Table 26-4, record the name of the icons, including a description of each icon, that can be found in the *My Network Places* window.
    ___c. Double-click the **Add Network Place** icon.
    ___d. Click on the **Browse** button.
    ___e. Double-click your **Workgroup** icon to expand the directory.
    ___f. Scroll through the list of computers connected to your network and double-click the computer that you used in Step 7 above to map the network drive.
    ___g. Scroll down and navigate to the folder you created that is labeled with the other first name.
    ___h. Click on the **New Folder** button.

PROCEDURE - 26

___ i. Type **Shared**, and then press the **ENTER** key. The *Browse* window should now appear similar to Figure 26-6.

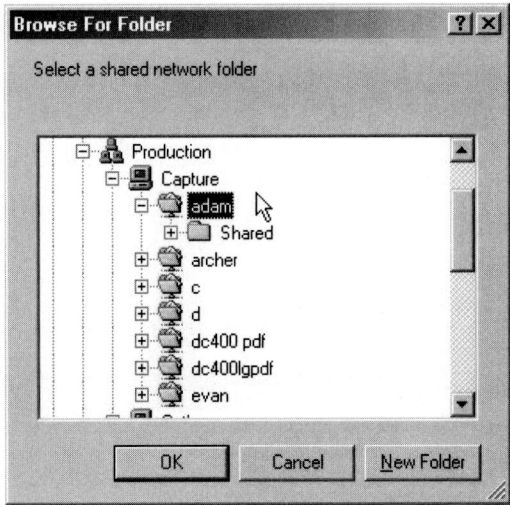

Figure 26-6: The Network Browse Window

___ j. Click on the **OK** button, and then click on the **Next** button to continue.
___ k. Type **Lab34 Sharing** and then click on the **Finish** button.
___ l. Close both windows that are now open on your desktop.
___ m. Double-click the **My Network Places** icon and list all the entries in Table 26-5.
___ n. Close all open windows and shut down the computer.

TABLES

Table 26-1

Listed Computer Name:	

Table 26-2

Change in Appearance:	

Table 26-3

"Access Type" Options:	

WINDOWS ME NETWORK OPERATIONS - 183

PROCEDURE - 26

Table 26-4

My Network Places Icons	
Icon Name	**Icon Description**

Table 26-5

Adding a Network Place	
Icon Name	**Icon Description**

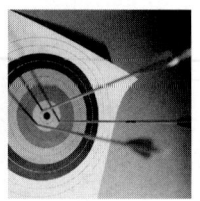

Feedback

LAB QUESTIONS

1. When you map a drive over a network, the mapped drive acts as though it is another drive that is physically in your system. True or False?

2. What two types of password-controlled access does Windows Me allow for a shared drive or folder?

3. What is a Network Place?

4. To be able to share files or folders on your computer with others in your network, you must first do what?

5. How do you know if you are mapped to another computer or directory?

LAB PROCEDURE 27

Windows Me Accessories

OBJECTIVES

1. Learn about Internet Connection Sharing.
2. Learn about Accessibility Options.
3. Learn about Regional Options.
4. Learn about Sounds and Multimedia.

Networking

RESOURCES

1. PC-compatible desktop/tower computer system — Customer-supplied desktop/tower hardware system **OR** Marcraft MC-8000 Computer Hardware Trainer **OR** suitable PC hardware trainer with Windows Millennium Edition installed
2. Sound card and speakers
3. Dial-up networking connection to an ISP
4. ISP username and password

DISCUSSION

This lab will explore some of the various system customization options in Windows 2000. Accessibility Options can be used to help people with audio and visual impairments. This feature can make sounds and show visual alerts at various keyboard events. Regional Options can change language and various country-specific settings on the computer. From Sounds and Multimedia you can change sounds for different events.

PROCEDURE

1. **Install Internet Connection Sharing**
   ___a. Boot the computer to Windows Millennium Edition.
   ___b. Navigate the path *Start/Settings/Control Panel* and double-click the **Add/Remove Programs** icon to open the *Add/Remove Programs* window.
   ___c. Click on the **Windows Setup** tab.
   ___d. Scroll down to **Communications** and click on it to highlight it.
   ___e. Click on the **Details** button.

WINDOWS ME ACCESSORIES - 185

PROCEDURE - 27

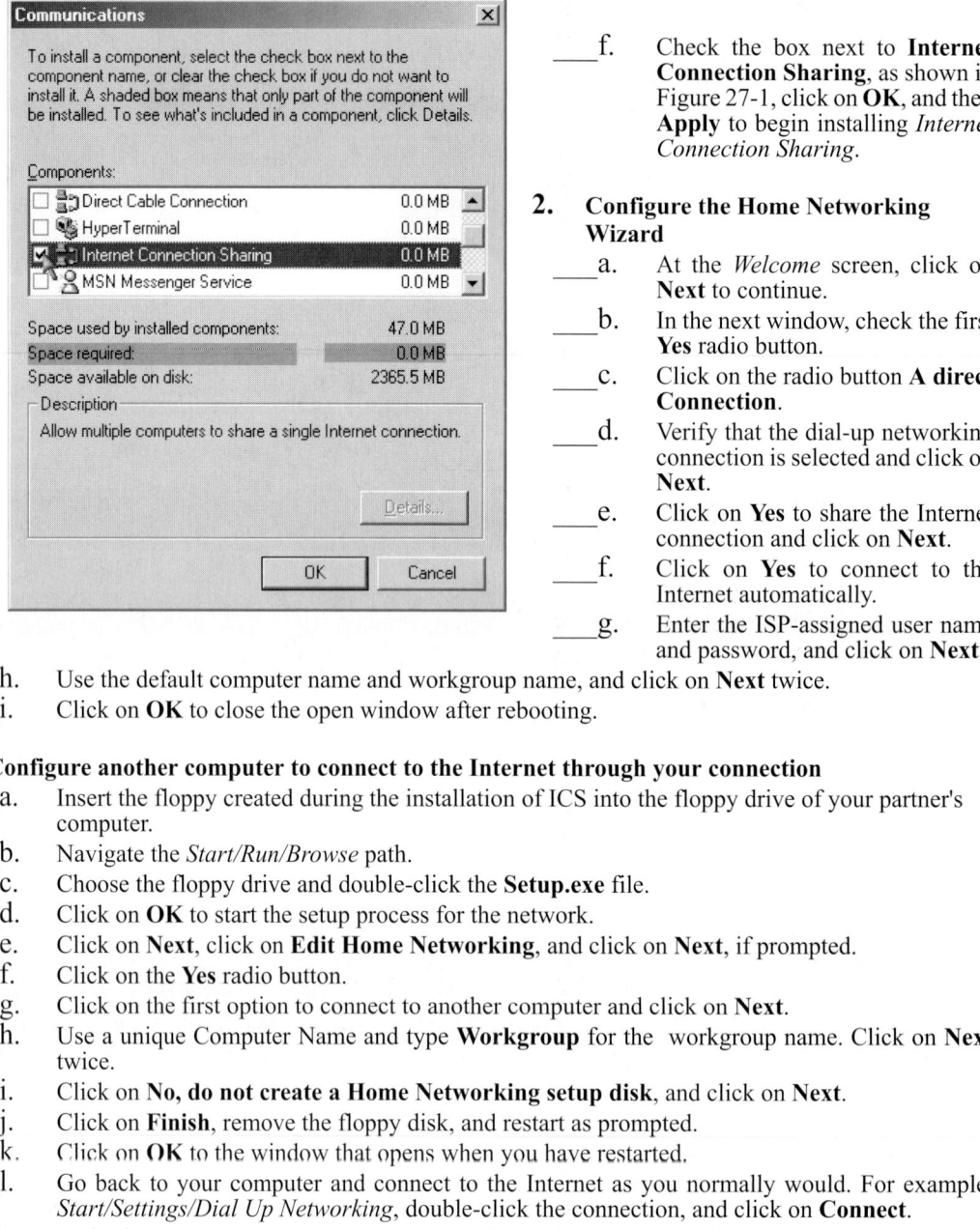

Figure 27-1:
Communications
Window with Internet
Connection Sharing
Selected

    ___f.   Check the box next to **Internet Connection Sharing**, as shown in Figure 27-1, click on **OK**, and then **Apply** to begin installing *Internet Connection Sharing*.

2. **Configure the Home Networking Wizard**
    ___a.   At the *Welcome* screen, click on **Next** to continue.
    ___b.   In the next window, check the first **Yes** radio button.
    ___c.   Click on the radio button **A direct Connection**.
    ___d.   Verify that the dial-up networking connection is selected and click on **Next**.
    ___e.   Click on **Yes** to share the Internet connection and click on **Next**.
    ___f.   Click on **Yes** to connect to the Internet automatically.
    ___g.   Enter the ISP-assigned user name and password, and click on **Next**.
    ___h.   Use the default computer name and workgroup name, and click on **Next** twice.
    ___i.   Click on **OK** to close the open window after rebooting.

3. **Configure another computer to connect to the Internet through your connection**
    ___a.   Insert the floppy created during the installation of ICS into the floppy drive of your partner's computer.
    ___b.   Navigate the *Start/Run/Browse* path.
    ___c.   Choose the floppy drive and double-click the **Setup.exe** file.
    ___d.   Click on **OK** to start the setup process for the network.
    ___e.   Click on **Next**, click on **Edit Home Networking**, and click on **Next**, if prompted.
    ___f.   Click on the **Yes** radio button.
    ___g.   Click on the first option to connect to another computer and click on **Next**.
    ___h.   Use a unique Computer Name and type **Workgroup** for the workgroup name. Click on **Next** twice.
    ___i.   Click on **No, do not create a Home Networking setup disk**, and click on **Next**.
    ___j.   Click on **Finish**, remove the floppy disk, and restart as prompted.
    ___k.   Click on **OK** to the window that opens when you have restarted.
    ___l.   Go back to your computer and connect to the Internet as you normally would. For example, *Start/Settings/Dial Up Networking*, double-click the connection, and click on **Connect**.
    ___m.   Go back to your partner's computer and open Internet Explorer to test a connection to the Internet.

4. **Uninstall Internet Connection Sharing**
    ___a.   On your computer, navigate the *Start/Settings/Control Panel/Add/Remove Programs* path.
    ___b.   Click on the **Windows Setup** tab.
    ___c.   Double-click on **Communications**.
    ___d.   Scroll down to *Internet Connection Sharing* and uncheck it.
    ___e.   Click on **OK** twice and restart the computer as prompted.

PROCEDURE - 27

5. **Accessibility Options**
   ___a. At the Windows Millennium Edition Control Panel, double-click on **Accessibility Options**.
   ___b. Double-click the **Display** tab. You will see a window similar to Figure 27-2.

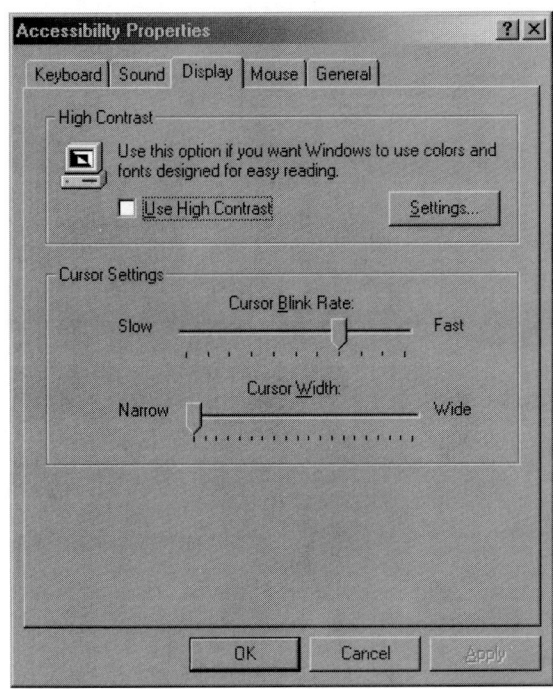

Figure 27-2: Accessibility Contrast Options

   ___c. Select **Use High Contrast**. Click on **Apply**.
   ___d. Record your observations in Table 27-1.
   ___e. Uncheck high contrast and click on **Apply** to restore to the original state. You may need to resize the Taskbar by dragging the edge back down to its original position.
   ___f. In the *Accessibility Properties* window click on the **Mouse** tab.
   ___g. Select **Use MouseKeys**, then click on **Apply**.
   ___h. Look at the keyboard and verify that the Num Lock light is on. If it is not, press the **NUM LOCK** key.
   ___i. There are arrow keys on the numeric keypad on the right-hand side of the keyboard. Up is 8, down is 2, left is 4, and right is 6. Press up and record your observations in Table 27-2.
   ___j. Uncheck *Use MouseKeys* and click on **Apply** to restore the option back to its original state.
   ___k. Click on **OK** to exit *Accessibility Options*.

6. **Regional Options**
   ___a. From the Windows Millennium Edition Control Panel double-click on **Regional Options**.
   ___b. Your window should be similar to Figure 27-3.

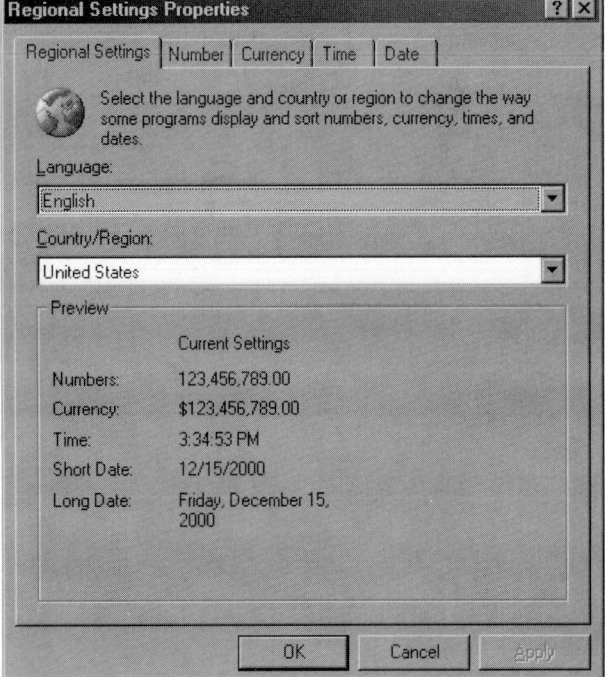

Figure 27-3: Regional Options

WINDOWS ME ACCESSORIES - 187

PROCEDURE - 27

    ___c.   Under the *Regional Settings* tab record your locale in Table 27-3.
    ___d.   Under the *Number* tab record the measurement system in Table 27-3.
    ___e.   Under the *Currency* tab record the currency symbol in Table 27-3.
    ___f.   Under the *Time* tab record the time style in Table 27-3.
    ___g.   Under the *Date* tab record the short date style in Table 27-3.
    ___h.   Click on **OK** to exit the *Regional Options*.

7.   **Sounds and Multimedia**
    ___a.   From the Windows Millennium Edition Control Panel double-click on **Sounds and Multimedia**.
    ___b.   You will see a window similar to Figure 27-4. Click on the **Critical Stop** event.

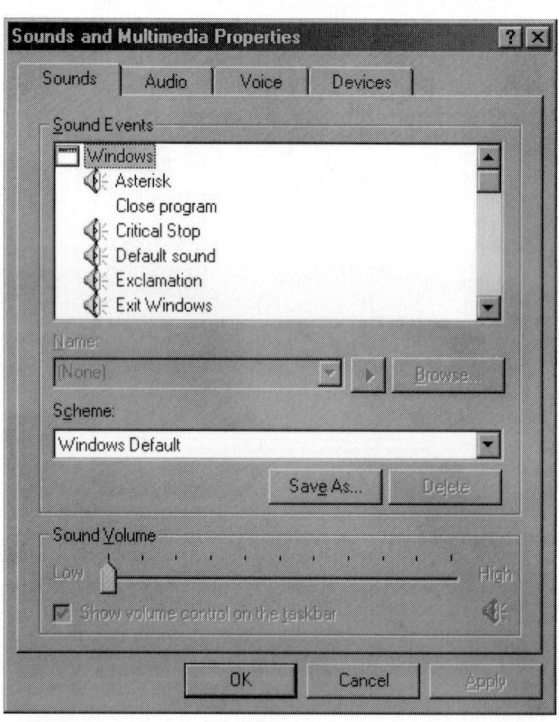

Figure 27-4: Sound and Multimedia Properties

    ___c.   Record the "Name:" in Table 27-4. This is the name of the sound file that Windows plays when the corresponding event has occurred.
    ___d.   If you have a sound card and speakers, click on the **Play** button and you will hear the sound.
    ___e.   Click on the **Audio** tab. Click on the **Preferred device** menu for sound playback and select your sound card.
    ___f.   Enter this information in Table 27-5.
    ___g.   Click on the **Advanced** tab under sound playback.
    ___h.   Record the speaker setup in Table 27-6.
    ___i.   Click on **OK** to close the *Advanced* window.
    ___j.   Click on the **Devices** tab.
    ___k.   Record the number of devices listed under Video Compression Codecs in Table 27-7.
    ___l.   Click on **OK** and close the *Sound and Multimedia Properties* window.

PROCEDURE - 27

TABLES

Table 27-1

Observations of High Contrast:	

Table 27-2

Observations of Pressing the UP (8) Key:	

Table 27-3

Locale:	
Measurement System:	
Currency Symbol:	
Time Style:	
Short Date Style:	

Table 27-4

"Critical Stop" Event Name:	

Table 27-5

Preferred Sound Device:	

Table 27-6

Speaker Setup:	

PROCEDURE - 27

Table 27-7

Number of Video Compression Devices:	

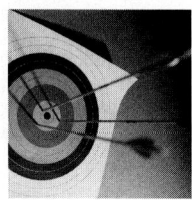

Feedback

LAB QUESTIONS

1. What features of accessibility were demonstrated in this lab?
2. Where would you go to change the language of the system?
3. The Regional Options/Date feature does what?
4. What is one way to change the hardware settings of an audio card in Windows Millennium Edition?

LAB PROCEDURE 28

Windows 2000 TCP/IP

OBJECTIVES

1. Configure the Command Prompt window to improve visibility.
2. Use the IPCONFIG utility to examine your current TCP/IP configuration.
3. Use the ARP utility to map IP addresses to physical MAC addresses.
4. Use the NETSTAT utility to examine all current network connections.
5. Use the NBTSTAT utility to resolve Windows computer names on the network.
6. Use the NET VIEW utility to list all shared devices on a network node.
7. Use the TRACERT utility to test data packet routing and timing.
8. Use the PING utility to test other network nodes.

Networking

RESOURCES

1. PC-compatible desktop/tower computer system — Customer-supplied desktop/tower hardware system **OR** Marcraft MC-8000 Computer Hardware Trainer **OR** suitable PC hardware trainer with 128 MB RAM
2. Windows 2000 operating system (installed)
3. Network Interface Card (installed)
4. Internet access through a network connection or modem

DISCUSSION

Windows provides several networking tools, called TCP/IP utilities, which can assist you in troubleshooting networking problems and determining how your network is performing. These tools are also present in Windows 2000. The functionality of the utilities will change depending on whether you are using a network server, a direct network connection via a modem, or a network workstation. Because of this variability, if a step does not function as described below, move on to the next step.

PROCEDURE - 28

Networking

PROCEDURE

As before, you will access these tools through the *Command Prompt* window. In this lab procedure you will modify the *MS-DOS Command Prompt* window to increase the visibility of the displayed information. When completed, you will use the IPCONFIG /all command to list all current network parameters. The ARP command will map your network host's IP address to a NIC's MAC address. You will use the NETSTAT command to identify your current network connections, and the NBTSTAT command to resolve the Windows computer names of the other nodes you are connected to on the network. The NET VIEW command will list the nodes on your LAN and the shared devices on one of these nodes. You will use the TRACERT command to test data packet routing to a remote host, and to examine the time required for it to travel between points. Finally, you will use the PING command to test for responsiveness from a network node.

NOTE: The information actually displayed when running these utilities will vary greatly depending on your particular network configuration. The examples provided below will not match your results.

1. **Modify the Command Prompt window to increase visibility**
    ___ a. Boot the computer into Windows 2000.
    ___ b. Navigate the path *Start/Programs/Accessories/Command Prompt* to open the *MS-DOS Command Prompt* window.
    ___ c. Right-click the Command Prompt title bar and select **Properties** from the pop-up contextual menu.
    ___ d. Click on the **Colors** tab.
    ___ e. Click on the white color selector box, as seen in Figure 28-1, to change the background to white.
    ___ f. Click on the **Screen Text** radio button to select it.
    ___ g. Click on the black color selector box to change the text color to black.
    ___ h. Click on the **OK** button to close the *Properties* window.
    ___ i. Click on the **OK** button to change the window properties for the current window only.

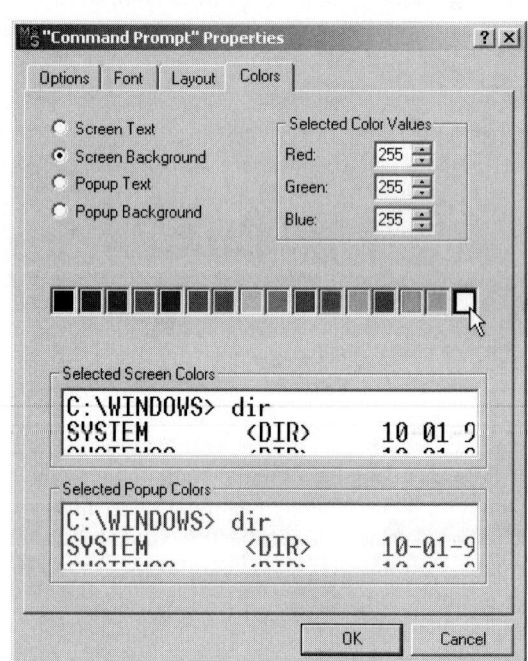

Figure 28-1: Command Prompt Properties Window

192 - LAB GROUP 3

PROCEDURE - 28

IPCONFIG

The IPCONFIG utility allows you to see your current IP address and other useful network configuration information. The command "IPCONFIG /all" will display the complete network information for the host computer you are using. As shown in Figure 28-2, this utility will identify the current network configuration, including the IP address and physical MAC address. If you are using DHCP to provide your IP address, you can use the "/release" and "/renew" switches to force the DHCP server to withdraw the current IP address lease, or drop the current lease and grab a new one.

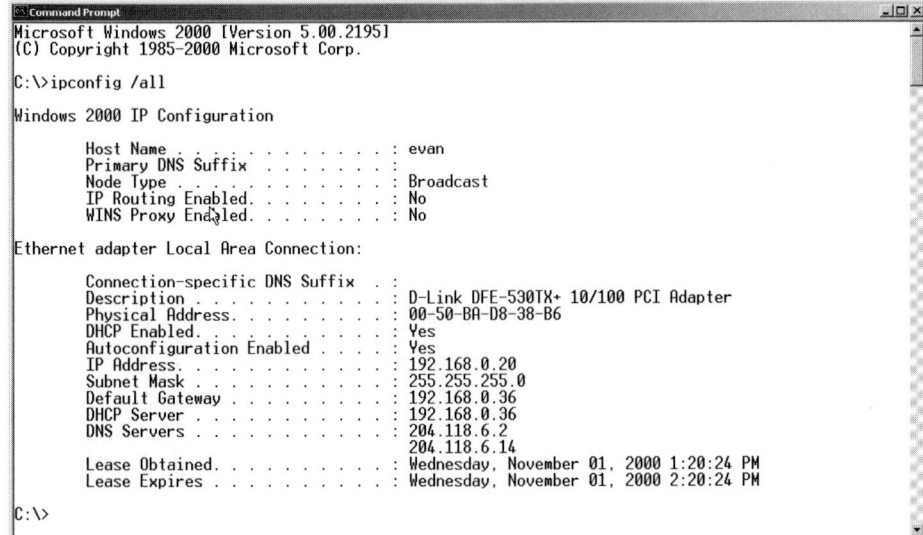

Figure 28-2: IPCONFIG /all

NOTE: IPCONFIG /all is used to display the current network configuration.

1. **Run IPCONFIG to display your network configuration**
    ___ a. At the MS-DOS command prompt, type **ipconfig ?** and press the **ENTER** key. Review the usage notes for IPCONFIG.
    ___ b. At the command prompt, type **ipconfig /all** and press the **ENTER** key.
    ___ c. Record the listed information for your client workstation in Table 28-1.

ARP

The Address Resolution Protocol (ARP) utility can be used to identify addressing information by examining the contents of the ARP caches on either the client or the server. It is primarily used to map IP addresses to physical MAC addresses.

1. **Run ARP to resolve your client and current network connections**
    ___ a. At the command prompt, type **arp** and press the **ENTER** key. Review the usage notes for ARP.

WINDOWS 2000 TCP/IP - 193

PROCEDURE - 28

____b. At the command prompt, type **arp -a** and press the **ENTER** key. This will show information similar to Figure 28-3.

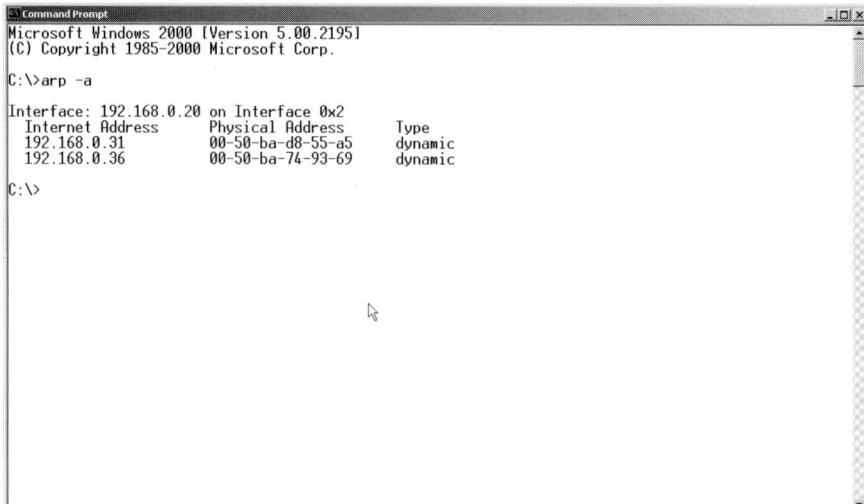

Figure 28-3: arp - a Command Prompt Window

NOTE: ARP is used to map IP addresses and physical MAC addresses.

____c. Record the IP address of your host computer, as shown in the Interface line, in Table 28-2.
____d. Record the IP and MAC addresses in Table 28-3.

NETSTAT

The command "netstat -e" displays the number of data packets transmitted and received, and the number of errors generated, as shown in Figure 28-4. The command "netstat -r" displays a list of all of the current connections and shows which are active.

NOTE: NETSTAT is used to display statistics about the current session.

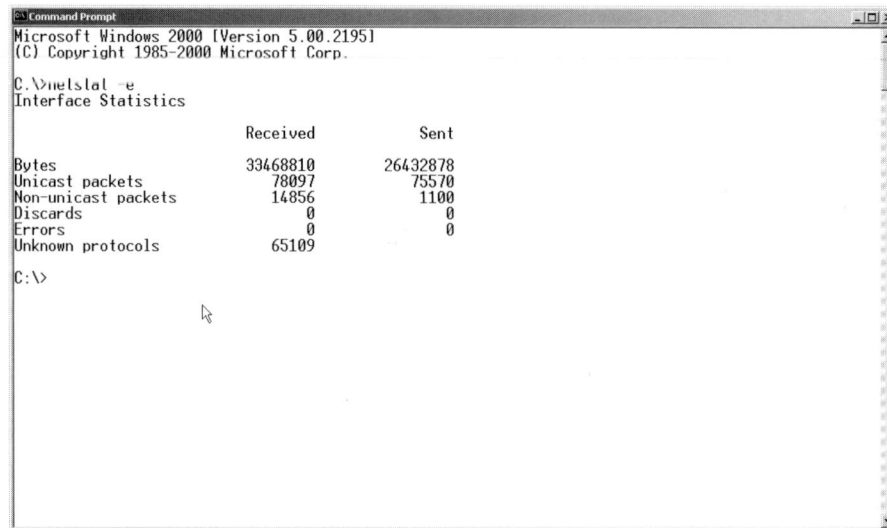

Figure 28-4: netstat - e Command Prompt Window

PROCEDURE - 28

1. **Run NETSTAT to examine the current network connection**
   ___ a. At the command prompt, type **netstat ?** and press the **ENTER** key. Review the usage notes for NETSTAT.
   ___ b. At the command prompt, type **netstat -e** and press the **ENTER** key to display packet statistics.
   ___ c. At the command prompt, type **netstat -r** and press the **ENTER** key. This will show your network connection information similar to Figure 28-5.

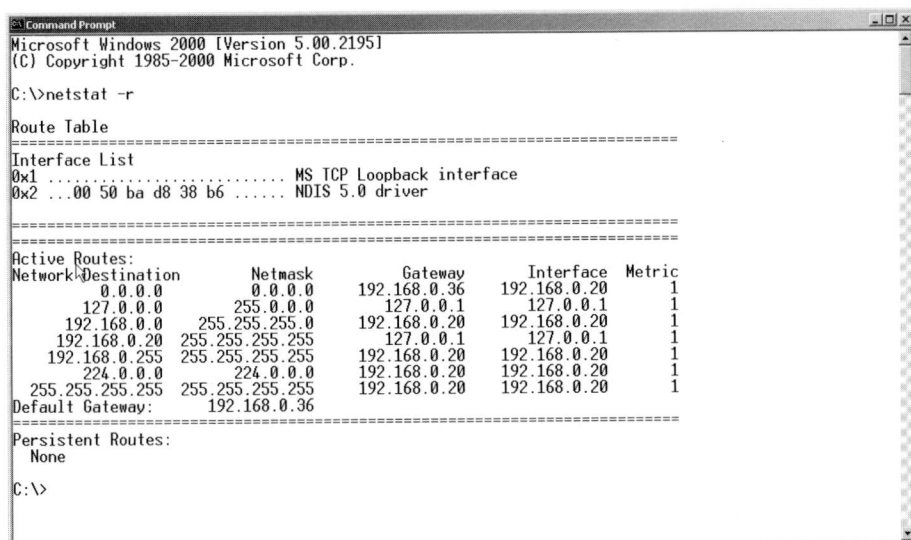

Figure 28-5: netstat -r Command Prompt Window

NBTSTAT

The NBTSTAT (NetBIOS over TCP STATistics) utility shows the Windows NetBIOS names for the connected computers, and lists their IP addresses and the status of the connection. This allows you to check connections made with the Windows Network Neighborhood tool. The "nbtstat -c" command displays the NetBIOS names of the hosts you are connected to, and the IP addresses they map to.

1. **Run NBTSTAT to resolve your client's current network connections**
   ___ a At the command prompt, type **nbtstat** and press the **ENTER** key. Review the usage notes for NBTSTAT.
   ___ b. At the command prompt, type **nbtstat -c** and press the **ENTER** key. This will show you remote host identification information similar to Figure 28-6.

WINDOWS 2000 TCP/IP - 195

PROCEDURE - 28

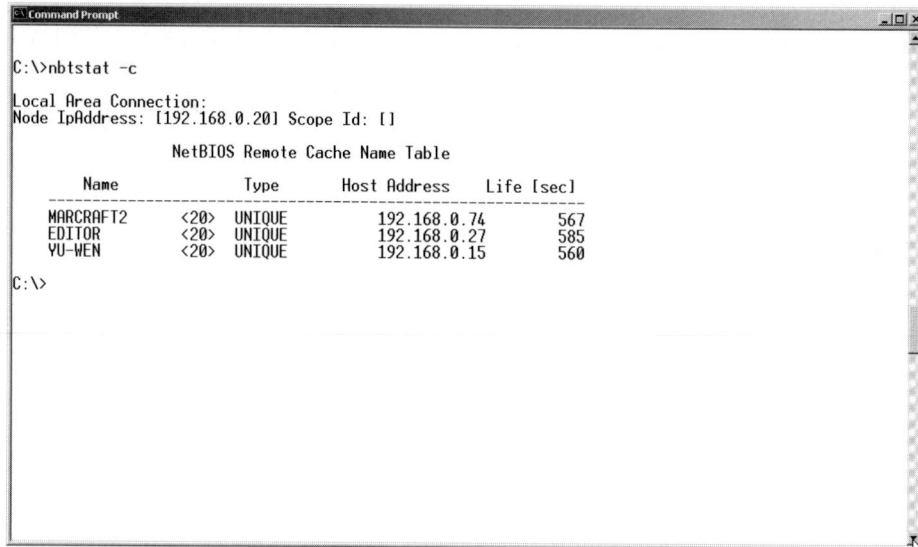

Figure 28-6: nbtstat -c Command Prompt Window

NET VIEW

The NET VIEW command lists all of the computers currently connected to your Local Area Network (LAN). It can also display all of the shared devices associated with a particular network host. The format for displaying shared devices is "net view *your server name*", where the server name is the actual NetBIOS name of the workstation or server you are connected to. For example, "net view \\accounting" will resolve a list of all of the shared devices supported by the server named "accounting".

1. **Run NET VIEW to list the nodes on the LAN and display the shared devices on a node**
   ___ a. At the command prompt, type **net view ?** and press the **ENTER** key. Review the usage notes for NET VIEW.
   ___ b. At the command prompt, type **net view** and press the **ENTER** key to list all of the nodes connected to your LAN. Your results should be similar to Figure 28-7.

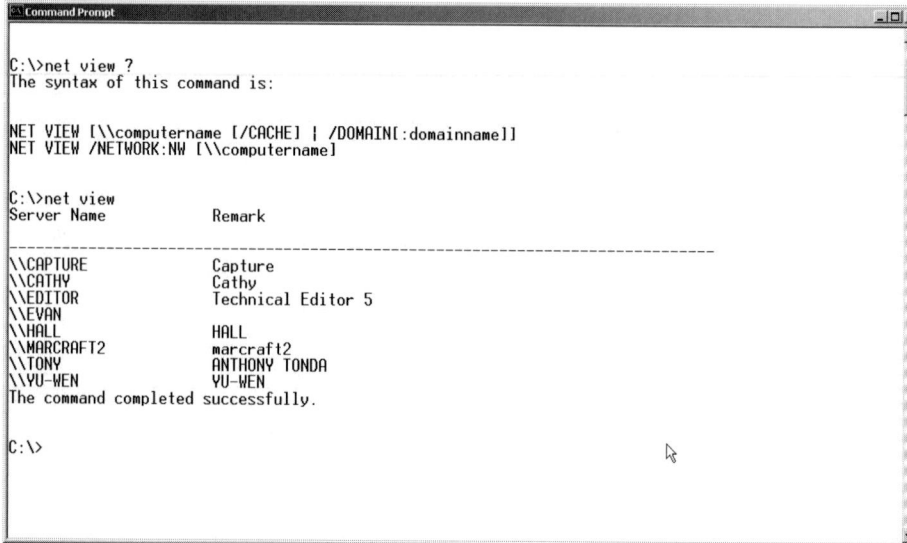

Figure 28-7: net view ? Command Prompt Window

196 - LAB GROUP 3

PROCEDURE - 28

____ c. Record the host names listed by NET VIEW in Table 28-4.
____ d. At the command prompt, type **net view** *host name* and press the **ENTER** key. In this command, you should replace *host name* with the NetBIOS name of one of the hosts listed in Table 28-4. This will show the shared devices on a particular host computer, as seen in the example shown in Figure 28-8.

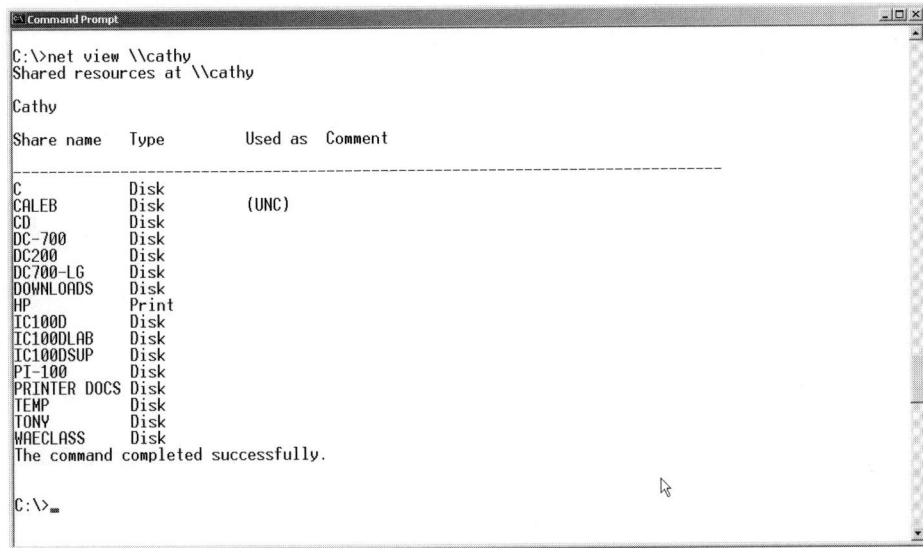

Figure 28-8: NET VIEW Command Prompt Window

TRACERT

The command "tracert *hostname*", where *hostname* is the IP address or DNS name of a host, will trace the path of a network connection to that remote host. This command will display the number of hops and the IP addresses of the routers that a data packet has traveled through in order to reach the remote host. It will also measure the time (in milliseconds) it takes for the data packet to travel from point to point on this route.

If you are having trouble connecting to a specific destination, the question then becomes: Is the problem at the destination, or at one of the routers along the way? TRACERT will detect whether a particular router along the current path is not functioning. If a router does not respond, the response time values are marked with an asterisk [*], indicating that the data packet timed out. TRACERT will also indicate if a router is slow. You can determine this by looking at the time it takes for a packet to get through a particular router. As you can see in Figure 28-9, the time delay is calculated three times for each router in the chain. The median of the three values should be used to evaluate the time it took to get the data packet through the router.

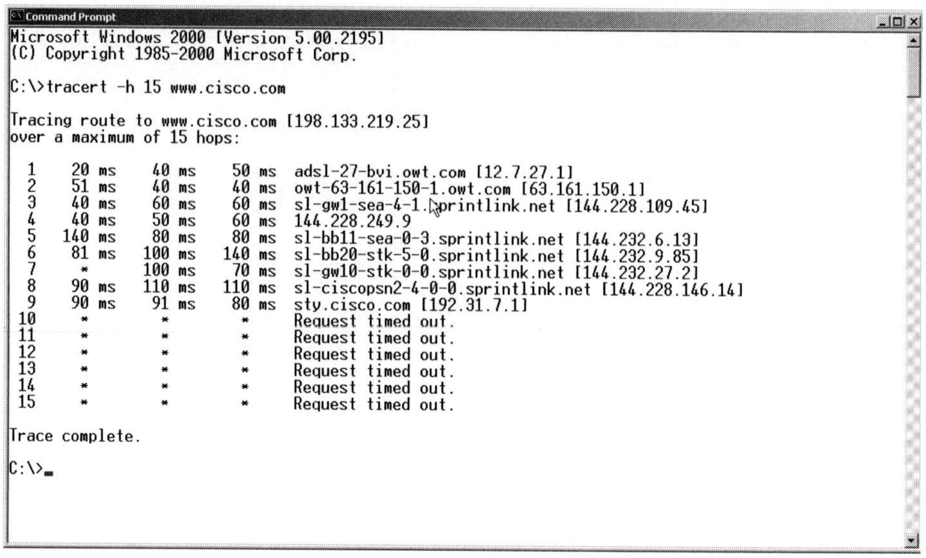

PROCEDURE - 28

Figure 28-9: TRACERT Command Prompt Window

```
Command Prompt
Microsoft Windows 2000 [Version 5.00.2195]
(C) Copyright 1985-2000 Microsoft Corp.

C:\>tracert -h 15 www.cisco.com

Tracing route to www.cisco.com [198.133.219.25]
over a maximum of 15 hops:

  1    20 ms    40 ms    50 ms  adsl-27-bvi.owt.com [12.7.27.1]
  2    51 ms    40 ms    40 ms  owt-63-161-150-1.owt.com [63.161.150.1]
  3    40 ms    60 ms    60 ms  sl-gw1-sea-4-1.sprintlink.net [144.228.109.45]
  4    40 ms    50 ms    60 ms  144.228.249.9
  5   140 ms    80 ms    80 ms  sl-bb11-sea-0-3.sprintlink.net [144.232.6.13]
  6    81 ms   100 ms   140 ms  sl-bb20-stk-5-0.sprintlink.net [144.232.9.85]
  7     *      100 ms    70 ms  sl-gw10-stk-0-0.sprintlink.net [144.232.27.2]
  8    90 ms   110 ms   110 ms  sl-ciscopsn2-4-0-0.sprintlink.net [144.228.146.14]
  9    90 ms    91 ms    80 ms  sty.cisco.com [192.31.7.1]
 10     *        *        *     Request timed out.
 11     *        *        *     Request timed out.
 12     *        *        *     Request timed out.
 13     *        *        *     Request timed out.
 14     *        *        *     Request timed out.
 15     *        *        *     Request timed out.

Trace complete.

C:\>_
```

1. **Run TRACERT to check a remote network connection**
   - a. At the command prompt, type **tracert** and press the **ENTER** key. Review the usage notes for TRACERT.
   - b. At the command prompt, type **tracert www.mic-inc.com** and press the **ENTER** key to trace the route to the Marcraft server.
   - c. Record the IP address associated with www.mic-inc.com in Table 28-5.

PING

The PING command is one of the key tools for troubleshooting TCP/IP. PING sends a data packet to a specified IP address and returns it to your machine. If the IP address is not currently active, you will receive a message stating that the transaction has timed out. If you are having trouble connecting to a network, PING can be used to test the functionality of TCP/IP on your own machine. If you are able to PING the loopback address (127.0.0.1) and your own network IP address, you can be fairly sure that TCP/IP on your host computer is working properly. The next step is to test the IP address for your network server and/or your default gateway. As a final test you can PING the IP address of a remote host server.

NOTE: Can't remember your IP address, or the IP address of the local server? Run IPCONFIG to get your IP address and the address of the host DNS server and gateway, or you can look up the data in Table 28-1.

1. **Run PING to check the status of a TCP/IP connection**
   - a. At the command prompt, type **ping** and press the **ENTER** key. Review the usage notes for PING.
   - b. At the command prompt, type **ping 127.0.0.1** and press the **ENTER** key to test TCP/IP on your local host computer.

PROCEDURE - 28

___ c. At the command prompt, type **ping xxx.xxx.xxx.xxx**, where *xxx.xxx.xxx.xxx* is the host IP address listed in Table 28-1. Now press the **ENTER** key to test your local TCP/IP connection. Your screen should appear similar to Figure 28-10.

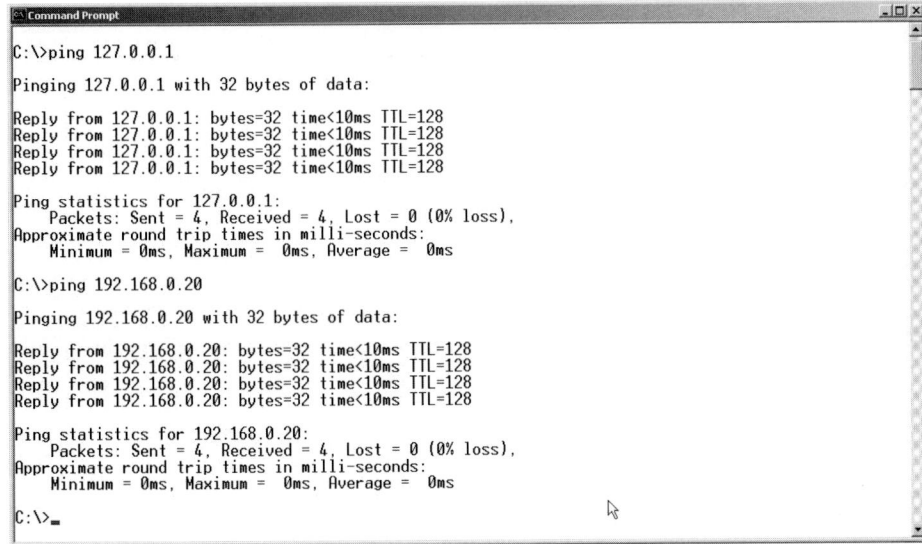

Figure 28-10: PING Command Prompt Window

___ d. At the command prompt, type **ping xxx.xxx.xxx.xxx**, where *xxx.xxx.xxx.xxx* is the IP address listed in Table 28-5. Press the **ENTER** key to test your connection to the remote server at Marcraft. You should see a screen similar to Figure 28-11.

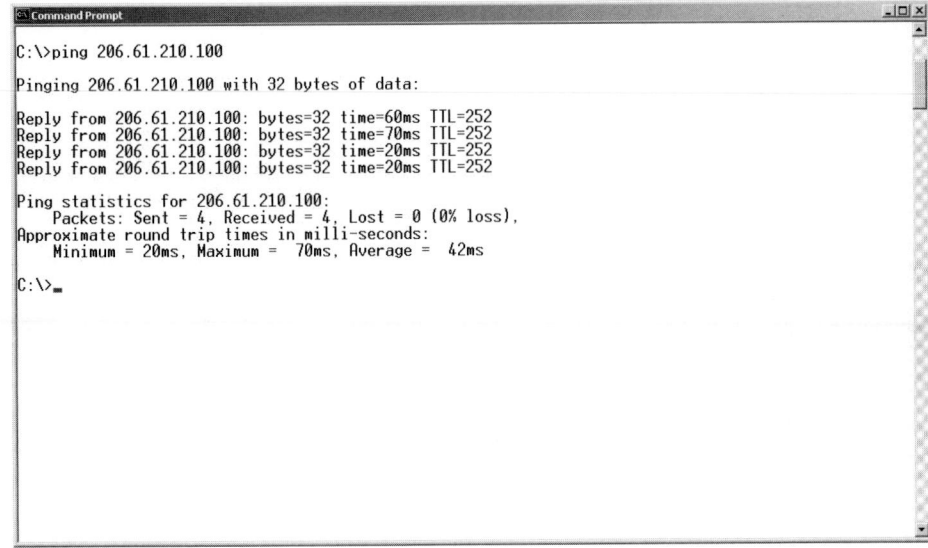

Figure 28-11: PINGing Command Prompt Window

___ e. Close all open windows, and shut down the computer.

WINDOWS 2000 TCP/IP - 199

PROCEDURE - 28

TABLES

Table 28-1

Host Name:	
Primary DNS Suffix:	
Node Type:	
IP Routing Enabled:	
WINS Proxy Enabled:	
Description:	
Physical Address:	
DHCP Enabled:	
Autoconfiguration Enabled:	
IP Address:	
Subnet Mask:	
Default Gateway:	
DHCP Server:	
DNS Servers:	
Lease Obtained:	
Lease Expires:	

Table 28-2

Host Computer Interface IP Address:	

PROCEDURE - 28

Table 28-3

IP and MAC Addresses		
IP Address	Physical MAC Address	Type

Table 28-4

Net View Host Names:	

Table 28-5

IP Address for www.mic-inc.com:	

PROCEDURE - 28

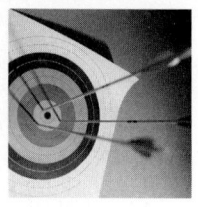

Feedback

LAB QUESTIONS

1. What command will display the connection path from your terminal to a remote Internet address?

2. Where do you enter the command to run a TCP/IP utility program?

3. What TCP/IP utility can be used to locate a slow router on a Wide Area Network such as the Internet?

4. Which command will resolve the IP and physical MAC addresses of the nodes connected to your network?

5. What TCP/IP utility can be used to identify the IP address of a site when given a DNS name?

LAB PROCEDURE 29

Windows 2000 Networking

OBJECTIVES

1. Share a folder and test access.
2. Share a printer and test printing.
3. Map a drive to a shared resource.
4. Add a Network Place.

Networking

RESOURCES

1. Two PC-compatible desktop/tower computer systems — Customer-supplied desktop/tower hardware systems **OR** Marcraft MC-8000 Computer Hardware Trainers **OR** suitable PC hardware trainers (with Windows 2000 installed) connected through a TCP/IP LAN
2. Internet Access for the "Add Network Place" section

DISCUSSION

This lab will perform some basic operations with peer-to-peer networks in Windows 2000. You will learn how to share folders, and check the ability of another user to connect and view the contents of that folder. Through "My Network Places" you can view contents of the LAN and create shortcuts to FTP sites. You will learn how to add a Network Place such as a File Transfer Protocol site, and how to map a drive to a folder that is shared on another computer in the Local Area Network (LAN).

PROCEDURE

1. **Share a folder**
    ___ a. On your local machine (Machine 1) boot to the Windows 2000 desktop.
    ___ b. Double-click on **My Computer**.
    ___ c. Double-click on **Local Disk (C:)**.
    ___ d. Create a new folder in the C: drive and name it **YOURNAME SHARED**.
    ___ e. Double-click the **YOURNAME SHARED** folder.
    ___ f. Create a text document by clicking on **File/New/Text Document** as in Figure 29-1.

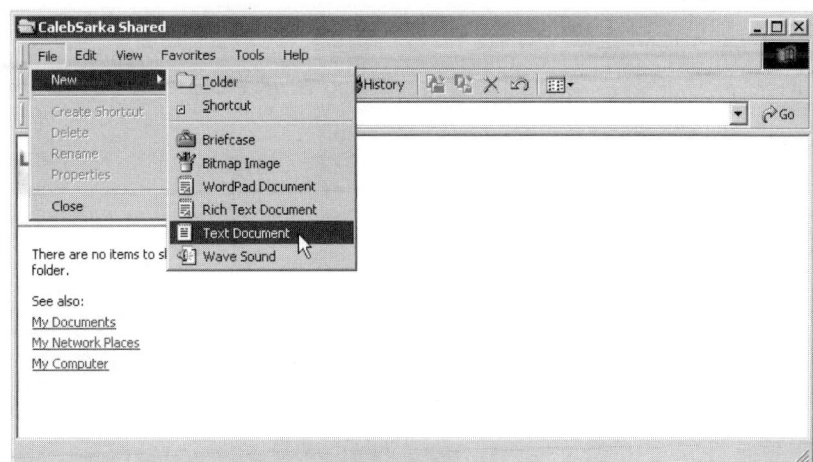

Figure 29-1: Create a Text Document

WINDOWS 2000 NETWORKING - 203

PROCEDURE - 29

    g. Use the default *New Text Document* by pressing the **ENTER** key.
    h. Click on the **Back** button in the top left-hand corner of the window.
    i. Right-click the **YOURNAME SHARED** folder and choose **Sharing**.
    j. Select the **Share this folder** radio button.
    k. Click on the **Permissions** button.
    l. A window similar to Figure 29-2 will open. The default "Everyone" group will be listed in the top pane of the window. From this pane you can add users and change their individual permissions in the bottom pane.
    m. Click on **OK** twice. The folder is now shared.

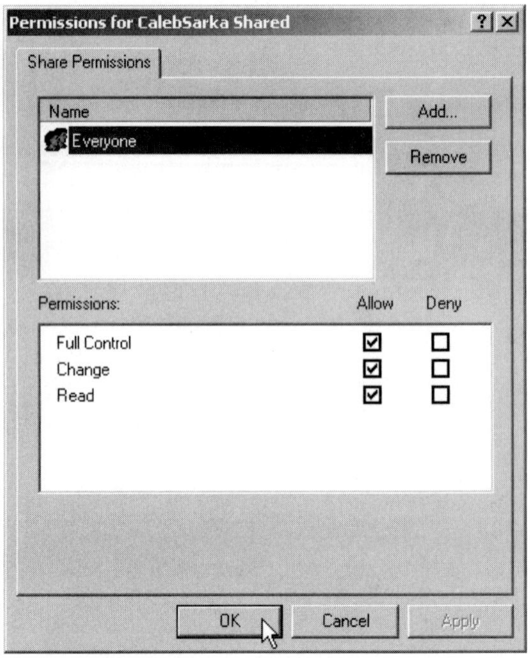

2. **Test access**
    a. On your partner's machine (Machine 2) boot to the Windows 2000 desktop.
    b. Double-click the **My Network Places** icon.
    c. Double-click on **Computers Near Me**. This displays the computers in your local workgroup.
    d. Look for the icon of (Machine 1) and double-click on it.
    e. You should see the folder that was just created and shared. Double-click on it and record its content in Table 29-1.
    f. You have just accessed a shared recourse over the LAN. Close all windows.

Figure 29-2: Sharing Permissions

3. **Share a printer**
    a. From your local computer (Machine 1) navigate the path *Start/Settings/Printers*.
    b. Right-click the printer that you installed earlier and choose **Sharing**.
    c. Click on the **Shared as** radio button as in Figure 29-3.
    d. Use the default name for the share, and then click on the **Additional Drivers** button.
    e. From this window you can select drivers for machines that may not have Windows 2000, and need to access the printer over a LAN. Click on **Cancel**.
    f. Click on **OK** to close the printer's *Properties* window.

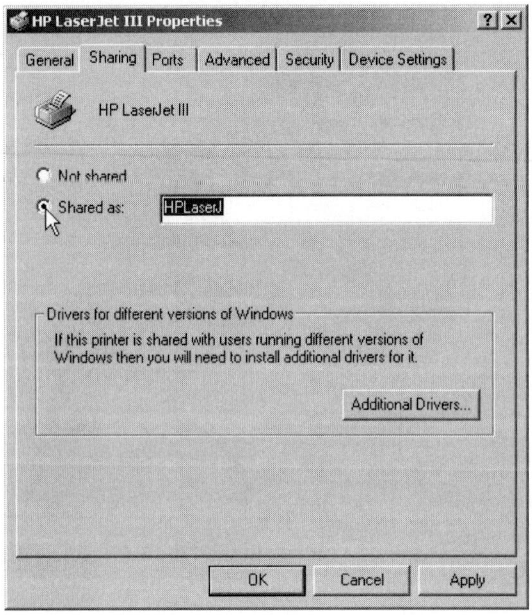

4. **Test printer access**
    a. From your partner's desktop (Machine 2) click on the **My Network Places** icon.
    b. Double-click on **Computers Near Me**.
    c. Look for the icon of (Machine 1) and double-click on it.
    d. Right-click the printer that you have just shared and select **Connect**.

Figure 29-3: Sharing a Printer

PROCEDURE - 29

___e. After a connection window similar to Figure 29-4 has appeared and closed, close all windows.

Figure 29-4: Connecting to a Printer

___f. Double-click the **My Computer** icon.
___g. Double-click the **Control Panel** icon.
___h. Double-click on **Printers**.
___i. Double-click the printer that you had connected to previously.
___j. From the Printer select **Properties**.
___k. Click on the **Print Test Page** button. The test page should now print from the printer attached to (Machine 1).
___l. Click on **OK** to close the dialog window that opens, and then click on **OK** to close the printer's *Properties* window.
___m. Close all windows.

5. **Map a drive to a shared resource**
   ___a. From your partner's desktop (Machine 2) click on the **My Network Places** icon.
   ___b. Double-click on **Computers Near Me**.
   ___c. Look for the icon of (Machine 1) and double-click on it.
   ___d. Look for the folder that was created and shared earlier (YOURNAME SHARED), and right-click on it, then select **Map Network Drive**. The window should look similar to Figure 29-5.

Figure 29-5: Map Network Drive

___e. For the *Drive:* field select the first available letter, E: for example. Record the drive letter selected in Table 29-2.
___f. Verify that the *Reconnect at logon* field is selected. This will map the drive to the shared resource every time that you log on to the LAN. Click on **Finish**.
___g. Close all windows. You have now mapped a drive to a shared resource.
___h. Verify the drive connection by double-clicking on **My Computer**. You will see the name of the folder you have just connected to, followed by the drive letter selected.
___i. Close all windows.

PROCEDURE - 29

6. **Add Network Place**
   ___ a. From the desktop of your computer double-click the **My Network Places** icon.
   ___ b. Double-click on **Add Network Place**.
   ___ c. The Add Network Place Wizard, similar to Figure 29-6, will appear. Click on the *some examples* hyperlink.

Figure 29-6: The Add Network Place Wizard

   ___ d. Read the three things that appear in the Examples list and record them in Table 29-3.
   ___ e. Type **ftp://ftp.microsoft.com** in the text box, and then click on **Next**.
   ___ f. Verify that the *Log on anonymously* field is checked. Most FTP sites allow an anonymous logon to view public files. Click on **Next**.
   ___ g. Enter "*Your Name's* connection to Microsoft's FTP server" in the text box and click on **Finish**.
   ___ h. The window should automatically open, similar to Figure 29-7. Record the number of items in Table 29-4.

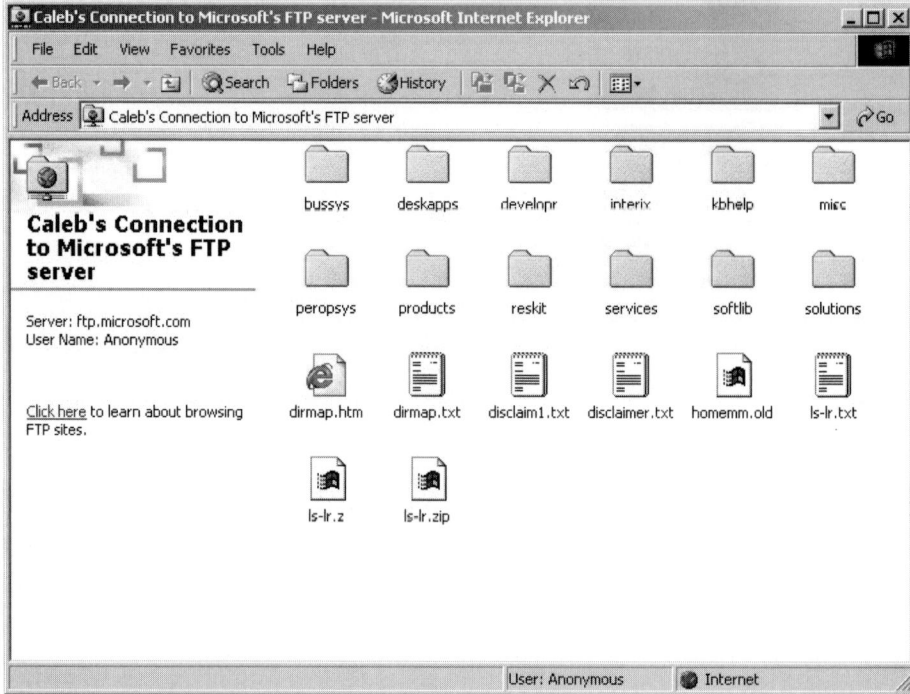

Figure 29-7: Connecting to the Microsoft FTP Server

206 - LAB GROUP 3

PROCEDURE - 29

___ i. Close the window and you should see My Network Places still open. Record any new items in Table 29-5.
___ j. Close all open windows and shut down the computer.

TABLES

Table 29-1

Content of Shared Folder:	

Table 29-2

Drive Letter Selected:	

Table 29-3

Network Place Examples:	

Table 29-4

Number of Items:	

Table 29-5

My Network Places - New Items:	

PROCEDURE - 29

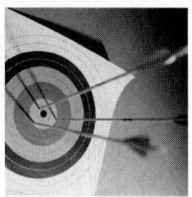

Feedback

LAB QUESTIONS

1. What is the default group added to a newly shared folder?
2. What can My Network Places be used for?
3. What does Computers Near Me display?
4. What are additional printer drivers used for?
5. Why is anonymous logon used?

LAB PROCEDURE 30

Windows XP TCP/IP Setup

OBJECTIVES

1. Install the TCP/IP protocol.
2. Administer clients, protocols, and services.
3. Set print and file sharing.
4. Administer bindings for the client.

Networking

RESOURCES

1. PC-compatible desktop/tower computer system — Customer-supplied desktop/tower hardware system **OR** Marcraft MC-8000 Computer Hardware Trainer **OR** suitable PC hardware trainer with 128 MB RAM, Windows XP operating system, and NIC installed
2. Internet access through a network connection or modem.
3. Internet Explorer 6.0
4. Windows XP CD-ROM

DISCUSSION

TCP/IP (Transmission Control Protocol/Internet Protocol) is used in many types of local area networks (LANs), but it is also used as the standard communications protocol for the Internet. TCP/IP is the most popular network protocol in use, primarily due to the fact that, unlike other network protocols (IPX/SPX, AppleTalk, etc.) no single vendor owns the rights to it. TCP/IP was originally created by the U.S. Department of Defense Advance Research Projects Agency (DARPA) to provide resilient service on networks that include a wide variety of computer types. Due to its beginnings as a protocol for military computer networks, TCP/IP is very resistant to hacking. Therefore, it is considered to be the most secure of all the network protocols. TCP/IP uses a system that assigns a unique number to every node on the network. This number is known as the IP address. All devices on a TCP/IP network need a unique IP address in order to function. An IP address is a set of four numbers that range in value between 0 and 255, and each number is separated by a period. It can be very time-consuming to manually assign IP addresses and subnet masks to every computer and device on the network. For this reason, many network administrators assign these IP addresses by automatic Dynamic Host Configuration Protocol (DHCP) addressing. DHCP enables the host server to automatically assign IP addresses and subnet masks every time a client computer begins a network session.

PROCEDURE - 30

Networking

PROCEDURE

1. **Open the TCP/IP Properties window**
   ___a. Turn on the computer.
   ___b. Right-click on the **My Network Places** icon on the desktop, then select **Properties** from the pop-up menu to open the *Network Connections* window.
   ___c. Right-click on the **Local Area Connection** icon and select **Properties** from the drop-down menu to open the *Local Area Connection Properties* window. It should appear similar to Figure 30-1.
   ___d. Click on the **Install** button to open the **Select Network Component Type** window.
   ___e. Click on **Protocol** to select it and then click on the **Add** button.
   ___f. Record the Network Protocols available in Table 30-1.
   ___g. Click on the **Cancel** button twice to return to the *Local Area Connection Properties* window.
   ___h. The *General* tab shows the current protocols, services, and clients installed on your computer. Record each of these items in Table 30-2.
   ___i. Get the appropriate TCP/IP network configuration information from your ISP, Network Administrator, or instructor and record this information in the appropriate locations in Table 30-3.

Figure 30-1: Local Area Connection Properties Window

2. **Record the current TCP/IP settings**
   ___a. Uncheck the box next to **Internet Protocol** (**TCP/IP**).
   ___b. Click on the **OK** button.
   ___c. Click on the **Yes** button when prompted for the removal of the other protocols.
   ___d. If you entered *Yes* for DHCP, click on the **Cancel** button and skip to Step 3.
   ___e. At the *General* tab, record the specified IP address and subnet mask in Table 30-4. Your screen should appear similar to Figure 30-2.

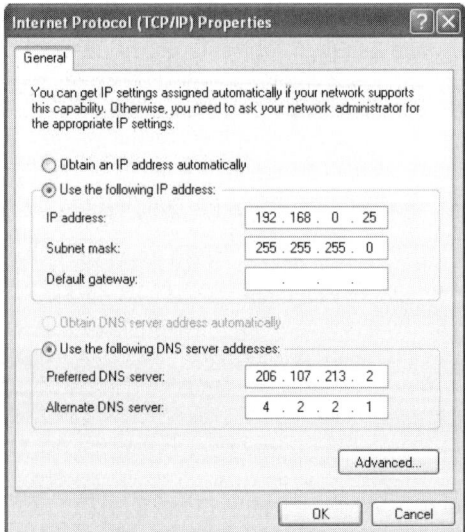

Figure 30-2: IP and Subnet Configuration Information

210 - LAB GROUP 3

PROCEDURE - 30

___f.   Click on the **Advanced** button to open the *Advanced TCP/IP Properties* window. It should appear similar to Figure 30-3.

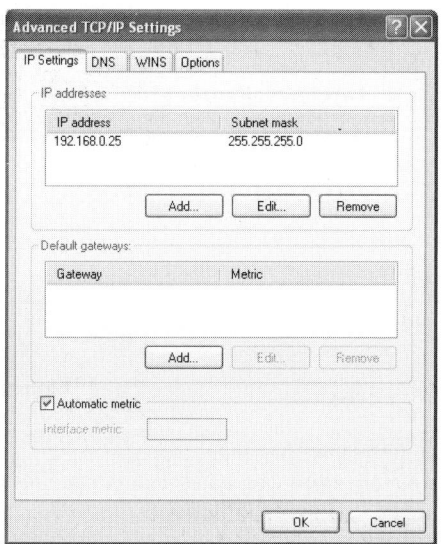

Figure 30-3:
Advanced TCP/IP
Properties Window

___g.   Click on the **DNS** tab and record the DNS server information, if any, in Table 30-4.
___h.   Click on the **Cancel** button to close the *Advanced TCP/IP Properties* window.
___i.   Click on the **Cancel** button to close the *Internet Protocol TCP/IP Properties* window.

3.   Delete the TCP/IP Protocol
___a.   Uncheck the box next to **Internet Protocol (TCP/IP)**.
___b.   Click on the **OK** button.
___c.   Click on the **Yes** button when prompted for the removal of the other protocols.

4.   Attempt to Access the Internet
___a.   Click on the **Internet Explorer** icon in the Quick Launch toolbar, to open Internet Explorer.
___b.   Close the message box that appears, and then close Internet Explorer.
___c.   Open Internet Explorer again.
___d.   Click on the **Refresh** button.
___e.   In Table 30-5, describe the message you receive.
___f.   Click on the **Connect** button. You should receive a message similar to the one in Figure 30-4.
___g.   Close all windows that are open.

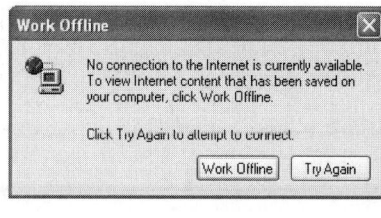

Figure 30-4: Unable to Connect to Internet Message

5.   Install the TCP/IP Protocol
___a.   Use the path *Start/Settings/Control Panel* to open the *Control Panel* window.
___b.   If the *Limited* view is presented, click on the *View all Control Panel options* hyperlink to see all of the *Control Panel* icons.
___c.   Double-click the **Network Connections** icon.
___d.   Double-click the **Local Area Connections** icon in the *Network Connections* window.

WINDOWS XP TCP/IP SETUP - 211

PROCEDURE - 30

    ___e.   Click on the **Support** tab, as shown in Figure 30-5.
    ___f.   In Table 30-6, record the information as it appears.
    ___g.   Click on the **General** tab again.
    ___h.   Click on the **Properties** button to open the *Local Area Connection Properties* window.
    ___i.   Place a checkmark next to **Internet Protocol (TCP/IP)** and the other options will automatically be selected as well.
    ___j.   Click on the **OK** button to install the TCP/IP protocol.

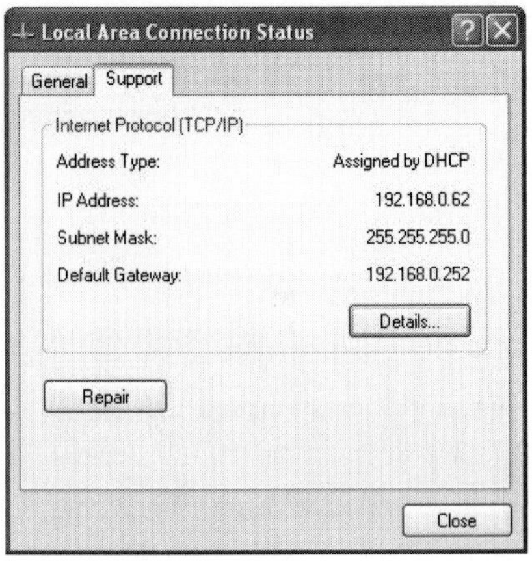

6. **Confirm the installation of the protocols**
    ___a.   In the *Local Area Status* window, click on the **Support** tab.
    ___b.   In Table 30-7, record the settings.
    ___c.   Click on the **Close** button.

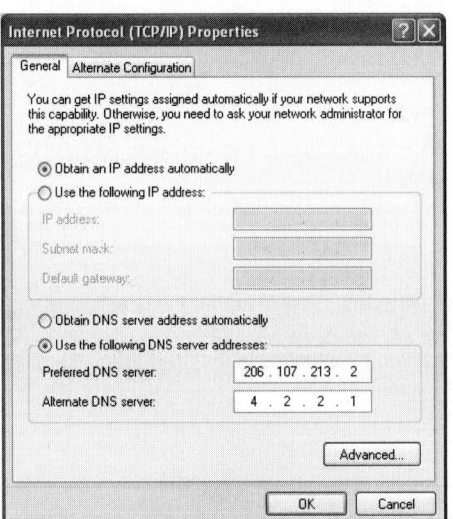

Figure 30-5: Support Tab

7. **Configure all TCP/IP settings**
    ___a.   If you are using DHCP, skip to Step i.
    ___b.   Right-click the **Local Area Connection** icon and select **Properties** from the drop-down menu.
    ___c.   Click on **Internet Protocol (TCP/IP)** to highlight it.
    ___d.   Click on the **Properties** button to open the *Internet Protocol (TCP/IP) Properties* window, as shown in Figure 30-6.

Figure 30-6: TCP/IP Properties Window

    ___e.   Enter the information that you collected from your instructor in the appropriate spaces.
    ___f.   Click on the **OK** button twice to confirm the configuration settings.
    ___g.   Turn off the computer.

PROCEDURE - 30

TABLES

Table 30-1: Network Protocols

Table 30-2: Current Protocols, Services, and Clients Installed

Table 30-3: DHCP

DHCP?	

Table 30-4: Assigned TCP/IP Configuration Settings

IP Address:	
Subnet Mask:	
Primary DNS Server:	
Secondary:	

Table 30-5

PROCEDURE - 30

Table 30-6

Address Type:	
IP Address:	
Subnet Mask:	
Default Gateway:	

Table 30-7

Address Type:	
IP Address:	
Subnet Mask:	
Default Gateway:	

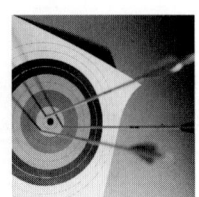

Feedback

LAB QUESTIONS

1. Which protocol is used to set the IP address?

2. For whom was TCP/IP created?

3. What system is used to automatically assign IP addresses and subnet masks to every computer and device on the network?

4. Which control panel is used to administer your network connection?

5. Name two advantages to using the TCP/IP protocol.

LAB PROCEDURE 31

Windows XP Network Operations

OBJECTIVES

1. Share drives, folders and files.
2. Set up drive mapping to a folder on another computer.
3. Connect to a shared network resource.
4. Add a Network Place.

Networking

RESOURCES

1. Two PC-compatible desktop/tower computer systems — Customer-supplied desktop/tower hardware systems **OR** Marcraft MC-8000 Computer Hardware Trainers **OR** suitable PC hardware trainers with 128 MB RAM, Windows XP operating system, and NIC installed
2. Working network connection

DISCUSSION

This lab will perform some basic operations with peer-to-peer networks in Windows 2000. You will learn how to share folders, and check the ability of another to connect and view the contents of that folder. Through "My Network Places" you can view contents of the LAN and create shortcuts to FTP sites. You will learn how to add a Network Place such as a File Transfer Protocol site, and how to map a drive to a folder that is shared on another computer in the Local Area Network (LAN).

PROCEDURE

1. **Share folders with other users of the network**
    ____ a. Open Windows Explorer.
    ____ b. Click on the plus sign (+) next to **My Computer** to expand the directory.
    ____ c. Double-click on the Local Disk (**C:**) drive to expand the directory tree.
    ____ d. With the C: drive highlighted, click on the **File** menu and select **New** and then **Folder**.
    ____ e. Type your first initial and last 4 characters of your last name, the word shared, and press the **ENTER** key.
    ____ f. Right-click your new folder and select **Sharing and security** from the pop-up menu.

PROCEDURE - 31

____g. Place a checkmark in the box next to **Share this folder on the network**, and uncheck the box next to **Allow network users to change my files**, shown in Figure 31-1.

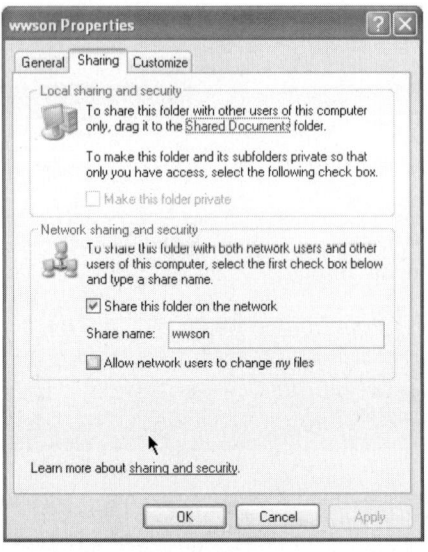

Figure 31-1: Sharing a folder on the Network

____h. Click on the **OK** button to save the shared settings.
____i. Click on the **Start** button and select **Run** from the menu.
____j. Type **Notepad** and click on the **OK** button to open the *Notepad* window.
____k. Type your name and your computer name in the *Notepad* window.
____l. Click on the *File* menu and select **Save As**.
____m. Click on the **My Computer** button on the left side of the *Save As* window.
____n. Double-click on the **C:** drive.

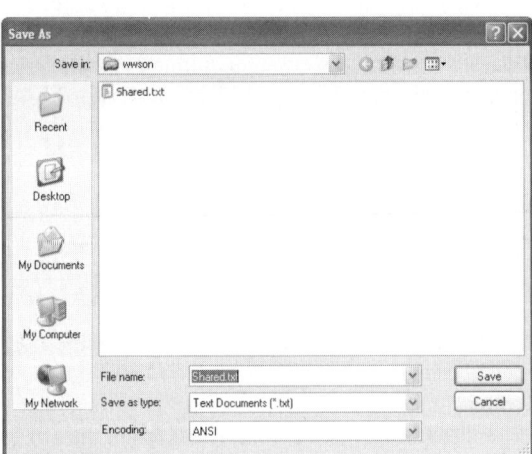

Figure 31-2: Creating and Saving a Text File to be Shared

____o. Double-click on the folder you just created.
____p. In the *File name:* text box, type **Shared.txt** and click on the **Save** button, as shown in Figure 31-2.
____q. Close all windows.

2. **Test access to the shared folder**
____a. Once your partner has finished the above steps, double-click on **My Network Places**.
____b. Double-click on **Entire Network**.

216 - LAB GROUP 3

PROCEDURE - 31

    ___ c.   Double-click on **Microsoft Windows Network**.
    ___ d.   Double-click on your workgroup or domain name.
    ___ e.   Look for the icon of your partner's computer and double-click it.
    ___ f.   You should see the folder that your partner created. Double-click on it and record the content of the folder in Table 31-1.
    ___ g.   You have just accessed a shared resource over the LAN. Close all windows.

3.   **Setting Full Access permissions for a shared folder**
    ___ a.   Double-click on **My Computer**.
    ___ b.   Double-click on the **C:** drive.
    ___ c.   Right-click your new folder and select **Sharing and security**.
    ___ d.   Place a checkmark next to **Allow network users to change my files**, as shown in Figure 31-3.
    ___ e.   Click on the **OK** button to save your settings and close the window.

NOTE: Now anyone can change the files that are in this folder.

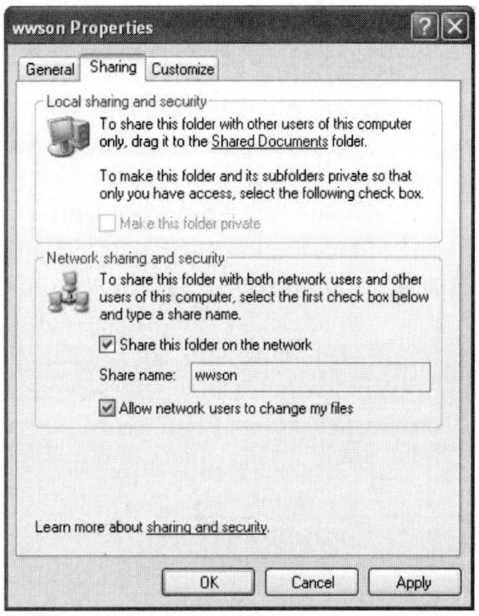

Figure 31-3: Allowing Users to Change Files

4.   **Share a printer**
    ___ a.   Go to the computer that is going to host the shared printer and navigate the *Start/Settings/Printers* path.
    ___ b.   Right-click on the computer that you installed the printer on previously and choose **Sharing**.

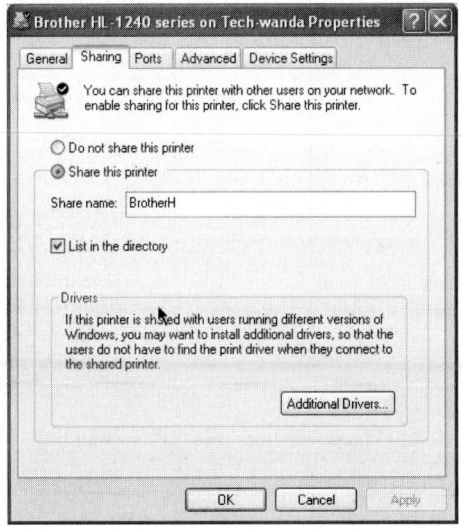

Figure 31-4: Sharing a Printer

    ___ c.   Click on the radio button next to **Share this printer**, as shown in Figure 31-4.
    ___ d.   Use the default name for the share.
    ___ e.   Click on the **Additional Drivers** button.
    ___ f.   From this window you can select drivers for machines that may not have Windows XP, and need to access the printer over a LAN. Click on the **Cancel** button.
    ___ g.   Click on the **OK** button to close the *Printer Properties* window.
    ___ h.   Close all other windows.

PROCEDURE - 31

5. **Test printer access**
   ___a. Go to your desktop and double-click on the **My Network Places** icon.
   ___b. Double-click on **Entire Network**.
   ___c. Double-click on **Microsoft Windows Network**.
   ___d. Double-click on your workgroup or domain name.
   ___e. Double-click on the name of the computer that hosts the printer that you just shared.
   ___f. Right-click the printer and select **Connect**.
   ___g. After a connection window similar to Figure 31-5 has appeared and closes, close all windows.
   ___h. Double-click the **My Computer** icon.
   ___i. Double-click the **Control Panel** icon.
   ___j. Double-click on **Printers and Faxes**.
   ___k. Double-click the printer that you had connected to previously.
   ___l. From the *Printer* select **Properties**.
   ___m. Click on the **Print Test Page** button. The test page should now print from the shared printer.
   ___n. Click on the **OK** button to close the dialog window that opens.
   ___o. Click on the **OK** button to close the *Printer Properties* window.
   ___p. Close all windows.

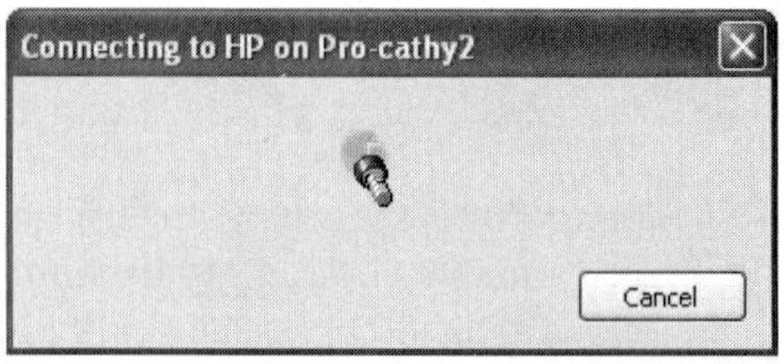

Figure 31-5: Connecting to a Shared Printer

6. **Map a network drive in Windows Explorer**
   ___a. Double-click on the **My Computer** icon on the desktop.
   ___b. Click on the **Tools** menu and select **Map Network Drive**.
   ___c. Click on the drop-down menu next to **Drive:** and make sure the next consecutive drive letter is chosen.
   ___d. Click on the **Browse** button as shown in Figure 31-6.
   ___e. Double-click on **Microsoft Windows Network** and then your workgroup or domain name.
   ___f. Double-click on the **C:** drive.
   ___g. Click on the folder that your partner created and shared, and then click on the **OK** button.
   ___h. Click on the check box next to **Reconnect at logon** in order to re-create the mapped drive, as shown in Figure 31-7.

Figure 31-6: Browsing to a Folder to Map to

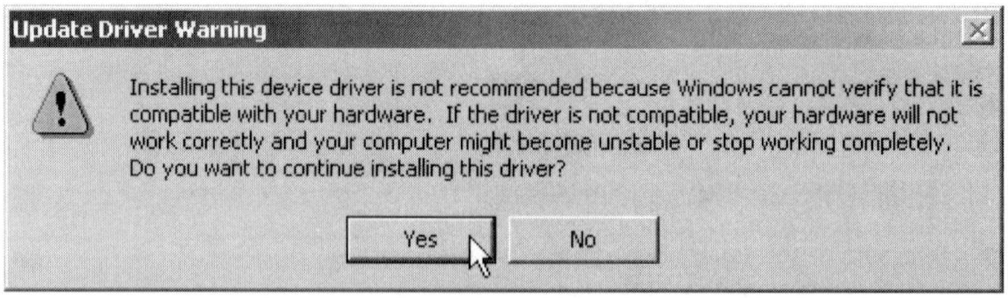

Figure 31-7: Reconnect at Logon Setting

   ___i. Click on the **Finish** button.
   ___j. Close all windows.

NOTE: You have now mapped a drive to a shared resource.

PROCEDURE - 31

    ___ k.   Verify the drive connection by double-clicking on **My Computer**. You will see the name of the folder you have just connected to, followed by the drive letter that it was given during the mapping under the *Network Drives* section.

    ___ l.   Close all windows.

7. Add Network Place

    ___ a.   From the desktop of your computer double-click the **My Network Places** icon.

    ___ b.   Double-click on **Add Network Place**.

    ___ c.   The *Add Network Place Wizard*, similar to Figure 31-8, will appear.

    ___ d.   Click on the **Next** button.

    ___ e.   Click on **Choose another network location** and click on the **Next** button.

    ___ f.   Read the Service Providers that appear in the next window and record them in Table 31-2.

    ___ g.   Click on the **View some examples** link below the text entry box.

    ___ h.   Take note of the types of places that can be added with this wizard.

    ___ i.   Type **ftp://ftp.microsoft.com** in the text box, and then click on the *Examples* link below the text entry box.

    ___ j.   Click on the **Next** button.

    ___ k.   Verify that the **Log on anonymously** field is checked. Most FTP sites allow an anonymous logon to view public files.

    ___ l.   Click on the **Next** button.

    ___ m.   Enter *Your Name's* **connection to Microsoft's FTP server** in the text box, substituting your name for the words *Your Name's*.

    ___ n.   Click on the **Finish** button.

    ___ o.   The Internet Explorer window should automatically open, similar to Figure 31-9. Record the number of items in Table 31-3.

Figure 31-8: Add a Network Place Wizard

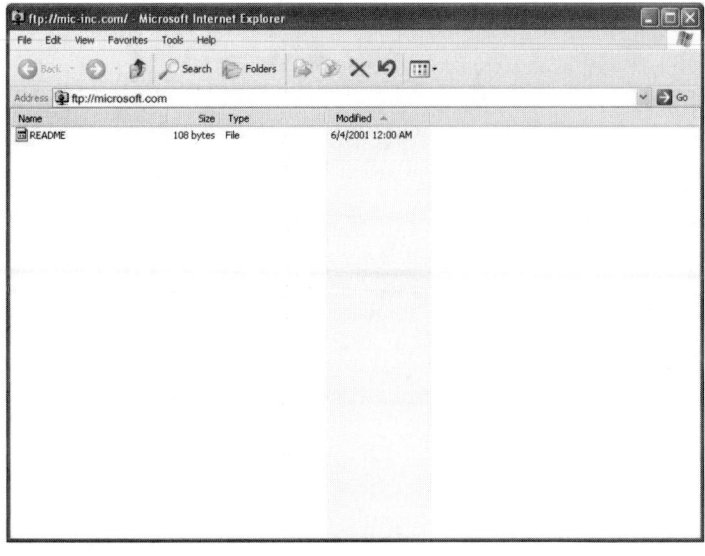

Figure 31-9: Internet Explorer Window

    ___ p.   Close the window and you should see My Network Places still open. Record any new items in Table 31-4.

    ___ q.   Close all open windows and shut down the computer.

PROCEDURE - 31

TABLES

Table 31-1

Content of Shared Folder:	

Table 31-2

Service Providers:	

Table 31-3

Number of Items:	

Table 31-4

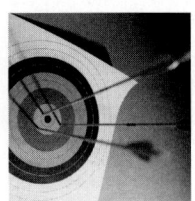

Feedback

LAB QUESTIONS

1. What can My Network Places be used for?

2. What are additional printer drivers used for?

3. When mapping a shared resource from another computer, what does it look and act like?

4. Why is anonymous logon used?

LAB PROCEDURE 32

Windows XP Remote Troubleshooting

Networking

OBJECTIVES

1. Set up MSN Messenger.
2. Add contacts to MSN Messenger.
3. Use Remote Assistance.

RESOURCES

1. Two PC-compatible desktop/tower computer systems — Customer-supplied desktop/tower hardware systems **OR** Marcraft MC-8000 Computer Hardware Trainers **OR** suitable PC hardware trainers with Windows XP Professional installed
2. Networked computers
3. Internet connection
4. MSN Messenger installed
5. 2 lab groups (must work together)

DISCUSSION

In Windows XP Microsoft has added a new feature for remote troubleshooting. When you combine the Windows XP operating system with Microsoft's MSN messenger you can now ask for assistance from someone you are chatting with or from Microsoft directly. In this procedure we will show you how to set up MSN Messenger and then how to get assistance while using the program.

PROCEDURE

1. **Set up MSN Messenger (done on both computers)**
   a. Boot to the Windows XP desktop.
   b. Click on **Start**, **My computer**.
   c. Insert the A+ Lab CD into the CD-ROM drive.
   d. Double-click on the CD-ROM drive (usually **d:** drive).
   e. Double-click on the file **MsnMsgs.Msi**. This will start the installation of MSN Messenger. If the repair or remove screen comes up, as in Figure 32-1, click on **Cancel** and **Yes** to confirm to cancel. Click on **Start**, **Windows Messenger** and continue at Step 2.

Figure 32-1: Repair or Remove

WINDOWS XP REMOTE TROUBLESHOOTING - 221

PROCEDURE - 32

___f. The Welcome to MSN Messenger Setup screen appears as in Figure 32-2. Click on **Next**.

Figure 32-2: MSN Messenger Setup

___g. The *End-User License Agreement (EULA)* screen appears as in Figure 32-3. Select that you agree to the terms and click on **Next**.

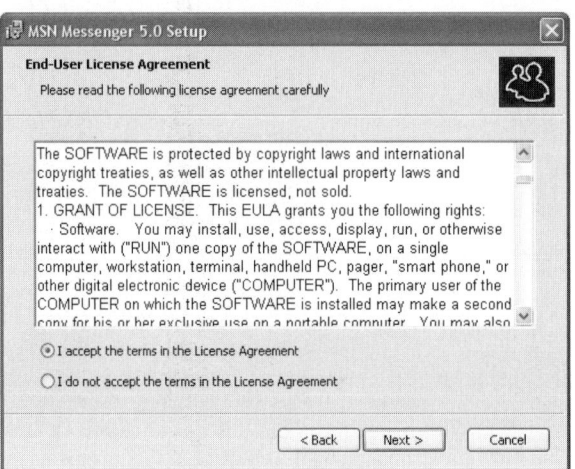

Figure 32-3: End-User License Agreement (EULA)

___h. MSN Messenger then installs the components as in Figure 32-4. When it has completed, click on **Finish**.

Figure 32-4: Installing Messenger

222 - LAB GROUP 3

PROCEDURE - 32

2. **Sign in to MSN Messenger**
   ___ a. MSN Messenger then appears as in Figure 32-5. Click on the **Sign In** button.
   ___ b. If it signs in automatically, skip to Step 3. If it asks for a password the password should be your school name. If not, ask your instructor.
   ___ c. If an account is not set up on the computer it will display the .NET Passport wizard as in Figure 32-6. Click on **Next**.

Figure 32-5: MSN Messenger

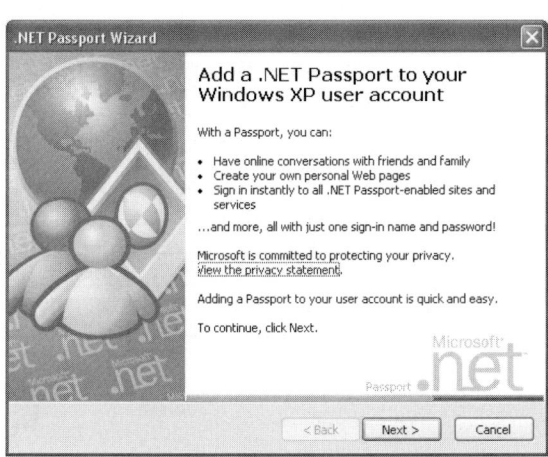

Figure 32-6: .NET Passport Wizard

___ d. Select **No, I would like to open a free MSN.com e-mail account now** and click on **Next**.
___ e. Enter your Name into the next screen and click on **Next**.
___ f. The *Where do you live?* screen will appear as in Figure 32-7. Fill it out for your school's address and click on **Next**.

___ g. The *Terms of Use* screen comes up as in Figure 32-8. Select that you agree to the terms and click on **Next**.

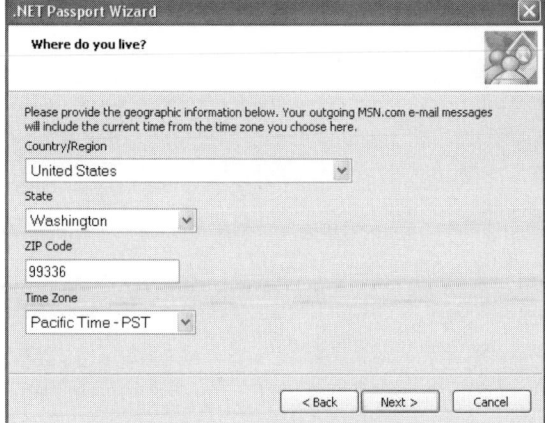

Figure 32-7: Where Do You Live?

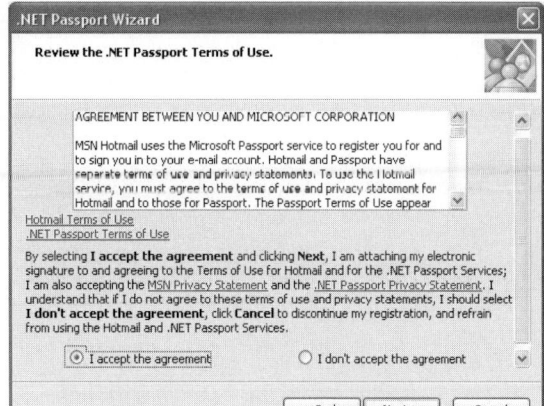

Figure 32-8: Terms of Use

PROCEDURE - 32

____ h. Fill out the information about yourself as in Figure 32-9.

____ i. Create an e-mail address in the next screen. Type in your school name and then your station number with no spaces, as in Figure 32-10, and click on **Next**.

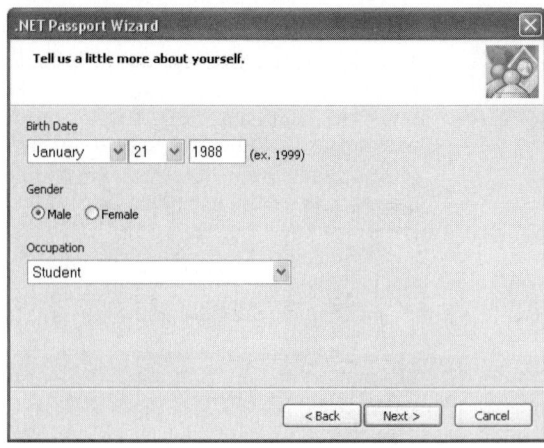

Figure 32-9: Your Information

Figure 32-10: Create an E-Mail Address

____ j. Create your password in the next screen that appears. Make the password the city that your school is located in with all the letters being in lowercase. For example, a school in Los Angeles could have the password of losangeles or la.

____ k. Notice that when you type the password the screen displays dots instead of the letters; this is normal for password encryption. For the secret question screen, choose **High school name?** as in Figure 32-11.

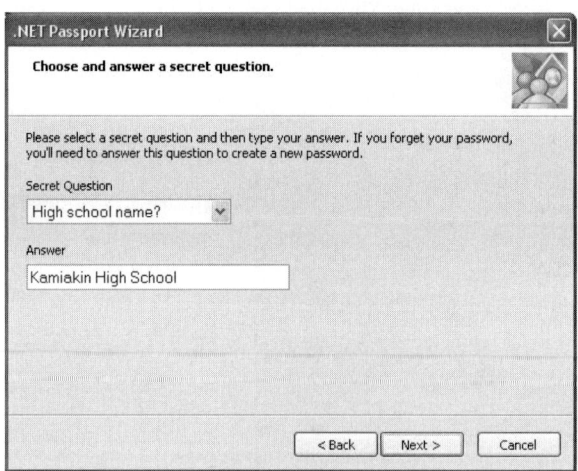

Figure 32-11: Secret Question

____ l. In the *Share your information* dialog box, leave all the boxes blank and click on **Next**.

____ m. In the *hotmail member directory* dialog box, deselect *Hotmail member directory* and click on **Next**.

____ n. Your done screen appears. Click on **Finish** to exit the .NET Passport Wizard. You should be signed in to MSN Messenger.

PROCEDURE - 32

3. **Add people to your contact list**
    ___ a. Click on **Add a Contact** under the **I want to…** section, as in Figure 32-12.
    ___ b. When the *How do you want to add the contact* dialog box comes up, make sure **by e-mail address or sign-in name** is selected and click on **Next**.
    ___ c. Get the name of the workstation of the lab group you are working with. It should be the school name and station number. Type it in the blank as shown in Figure 32-13.

Figure 32-12: MSN Messenger

Figure 32-13: Add a Contact

    ___ d. You will get a success message stating that the contact has been added. If not, check to make sure it is spelled correctly on both machines. Click on **Finish**.
    ___ e. You will now have a contact in your group. If the contact is green, double-click on the contact. If the contact is red, have the other lab group sign into MSN Messenger and wait until it turns green.
    ___ f. You will get a conversation dialog box, as in Figure 32-14. Type **hi** and press the **ENTER** key. This will send the message "hi".

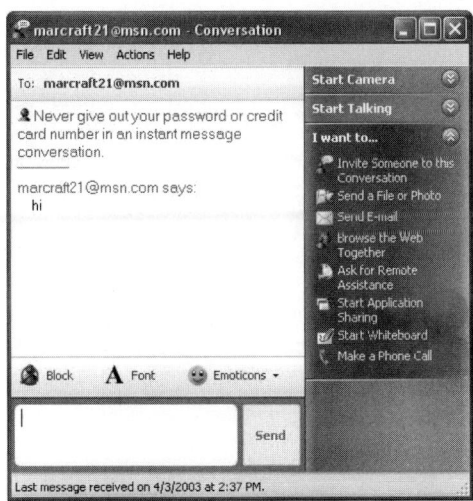

Figure 32-14: Conversion Dialog Box

4. **Get remote assistance using MSN messenger**
    ___ a. In the *conversation* dialog box, under the *I want to…* section, click on **Ask for Remote Assistance**.

WINDOWS XP REMOTE TROUBLESHOOTING - 225

PROCEDURE - 32

The computer sending the message will get the message stating that you sent an invitation to use remote assistance. The remote computer will get the message asking them to either accept or decline the invitation. These messages are shown in Figure 32-15.

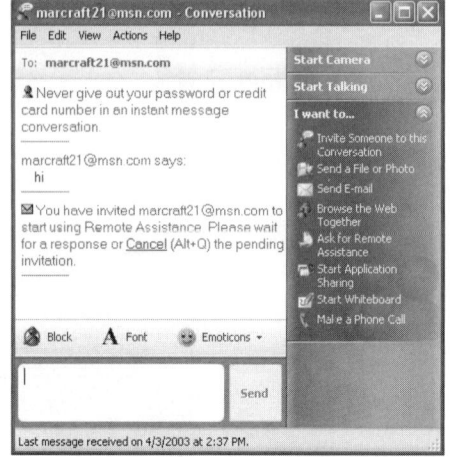 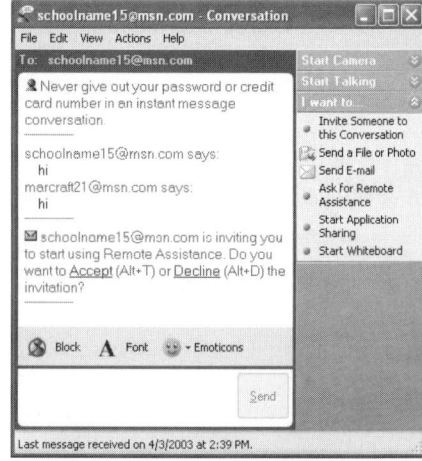

Figure 32-15: Remote Assistance Screens

____ b.   Click on the **Accept** link to use remote assistance.
____ c.   The computers then try to connect to each other to use Remote Assistance, as shown in Figure 32-16.
____ d.   There will be a window asking if you would like to allow the person to view your screen and chat with you. Click on **Yes** to allow this as in Figure 32-17.

Figure 32-16: Attempting to Connect Window

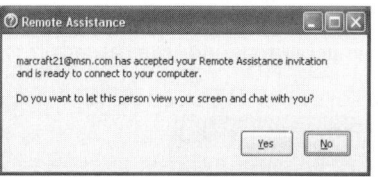

Figure 32-17: Allow Viewing of Screen

____ e.   Once connected you should get *Remote Assistance* window. Click on **Scale to Window** and now your display should look similar to Figure 32-18.

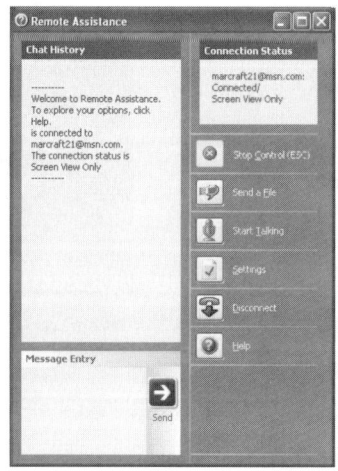

Figure 32-18: Remote Assistance

226 - LAB GROUP 3

PROCEDURE - 32

___ f. Click on **Take Control** in the upper-left corner to take control of the machine. You should see a screen similar to Figure 32-19 on each machine. The remote user logs onto the machine and shares control.

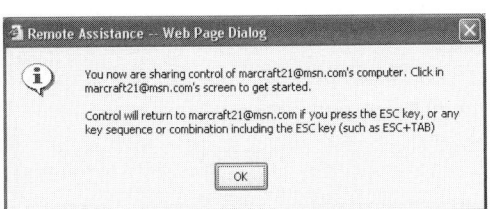

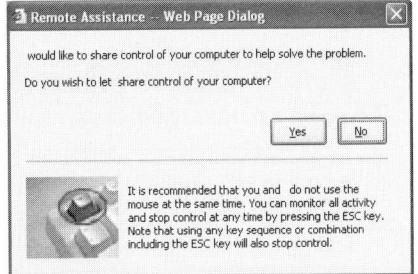

Figure 32-19: Web Page Dialog Box – Sharing Control

___ g. Click on **Start**, **Control Panel** to bring up Control Panel in the *Remote Assistance* window.
___ h. In Control Panel, click on **Performance and Maintenance** and then click on the **System** icon. You should end up on the *System Properties* screen for the other computer as in Figure 32-20.

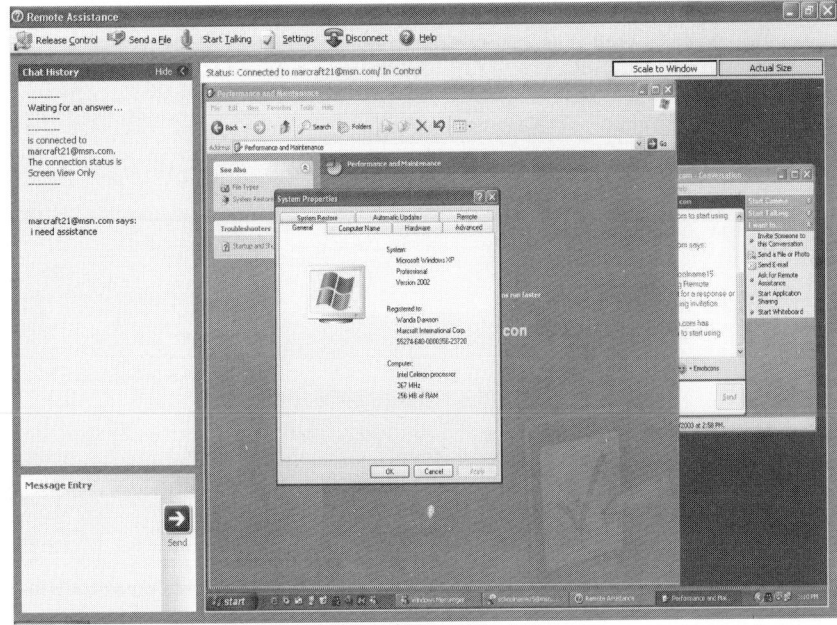

Figure 32-20: Remote Assistance – System Properties

___ i. Click on the **Hardware** tab and then **Device Manager** to open Device Manager. This is where you would be able to reinstall all drivers by using Remote Assistance.
___ j. Since everything is working properly, everything in the window appears normal. Click on **Release control** in the upper-left corner.
___ k. Now click on **Disconnect** to stop using Remote Assistance. You should receive a message similar to Figure 32-21 on both machines.
___ l. Close all open windows.

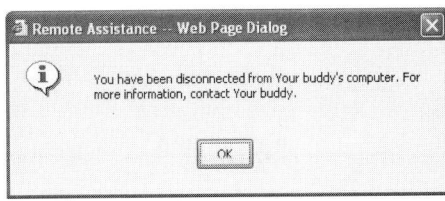

Figure 32-21: Disconnected from Remote Assistance

WINDOWS XP REMOTE TROUBLESHOOTING - 227

PROCEDURE - 32

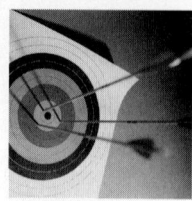

Feedback

LAB QUESTIONS

1. How do you set up MSN Messenger?
2. How do you add contacts to MSN Messenger?
3. How do you ask for remote assistance using MSN Messenger?
4. Can a remote user take control of your system without your knowledge?
5. Can you change the driver of a modem from a remote connection using Windows XP?

LAB PROCEDURE 33

Internet Client Setup for IE 6.0

Networking

OBJECTIVES

1. Run the Internet Explorer browser client.
2. Browse the Internet.
3. Configure the Outlook Express e-mail client.
4. Check your e-mail.
5. Configure Internet Explorer.

RESOURCES

1. Two PC-compatible desktop/tower computer systems — Customer-supplied desktop/tower hardware systems **OR** Marcraft MC-8000 Computer Hardware Trainers **OR** suitable PC hardware trainers with Windows XP Operating System Installation CD and NIC installed
2. Internet access through a network connection
3. A valid e-mail account
4. Internet account configuration information from your instructor, network administrator, or ISP

DISCUSSION

One of the fastest growing areas of microcomputer use is in the field of wide area networking. The advent of the World Wide Web, and the use of associated client applications called web browsers, has enabled millions of non-technical users to access the Internet. This, in turn, has led to a greater need for web-related technical assistance.

A successful computer technician must have the ability to identify concepts and capabilities relating to the Internet and basic procedures for setting up a system for Internet access. That is the purpose of this lab. The subsequent labs will cover Internet-related topics such as Telnet, FTP, and the Internet domain name system.

The most widely used web browser applications are Microsoft's Internet Explorer (IE) and Netscape's Navigator. Both of these applications are provided free for educational or personal noncommercial use, and can be downloaded from the company's web site. Of course, you will need to have a web browser already installed and configured in order to download these browsers.

Fortunately, Windows XP comes with IE already installed as part of the operating system. Using an Internet browser to locate and download applications, demos, drivers, and patches is one of the primary skills needed by every computer technician.

PROCEDURE - 33

Networking

PROCEDURE

In this lab procedure you will configure your network Internet browser and e-mail clients. In order to fill in some of these parameters, you will need to acquire information from your ISP, instructor, or network administrator. Then you will browse the Internet using the Internet Explorer 6.0 (IE6) web browser, as shown in Figure 33-1. You will then configure your e-mail client (Outlook Express) and check your e-mail.

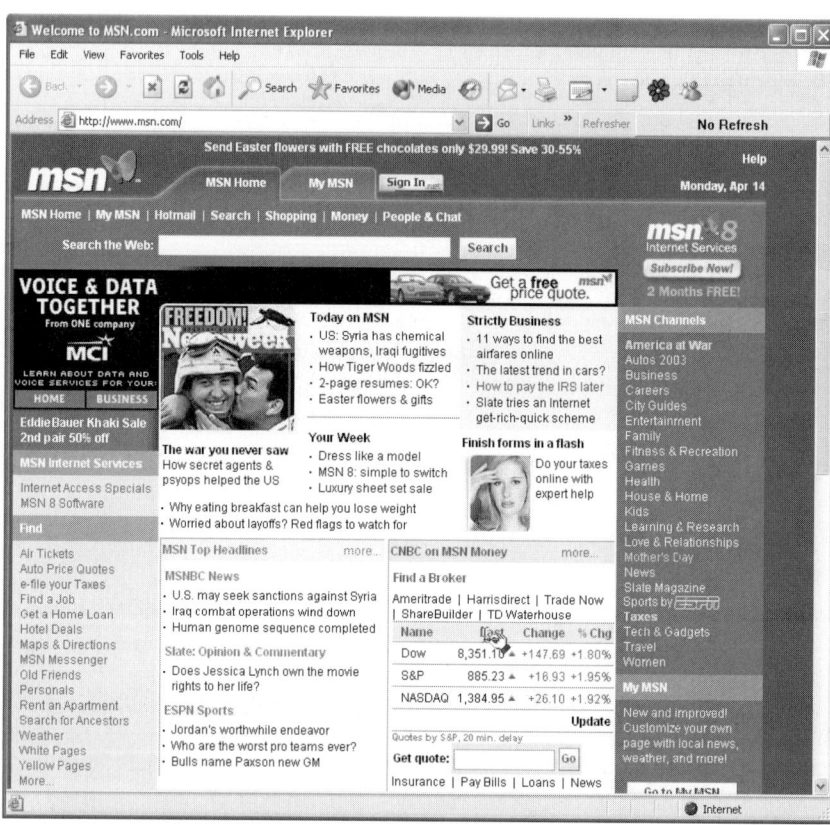

**Figure 33-1:
Internet Explorer
Web Browser**

If you are working in a classroom environment, it may be necessary to uninstall these features from the system for the next class. In this case, consult with your instructor before uninstalling anything from the system.

1. **Record the configuration information for your Internet network connection**
    ___ a. Boot up the computer.
    ___ b. Record the Internet configuration information you received from your instructor, network administrator, or ISP in Table 33-3.

2. **Run Internet Explorer**
    ___ a. Double-click the **Internet Explorer** icon on your desktop.
    ___ b. In the *Windows XP - Microsoft Internet Explorer* window, click on the **Maximize** button in the upper-right corner.
    ___ c. Click on the **Help** menu and select **About Internet Explorer**.
    ___ d. Record the current version number in Table 33-1.
    ___ e. Click on the **OK** button to close the *About Internet Explorer* window.
    ___ f. Close Internet Explorer.

230 - LAB GROUP 3

PROCEDURE - 33

3. **Explore the Internet with the Internet Explorer browser**
   ___a. Click on the **Start** button and select **Run** from the *Start* menu.
   ___b. In the *Open* box, type **www.arstechnica.com** and then click on the **OK** button.
   ___c. Press the **CTRL+D** keys simultaneously to add the current page to your *Favorites* list.

4. **Search the Internet to find a driver for an HP DeskJet 6127 printer**
   ___a. Click on the **Address** box and type **www.hp.com** to access the Hewlett-Packard website.
   ___b. Press the **ENTER** key.
   ___c. Click on the link labeled **support & drivers** as shown in Figure 33-2.

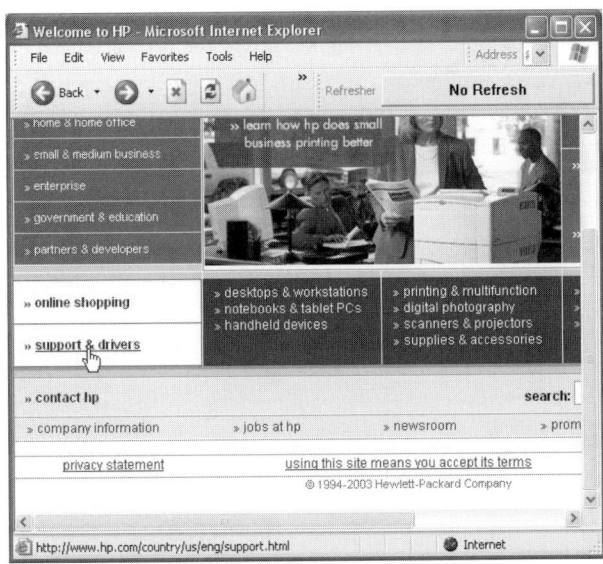

Figure 33-2: Selecting the Drivers Link from the HP Website

   ___d. Click on the link labeled **HP driver downloads, software updates and patches**.
   ___e. Scroll down the list of company names and click on the hyperlink labeled **Hewlett Packard**.
   ___f. In the box labeled *Enter model product number:* type **DeskJet 6127** and click on the double arrows to the right.
   ___g. Select your operating system by clicking on the **Microsoft Windows XP** link.
   ___h. Click on the **hp deskjet 6127 printer software/driver: Corporate users - Network and USB** link.
   ___i. Scroll down and click on the **download now** button.
   ___j. Click on the **Save** button when the *File Download* box appears.
   ___k. Save the file to your *Download* directory.

5. **Find a map showing the location of Marcraft International, Inc.**
   ___a. Click on the **Address** box, type **www.yahoo.com**, and press the **ENTER** key.
   ___b. In the list of site features, click on **Maps** as shown in Figure 33-3.

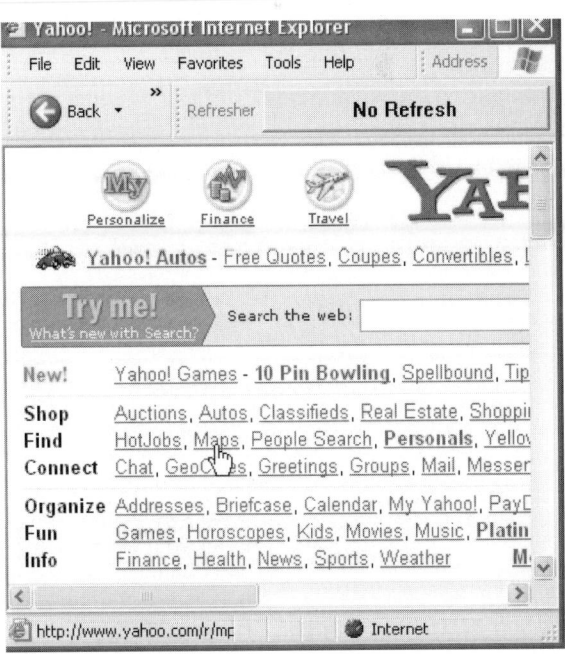

Figure 33-3: Selecting the Maps Link at Yahoo.com

INTERNET CLIENT SETUP FOR IE 6.0 - 231

PROCEDURE - 33

___c. In the *Address* box type **100 N. Morain St**.
___d. In the *City/State/Zip* box type **Kennewick, WA 99336**.
___e. Click on the **Get Map** button.
___f. When the page finishes downloading, press the F11 key on your keyboard to view the full screen image.

NOTE: There are various features to enlarge or reduce the map size and detail. The area viewed can also be shifted in any direction by clicking on the arrow next to the compass direction.

___g. Click on the link labeled **Driving Directions: To this location** as shown in Figure 33-4.

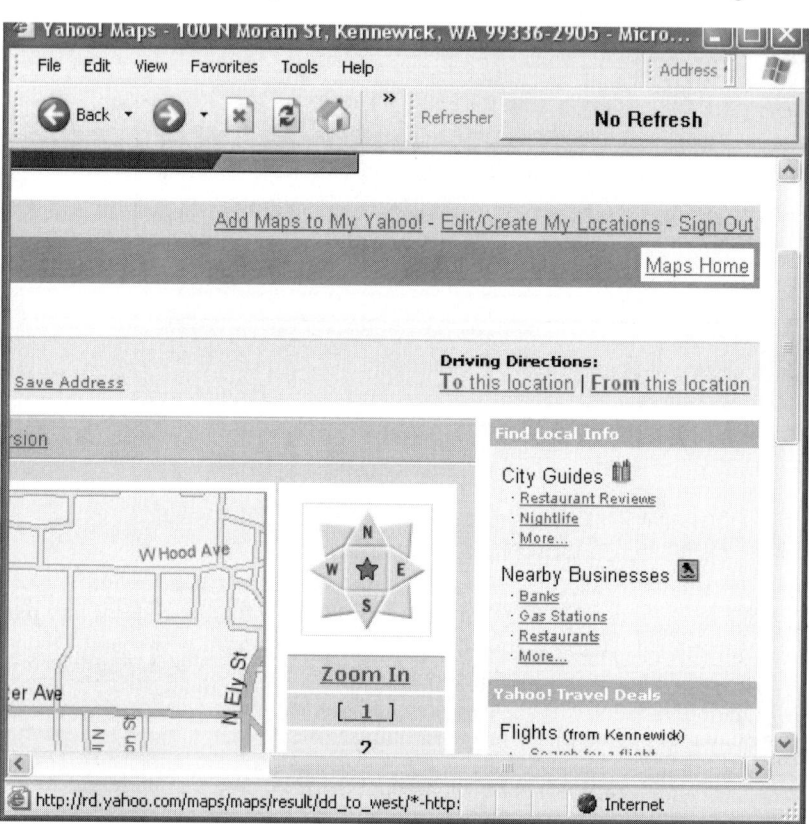

Figure 33-4: Selecting Driving Directions

___h. Enter the address of your current location in the **Enter a Starting Address** section.
___i. Click on the **Get Directions** button.
___j. Record the distance to Marcraft in Table 33-2.

6. **Configure the Outlook Express e-mail client**
    ___a. Click on the **Outlook Express** icon in the *Quick Launch* toolbar at the bottom of the screen.
    ___b. Click on the **Tools** menu and select **Accounts**.
    ___c. On the **Mail** tab, click on the **Add** button and select **Mail**.
    ___d. Enter your name as listed in Table 33-3a into the *Display name* box, then click on the **Next** button.
    ___e. Enter your e-mail address as listed in Table 33-3b into the *E-mail address* box, then click on the **Next** button.
    ___f. Enter your POP3 server name or address as listed in Table 33-3c into the *Incoming mail* box.
    ___g. Enter your SMTP server address as listed in Table 33-3d into the *Outgoing mail* box. Click on the **Next** button to continue.

PROCEDURE - 33

    ___h.   Enter your POP3 Login Name as listed in Table 33-3e into the *Account name* box.
    ___i.   Enter your POP3 password as listed in Table 33-3f into the *Password* box, then click on the **Next** button.
    ___j.   Click on the **Finish** button to continue.
    ___k.   Click on the **Close** button.

7.   **Use and configure the Outlook Express mail client**
    ___a.   Click on the **Maximize** button in the upper-right corner.
    ___b.   Click on the **Send/Receive** button in the toolbar.
    ___c.   Click on the **Tools** menu and select **Options.**
    ___d.   Click on the **Maintenance** tab in the *Options* window.
    ___e.   Click on the check box to select **Empty messages from the 'Deleted Items' folder on exit** as shown in Figure 33-5.

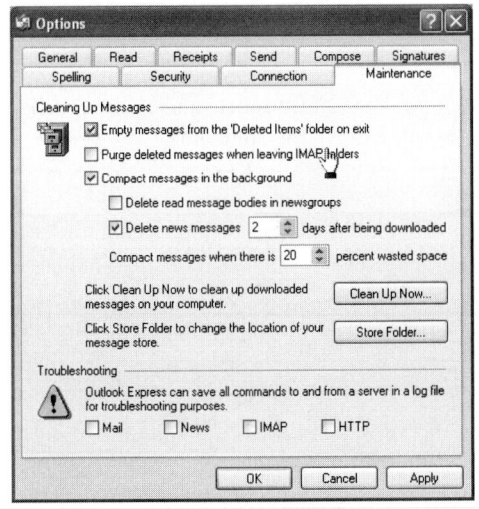

Figure 33-5: The Empty messages form Deleted Items Setting

    ___f.   Click on the **OK** button.
    ___g.   Close Outlook Express.

8.   **Configure the Internet Explorer browser**
    ___a.   Click on the **Internet Explorer** icon in the Taskbar to open IE.
    ___b.   Press the **F11** key to return to standard view.
    ___c.   Click on the **Address** box, type **www.zdnet.com/zdnn/**, and press the **ENTER** key.
    ___d.   Click on the **Tools** menu and select **Internet Options**.
    ___e.   Click on the **General** tab, and under *Home page* click on the **Use Current** button.
    ___f.   Click on the **Apply** button to make ZDNet News your home page.
    ___g.   Click on the **Advanced** tab.
    ___h.   Scroll down to locate the *Use inline AutoComplete* function, and then click on the check box to select it, as shown in Figure 33-6.

PROCEDURE - 33

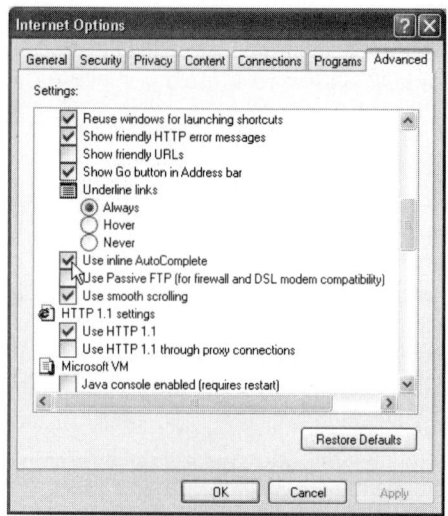

Figure 33-6: Select AutoComplete

   ___i.   Click on the **OK** button to turn on AutoComplete and exit the *Internet Options* window.
   ___j.   Close all open windows and shut down the computer.

TABLES

Table 33-1

Version Number:	

Table 33-2

Distance to Marcraft:	

Table 33-3

a.) Name:	
b.) E-mail Address:	
c.) POP3 Server Address:	
d.) SMTP Server Address:	
e.) POP3 Login Name:	
f.) POP3 Password:	

PROCEDURE - 33

LAB QUESTIONS

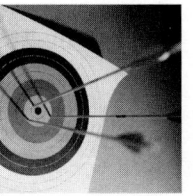

Feedback

1. List five of the required configuration items that must be obtained from your ISP or network administrator when you are setting up Internet client applications.

2. State at least one Internet-related skill that is used by computer technicians.

3. What kind of Internet site is Yahoo.com?

    Hint: Click on Company Info at the bottom of www.yahoo.com.

4. How do you open the window that controls the advanced settings for Internet Explorer?

5. How do you set the current web page as your home page?

LAB PROCEDURE 34

Windows Me FTP/Telnet

OBJECTIVES

1. Install the HyperTerminal telnet client.
2. Use HyperTerminal to access a remote server.
3. Use the Windows FTP client to access a FTP site.
4. Log on to a public FTP site.
5. Download an ASCII text file and a binary file.
6. Use the Internet Explorer FTP client to download a file.
7. Install the WinZip compression utility.
8. Install the LeechFTP client.
9. Download and upload files using a graphical FTP client.

Networking

RESOURCES

1. PC-compatible desktop/tower computer system — Customer-supplied desktop/tower hardware system **OR** Marcraft MC-8000 Computer Hardware Trainer **OR** suitable PC hardware trainer with 64 MB RAM
2. Windows Me operating system (installed)
3. Internet access through a network connection or modem

DISCUSSION

Telnet is a service you can use to "TELephone - NETwork" with a remote computer. For example, if you were a sports reporter for the New York Times newspaper, and you were watching the Yankees play the Braves at Turner Field in Atlanta, Georgia, you could "telnet" to the computer at the Times office in New York City, and enter your story immediately from this remote location. The information would be presented on the screen of your portable computer, just as if you were back at your desk in New York. This type of remote system access usually uses terminal-emulation software to create a compatible interface for a completely different kind of computer. Typically, a Windows computer is used to access and use a UNIX/LINUX system. You should note that Telnet will only be able to access those host servers that have been pre-configured to support the telnet protocol.

NOTE: The layout and procedures at web, Telnet, and FTP sites can change fairly often. The instructions below may have to be modified to comply with those changes. Even so, the basic structure of these sites and the applications you download will be similar to the steps used in this lab procedure.

PROCEDURE - 34

Networking

PROCEDURE

For the following procedure you will install the Windows HyperTerminal telnet client, configure it, and use it to log on to a public telnet site.

NOTE: If you already have HyperTerminal installed on your computer, you may skip to Step 2.

1. **Install the Windows HyperTerminal telnet client**
   ___ a. Boot to the Windows Me desktop.
   ___ b. Navigate the path *Start/Settings/Control Panel* and open the **Add/Remove Programs Wizard**.
   ___ c. Click on the **Windows Setup** tab.
   ___ d. In the *Components* window, double-click on **Communications**.
   ___ e. Click to select the check box next to **HyperTerminal**.
   ___ f. Click on the **OK** button.
   ___ g. Click on the **OK** button to begin installation.

2. **Set up a telnet session using HyperTerminal**
   ___ a. Navigate the path *Start/Programs/Accessories/Communications* and select **HyperTerminal** to run it.

   NOTE: If you are using a LAN connection and do not have a modem installed, you may be asked to install one. Just cancel this and continue.

   ___ b. In the *New Connection* window type **Aztec-ASU** into the *Name* box, then click on the **OK** button.
   ___ c. In the *Connect to* window, click on the triangle to open the drop-down menu next to the Connect Using box. Select your modem if you are using one to connect to the Internet. If you are using a LAN connection to the Internet, select TCP/IP (Winsock).
   ___ d. In the *Host address* box, type **aztec2.asu.edu**, and then click on the **OK** button.
   ___ e. Maximize the *HyperTerminal* window.

3. **Use telnet to log in to the AzTeC server**
   ___ a. Read the welcome section, then record the full name for the abbreviation AzTeC in Table 34-1.
   ___ b. Record the provided login name in Table 34-2.
   ___ c. Record the provided password in Table 34-3.
   ___ d. At the login prompt type **guest**, and press the **ENTER** key. Your screen should be similar to Figure 34-1.
   ___ e. At the password prompt, type **visitor** and press the **ENTER** key.
   ___ f. Follow the prompts until you see the main menu.
   ___ g. Explore AzTeC.
   ___ h. Close HyperTerminal.
   ___ i. When asked if you are sure, click on the **Yes** button.

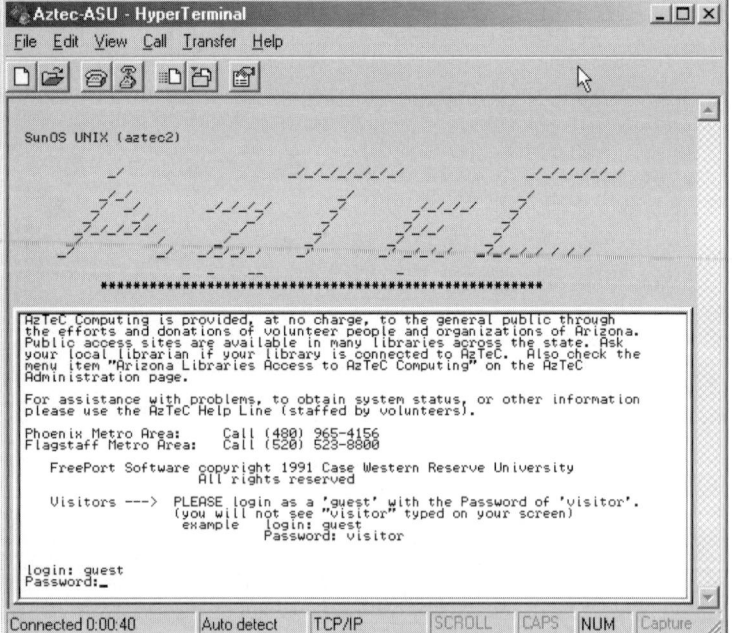

Figure 34-1: The AzTeC-ASU Welcome Screen

PROCEDURE - 34

Transferring Files Using an FTP Client

FTP (File Transfer Protocol) is an older communication protocol used to transfer files over a remote network connection. Before the creation of the World Wide Web, almost all files were moved in this manner. The widest use of FTP today is for downloading software. For example, almost all manufacturers have a download page on their web site. At this page you can download a demo, a shareware or freeware version of their product, or the latest driver, revision, or patch for a product.

FTP is also a good tool for troubleshooting a TCP/IP connection. First, if a file can be sent or received, the connection is good. Second, the information collected during the transfer of a large file is the best way to evaluate the speed of a particular connection. It should be noted that FTP will only work on host servers that are configured to support the FTP protocol. Standard HTTP web servers will not normally allow you to use FTP to access the files on the system.

The procedure used to log on to a public FTP site is very simple. Typically, you will be asked to enter a login name and password. Traditionally, users could log on to a public FTP site by using "anonymous" FTP. This means that a user would enter "anonymous" for the requested login name, and "anonymous" for the password. This would allow the user limited guest privileges to use the site. Currently, most sites that allow anonymous FTP use "ftp" for the login name, and the most common requested password is your e-mail address.

Windows has a very simple FTP client that can be accessed through the Start menu by choosing Run and typing **ftp**, or by entering **ftp** at the MS-DOS command prompt. If you wish to use this client to transfer ASCII text files, all you have to do is navigate to the file's location and type **get** *filename* at the ftp prompt. This won't work with non-text files that have extensions such as .exe, .jpg, .pdf, and so on. In order to download these types of files you will have to switch to binary mode. To do this you will need to type **binary** at the FTP prompt. After you are finished you can switch back to ASCII mode by typing **ascii** at the FTP prompt. After finishing, the downloaded files can be found in the directory from which you accessed FTP.

Fortunately, in most cases you should not need to use this awkward Windows utility. Most web browsers, such as IE and Navigator, have built-in FTP capability. This allows the web site visitor to use pre-created FTP tasks without having to do anything other than point and click on a hyperlink. While these predefined tasks can be very helpful to the user, if you wish to do anything more than the simplest of FTP tasks, it might be best to upgrade to a graphical FTP client. Fortunately, there are several excellent freeware and shareware FTP clients available, such as LeechFTP, WS_FTP LE, CuteFTP, and FTP Voyager. These FTP clients automatically identify the type of file you are transferring (text or binary) and use the appropriate download method. These graphical FTP clients have intuitive interfaces that use drag-and-drop and standard Windows-like navigation to make it very easy to transfer files.

Many files at FTP sites are available for download as compressed archive files, most commonly in the .zip, .tar, .sit, .bin, or .hqx formats. In order to decompress these files after download, you will need to have a utility such as WinZip, PKZip, or Expander installed on your computer. These compression utilities can be downloaded from a shareware download web site, such as *download.com* or *tucows.com*.

In the next part of this lab you will install the WinZip archive utility and the LeechFTP client. You will use the Windows FTP client to access the Marcraft public FTP site and download an ASCII text file and a binary file, and then use the Internet Explorer FTP client to download a file. Finally, you will download and upload files using the Leech FTP client.

1. **Access the Marcraft public FTP site**
   ___a. Navigate the path *Start/Programs/Accessories* to open the *MS-DOS command prompt* window.
   ___b. At the MS-DOS command prompt, type **cd c:\downloads** and press the **ENTER** key to change to your downloads directory. If your *DOWNLOADS* folder is not at this location, just navigate to an appropriate directory.
   ___c. At the MS-DOS command prompt, type **ftp ftp.mic-inc.com** and press the **ENTER** key.

PROCEDURE - 34

___ d. At the User prompt type **anonymous** and press the **ENTER** key.
___ e. At the password prompt type your e-mail address and press the **ENTER** key.
___ f. At the FTP prompt type **ls** and press the **ENTER** key to list the files in the directory.
___ g. At the FTP prompt type **cd pub** and press the **ENTER** key to change to the pub directory.
___ h. At the FTP prompt type **ls** and press the **ENTER** key to list the files in the directory.
___ i. At the FTP prompt type **cd downloads** and press the **ENTER** key to change to the downloads directory. Your screen should be similar to Figure 34-2.

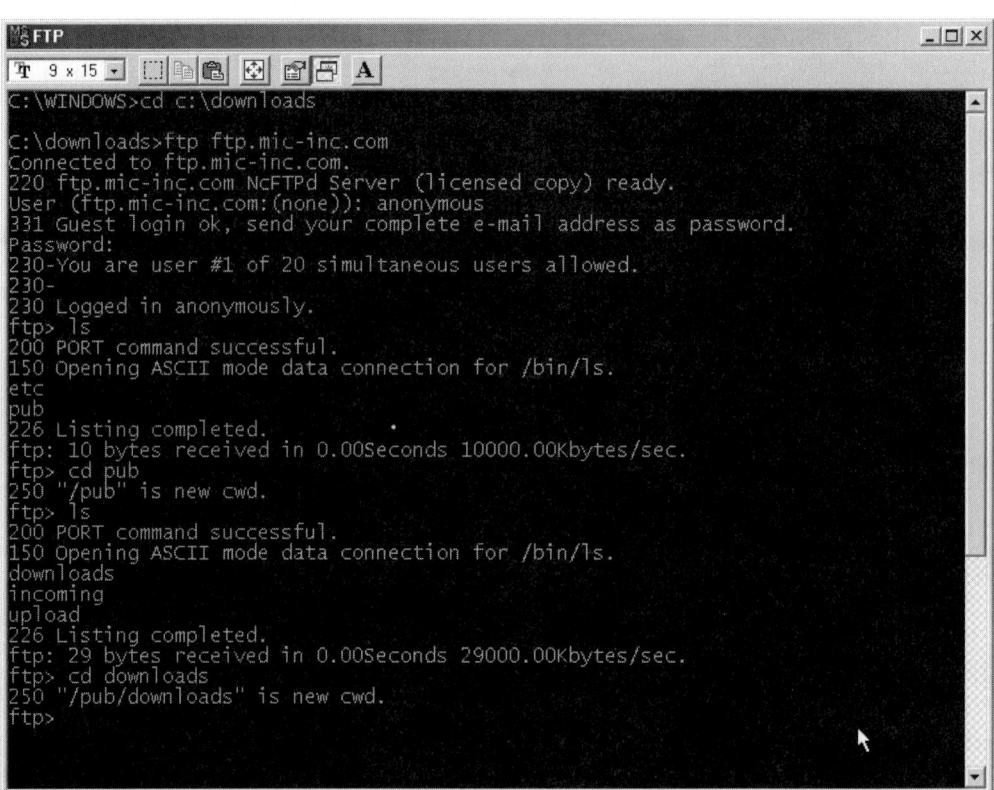

Figure 34-2: The Windows FTP Client

2. **Download a text and binary file with FTP**
   ___ a. At the FTP prompt type **get test1.txt** and press the **ENTER** key to download an ASCII text file.
   ___ b. In Table 34-4 record the bytes received, time, and speed of the download.

3. **Download a binary file with FTP**
   ___ a. At the FTP prompt type **binary** and press the **ENTER** key to switch to binary format.
   ___ b. At the FTP prompt type **get marcraft.gif** and press the **ENTER** key to download a binary file (in this case a GIF image).
   ___ c. At the FTP prompt type **get lftp13.zip** and press the **ENTER** key to download a binary file (in this case an FTP client program).
   ___ d. When the download is done record the bytes received, time, and speed of the download in Table 34-5.
   ___ e. At the FTP prompt type **ascii** and press the **ENTER** key to switch back to ASCII text format.
   ___ f. At the FTP prompt type **quit** and press the **ENTER** key to switch back to ASCII text format.
   ___ g. At the MS-DOS command prompt, type **dir** and press the **ENTER** key to view the content of your downloads directory.
   ___ h. At the MS-DOS command prompt, type **exit** and press the **ENTER** key to return to Windows.

PROCEDURE - 34

4. Use the Internet Explorer FTP client to download the WinZip installation file
  ___a. Navigate the path *Start/Run* to open the *Run* window.
  ___b. In the *Open* box type **www.winzip.com** and press the **ENTER** key.
  ___c. Click on the hyperlink labeled *Download*.
  ___d. Click on the link labeled *Download WinZip*.
  ___e. Select the **Save this program to disk** radio button, and then click on the **OK** button.
  ___f. Navigate to your *DOWNLOADS* folder and then click on the **Save** button.
  ___g. When the file is done downloading, click on the **Close** button.

NOTE: If you already have WinZip installed on your computer, you may skip to Step 6.

5. Install the WinZip compression utility
  ___a. Open Windows Explorer and navigate to your *C:\DOWNLOADS* folder.

NOTE: If your DOWNLOADS folder is not at this location, just navigate to an appropriate directory.

  ___b. Double-click the file **winzip80.exe** to begin.
  ___c. Click on the **Setup** button to begin the installation of WinZip, and then click on **OK** to use the default location for installing the program.
  ___d. Click on the **Next** button to continue, and then click on the **Yes** button to accept the license agreement.
  ___e. Click on the **Next** button if you are familiar with programs such as WinZip. Otherwise, view the Help information before clicking on the **Next** button.
  ___f. Click on the radio button next to the **Start with WinZip Classic** option, and then click on the **Next** button.
  ___g. Select **Express Setup** and click on the **Next** button.
  ___h. Click on the **Next** button to associate WinZip with all supported archive file types.
  ___i. When the installation completes, click on the **Finish** button, and then close the *Tip of the Day* window.

6. Install the LeechFTP client
  ___a. In the Taskbar, click on the **Downloads** button to bring it to the front.
  ___b. Double-click the installation file **lftp13.zip**.
  ___c. If the *WinZip license* window appears, click on the **I Agree** button to continue.
  ___d. Double-click the file **Setup.exe** in the *WinZip* window, and then click on the **OK** button to begin.
  ___e. Click on the **Next** button in the *LeechFTP1.3 Installation* window, and then click on the **Next** button to accept the *DEFAULT* folder.
  ___f. Click on the **Finished** button when the installation process is done.

7. Run the LeechFTP client and log on to ftp.mic-inc.com
  ___a. Navigate the path *Start/Programs/LeechFTP* to run LeechFTP.
  ___b. At the left side panel, click on the **Threads** tab.
  ___c. In the center panel, double-click the folder with a blue arrow and labeled ".." to go up one level in the directory tree.
  ___d. Again, in the center panel, double-click the folder with a blue arrow and labeled ".." to go up to the C:\ root directory.
  ___e. In the central panel, double-click on your personal *DOWNLOADS* folder to open it. If your *DOWNLOADS* folder is not at this location, just navigate to an appropriate directory.
  ___f. Click on the **lightning bolt** button in the toolbar to start a new FTP connection.
  ___g. Type **ftp.mic-inc.com** in the *Host or URL* box, and then click on the **OK** button.
  ___h. In the right panel, double-click the folder labeled *PUB* to open it.

PROCEDURE - 34

___i. Click on the **Remote** menu, then click on **Add Bookmark** and type **Marcraft** into the bookmark description box, and then click on the **OK** button. Your screen should now appear similar to Figure 34-3.

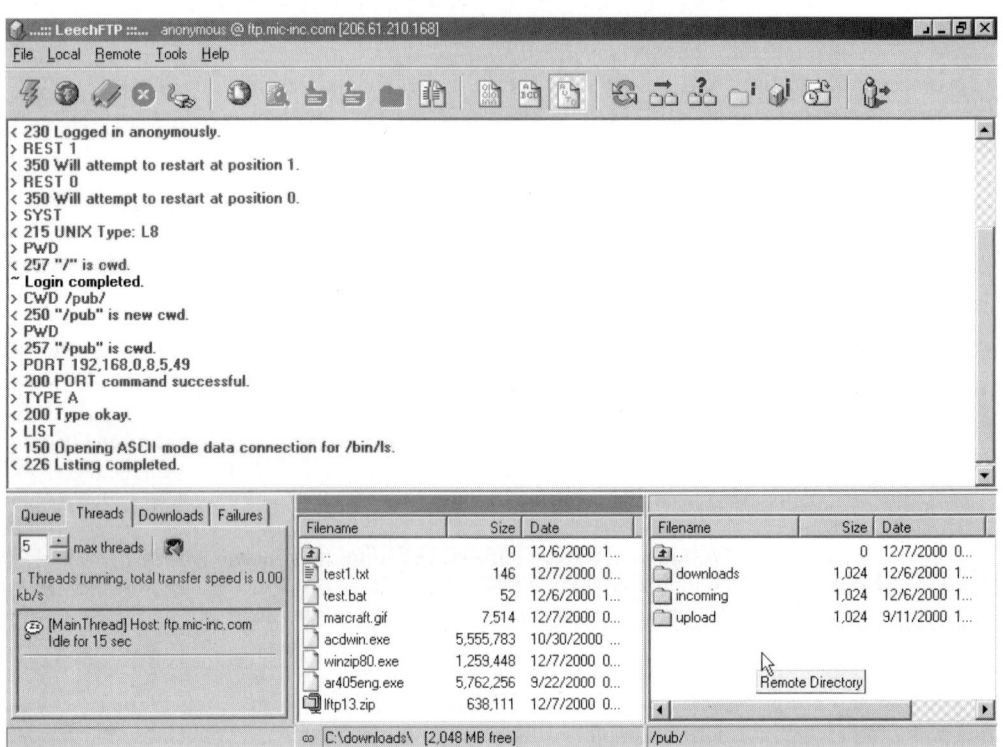

Figure 34-3: The LeechFTP Window

NOTE: You should make a bookmark every time you visit a new FTP site. If at any time the FTP server disconnects you, just log on again by clicking on the Show Bookmarks button (on the toolbar, third from the left), then double-clicking the bookmark you created for that particular FTP site.

8. **Download and examine a text file using LeechFTP**
   ___a. In the right panel, double-click the folder labeled **DOWNLOADS** to open this directory.
   ___b. Click and hold the file **dirmap.txt**, and then drag-and-drop it over the center panel, which represents your personal downloads directory.
   ___c. Double-click the file **dirmap.txt** in your center panel, and then read the content of this file.
   ___d. Click on the **Disconnect from remote host** button (looks like a power plug) in the toolbar if you are still connected.
   ___e. Click on the **Normal Connect** button (lightning bolt).
   ___f. In the *Host or URL* box type **ftp.microsoft.com**, then click on the **OK** button.

NOTE: If a confirmation window appears, click on OK to continue.

   ___g. Click on the **Remote** menu in the toolbar and select **Add Bookmark**.
   ___h. Type **Microsoft** into the box, and then click on **OK**.
   ___i. Using the directory map from *dirmap.txt*, navigate to the */deskapps/games* directory.
   ___j. Right-click the file *readme.txt* and select **View File** from the pop-up menu.
   ___k. Read the description under *Public*, then close the *readme.txt* window.
   ___l. Double-click the folder labeled **PUBLIC** to open it.
   ___m. Double-click the folder labeled **BASEBALL2001** to open it.

PROCEDURE - 34

____n. Click on the **Change Remote Directory** button (looks like two folders with an arrow over it) in the toolbar.
____o. In Table 34-6, record the FTP site address and the path you must navigate in order to reach the baseball 2001 game demo.
____p. Click on the **Cancel** button to close the *Change Remote Directory* window.

9. Download a video file from the Marcraft FTP site
____a. From the **File** menu select **Disconnect**.
____b. Click on the **Show Bookmarks** button on the toolbar.
____c. Double-click on **Marcraft** in the *Bookmarks* window.
____d. In the right panel, double-click the folder labeled **DOWNLOADS** to open this directory.
____e. In the right panel, click on the file **dwnld.avi**, and then drag-and-drop it into your personal *DOWNLOADS* folder (center panel). Downloading this file should take a maximum of 8 minutes (check the progress display in the *Threads* tab).
____f. After downloading is finished, double-click the file **dwnld.avi** in the center panel. The *Windows Media Player* window will appear displaying a video similar to Figure 34-4.

NOTE: If you do not have a sound card installed on your system, you may be presented with an error message explaining that the sound cannot be played. Click on the Close button to begin playing the video portion of the file.

Figure 34-4: Windows Media Player Window with DWNLD.AVI Displayed

NOTE: If the proper multimedia codec (<u>co</u>ding and <u>dec</u>oding file) is not installed on your system, you will be prompted with a dialog box asking permission to install the codec. If so, click on Yes to continue.

____g. After viewing the video, close the window.

10. Create a test file for uploading
____a. On the Taskbar, click on the **dirmap.txt - Notepad** button.
____b. Click on **File** and then select **New**.
____c. Type **This is an FTP upload test by *yourname***.
____d. Click on **File** and select **Save As** from the *File* menu.
____e. Type **upld*xxx*** in the File name box (where *xxx* are your initials), and then click on the **Save** button.

PROCEDURE - 34

NOTE: Make sure that this file is saved in the correct directory, so that you do not have to search for it later.

11. Upload a file using LeechFTP
  ___ a. On the Taskbar, click on the **LeechFTP** button.

NOTE: If you have become disconnected, click on the Show Bookmarks button. In the Bookmarks window, double-click on Marcraft to reconnect.

  ___ b. In the right panel, scroll to the right and read the permission flags for the *UPLOAD* and *INCOMING* directories. Record these permission flags in Table 34-7.

NOTE: There are two upload folders in the right panel. The INCOMING folder is for the general public and the UPLOAD folder is for the site administrator.

  ___ c. In the right panel, double-click the **DOWNLOADS** folder.
  ___ d. In the center panel, click on the **upld*xxx*.txt** text file, and then drag-and-drop it into the right panel (into the *DOWNLOADS* directory).
  ___ e. Record the resulting error messages in Table 34-8.
  ___ f. Click on the **Change remote directory** button in the toolbar.
  ___ g. Click on the **UPLOAD** folder to highlight it, and then click on the **Change Directory** button.
  ___ h. In the center panel, click on the **upld*xxx*.txt** text file, and then drag-and-drop it into the right panel (into the *UPLOAD* directory).
  ___ i. Record the resulting error messages in Table 34-9.
  ___ j. Click on the **Change remote directory** button in the toolbar.
  ___ k. Click on the **INCOMING** folder to highlight it, and then click on the **Change directory** button.
  ___ l. In the center panel, click on the **upld*xxx*.txt** text file, and then drag-and-drop it into the right panel (into the *INCOMING* directory).
  ___ m. Record the resulting messages in Table 34-10.
  ___ n. Click on the words **refresh needed** at the top of the right panel to highlight them.
  ___ o. In the toolbar, click on the **Refresh** button (appears as two green arrows going in a circle) to refresh your directory list.
  ___ p. Disconnect and exit LeechFTP, and then shut down your computer.

TABLES

Table 34-1

Full Name:	

Table 34-2

Provided Login Name:	

Table 34-3

Provided Password:	

PROCEDURE - 34

Table 34-4

ASCII Text File	
Bytes Received:	
Time to Download:	
Speed of Download:	

Table 34-5

Binary File	
Bytes Received:	
Time to Download:	
Speed of Download:	

Table 34-6

FTP Site Address:	
Path:	

Table 34-7

Permission Flags	
Upload Directory:	
Incoming Directory:	

Table 34-8

Download Error Messages:	

PROCEDURE - 34

Table 34-9

Upload Error Messages:	

Table 34-10

Incoming Directory Messages:	

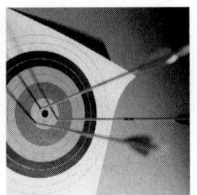

Feedback

LAB QUESTIONS

1. What kind of software is used to simulate a computer interface on a remote telnet connection?
2. Who owns the telnet server you used in this lab procedure?
3. What is the most accurate means of testing the speed of a network connection?
4. What is anonymous FTP?
5. Name one freeware graphical FTP client.

LAB PROCEDURE 35

Windows Me Internet Domain Names

OBJECTIVES

1. Examine the navigation functions of the Microsoft Internet Explorer (IE) web browser.
2. Visit Internet sites by FQDN.
3. Visit Internet sites by IP address.
4. Visit Internet sites by URL.
5. Use the TCP/IP utility NETSTAT to view the address of an Internet connection, including the port number.
6. Use the TCP/IP utility TRACERT to view a trace of your connection.

Networking

RESOURCES

1. PC-compatible desktop/tower computer system—Customer-supplied desktop/tower hardware system **OR** Marcraft MC-8000 Computer Hardware Trainer **OR** suitable PC hardware trainer with 64 MB RAM
2. Windows Me operating system (installed)
3. Internet access through a network connection or modem
4. Internet Explorer (installed)

DISCUSSION

The Domain Name System (DNS) was created in 1984 in order to make navigation on the Internet easier. DNS allows you to enter the logical name (e.g., www.microsoft.com), which is easy to remember and will rarely change, instead of the formal IP address (e.g., 207.68.137.36), which may change quite frequently. You experience DNS in action every time you visit an Internet web page. The page's readable Internet address usually appears in the Address bar of the browser. Since computers on the web actually connect by means of numeric IP addresses and not by name, DNS must map a particular Internet address (e.g., www.mic-inc.com) to a specific IP address number (e.g., 206.61.210.100).

When you enter the address www.microsoft.com, you will first be directed to a root DNS server that knows all of the .COM entries on the Internet. The root DNS server provides the IP addresses of all of the DNS servers that provide services to the microsoft.com domain. Now you will be put in contact with one of the microsoft.com DNS servers to get the IP address for the *www.microsoft.com* web server.

DNS uses a human-readable name called a Fully Qualified Domain Name (FQDN). An FQDN includes a computer's host name and the associated domain name. For example, given a local host server with a name of "accounting", and your network with a domain name of "mic-inc.com", the FQDN would be "accounting.mic-inc.com"; or, if the host is a World Wide Web server, the FQDN would be usually be "*www.mic-inc.com*".

NOTE: *Although DNS names are not case sensitive, they are usually written in lowercase.*

PROCEDURE - 35

The FQDN suffix, technically known as the top-level domain, defines the type of organization or country of origin associated with an address. Generally, commercial site addresses end with .com, government sites end with .gov, military sites end with .mil, educational institutions end with .edu, and non-profit organization sites end in .org. Sites from locations outside the United States end with a two-letter suffix, such as .uk for the United Kingdom (Britain) and .ca for Canada.

The format for reading the host and domain information from the IP address is defined when you use a subnet mask. For example, by using the most typical subnet mask, a Class C (255.255.255.0), you instruct TCP/IP to read the first three sets of numbers in the IP address as the domain name, and the last set would designate the address of a host computer on the network. For example, if ftp.microsoft.com is associated with the IP address 207.68.137.36, the first three numbers (207.68.137.xxx) would designate the commercial domain "microsoft.com", and the last number (xxx.xxx.xxx.36) would designate the host FTP server "ftp".

DNS will map an FQDN to the IP address of a specific server or host computer. But in order to reach a specific file on the web site you must enter a string of information called a Uniform Resource Locator (URL). For example, the URL **http://www.yale.edu:80/admissions/index.html** provides the following information:

http://	This host server uses the Hyper-Text Transfer Protocol.
www	This is a World Wide Web server.
yale	This web server provides services for Yale University.
edu	This is an educational institution.
:80	This is the number of the port accessed on this server.
/admissions	This is the name of the subdirectory being accessed; in this case, the Admissions Department.
/index.html	This is the name of the file to be displayed.

Networking

PROCEDURE

In this lab procedure you will navigate a browser to a web site using an FQDN, an IP address, and a URL. You will then download a file and examine the connection address using the NETSTAT and TRACERT TCP/IP utilities.

NOTE: Over time, the IP addresses and hyperlinks used in this lab are subject to change. Try to follow along as best you can using the links provided.

1. **Run the Internet Explorer browser**
    ___ a. Boot to the Windows Me desktop.
    ___ b. Click on the **Internet Explorer** icon on the Quick Launch toolbar.

2. **Navigate the World Wide Web using an FQDN**
    ___ a. Click in the *Address* box to highlight the current address.
    ___ b. Type **www.cisco.com** into the box and press the **ENTER** key. This homepage should be similar to Figure 35-1.

PROCEDURE - 35

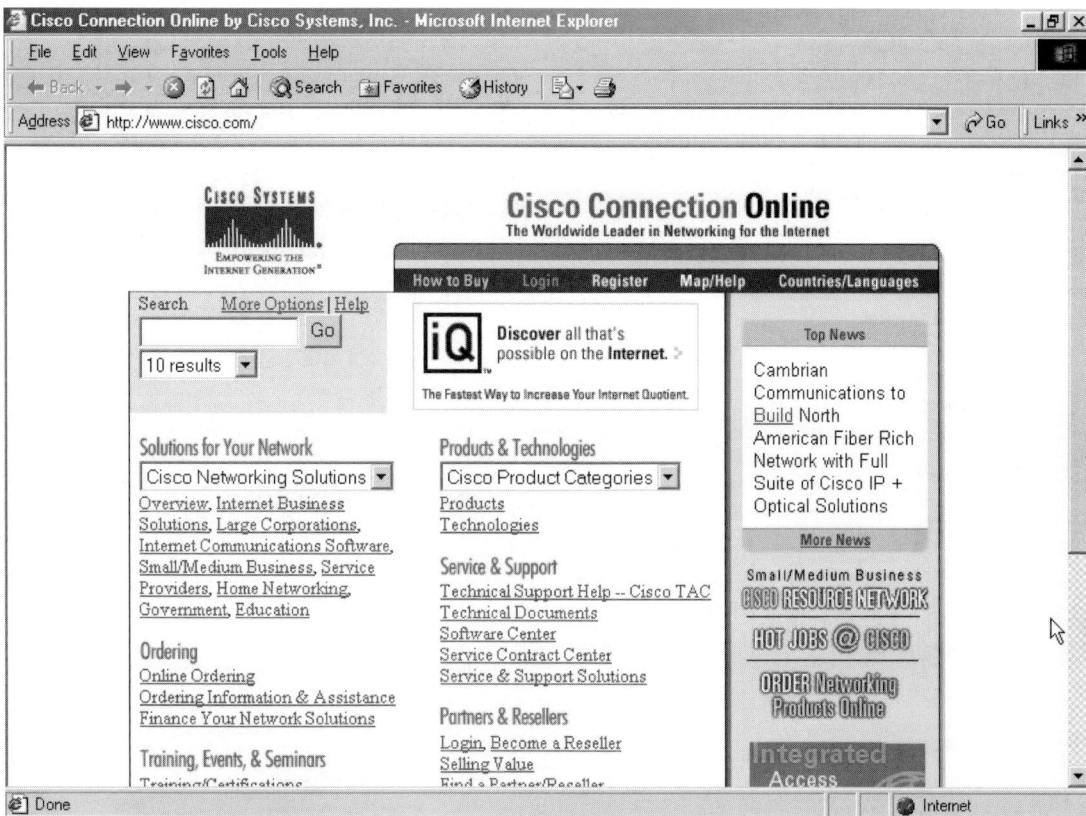

Figure 35-1: The Cisco Homepage

    c.   Record the address shown in the Address box in Table 35-1.
    d.   Locate and click on the link to the *Map/Help* page.
    e.   Record the address shown in the *Address* box in Table 35-2.
    f.   Click in the *Address* box to highlight the current address.
    g.   Type **www.windowsupdate.com** into the box and press the **ENTER** key.
    h.   Record the address shown in the *Address* box in Table 35-3.

3.   **Navigate the World Wide Web using an IP address**
    a.   Click in the *Address* box to highlight the current address.
    b.   Type **206.61.210.100** into the box and press the **ENTER** key. This homepage should be similar to Figure 35-2.
    c.   Record the name of the company, and the FQDN address shown in the *Address* box in Table 35-4.
    d.   Click in the *Address* box to highlight the current address.
    e.   Type **198.133.219.25** into the box and press the **ENTER** key.

PROCEDURE - 35

Figure 35-2: The Marcraft Homepage

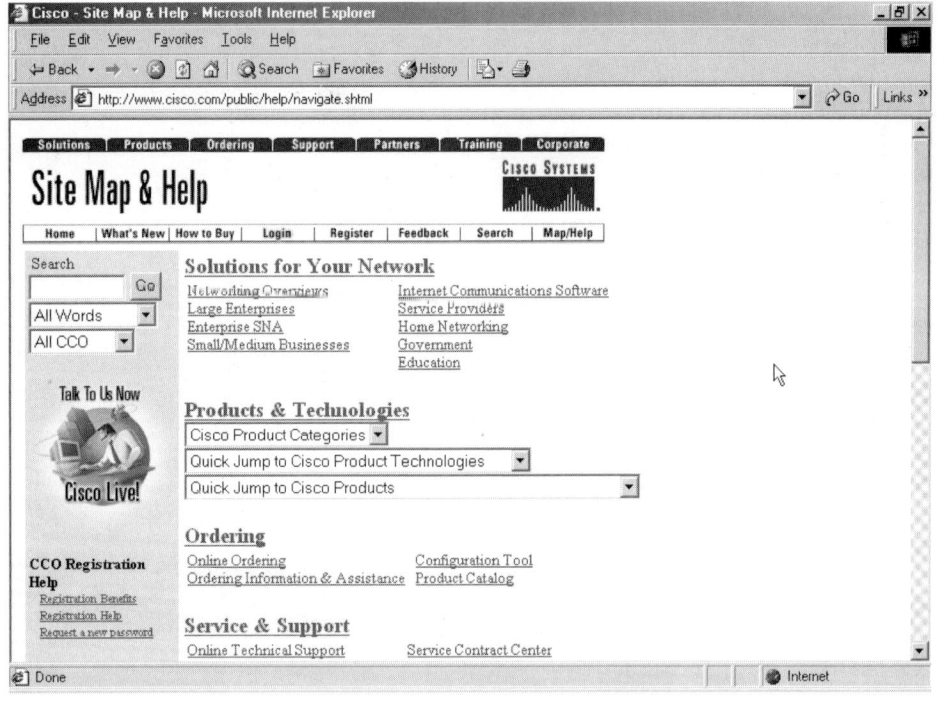

Figure 35-3: The Cisco Site Map

4. **Navigate the World Wide Web using a URL**

   ____ a. Click in the *Address* box to highlight the current address.

   ____ b. Type the address you recorded in Table 35-2 into the box and press the **ENTER** key. The web page should be similar to Figure 35-3.

PROCEDURE - 35

5. **Establish an active Internet connection by downloading a file**
   ___a. Click in the *Address* box to highlight the current address.
   ___b. Type **www.tucows.com** into the box and press the **ENTER** key to go to the Tucows download site.
   ___c. Click on the link labeled *Games*.
   ___d. Choose your region from the list, then click on the link for the nearest mirror server.
   ___e. In the Games navigation bar to the left, click on the link labeled *Download Software*.
   ___f. In the Action section, click on the link labeled *First Person Shooters*.
   ___g. Click on the link labeled *Download Now* for the first listed file.
   ___h. Click on the **OK** button and then click on the **Save** button to begin downloading the file.

6. **Open the MS-DOS Prompt window and run the NETSTAT utility**
   ___a. Minimize windows to view the desktop and double-click the **MS-DOS Prompt shortcut** to open it.
   ___b. Type **netstat** at the prompt and press the **ENTER** key.
   ___c. Record the Foreign Addresses of all connections in Table 35-5.
   ___d. Type **netstat -n** at the prompt and press the **ENTER** key. The window should appear similar to Figure 35-4.
   ___e. Record the Foreign Addresses of all connections in Table 35-6.

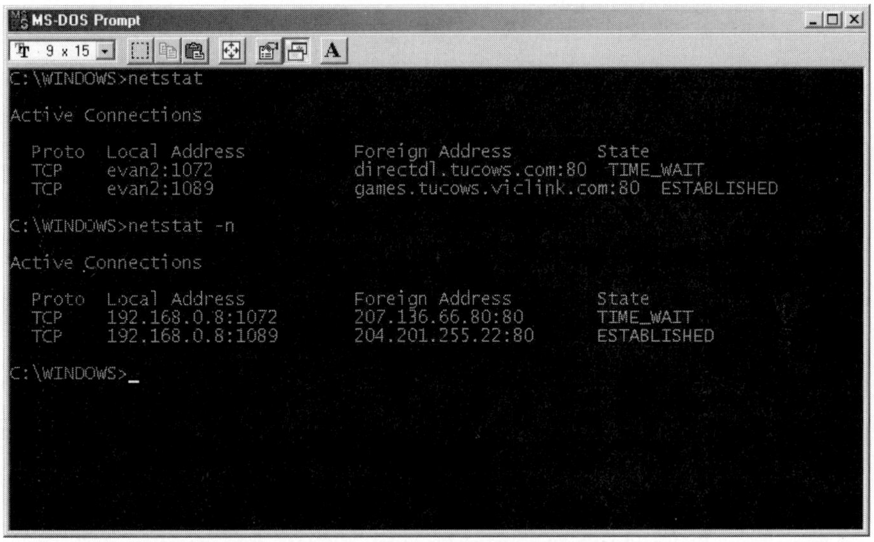

Figure 35-4: The NETSTAT Information

7. **Run the TRACERT utility**
   ___a. Type **tracert -h 10 FQDN** at the command prompt, where *FQDN* is the bottom FQDN address you recorded in Table 35-5. Press the **ENTER** key.
   ___b. Record the IP address associated with the FQDN you just entered in Table 35-7.
   ___c. Close the *MS-DOS Prompt* window, and cancel or finish the download.
   ___d. Close all open windows, and shut down the computer.

TABLES

Table 35-1

Cisco Homepage Address:	

Table 35-2

Map/Help Page Address:	

PROCEDURE - 35

Table 35-3

Windows Update Page Address:	

Table 35-4

Company Name:	
FQDN Address:	

Table 35-5

NETSTAT Connections	
Foreign Addresses:	

Table 35-6

NETSTAT -N Connections	
Foreign Addresses:	

Table 35-7

FQDN IP Address:	.

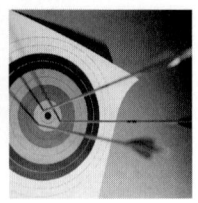

Feedback

LAB QUESTIONS

1. What two parts make up an FQDN?
2. Name three common domain suffixes.
3. What additional information does a URL show, compared to an FQDN?
4. What does a subnet mask do?
5. What happens in the DNS system when you enter a FQDN address in your web browser's Address box?

SYSTEM MAINTENANCE

LAB PROCEDURE 36

Windows Me Software Version Update Management

OBJECTIVES

1. Use the Windows Update utility to manage Windows.
2. Use an application's upgrade feature to automatically obtain and install the latest version.
3. Manually download and install the most recent display driver.

Software

RESOURCES

1. PC-compatible desktop/tower computer system — Customer-supplied desktop/tower hardware system **OR** Marcraft MC-8000 Computer Hardware Trainer **OR** suitable PC hardware trainer with 64 MB RAM
2. Windows Me operating system (installed)
3. Internet access through a network connection or modem
4. Internet Explorer 5.0 (installed)
5. Windows Me CD-ROM

DISCUSSION

The software on your computer will become outdated more frequently than you might imagine. Most applications or drivers should be upgraded or patched at least once every six months. Upgrades are new versions of a program containing significant changes in functionality from the old version. Patches replace or repair program files in order to fix small bugs in the application, and should be located and installed fairly often. Therefore, an important part of managing any computer system is to conduct periodic updates. Approximately once a month, you should check to see if there are any new updates that need to be downloaded and installed. To make this task easier, you should create a list of the current versions of every major device driver and application on your system, similar to the one shown in Figure 36-1.

There are several different methods to examine the version information of an application. The easiest, but least informative, is to right-click the .exe file itself and select *Properties* from the pop-up menu. Running the application, then selecting *About* from the *Help* menu will usually access the most comprehensive information on a particular application.

Many applications have an automatic update feature that can be accessed via the *Help* menu. This feature will typically access the Internet and navigate to the appropriate company's web page. Some versions of this feature will actually find, download, and install any needed updates automatically.

PROCEDURE - 36

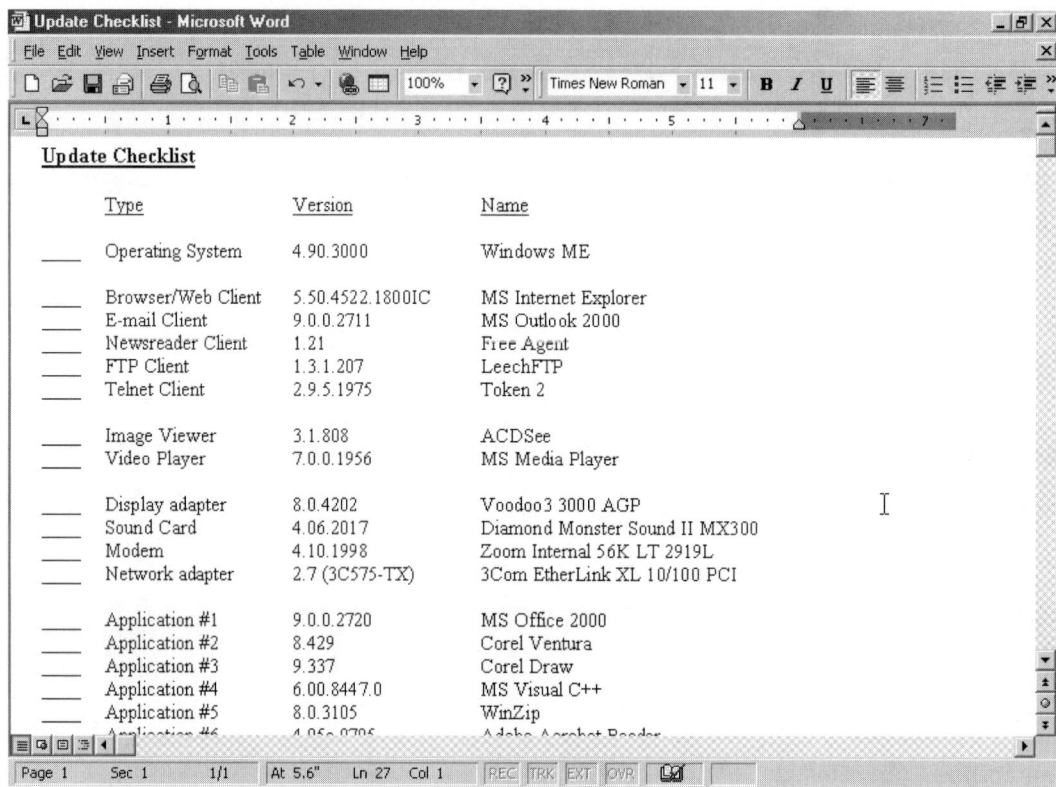

Figure 36-1: Update Checklist

Upgrades or patches to the operating system itself are best done through the built-in Windows Update feature. When you run Windows Update (if you can connect to the Internet), your web browser will open the Microsoft Windows Update web site, displaying a list of possible updates for you to download and install. You should use this feature at least once a month to make certain that you are not missing any vital patches needed for a bug or security fix.

Software

PROCEDURE

Updating Windows Me

The first item on any update checklist should be the operating system. For this procedure we will use the Windows Update feature of Windows Me to select, download, and install items for the operating system.

1. **Run Windows Update**
   ___ a. Boot to the Windows Me desktop.
   ___ b. Click on **Start** and select **Windows Update** from the *Start* menu.
   ___ c. Maximize the *Internet Explorer* window.

256 - LAB GROUP 4

PROCEDURE - 36

2. **Select and download the Windows Me critical update**

    ___ a. At the *Windows Update* web page, click on the hyperlink labeled *Product Updates*. If prompted to install MS WIN Update Active Setup, click on the **Yes** button. The screen that is displayed should appear similar to Figure 36-2.

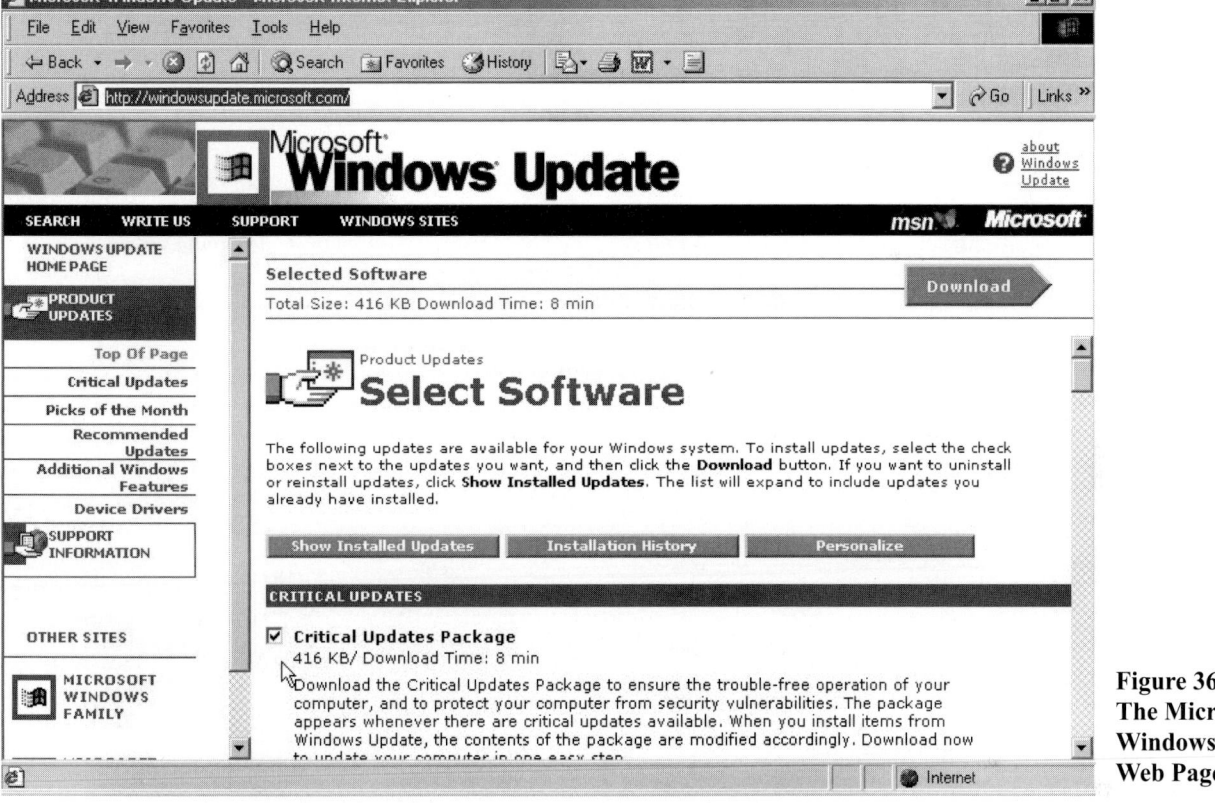

Figure 36-2: The Microsoft Windows Update Web Page

    ___ b. If you already have a critical update automatically selected, skip to Step d.
    ___ c. Scroll down to the RECOMMENDED UPDATES section, and then select the first item (i.e., click on the check box).
    ___ d. Record the name of the file, the file size, and the predicted download time in Table 36-1.
    ___ e. Click on the hyperlink button labeled *Download*.
    ___ f. At the next page, click on the hyperlink button labeled *Start Download*.
    ___ g. At the license window click on the **Yes** button.

NOTE: Different installation applications may have different steps to go through. Just follow the instructions appearing on the screen.

    ___ h. If prompted to Restart now, click on the **Yes** button.
    ___ i. If you are not prompted to restart your computer when the download and installation are complete, click on the hyperlink button labeled *Back*.
    ___ j. After reboot, read any help notices and then close all windows to return to the desktop.

PROCEDURE - 36

Using an Application's Upgrade Feature

Most current applications have a built-in update feature. At a minimum, this feature will access the manufacturer's web site, which will usually contain updates, patches, or technical support information. At this point you would look for a link that will download the needed installation file. Fortunately, it is becoming more common for applications to have an automatic update feature. When executed, usually by selecting an item from a menu, this feature will automatically connect, find, download, and install any needed updates. For example, Apple's QuickTime Player, Microsoft's Windows Media Player, and Real's RealPlayer all have this feature.

NOTE: The navigation and layout of a web site will change fairly frequently. You may have to modify your point-and-click sequences to match what you experience. The same is true for installation programs: The actual button labels and sequence may change slightly from version to version.

1. **Run the update feature for Microsoft Windows Media Player**
    ___a.   On the desktop, double-click the **Windows Media Player** icon to run it.
    ___b.   Click on the **Help** menu and select **About Windows Media Player**.
    ___c.   Record the version number in Table 36-2.
    ___d.   Click on the **Help** menu and select **Check For Player Upgrades** as shown in Figure 36-3.

Figure 36-3: Select the Media Player Automatic Update Feature

PROCEDURE - 36

___ e. At the *Windows Media Component Setup* window, as shown in Figure 36-4, click on the **Next** button to continue.

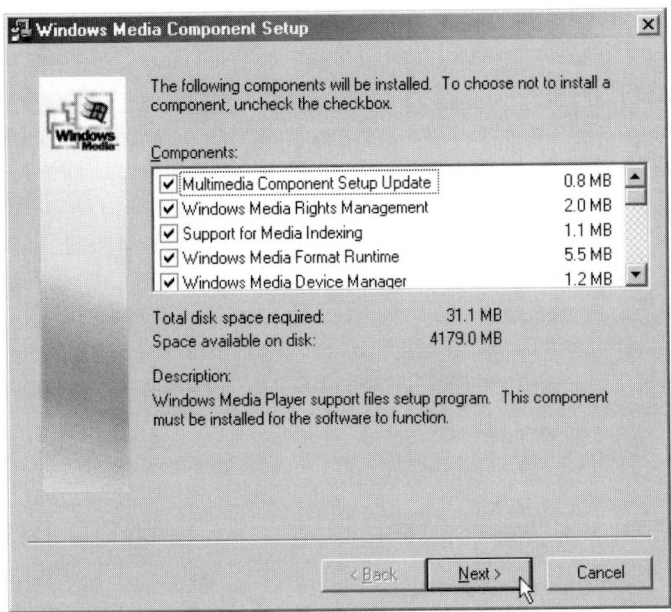

Figure 36-4: The Windows Media Component Setup Window

NOTE: If this is the first time you are updating Windows Media Player you might have as much as 40 MB of files to download and install. If you only have a 56K modem connection this could take over 2 hours to download. In this case, select only those components that can be downloaded in less than 10 minutes. This means that you should select items that add up to no more than 3 MB.

___ f. Click on the **Next** button to begin installation of the needed updates.
___ g. When setup has completed, click on the **Finish** button to restart your computer.
___ h. Run Windows Media Player by double-clicking the desktop icon.
___ i. Click on the **Return to Full Mode** button in the lower right corner to open the full *Media Player* window.
___ j. Click on the **Help** menu and select **About Windows Media Player.**
___ k. Record the version number in Table 36-3.
___ l. Close Windows Media Player.

Manually Downloading and Installing a Driver Update

Most device drivers, and many utility programs and older applications, require you to manually search for, download, and install any needed updates. Particularly with drivers, you will need to monitor the manufacturer's web site for updates to your current setup. Drivers are updated very frequently, so there is probably a newer driver than the one you have, even if you just bought the piece of hardware. This is why a checklist, such as the one shown in Figure 36-1, can be very helpful in managing driver updates.

PROCEDURE - 36

In order to make your search easier, you should try to find out the name of the manufacturer, the product model number, and, if possible, the name of the current driver. You must also be aware of which operating system will be using this driver. The most detailed information about your drivers can usually be acquired by opening up the system Control Panel from *Settings* on the *Start* menu. The *System Properties* window is a control center for all the hardware in your PC and the software drivers that control it. Select the *Device Manager* tab to see a list of all the kinds of devices on your system. Highlight the item you are interested in and click on the *Properties* button. Click on the *Driver* tab and then click on the *Driver File Details* button to access detailed information about the driver. The exceptions to this are your printer drivers, which can be found by using the path *Start/Settings/Printers*, right-clicking on the printer, and selecting *Properties* from the pop-up menu.

NOTE: Sometimes the company listed on the component is not the manufacturer who built the component. If you are having trouble determining the manufacturer, a good way to find out is by tracking the FCC ID located on the component. The FCC ID is a set of numbers issued by the U.S. Federal Communications Commission and should be on almost every piece of computer equipment. It usually says "FCCID:" right on the component. You can enter this number in the database search form located at http://www.fcc.gov/oet/fccid/. This should tell you the manufacturer of your component. If the search returns nothing, try removing the last letter or number from the FCC ID and try again, or enter just the first three letters, which is usually the company indicator.

Once you have identified the manufacturer of your device, you must locate the download page on the manufacturer's web site. A good place to start looking is a web site such as WinDrivers.com (*http://www.windrivers.com*). If the manufacturer is very obscure, you can look up the manufacturer by searching for the company name at a search site such as Yahoo.com (*http://dir.yahoo.com/Computers_and_Internet/Hardware/*).

For this lab you will be searching for a display driver, so here is a list of web pages for the manufacturers of the most commonly encountered video cards:

3dfx	*http://www.3dfxgamers.com/*
ASUS	*http://www.asus.com/products/software1.html*
ATI	*http://support.ati.com/drivers/*
Cirrus Logic	*http://www.cirrus.com/Drivers/*
Creative Labs	*http://www.creative.com/support/files/download.asp*
Diamond	*http://www.diamondmm.com/*
ELSA	*http://domino.elsa.de/internet/ElsaFileArea.nsf*
Hercules	*http://us.hercules.com/*
Matrox	*http://www.matrox.com/mga/support/drivers/*
SiS	*http://www.sis.com.tw/support/download/driver1.htm*
STB	*http://www.stb.com/drivers/*
S3	*http://www.s3.com/*
Trident	*http://www.trid.com/videocomm/download/download.htm*

Although most manufacturers will provide an installation program for you to download, some will require you to install the driver file manually. Typically there are instructions for installing the driver in a Readme or help file accompanying the driver. You'll have to copy the driver file into a particular folder on your hard drive, or unzip a bunch of files, and then install the driver manually.

PROCEDURE - 36

The most common method of installing a driver manually involves using the Device Manager located in the system Control Panel. Just locate the particular device's properties window as mentioned above, click on the *Driver* tab, and then click on the *Update Driver* button. Another method that is sometimes seen requires the user to locate an .INF file among the downloaded items. Just right-click the .INF file and select Install from the pop-up menu. A script is run that places the needed driver components in their proper place.

Printers are a little different. The easiest way to install a new printer driver is to open the *Printers* icon in the Control Panel folder, then double-click the *Add New Printer* icon. A wizard will pop up to guide you through the process. When you get to the dialog listing all the printer types, just click on the *Have Disk* button instead of picking a printer. Even if your printer is listed, you will want to install the new driver you just got rather than the one that is listed. The Add Printer wizard will smoothly handle the rest of the installation.

In the following steps you will locate, download, and install a driver update for your video card.

1. **Examine your current display adapter driver**
   ___a. Navigate the path *Start/Settings/Control Panel* and then double-click the **System** icon.
   ___b. Select the **Device Manager** tab.
   ___c. Click on the plus [+] button next to **Display adapters** to reveal the display driver.
   ___d. Double-click the name of the display driver to open the display adapter properties window.
   ___e. Record the driver name and manufacturer in Table 36-4.
   ___f. Click on the **Driver** tab, and then click on the **Driver File Details** button.
   ___g. Record the file version in Table 36-4.
   ___h. Right-click the desktop, select **Properties**, and click on the **Settings** tab.
   ___i. Click on the **Advanced** button, and then click on the **Adapter** tab. You will see a window similar

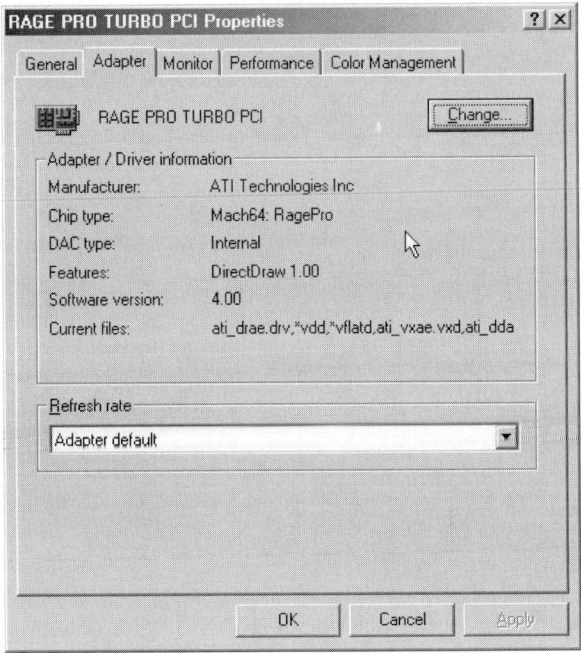

Figure 36-5: Display Adapter Properties

   to Figure 36-5.
   ___j. Record the chip type and current files in Table 36-4.

PROCEDURE - 36

2. Locate the appropriate driver update at the manufacturer's web site.
___a. Open Internet Explorer and navigate to the video card manufacturer's web site.

NOTE: Refer to the above list of manufacturers' web sites, or get the information from your instructor, if necessary.

___b. Click on the appropriate link, or links, to begin downloading the latest version of your driver (*ragedriver.exe* as an example).

> **WARNING**
>
> Make certain that you have selected the correct driver for your video card. Installing the wrong driver will usually require you to boot into Safe Mode, and then reinstall a default driver from the Windows Me CD-ROM.

3. Download the driver update
___a. Save the driver upgrade installation file(s) to your *C:\DOWNLOADS* folder.
___b. When the download is finished, if it is an archive file (.ZIP), allow WinZip to extract the files to your *DOWNLOADS* folder; otherwise just save it to your *DOWNLOADS* folder.
___c. Close Internet Explorer.

4. Automatically install the driver
___a. If your download is not an automatic installation file, skip to Step 5.
___b. If the driver you downloaded comes as an executable file (.EXE) run the file and follow the steps to install the driver automatically.
___c. When finished, skip to Step 6.

5. Manually install the new driver
___a. In the Video driver properties window, click on the **Change** button to begin manual installation of the driver.
___b. Click on the radio button to select **Specify the location of the driver (Advanced)**, and then click on the **Next** button to run the *Update Device Driver Wizard*.
___c. Click on the check box to select **Specify a location**.
___d. Click on the **Browse** button and navigate to your downloaded driver files (these should be in *C:\DOWNLOADS*) in the *Browse for Folder* window, and then click on the **OK** button.
___e. Click on the **Next** button to continue.
___f. After your new driver is located, click on the **Next** button.
___g. Click on the **Finish** button to begin installation of the new driver.
___h. If you are warned about installing a third-party driver, confirm to proceed.
___i. When your driver has successfully installed, close all windows and restart your computer as prompted.

6. Examine your new display driver
___a. Navigate the path *Start/Settings/Control Panel* and then double-click the **System** icon.
___b. Click on the plus [+] button next to **Display adapters** to reveal the display driver.
___c. Double-click the name of the display driver to open the display adapter properties window.
___d. Click on the **Driver** tab, and then click on the **Driver File Details** button.
___e. Record the driver name, file version, and the name of the current driver files in Table 36-5.
___f. Close all open windows and shut down the computer.

TABLES

Table 36-1

File Name:	
File Size:	
Predicted Download Time:	

Table 36-2

Windows Media Player Version Before Upgrade:	

Table 36-3

Windows Media Player Version After Upgrade:	

Table 36-4

Display Adapter	
Driver Name:	
Manufacturer:	
Driver File Version:	
Chip Type:	
Current Driver Files:	

PROCEDURE - 36

Table 36-5

Display Driver Updates	
Driver Name:	
Driver File Version:	
Current Driver Files:	

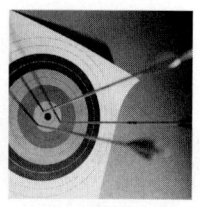

Feedback

LAB QUESTIONS

1. How often should you check for upgrades or patches for your most important software?
2. How would you find the version number of a device driver?
3. What type of device drivers are not managed by Device Manager in the system Control Panel?
4. Where can you usually find the most detailed information about an application?
5. How do you check for an upgrade or patch for Windows operating systems?

LAB PROCEDURE 37

Windows 2000 Software Version Update Management

OBJECTIVES

1. Upgrade to the latest Internet Explorer.
2. Install a Windows 2000 Service Pack.
3. Add Windows Media Player.
4. Remove Windows Media Player.

Software

RESOURCES

1. PC-compatible desktop/tower computer system — Customer-supplied desktop/tower hardware system **OR** Marcraft MC-8000 Computer Hardware Trainer **OR** suitable PC hardware trainer with Windows 2000 installed
2. Internet access through a network connection or modem

DISCUSSION

Windows 2000 needs to be updated periodically, just like Windows Me. Once a month you should check to see if there are any new updates that need to be downloaded and installed. An application's internal information display can be helpful in determining its version. Usually, you run the application and select About from the Help menu to access this feature. This feature may access the Internet and automatically find, download, and install any needed updates.

Upgrades, updates, or patches to the operating system itself are best done through the built-in Windows Update feature. Clicking on Start/Windows Update can access Windows Update. If you are connected to the Internet, this will connect you directly to the Microsoft web site and show you a list of possible downloads for you to access. You should use this feature at least once a month to make certain that you are not missing any vital patches needed for a bug or security fix. In this lab we will use this feature to add three things to the computer: Windows Media Player, the latest Internet Explorer, and a Windows 2000 Service Pack.

PROCEDURE

NOTE: This lab's time for completion will vary greatly depending on the bandwidth of the user's Internet connection. For the Service Pack section you may use the CD version instead of downloading the 15 MB file.

1. **Install Internet Explorer through Windows Update**
   ___a. Boot the computer to Windows 2000.
   ___b. From the Windows 2000 desktop, click on **Start/Windows Update**.

PROCEDURE - 37

____c. The browser will open and go to *windowsupdate.microsoft.com*. You will see a window similar to Figure 37-1. Click on **Product Updates**.

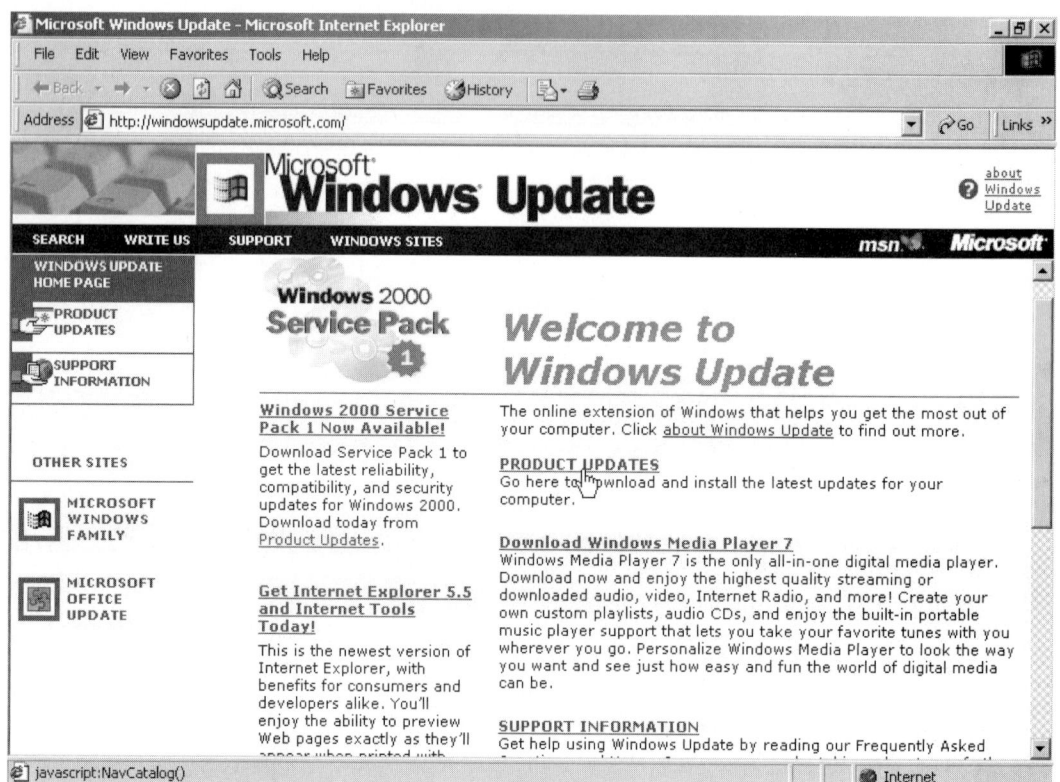

Figure 37-1: Windows Update

NOTE: The following procedures in this Step may vary over time.

____d. If this is the first time the computer has visited the page you will be receive a security warning. It asks if you want to install and run "Microsoft Active Setup". Click on **Yes**.

____e. Windows will check for available updates. Uncheck **Critical Updates package**, if it is selected. You can download this at a later time.

____f. Scroll down and look for the latest Internet Explorer. You may need to click on the **Show Installed Updates** button.

____g. Place a check next to **IE** and click on the **Download** button. You may get a warning similar to Figure 37-2. Click on **OK**.

____h. Click on the **Download** button again.

____i. Click on **Start Download**.

____j. Click on **Yes** to the terms of the License Agreement.

____k. You will see a download progress window. After the window has completed you will see the Internet Explorer License agreement once again. Click on the radio button next to **I accept the agreement** and click on **Next**.

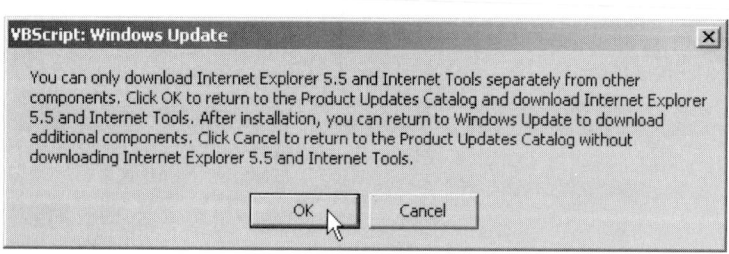

Figure 37-2: Separate Download of the Browser

PROCEDURE - 37

___l. The *Windows 2000 Install - 6.0MB* option appears. Click on **Next**. The download of components will appear similar to Figure 37-3.

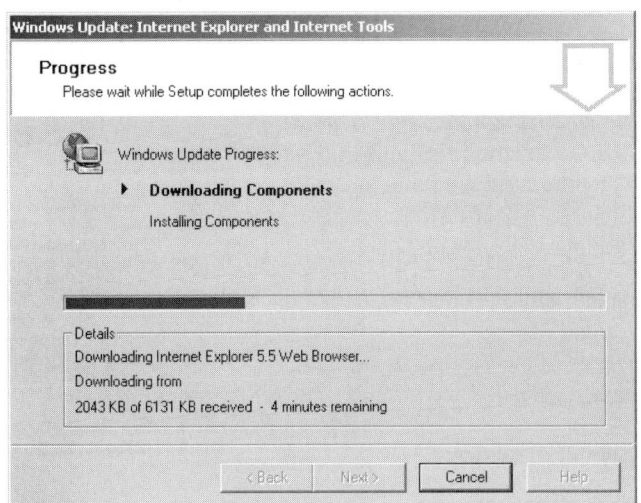

Figure 37-3: Download and Install Components

___m. After the program has downloaded and installed choose **Yes** to restart now.
___n. When Windows restarts, Browsing Services, Internet Tools, and System Services will be set up.

2. **Install Service Pack through Windows Update**
   ___a. Repeat Steps 1a-d to go to **Product Updates** in *Windows Update*.
   ___b. Scroll down and look for the latest Windows 2000 Service Pack. You may need to click on the **Show Installed Updates** button.
   ___c. You may get a warning about installing the Service Pack separately. Click on **OK**.
   ___d. Click on the **Download** button.
   ___e. Click on **Start Download**.
   ___f. Click on **Yes** to the terms of the License Agreement
   ___g. You will see a download progress window. After the download has completed you will see a window similar to Figure 37-4. Click a check next to **Accept the License Agreement**.

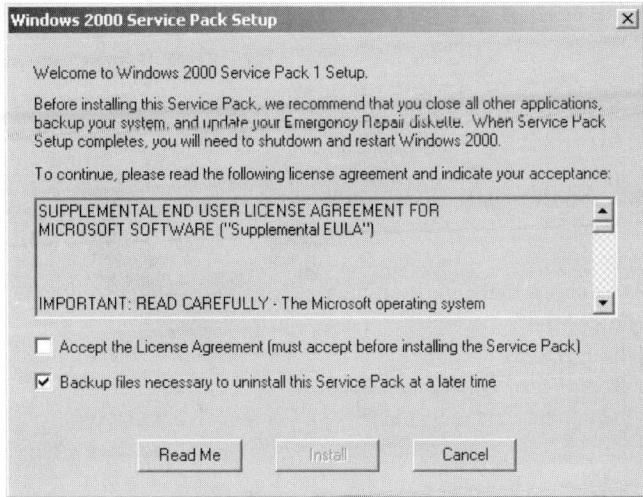

Figure 37-4: Windows 2000 Service Pack License Agreement

WINDOWS 2000 SOFTWARE VERSION UPDATE MANAGEMENT - 267

PROCEDURE - 37

___h. Uncheck **Backup files necessary to uninstall this Service Pack at a later time**.
___i. Click on **Install**. The download will begin; it may take a long time depending on your Internet connection bandwidth. The file is about 15 MB in size.
___j. When the download and install have completed click on **Exit** to restart the computer.
___k. When prompted click on **Yes** to restart now.

3. **Install Windows Media Player through Windows Update**
___a. Repeat Steps 1a-d to go to **Product Updates** in *Windows Update*.
___b. Scroll down and look for the latest Windows Media Player. You may need to click on the **Show Installed Updates** button.
___c. Place a check next to the **Media Player** and record its name, size, and download time in Table 37-1.
___d. Click on the **Download** button.
___e. Click on **Start Download**.
___f. Click on **Yes** to the terms of the License Agreement.
___g. After the program has downloaded and installed you will be prompted to restart. Click on **Yes** to restart now.
___h. After the computer has restarted record any new shortcuts on the desktop in Table 37-2.

4. **Remove Windows Media Player through Add/Remove Programs**
___a. From the Windows 2000 Desktop click on **Start/Settings** and select **Control Panel**.
___b. Double-click on **Add/Remove Programs**. You will see a window similar to Figure 37-5.

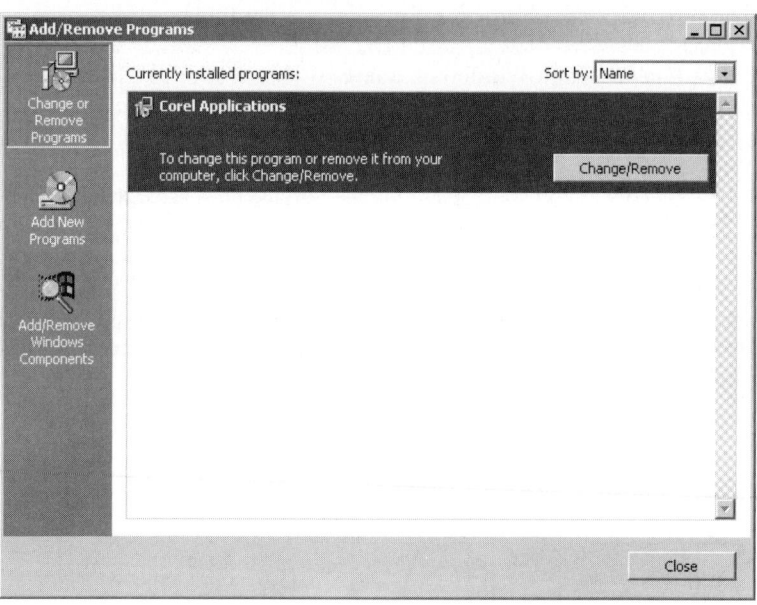

Figure 37-5: Add/Remove Programs

___c. Record the three buttons that appear on the left-hand side of the window in Table 37-3.
___d. Click on **Windows Media Player** if it is not selected already.
___e. Click on the **Change/Remove** button.
___f. The *Windows Media Component Setup* window will appear. Click on **Next**.
___g. Select all the components in the list displayed. Click on **Next** twice.
___h. When the uninstall has completed the computer will restart. Click on **Finish**. The computer will restart.

PROCEDURE - 37

5. **Use an application's Upgrade feature**
   ___a. When you uninstalled Media Player, Windows retained the previous version of Media Player. A shortcut to an older version (6.4) included with Windows should be on the desktop. Double-click on it. If the shortcut is not present it can be accessed through *C:\Program Files\Windows Media Player\mplayer2.exe*.
   ___b. Click on **Help/Check for Player Upgrade**. You will see a window similar to Figure 37-6.
   ___c. After the program has checked for a new version it should tell you your current version and the new version. Record these values in Table 37-4.

   NOTE: At this point you could click on Upgrade Now and follow the prompts to install the media player.

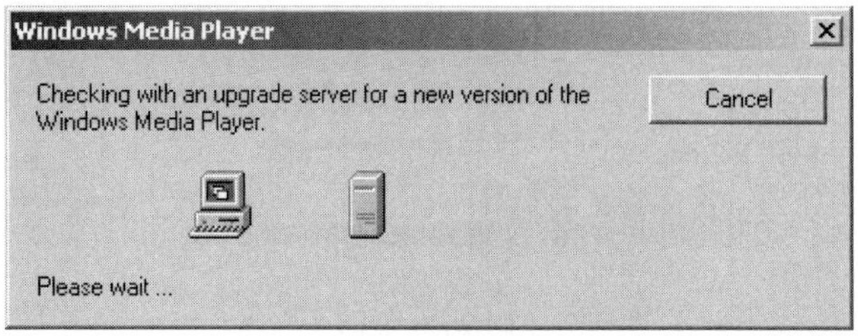

   Figure 37-6: Separate Download of the Browser

   ___d. Click on **Don't Upgrade**.
   ___e. Close all open windows and shut down the computer.

TABLES

Table 37-1

Windows Media Player Update	
Update File Name:	
Update File Size:	
Download Time:	

Table 37-2

New Desktop Shortcuts:	

Table 37-3

Three Buttons:	

WINDOWS 2000 SOFTWARE VERSION UPDATE MANAGEMENT - 269

PROCEDURE - 37

Table 37-4

Current Version:	
New Version:	

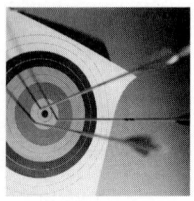

Feedback

LAB QUESTIONS

1. Where do most applications display their version number?
2. What web address does Microsoft use for updating their Windows products?
3. Can the version of IE used in this lab be downloaded and installed simultaneously with other components?
4. What are two ways to upgrade Windows Media Player?
5. Where would you go to uninstall Windows Media Player?

LAB PROCEDURE 38

Windows XP Software Version Update Management

OBJECTIVES

1. Upgrade Windows Media Player.
2. Install a Windows XP Service Pack.
3. Upgrade to the latest Internet Explorer.
4. Upgrade DirectX Software.

Software

RESOURCES

1. PC-compatible desktop/tower computer system — Customer-supplied desktop/tower hardware system **OR** Marcraft MC-8000 Computer Hardware Trainer **OR** suitable PC hardware trainer with Windows XP Operating System Installation CD and NIC installed
2. Internet access through a network connection

DISCUSSION

Windows XP needs to be updated periodically, just like Windows Me and Windows 2000. This can be done manually by the user, or automatically by the system. Either way, it is important that it be done consistently at least once a month.

An application's internal information display can be helpful in determining its version. Usually, you run the application and select *About* from the *Help* menu to access this feature. This feature may access the Internet and automatically find, download, and install any needed updates.

Upgrades, updates, or patches to the operating system itself are best done through the built-in *Windows Update* feature. Clicking on *Start/Windows Update* can access the Windows Update web site. If you are connected to the Internet, this will connect you directly to the Microsoft web site and show you a list of possible downloads for you to access. Once again, you should use this feature at least once a month to make certain that you are not missing any vital patches needed to fix a newly discovered bug or security flaw.

PROCEDURE

NOTE: This lab's time for completion will vary greatly depending on the bandwidth of the user's Internet connection.

1. **Install Internet Explorer through Windows Update**
   ___ a. Boot up the computer.

PROCEDURE - 38

____ b. From the Windows XP desktop, click on the **Start** button, **All Programs**, and then select **Windows Update.**

The browser will open and go to *windowsupdate.microsoft.com*. You will see a window similar to Figure 38-1.

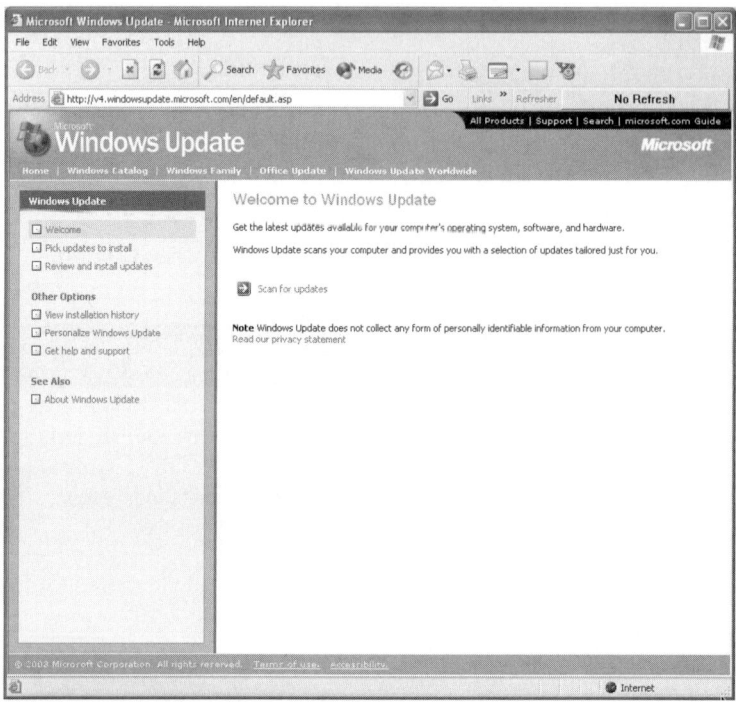

Figure 38-1: Windows Update Web Site

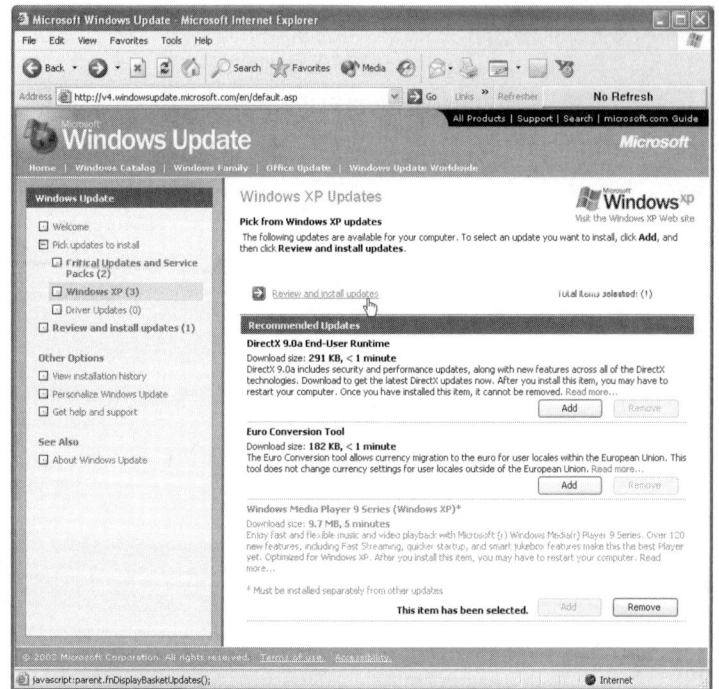

Figure 38-2: Accepting Licensing Agreement

____ c. On the left side of the screen, click on **Pick updates to install**.

NOTE: The following procedures in this Step may vary over time.

____ d. If this is the first time the computer has visited the page you will receive a security warning. It asks if you want to install and run "Microsoft Active Setup". Click on the **Yes** button.

____ e. Click on **Windows XP** in the list on the left side to show the operating system updates that are not critical.

____ f. Scroll down and look for the latest *Internet Explorer* selection.

____ g. Click on the **Add** button to add **Internet Explorer** to the selection, if available.

____ h. Click on **Review and install updates**, as shown in Figure 38-2.

____ i. Click on the **Install Now** button to begin the installation.

____ j. Click on the **Accept** button to accept the terms of the License Agreement.

PROCEDURE - 38

NOTE: You will see a download progress window. After the window has completed you will see the Internet Explorer license agreement once again.

___k. Click on the radio button next to **I accept the agreement** and click on the **Next** button.
___l. Click on the **Next** button to begin the download.
___m. After the program has downloaded and installed, click on the **Yes** button to restart the computer.

NOTE: When Windows restarts, Browsing Services, Internet Tools, and System Services will be set up.

2. Install the Windows XP Service Pack through Windows Update

NOTE: If the Service Pack is not available, it is already installed. Skip to Step 4.

___a. Repeat Steps 1a-c to go to the *Windows Update* site.
___b. Click on **Critical Updates and Service Packs** on the left side of the screen.
___c. Select the latest Windows XP Service Pack from the list by clicking on the **Add** button, if it isn't already selected.
___d. Click on **Review and install updates**.
___e. In the next screen, you will get a warning about installing the Service Pack separately. Click on the **OK** button.
___f. Click on the **Install Now** button as shown in Figure 38-3.
___g. Click on the **Accept** button, as shown in Figure 38-4, to accept the licensing agreement.

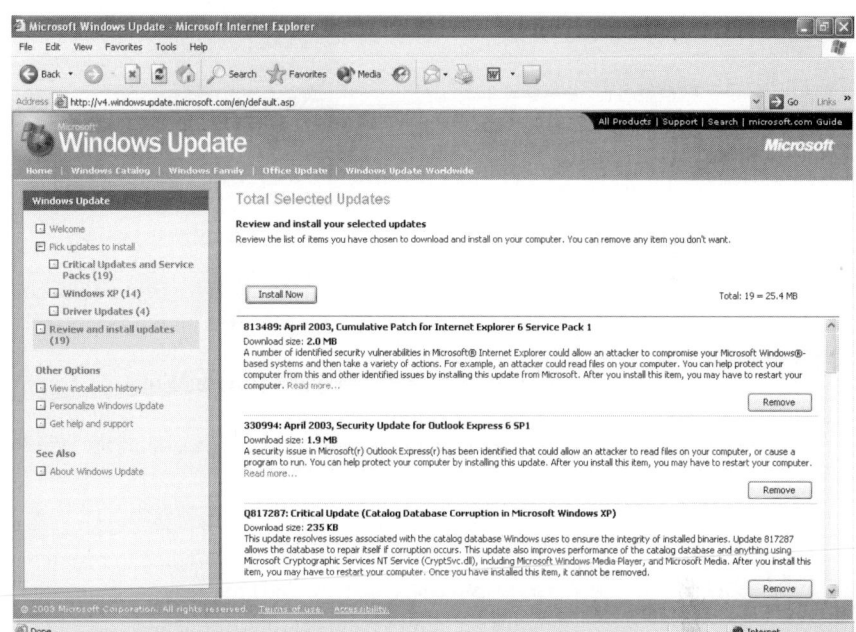

Figure 38-3: Installing Service Packs

Figure 38-4: Accepting the Manufacturer's Terms

PROCEDURE - 38

    ___h.   Click on the **Next** button when the *Windows XP Service Pack Setup Wizard* window appears.
    ___i.   Click on the **I Agree** radio button and then click on the **Next** button to accept the license agreement, as shown in Figure 38-5.

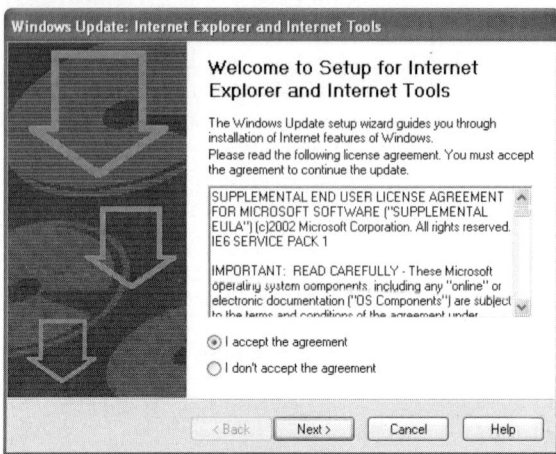

Figure 38-5: Accepting Microsoft's Licensing Agreement

    ___j.   Select the default of **Archiving Files** necessary to uninstall this Service Pack at a later time, and then click on the **Next** button.
    ___k.   When the download and install have completed, click on the **Exit** button.
    ___l.   When prompted, click on the **Yes** button to restart the computer.

3. Install Windows Media Player through Windows Update
    ___a.   Repeat Steps 1a-c to go to the *Windows Update* site.
    ___b.   Click on **Windows XP** on the left side of the window to show the non-critical updates that are available.
    ___c.   Scroll down to the latest *Windows Media Player* update and click on the **Add** button to add it to your selected updates.
    ___d.   Click on the **Yes** button when prompted to install this update by itself.
    ___e.   Record the size and download time for this update in Table 38-1.
    ___f.   Click on **Review and install updates**.
    ___g.   Click on the **Install Now** button.
    ___h.   Click on the **Accept** button to accept the terms of the license agreement.
    ___i.   After the program has finished downloading, the installation process will begin. Click on the **I Accept** button.
    ___j.   Click on the **Next** button, at the *Welcome* screen.
    ___k.   Accept the default settings and click on the **Next** button.
    ___l.   Click on the **Finish** button to complete the installation.

4. Installing the DirectX Software Upgrade
    ___a.   Go to the *Windows Update* web site again.
    ___b.   Click on **Windows XP** on the left side of the screen.
    ___c.   Click on the **Add** button to select the latest *DirectX* upgrade.
    ___d.   Click on **Review and install all updates**.
    ___e.   Click on the **Install Now** button.
    ___f.   Click on the **Accept** button, and the installation begins.
    ___g.   When the installation is finished, click on the **OK** button to reboot the computer.

PROCEDURE - 38

TABLES

Table 38-1

Windows Media Player Update	
Update File Size:	
Download Time:	

LAB QUESTIONS

1. Where do most applications display their version number?

2. What web address does Microsoft use for updating their Windows products?

3. Can the version of IE used in this lab be downloaded and installed simultaneously with other components?

4. What are the three types of updates available on the Windows Update web site?

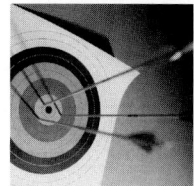

Feedback

LAB PROCEDURE 39

Windows Me OS Faults

OBJECTIVES

1. Delete several system files.
2. Observe different signs of a failing operating system.
3. Determine what specific faults cause the computer to respond in certain ways.

Troubleshooting

RESOURCES

1. PC-compatible desktop/tower computer system — Customer-supplied desktop/tower hardware system **OR** Marcraft MC-8000 Computer Hardware Trainer **OR** suitable PC hardware trainer with Windows Millennium Edition installed
2. Two blank floppy disks
3. Windows Millennium Edition Startup disk

NOTE: This lab procedure will only work properly if Windows Me is the ONLY operating system installed on the Windows Me computer.

DISCUSSION

Everyone at one time or another will turn on their computer and receive some strange message telling them that something is corrupt and Windows needs to be reinstalled. There are a few changes in the way Windows Me and Windows 2000 handle their system files, compared to Windows 98, that help eliminate the occurrence of these messages. You should still be familiar with these messages and their meaning in case you do run across one of them. It could mean the difference between wiping out an entire hard drive to reinstall Windows, and simply copying a system file from another computer onto your computer. With Windows Me, the new System Restore feature pretty much takes care of the operating system itself. It is still a good idea to know how to manually remove and restore system files.

PROCEDURE

1. **Set Explorer to "Show all files"**
   ___a. Boot the computer to Windows Millennium Edition.
   ___b. Open Windows Explorer and click on the **C: drive** to highlight it.
   ___c. Click on the **Tools** menu and select **Folder Options**.

PROCEDURE - 39

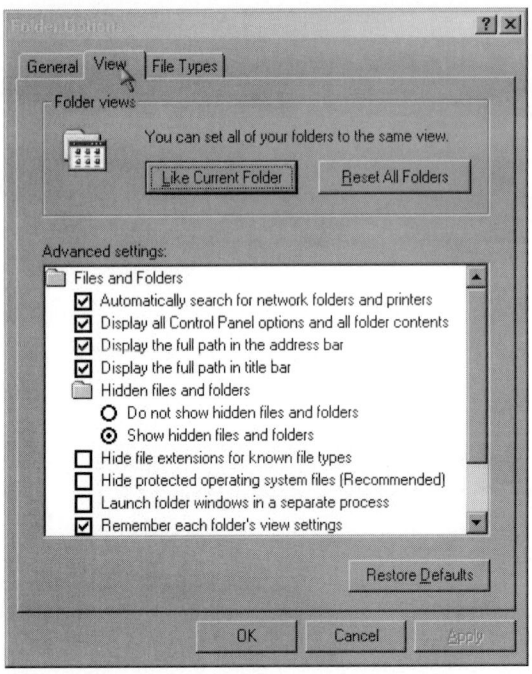

Figure 39-1: The View Tab

    ___d.   Click on the **View** tab, as shown in Figure 39-1.
    ___e.   In the *Advanced settings* box, place a check next to **Show hidden files and folders** and uncheck *Hide file extensions for known file types*.
    ___f.   Click on **Apply**, then **OK** to close the *Folder Options* window.

2. **Back up the system files that we'll be removing in this procedure to disable the operating system**
    ___a.   Place a blank floppy disk into the floppy drive.
    ___b.   With the C: drive highlighted, scroll down to **io.sys** and click on it once.
    ___c.   Click on the **Edit** menu and select **Copy**.
    ___d.   Click on the **Floppy (A:) drive** to highlight it.
    ___e.   Click on the **Edit** menu again, and select Paste.
    ___f.   Click on the **WINDOWS** folder to highlight it.
    ___g.   Press and hold the **CTRL** key down and click on **explorer.exe**, **ifshlp.sys**, and **system.ini**.
    ___h.   Click on the **Edit** menu and select **Copy**.
    ___i.   Place the cursor on the **Floppy (A:) drive** and click on it to highlight it.
    ___j.   Click on **Edit** again and select **Paste**.

3. **Selected file removal (removing *io.sys*)**
    ___a.   Click on the **C:\ drive** to highlight it.
    ___b.   On the right side, right-click **io.sys** and choose **Delete**.
    ___c.   Remove the floppy from the disk drive and reboot the computer.
    ___d.   Record the results in Table 39-1.
    ___e.   Put the backup floppy disk into the floppy drive and press **ENTER** to finish booting to Windows.
    ___f.   Copy **io.sys** from the floppy drive to the C: drive.
    ___g.   Reboot the computer.

4. **Remove protected system files**
    ___a.   Click on the Windows **SYSTEM** folder to highlight it.
    ___b.   On the right-hand side of the screen, right-click the file called **Vredir.vxd** and select **Delete**.
    ___c.   Notice that within approximately 5 seconds, the file reappears in the directory from which it was removed!
    ___d.   Repeat Step b above for the following files: **Vnetsup.vxd**, **Vtcp.386**, and **Vnbt.386**.
    ___e.   Check the *C:\WINDOWS\SYSTEM* folder to see how many of these files have reappeared.
    ___f.   Open the Recycle Bin in the *Explore* mode.
    ___g.   Click on the **Edit** menu and choose **Select All**.
    ___h.   Right-click the highlighted area and click on **Restore** to restore every file into its proper folder.

5. **Remove *system.ini***
    ___a.   Click on the **WINDOWS** folder to highlight it.
    ___b.   Right-click **system.ini** on the right side and choose **Delete**.
    ___c.   Reboot the computer and record the results in Table 39-2.
    ___d.   Insert the floppy into the floppy drive and boot to Windows Millennium Edition.
    ___e.   Copy **system.ini** from the floppy disk to the *C:\WINDOWS* folder.
    ___f.   Remove the floppy disk and reboot the computer.

PROCEDURE - 39

6. **Remove** *explorer.exe*
    - ___a. Insert the Windows Me Startup disk into the floppy drive and reboot the computer.
    - ___b. At the *Startup* menu, press **SHIFT + F5** to get the command prompt.
    - ___c. At the A: prompt, type **del C:\Windows\explorer.exe**.
    - ___d. Remove the Startup disk and reboot the computer.
    - ___e. Record the results in Table 39-3.
    - ___f. Press the **ENTER** key.
    - ___g. Insert the Windows Me Startup disk and reboot the computer.
    - ___h. At the *Startup* menu, press **SHIFT + F5** to get the command prompt.
    - ___i. Switch disks, type **copy Explorer.exe c:\Windows**, and press **ENTER**.
    - ___j. Remove the floppy and reboot.

7. **Remove** *ifshlp.sys*
    - ___a. In the Windows directory, right-click **ifshlp.sys** and choose **Delete**.
    - ___b. Reboot the computer.
    - ___c. Record the results in Table 39-4.
    - ___d. Insert the Startup disk and reboot.
    - ___e. At the *Startup* menu, press **SHIFT + F5** to get the command prompt.
    - ___f. Switch disks and copy **ifshlp.sys** to *C:\WINDOWS*.
    - ___g. Remove the floppy disk and reboot.
    - ___h. Close all open windows, and shut down the computer.

TABLES

Table 39-1

Result of Missing io.sys:	

Table 39-2

Results of Missing system.ini:	

Table 39-3

Results of Missing explorer.exe:	

PROCEDURE - 39

Table 39-4

Results of Missing ifshlp.sys:	

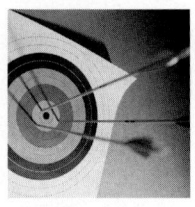

Feedback

LAB QUESTIONS

1. Why can't *explorer.exe* be removed from within Windows?
2. From the results of the procedure, what conditions would you expect to encounter if the io.sys file becomes corrupt?
3. How does the Windows Me operating system respond to missing files in the System folder?
4. What type of error might lead you to suspect that the system.ini file is missing or corrupt?
5. Which Windows Me location must be accessed to check for hidden and system files on the disk drive?

LAB PROCEDURE 40

Windows 2000 OS Faults

OBJECTIVES

1. Delete *boot.ini*.
2. Make a shortcut point to an incorrect location.
3. View automatic restoration of Windows programs.
4. Change a file type association.
5. Edit Registry to run an invalid file at startup.
6. Assign bad drivers to network and video cards.

Troubleshooting

RESOURCES

1. PC-compatible desktop/tower computer system — Customer-supplied desktop/tower hardware system **OR** Marcraft MC-8000 Computer Hardware Trainer **OR** suitable PC hardware trainer with Windows 2000 installed
2. Drivers for the Plug and Play network card
3. LAN connection

NOTE: This lab procedure will work properly only if Windows 2000 is the ONLY operating system installed on the Windows 2000 computer.

DISCUSSION

Windows 2000.0 is the most stable operating system yet. It is harder to "break" than previous Microsoft operating systems such as NT 4.0 or Windows 98. One can delete *arcldr.exe*, *arcsetup.exe*, *autoexec.bat*, *boot.ini*, *config.sys*, *io.sys*, and *msdos.sys* and Windows will still start. If you create a shortcut to a file and then move the file, Windows will search for that file upon execution of the shortcut. If you rename a file, shortcuts pointing to it will be modified so that they still point to it. If you delete files that came with Windows (such as Net Meeting) they will be restored automatically. You cannot rename running Windows files such as Windows Explorer or .dll files. This would cause a fault in Windows.

Some actions can be fatal however. If you delete significant amounts of information from the Registry, you will need to re-install Windows. If you delete ntldr or ntdetect, you will need to run an emergency repair. If you install the wrong driver for an expansion card, you will need to install the correct driver.

PROCEDURE

1. ***Boot.ini***
   ___ a. Boot the computer to Windows 2000 and from the desktop double-click the **My Computer** icon.

WINDOWS 2000 OS FAULTS - 281

PROCEDURE - 40

___ b. Double-click the **C: Drive**.
___ c. Click on **Tools/Folder Options**.
___ d. Click on the **View** tab.
___ e. You need to view all files, so click the radio button next to **Show hidden files and folders**.
___ f. Uncheck *Hide file extensions for known file types* and uncheck *Hide protected operating system files (Recommended)*.
___ g. You will get a warning similar to Figure 40-1. Read the warning and click on **Yes**.

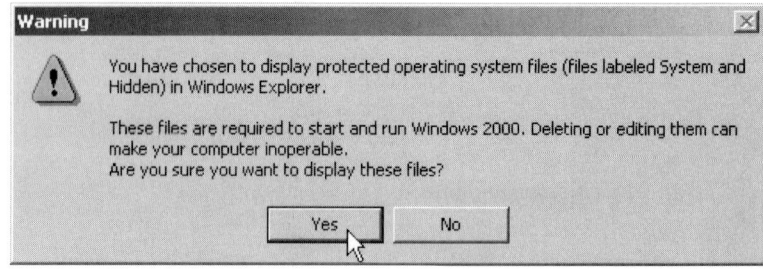

Figure 40-1: Display Protected Operating System Files

___ h. Click on **OK** to close the *Folder Options* windows.
___ i. Record your observations about what you can now view in C: in Table 40-1.
___ j. Right-click on **boot.ini** and select **Delete**.
___ k. Confirm the File Delete by clicking on **Yes**.
___ l. Close all windows and restart the computer.
___ m. When Windows is restarting record the message that appears at the beginning of startup in Table 40-2.
___ n. Once Windows has restarted double-click the **Recycle Bin**.
___ o. Right-click on **boot.ini** and click Restore.
___ p. Confirm moving the system file by clicking on **Yes**.
___ q. Close the Recycle Bin.

2. **Shortcut problems**
___ a. Right-click the desktop and click **New/Text Document**.
___ b. Right-click the **New Text Document** and click on **Copy**.
___ c. Right-click the desktop and click on **Paste Shortcut**.
___ d. Double-click the shortcut and you will see *Notepad* viewing *New Text Document.txt*.
___ e. Close the window.
___ f. Right-click the **New Text Document** (not the shortcut) and click on **Cut**.
___ g. Double-click the **My Computer** icon.
___ h. Double-click on **C:**.
___ i. Right-click in any blank space and click on **Paste**.
___ j. Close the window.
___ k. Double-click the shortcut. Record what happens in Table 40-3.
___ l. Close all windows.
___ m. As before, go through *My Computer*, but this time delete **New Text Document.txt** from (C:).
___ n. Double-click the shortcut to **New Text Document.txt**. You will see a window similar to Figure 40-2. Click on **Yes** to delete the shortcut.

Figure 40-2: Delete an Invalid Shortcut

PROCEDURE - 40

___o. Right-click the **Recycle Bin** and click on **Empty Recycle Bi**n.
___p. Confirm the file delete by clicking on **Yes**.

3. **Automatic restoration of Windows components**
   ___a. From the desktop double-click the **My Computer** icon.
   ___b. Double-click on **(C:)**.
   ___c. Double-click the **PROGRAM FILES** folder.
   ___d. If necessary click on **Show Files to view the contents of the folder**.
   ___e. Double-click the **NETMEETING** folder.
   ___f. Right-click on **conf.exe** (the execution file for Net Meeting) and click on **Rename**.
   ___g. Rename the program to **conf.exx** and press ENTER.
   ___h. You will get a Rename warning similar to Figure 40-3. Click on **Yes**.

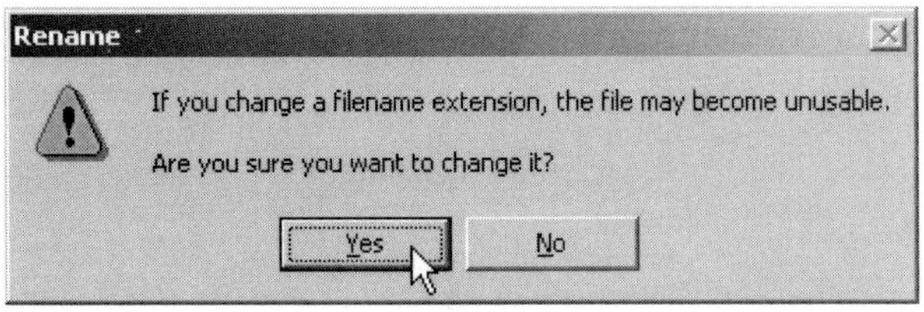

Figure 40-3: Rename Warning

   ___i. Wait approximately 10 seconds and record your observations about the folder's contents in Table 40-4.
   ___j. Delete the file **conf.exx**.
   ___k. Right-click on one of the .dll files in the folder and delete it. Use *nmchat.dll*, for example.
   ___l. Wait 10 seconds and record your observations about the folder's contents in Table 40-5.
   ___m. Close all windows.

4. **File type association**
   ___a. From the Windows 2000 desktop double-click the **My Documents** icon.
   ___b. Click on **File/New/Text Document**.
   ___c. Use the default *New Text Document.txt* filename and open the document by double-clicking the icon.
   ___d. Type **This is a test** in the document.
   ___e. Close the document and click on **Yes** to save the changes.
   ___f. From the *My Documents Folder* window click on **Tools/Folder Options**. This menu can be accessed from any folder in the Windows Explorer.
   ___g. Click on the **File Types** tab. You will see a window similar to Figure 40-4.
   ___h. Look for the extension "TXT" by scrolling down in the *Registered file types* field.
   ___i. Click on the **TXT** extension and record its File Type in Table 40-6.
   ___j. In the lower portion of the window is a short explanation of the extension. Record the name of the program that TXT "Opens with" in Table 40-7.
   ___k. Click on the **Change** button.

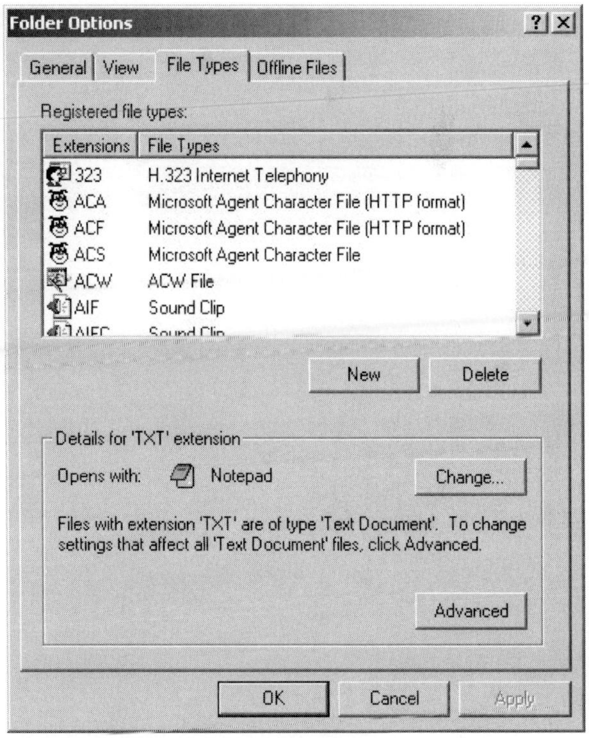

Figure 40-4: File Type Associations

WINDOWS 2000 OS FAULTS - 283

PROCEDURE - 40

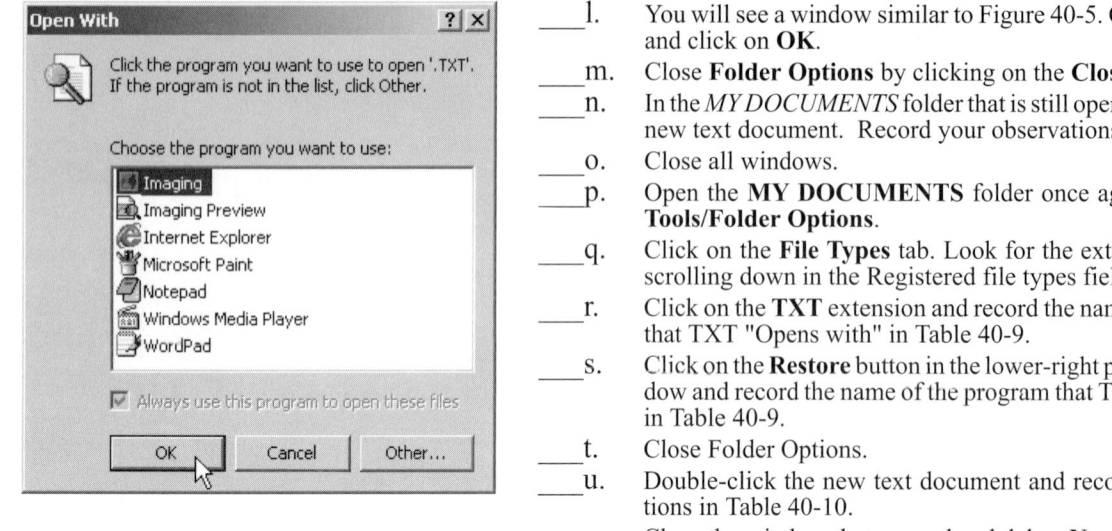

Figure 40-5: New File Type Association

___ l. You will see a window similar to Figure 40-5. Click on **Imaging** and click on **OK**.
___ m. Close **Folder Options** by clicking on the **Close** button.
___ n. In the *MY DOCUMENTS* folder that is still open double-click the new text document. Record your observations in Table 40-8.
___ o. Close all windows.
___ p. Open the **MY DOCUMENTS** folder once again and click on **Tools/Folder Options**.
___ q. Click on the **File Types** tab. Look for the extension "TXT" by scrolling down in the Registered file types field.
___ r. Click on the **TXT** extension and record the name of the program that TXT "Opens with" in Table 40-9.
___ s. Click on the **Restore** button in the lower-right portion of the window and record the name of the program that TXT "Opens with" in Table 40-9.
___ t. Close Folder Options.
___ u. Double-click the new text document and record your observations in Table 40-10.
___ v. Close the window that opened and delete **New Text Document.txt**.

5. **Invalid shortcut at startup**
   ___ a. Right-click the desktop and click on **New/Bitmap Image**.
   ___ b. Right-drag the new bitmap image through *Start/Programs/Startup* and release the mouse button. Select **Create Shortcut(s) Here** from the window that opens. The screen should look similar to Figure 40-6.

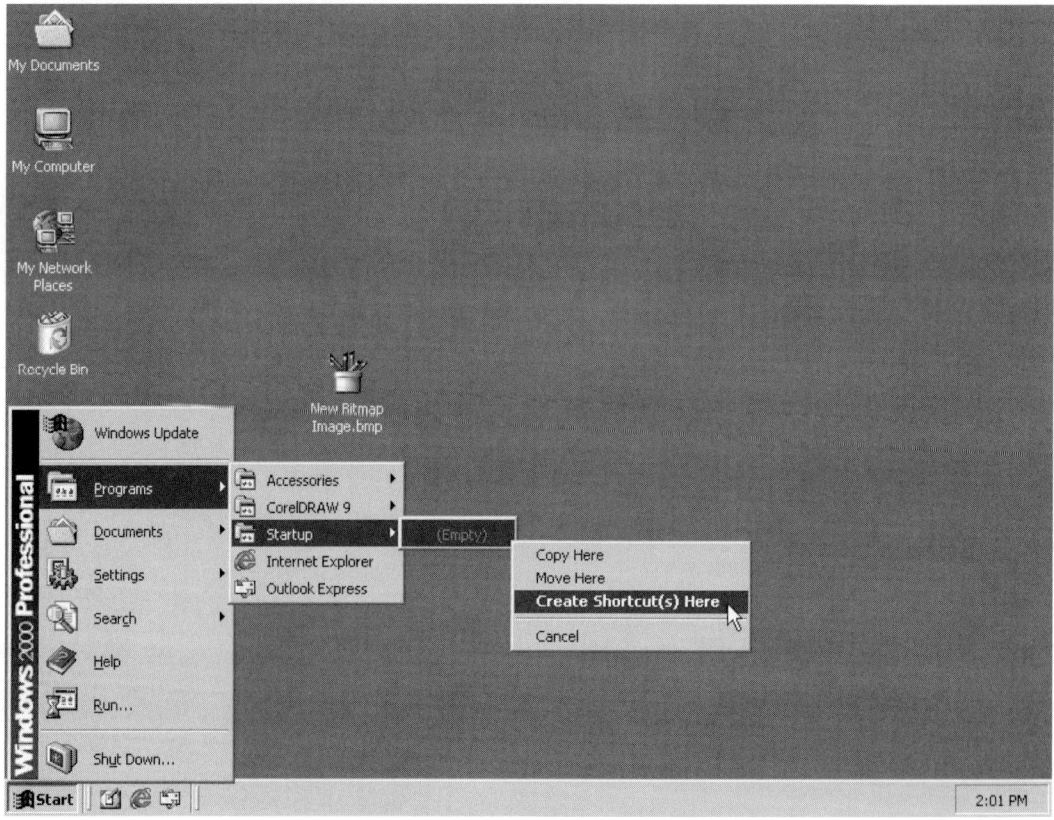

Figure 40-6: Create a Shortcut

284 - LAB GROUP 4

PROCEDURE - 40

___c. You now have a shortcut to open the bitmap image at startup.
___d. From the desktop delete the **New Bitmap Image.bmp**.
___e. Close all windows and restart the computer.
___f. Record your observations when Windows has restarted in Table 40-11.
___g. Close any open windows.
___h. Click on **Start/Programs/Startup**. Right-click on **Shortcut to New Bitmap Image.bmp** and click on **Delete**.
___i. Click on **Yes** to confirm the deletion.

6. **Incorrect network adapter drivers**
   ___a. From the Windows 2000 desktop double-click the **My Network Places** icon.
   ___b. Double-click on **Computers Near Me**.
   ___c. Record your observations in Table 40-12.
   ___d. Close all windows.
   ___e. Go to Device Manager by navigating the *Start/Settings/Control Panel* path. Double-click the **System** icon.
   ___f. Click on the **Hardware** tab, and then click on **Device Manager**.
   ___g. Expand **Network adapters**. Record the name of your adapter in Table 40-13. Right-click on your adapter and click on **Properties**.
   ___h. Click on the **Driver** tab.
   ___i. Click on **Update Driver**.
   ___j. Click on **Next**.
   ___k. Click on **Display a list of the known drivers for this device...** and click **Next**.
   ___l. Click on **Show all hardware of this device class**.
   ___m. Choose a different Manufacturer from the Manufacturers list and choose any Network Adapter. The point is to choose an incorrect driver.
   ___n. Click on **Next**.
   ___o. You will see a window similar to Figure 40-7. Click on **Yes**.

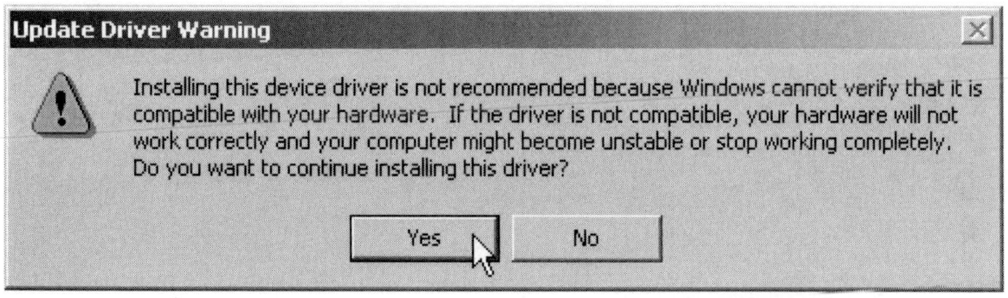

Figure 40-7: Incorrect Driver Warning

   ___p. Click on **Next** and click on **Finish**.
   ___q. Close the properties of the adapter and restart as prompted.
   ___r. When Windows has restarted double-click on **My Network Places** and double-click on **Computers Near Me**.
   ___s. Record your observations in Table 40-14.
   ___t. Close all windows. At this point you can install the correct drivers for the network card by using Plug and Play or the drivers provided by the manufacturer.
   ___u. Repeat Steps e and f. Right-click on your adapter and click on **Uninstall**.
   ___v. Click on **OK** to confirm the device removal. Right-click the computer name and select **Scan for Hardware changes**.
   ___w. The following step will vary because Windows may not have the drivers built in. The new drivers will be installed automatically for the Plug and Play network adapter. You may need to follow the Wizard to install the driver provided by the manufacturer. When the correct driver is installed you may close all windows.
   ___x. Restart the computer and enter *Computers Near Me* as before.

PROCEDURE - 40

    ___y.   Record your observations in Table 40-15.
    ___z.   Close all windows.

7. **Incorrect video adapter drivers**
   - ___a. Enter into *Device Manager* as in previous steps.
   - ___b. Expand **Display adapters**.
   - ___c. Record the name of your adapter in Table 40-16.
   - ___d. Right-click the adapter and click on **Properties**.
   - ___e. Click on the **Driver** tab.
   - ___f. Click on **Update Driver**.
   - ___g. Click on **Next**.
   - ___h. Click on **Display a list of the known drivers for this device...** and click on **Next**.
   - ___i. Click on **Show all hardware of the device class**.
   - ___j. Choose a different Manufacturer from the Manufacturers list and choose any Network Adapter. Click on **Next**.
   - ___k. Click on **Yes** to the incorrect driver warning window.
   - ___l. Click on **Next** and click on **Finish**.
   - ___m. Close the video adapter's properties and restart as prompted.
   - ___n. When Windows has restarted record your observations about the desktop in Table 40-17.
   - ___o. You can now reinstall the correct drivers for the video card. Enter *Device Manager* as before.
   - ___p. Right-click the video adapter and click on **Properties**.
   - ___q. From the *General* tab record the Device status in Table 40-18.
   - ___r. Close the video adapter's properties.
   - ___s. Right-click the video adapter and click on **Uninstall**.
   - ___t. Click on **OK** to confirm the device removal. Right-click the computer name and select **Scan for Hardware changes**.
   - ___u. The new drivers will be installed for the Plug and Play video adapter.

   NOTE: The following step will vary because Windows may not have the drivers built in. The new driver will be installed automatically for the Plug and Play video adapter. You may need to follow the Wizard to install the drivers provided by the manufacturer. When the correct driver is installed you may close all windows and restart as prompted.

   - ___v. When Windows has restarted record your observations about the desktop in Table 40-19.

TABLES

Table 40-1

Observations:	

Table 40-2

New Message at Startup:	

PROCEDURE - 40

Table 40-3

Observations:	

Table 40-4

Observations:	

Table 40-5

Observations:	

Table 40-6

TXT File Type:	

Table 40-7

TXT File Opens with:	

Table 40-8

Observations:	

Table 40-9

Before Restore TXT File Opens with:	
After Restore TXT File Opens with:	

Table 40-10

Observations:	

Table 40-11

Observations at Startup:	

WINDOWS 2000 OS FAULTS - 287

PROCEDURE - 40

Table 40-12

| Network Observations: | |

Table 40-13

| Network Adapter Name: | |

Table 40-14

| Network Observations: | |

Table 40-15

| Network Observations: | |

Table 40-16

| Display Adapter Name: | |

Table 40-17

| Desktop Observations: | |

Table 40-18

| Video Adapter Device Status: | |

Table 40-19

| Desktop Changes: | |

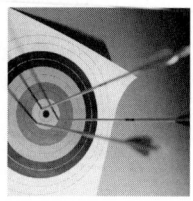

Feedback

LAB QUESTIONS

1. What happens to the icon in Device Manager when an incorrect driver is installed for the network adapter?

2. What type of mode did Windows enter when you installed an incorrect video driver?

3. How many options were there in the Folder Options/View window?

4. How long did it take for Windows to automatically restore a file that you renamed?

5. What is a possible reason for receiving a Problem with Shortcut window?

288 - LAB GROUP 4

LAB PROCEDURE 41

Windows XP OS Faults

OBJECTIVES

1. Delete *boot.ini*.
2. Make a shortcut point to an incorrect location.
3. View automatic restoration of Windows programs.
4. Change a file type association.
5. Edit Registry to run an invalid file at startup.

Software

RESOURCES

1. PC-compatible desktop/tower computer system — Customer-supplied desktop/tower hardware system **OR** Marcraft MC-8000 Computer Hardware Trainer **OR** suitable PC hardware trainer with Windows XP Operating System Installation CD and NIC installed
2. Internet access through a network connection or modem
3. Drivers for the Plug and Play network card

NOTE: This lab procedure will work properly only if Windows XP is the ONLY operating system installed on the Windows XP computer.

DISCUSSION

Windows XP is the most stable operating system yet. It is harder to "break" than previous Microsoft operating systems such as NT 4.0 or Windows Me. One can delete *arcldr.exe, arcsetup.exe, autoexec.bat, boot.ini, config.sys, io.sys,* and *msdos.sys* and Windows will still start. If you create a shortcut to a file and then move the file, Windows will search for that file upon execution of the shortcut. If you rename a file, shortcuts pointing to it will be modified so that they still point to it.

If you delete files that came with Windows (such as Net Meeting) they will be restored automatically. You cannot rename running Windows files such as Windows Explorer or .dll files. This would cause a fault in Windows.

Some actions can be fatal, however. If you delete significant amounts of information from the Registry you will need to re-install Windows. If you delete ntldr or ntdetect you will need to run an emergency repair. If you install the wrong driver for an expansion card you will need to install the correct driver.

PROCEDURE - 41

PROCEDURE

1. **Boot.ini**
   ___a. Boot the computer to Windows XP and from the desktop double-click on the **My Computer** icon.
   ___b. Double-click the **C:** Drive.
   ___c. Click on the *Tools* menu and select **Folder Options**.
   ___d. Click on the **View** tab.
   ___e. You need to view all files, so click on the radio button next to **Show hidden files and folders**.
   ___f. Uncheck **Hide file extensions for known file types** and uncheck **Hide Protected operating system files (Recommended).**
   ___g. You will get a warning similar to Figure 41-1. Read the warning and click on the **Yes** button.

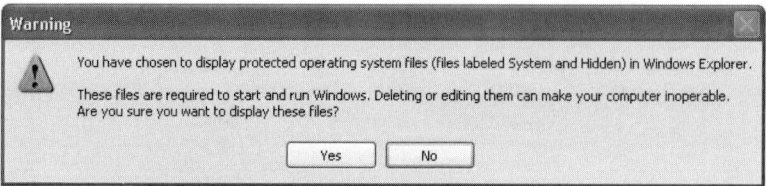

Figure 41-1: Warning Screen

   ___h. Click on the **OK** button to close the *Folder Options* windows.
   ___i. Record your observations about what you can now view in C: in Table 41-1.
   ___j. Right-click on the file named **boot.ini** and select **Copy**.
   ___k. Right-click on the **Windows** folder and select **Paste**.
   ___l. Right-click on the file named **boot.ini** in the C:\ drive again, and select **Delete**.
   ___m. Confirm the File Delete by clicking on the **Yes** button.
   ___n. Close all windows and restart the computer.
   ___o. When Windows is restarting record the message that appears at the beginning of startup in Table 41-2.
   ___p. Once Windows has restarted double-click the **MyComputer** icon.
   ___q. Double-click on the **C:** drive.
   ___r. Double-click on the **Windows** folder.
   ___s. Right-click on the file named **boot.ini** and select **Copy**.
   ___t. Right-click on the **C:** drive and select **Paste**.
   ___u. Close all windows.

2. **Shortcut problems**
   ___a. Right-click the desktop and select **New** and then **Text Document**.
   ___b. Accept the default name for the file.
   ___c. Right-click the New Text Document and select **Copy**.
   ___d. Right-click the desktop and select **Paste Shortcut**.
   ___e. Double-click the shortcut and you will see *Notepad* viewing *New Text Document.tx*t.
   ___f. Right-click the **New Text Document** (not the shortcut) and select **Cut**.
   ___g. Double-click the **My Computer** icon.
   ___h. Double-click on the **C:** drive.
   ___i. Right-click in any blank space and select **Paste**.
   ___j. Close the window.
   ___k. Double-click the shortcut and record what happens in Table 41-3.
   ___l. Close the window.
   ___m. As before, go through **My Computer** and double-click on **C:**.

290 - LAB GROUP 4

PROCEDURE - 41

___ n. Right-click on **New Text Document** and select **Delete**.
___ o. Click on **Yes** to send it to the Recycle Bin.
___ p. Close the window.
___ q. Double-click the shortcut to **New Text Document. txt**. You will see a window similar to Figure 41-2. Click on the **Delete it** button to delete the shortcut.
___ r. Right-click the **Recycle Bin** and click on **Empty Recycle Bin**.
___ s. Confirm the file delete by clicking on the **Yes** button.

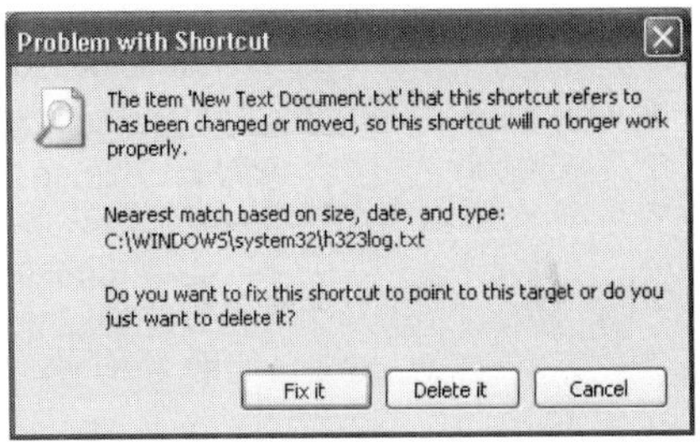

Figure 41-2: Problem with Shortcut

3. **Automatic restoration of Windows components**
___ a. From the desktop double-click the **My Computer** icon.
___ b. Double-click on the **(C:\)** drive.
___ c. Double-click the **Program Files** folder.
___ d. If necessary, click on **Show Files** to view the contents of the folder.
___ e. Double-click the **Netmeeting** folder.
___ f. Right-click on **conf.exe** (the execution file for Net Meeting) and select **Rename**.
___ g. Rename the program to **conf.exx** and press the **ENTER** key.
___ h. You will get a Rename warning similar to Figure 41-3. Click on the **Yes** button.

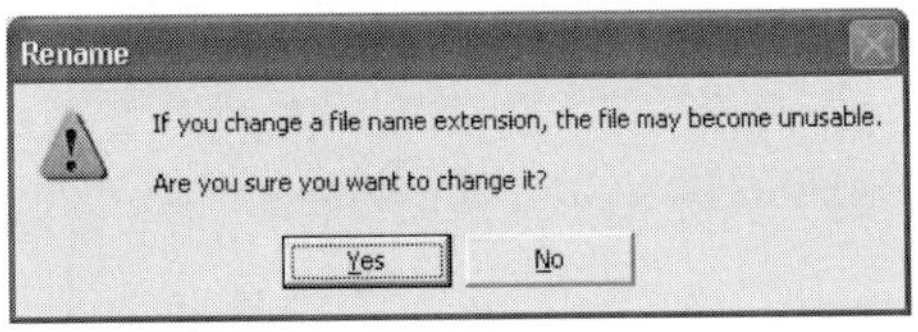

Figure 41-3: Rename File Extension

___ i. Wait approximately 10 seconds and record your observations about the folder's content in Table 41-4.

NOTE: The file conf.exe should be re-created at the bottom of the screen.

___ j. Delete the file **conf.exx**.
___ k. Right-click on one of the .dll files in the folder and delete it. Use **nmchat.dll**, for example.
___ l. Wait 10 seconds and record your observations about the folder's content in Table 41-5.
___ m. Close all windows.

4. **File type association**
___ a. From the Windows XP desktop double-click the **My Documents** icon.
___ b. Click on the **File** menu and select **New** and then **Text Document**.
___ c. Use the default *New Text Document.txt* filename and open the document by double-clicking the icon.
___ d. Type **This is a test** in the document.
___ e. Close the document and click on the **Yes** button to save the changes.
___ f. From the *My Documents Folder* window, click on the *Tools* menu and select **Folder Options**.
___ g. Click on the **File Types** tab. You will see a window similar to Figure 41-4.

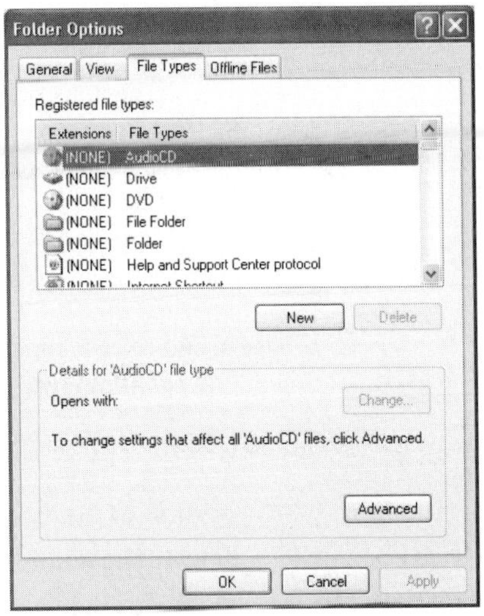

Figure 41-4: File Types

PROCEDURE - 41

___h. Look for the extension **TXT** by scrolling down in the *Registered file types* field.
___i. Click on the **TXT** extension and record its File Type in Table 41-6.
___j. A short explanation of the extension is located in the lower portion of the window. Record the name of the program that opens files with a TXT extension in Table 41-6.
___k. Click on the **Change** button.
___l. You will see a window similar to Figure 41-5. Select **Windows Picture and Fax Viewer** and click on the **OK** button.

Figure 41-5:
Open With Dialog Box

___m. Click on the **Close** button to close the *Folder Options* window.
___n. Double-click on **New Text Document.txt** in the *My Documents* folder.
___o. Record your observations in Table 41-7.
___p. Close all windows.
___q. Open the **My Documents** folder once again.
___r. Click on the *Tools* menu and select **Folder Options**.
___s. Click on the **File Types** tab and look for the extension **TXT** by scrolling down in the *Registered file types* field.
___t. Click on the **TXT** extension.
___u. Click on the **Restore** button in the lower-right portion of the window, and the program that opens files with a .txt extension will be changed back to Notepad.
___v. Close the *Folder Options* window.
___w. Close the *My Documents* window.

5. **Invalid shortcut at startup**
___a. Right-click the desktop and select **New** and then **Bitmap Image**.
___b. Right-click and drag the new bitmap image through the **Start** menu, over **Programs**, and down to **Startup**, and release the mouse button.
___c. Select **Create Shortcut(s) Here** from the pop-up menu.

NOTE: You now have a shortcut to open the bitmap image at startup.

___d. From the desktop delete the **New Bitmap Image.bmp** file.
___e. Close all windows and restart the computer.
___f. Record your observations when Windows has restarted in Table 41-8.
___g. Close any open windows.

PROCEDURE - 41

____ h. Click on the **Start** button and go to *Programs* and then *Startup*. Right-click on **Shortcut to New Bitmap Image.bmp** and select **Delete**.
____ i. Click on the **Yes** button to confirm the deletion.

TABLES

Table 41-1

Table 41-2

Table 41-3

Table 41-4

Table 41-5

Table 41-6

Extension	File type	Opens with

Table 41-7

WINDOWS XP OS FAULTS

PROCEDURE - 41

Table 41-8

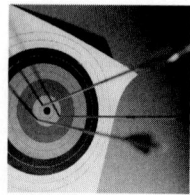

Feedback

LAB QUESTIONS

1. How many options for hiding files and folders were there in the *Folder Options/View* window?

2. How long did it take for Windows to automatically restore a file that you renamed?

3. What is a possible reason for receiving a *Problem with Shortcut* window?

4. What happens if a file's association somehow gets changed to the wrong program?